JSTL in Action

JSTL in Action

SHAWN BAYERN

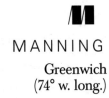

MANNING

Greenwich
(74° w. long.)

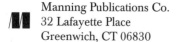

Manning Publications Co.   Copyeditor: Tiffany Taylor
32 Lafayette Place   Typesetter: Denis Dalinnik
Greenwich, CT 06830   Cover designer: Leslie Haimes

ISBN 1-930110-52-9 (alk. paper)

Printed in the United States of America

1 2 3 4 5 6 7 8 9 10 – VHG – 05 04 03 02

For my future wife and kids,
who, when I meet and conceive them,
respectively,
will likely be my love and my inspiration

brief contents

contents

preface

I originally got involved in creating the JSTL in Action (JSTL) when Eduardo Pelegri-Llopart at Sun noticed my emails on an Apache Jakarta mailing list and thought I needed something to keep me busy.

This wasn't strictly true—I already had quite enough on my plate—but I soon found myself growing more and more interested in JSP tag libraries and the JSTL effort. Soon, I was spending a good portion of my waking hours on it (and some nonwaking hours, too).

If you like to design things, then helping to create a new standard and managing its reference implementation are thrilling tasks. Working with the Java Community Process means you meet bright, engaging people from all over the world, and then spend hundreds of hours arguing with them about technical details. Like most of my idiosyncratic pastimes (such as purchasing high-efficiency air filters or watching the British Parliament on television), it might be hard to explain why I've had so much fun with the Java Community Process—but it's been a blast.

However, I don't think my enjoyment of the process alone explains my enthusiasm for JSTL. Rather, JSTL has a special appeal because its goal is to make JSP, and web development in general, more accessible. Just as important, JSTL's design reminds me why I like Java in the first place. It's maintainable, based on thoughtful, careful principles, and easy to use. JSTL takes Java's and JSP's advantages, packages them, and places them in your reach even if you don't know how to program yet.

This book will show you how to make the most of JSTL. It begins without assuming you know anything more than HTML, and it gently introduces you to all the principles you'll need to produce flexible, powerful web pages. The goal of this book isn't to satisfy my own ego by showing you how subtle and tricky technology can be, but instead to equip you to handle any JSTL-related issue that arises when you produce real-world, dynamic web sites. If you read an example in this book and think, "I didn't realize it could be so easy," then JSTL has done its job—and so have I.

acknowledgments

Authors often wax sentimental when their books go to press. I think that's because writing computer books leads some people to turn to alcohol, quit their jobs, and start wandering the wild.

My experience wasn't anything like this. In fact, writing this book was a lot of fun, and I'd do it all again (as soon as my wrists heal). Still, even a book that's fun to write isn't produced in a vacuum, and it depends on the efforts and ideas of many people.

I'd particularly like to thank Pierre Delisle, the specification lead for JSTL, for his friendship, guidance, and trust. Pierre encouraged me to write this book, and he's also the one who asked me to lead the JSTL reference-implementation effort. I used up all the French I know thanking Pierre in my last book, so for now, I'll stick with English and just say that it's been fun and that I'll miss our long nights and email storms—at least, until JSTL 1.1!

I'd also particularly like to thank Marjan Bace for a wonderful author-publisher relationship and for countless suggestions that made this book meaningfully better. With his sharp sense of the industry, I couldn't have asked for a better guide. Just as important, he's kept things fun, and has set a great tone for all of Manning. After just one phone conversation with Marjan, I knew I'd found the publisher I wanted to work with.

The JSTL spec wouldn't exist without the JSR-052 Expert Group. If all expert groups were as good as this one, diplomats and ambassadors would use the Java Community Process as an example of how to bring people together from around the world and solve difficult problems. Thanks in particular to the superb JSTL RI team: Justy Horwat and Jan Luehe, with important contributions from Nathan Abramson and Hans Bergsten (my competing JSP author!). I'm also indebted to the JSP 1.3 spec leads, Eduardo Pelegri and Mark Roth, for making sure key JSP features were ready for JSTL on time.

Thanks to Ted Kennedy for coordinating the book's reviews and managing an amazing volume of useful and encouraging feedback from the likes of Monte Glenn Gardner, Henri Yandell, Dean Riechman, Lance Andersen, Vimal Kansal, Phil Hanna, Gal Shachor, Ian Jagger, Igor Fedulov, James McGovern, Rizwan Lodhi, and James Strachan. Thanks to all of you—even the ones who objected to my off-beat humor. Thanks especially to Martin Cooper for his insightful technical proofing and to Tiffany Taylor for outstanding copyediting work.

Thanks to the production crew—particularly Mary Piergies, Syd Brown, and Denis Dalinnik—and to Lianna Wlasiuk and Alex Garrett for some useful early comments. Finally, thanks to Manning's publicist, Helen Trimes, who might very well be the reason you're reading this book.

I also want to mention a few people from Yale. Thanks to my friend David Davies for his generic-sounding name, which I've used in many examples throughout the book. Thanks also to my colleagues at Yale who, unlike David, *didn't* leave to go off to business school—particularly Andy Newman, Nick Rawlings, Susan Bramhall, Howard Gilbert, and Peter Furmonavicius, for whom "Peter's Junk-Mail Service" from chapter 11 is named. The eccentric members of the +@essentially.net mailing list offered some useful minor comments too; I think they collectively had a positive effect on about a dozen words in this manuscript. Thanks, guys.

Of course, I want to thank my parents. If they make it through chapter 1, I'll be delighted.

And thanks to you for reading all the way through the acknowledgments. But I have to say, you'll learn more from the book's technical content. Get back to work!

about this book

Like JSTL, this book is aimed at both programmers and nonprogrammers. Parts 1, 2, and 3 are accessible to page authors who start out with nothing more than HTML. Part 4 is intended for Java programmers—and ambitious page authors who want to learn more about how JSTL works behind the scenes.

In part 1, we look broadly at the Web and at two technologies that are important foundations to JSTL: JavaServer Pages (JSP) and the Extensible Markup Language (XML).

In part 2, we delve into JSTL's depths. Chapters 3, 4, and 5 lay the necessary groundwork by discussing JSTL's expression language, conditions, and loops. Chapters 6 through 10 discuss the more exciting features of JSTL: database access, XML manipulation, text importing and formatting, and so forth.

In part 3 (chapters 11, 12, and 13), we look at progressively more complete and integrated examples of JSTL in action. We start with common, stand-alone tasks and move to an example of organizing an entire site—a web portal—using JSTL.

Finally, part 4 discusses how to configure JSTL, integrate Java code, and even write custom tags using JSTL's API.

The appendices contain reference material. Appendix A is a brief summary of all of JSTL's tags. Appendix B lists JSTL's API and goes into detail about some of its advanced features. Appendix C describes the basics of SQL to help you follow some of the book's examples, and appendix D lists online and printed references.

How to approach the book

If you're a web-page author who knows HTML, you'll probably want to start at the beginning. Chapters 1 and 2 will be particularly useful to you, and you can read the rest of the book in order, stopping somewhere around chapter 14 if the material becomes less interesting to you. If you already know JavaScript, pay special attention to chapter 3, because you'll need to master the details of JSTL's expression language. JavaScript won't help you produce dynamic server-side logic in this environment. If you don't know SQL, appendix C will help you follow the book's database examples.

If you're an experienced Java programmer looking to master JSTL in order to use or teach it, you can probably skip part 1. You might want to begin by focusing on the expression language in chapter 3. Chapters 4 and 5 will be a breeze, but the rest of part 2 should be useful in orienting you to JSTL's tag-set. The examples in part 3 will be useful, and part 4 is specially intended for you. Also, appendix B is both a thorough reference and an indispensable introduction to some of JSTL's advanced features.

If you have a background in JSP but aren't familiar with Java, then parts 2 and 3 will be particularly useful to you. Also, the beginning of chapter 14—integrating JSTL with scriptlets—might be helpful.

In general, the book gets more advanced as it moves forward. Most readers will gain less by reading the book backward (but if you find any interesting hidden messages that way, be sure to let me know).

Conventions

By and large, the book is self-explanatory. I've followed a few conventions throughout the book that should help illuminate some material; a general convention suggests that I list them here. They include:

- *Boldface type*

  In code listings, I use **boldface type** to differentiate dynamic code (JSTL tags) from static text (including HTML tags). This distinction is useful because they look the same on the surface, so they can easily blur, especially late at night. Also, a few examples use a JSTL tag *within* an HTML tag, and boldface is helpful to make sure the JSTL tag stands out.

- *Other type styles*

  I occasionally use *italics* when introducing a term I want you to remember—or a word that I'd accompany with a bang on the table if I were speaking to you in person (and if there were a table present). Courier font marks tag names (for HTML, XML, or JSTL tags), tag attributes, scoped-variable names, and other words that normally appear within code.

- *Tables for tags*

Just like HTML tags, JSTL tags have *attributes* that let you modify the tags' behavior. For instance, in the tag `<fmt:formatNumber type="currency"/>`, the text `type="currency"` is an attribute. I've listed tag attributes in tables that have a consistent format. Here's an example:

`<c:spam>` **tag attributes**

Attribute	Description	Required	Default
email	Email address to send junk email to	Yes	*None*
subject	Subject of the junk-email message	No	`"Long distance service for less."`
message	Body of the junk-email message	No	*Body*

This sample table shows a few things. First, tables for tag attributes have a "tag" icon to help you find them. Such tables have four columns describing the attribute name, a brief description of each attribute, information about whether the attribute must be specified for each use of the tag, and information about the default value of the attribute if you don't specify a value. If the Default column contains *None*, the attribute has no default. If this column contains *Body*, the default value comes from the tag's body. (See chapter 2 for more information about tags, attributes, and bodies. Note that `<c:spam>` is, of course, not a real JSTL tag—although given the number of applications that send out junk mail, there's clearly a need for it; perhaps we'll see it in JSTL 1.1.)

- *Highlighting*

I highlight sections of code samples whenever I feel like it, usually to draw your attention to a part of the code sample that has changed. Highlighting isn't consistent; it's there only when I think it will be useful.

- *Code annotations*

Some longer examples are annotated using bullets like this: ❽. These are often tied to paragraphs that follow and amplify the code.

- *Call-out boxes*

Occasionally, I draw your attention to a Note, Tip, or Warning using a noticeable box in the middle of the page. To be honest, I do this just because other books do it; fortunately, I use these boxes sparingly.

Source code

All of the source code is downloadable from http://www.manning.com/bayern. I typed it all in so that you don't have to. Don't thank me too much, because I had to type it into the manuscript anyway. Visit http://www.manning.com/bayern to download the code. It's available in a number of convenient formats, including a ready-to-use bundle that can get you up and running quickly, even if you haven't yet set up a JSP container.

Author online

I spend a lot of time online, and now, having written this book, I'm eager to discuss it with you and answer any questions you have about it.

Manning has set up an Author Online forum for *JSTL in Action* to make it easy for you to communicate with me and other readers. The Author Online forum is great if you have any questions or comments about the book (or even if you just want to hold me accountable for one of my jokes). To access the Author Online forum, visit http://www.manning.com/bayern. This page will help you register, read other people's messages, and post your own questions and answers.

about the cover illustration

The figure on the cover of this book is called a "Baniana," which, as far as we can tell, refers to the wife of an Indian merchant who, while making his fortune in that country, is not a permanent resident of India. The illustration is taken from a Spanish compendium of regional dress customs first published in Madrid in 1799.

Those who know how quickly programming languages evolve might be pleased to reflect on the changes that natural human language constantly undergo: the descriptions that come with this source material are only about two hundred years old, but they are not all easily translated by speakers of modern Spanish. Some captions that accompany the illustrations contain words that are archaic but can be found in dictionaries; others have now disappeared, not only from the oral language but also from common written sources.

The title page of the Spanish compendium states:

> *Coleccion general de los Trages que usan actualmente todas las Nacionas del Mundo desubierto, dibujados y grabados con la mayor exactitud por R.M.V.A.R.. Obra muy util y en special para los que tienen la del viajero universal*

which we translate, as literally as possible, thus:

> *General collection of costumes currently used in the nations of the known world, designed and printed with great exactitude by R.M.V.A.R. This work is very useful especially for those who hold themselves to be universal travelers*

Although nothing is known of the designers, engravers, and workers who colored this illustration by hand, the "exactitude" of their execution is evident in this drawing. The "Baniana" is just one of many figures in this colorful collection. Their diversity speaks vividly of the uniqueness and individuality of the world's towns and regions just 200 years ago. This was a time when the dress codes of two regions separated by a few dozen miles identified people uniquely as belonging to one or the other. The collection brings to life a sense of isolation and distance of that period and of every other historic period except our own hyperkinetic present.

Dress codes have changed since then and the diversity by region, so rich at the time, has faded away. It is now often hard to tell the inhabitant of one continent from another. Perhaps, trying to view it optimistically, we have traded a cultural and visual diversity for a more varied personal life. Or a more varied and interesting intellectual and technical life.

We at Manning celebrate the inventiveness, the initiative, and the fun of the computer business with book covers based on the rich diversity of regional life of two centuries ago brought back to life by the pictures from this collection.

Part 1

Background

Welcome to *JSTL in Action*, a guide to everything you'll need to know about JSTL. In the first part of this book, we explore what JSTL is and how it works. We start by discussing the simple ideas behind *dynamic content* on the Web.

After that, we look at some of the differences between HTML and XML. This topic is important because JSTL uses an XML-like syntax, so you'll need to be aware of its rules. Toward the end of part 1, we also discuss the basics of JavaServer Pages (JSP), the broader language that JSTL is based on.

Part 1 takes for granted only a basic knowledge of HTML. This book is designed to be a gentle but complete introduction to JSTL, and it doesn't assume you're familiar with any other programming or web-design languages. Part 1 lays a foundation so that you have all the tools you need to jump in and begin designing dynamic web pages.

Dynamic web sites

This chapter covers...

- Ideas behind dynamic web content
- What JSTL looks like
- Requirements for running JSTL
- JSTL's role in web applications

Welcome to *JSTL in Action*. This book will teach you how to design dynamic web pages using JSTL, the JSTL in Action.

When you write a page in the Hypertext Markup Language (HTML), it looks the same every time a browser loads it. Actually, that's not quite true; it probably looks slightly different in each browser where you view it—and on each operating system, too. But this sort of haphazard change isn't what I mean when I say *dynamic content*. I mean pages that are responsive to users' needs—pages that present customized information, let the viewer interact, and even print information from databases and XML files.

I've designed this book to be a gentle but complete introduction to all of JSTL. You don't need to start with anything more than a familiarity with HTML. This chapter and the next give you all the necessary background to begin writing practical, exciting pages.

1.1 *The boring life of a web browser*

Many new designers of dynamic web pages make the same mistake: they think that for a web page to be interesting or interactive, it needs to send some program code—like JavaScript—out to web browsers. In fact, most of the interesting software on the Web runs on servers. The Web is based on a model of software design called *client/server*, which is just a pretentious way of describing the computers in figure 1.1. All the term *client/server* means is that a bunch of machines, like desktops and Personal Digital Assistants (PDAs), can access a big machine, like a web server, to retrieve or submit information.

To picture how the Web works, imagine that you call up a friend for directions to his house. After you ask for directions, he pauses a moment and says, "Sure, just give me a minute." Then, about a minute later, he comes back to the phone and gives you directions.

During the minute your friend is away, you have no idea what he's really doing. Perhaps he's just answering another phone line and doesn't really need 60 seconds to figure out how to give you directions to his home. Maybe he needs to check something—he might be asking his wife which way North is. The point is, the procedure your friend follows—his implementation details, so to speak—aren't accessible to you. If he's looking at a map, you might never know. If he is indeed talking to his wife, you have no idea if he's using English or Swedish. And if his wife has her own private source of information (perhaps she's cheating on your friend), you're not even close to finding *that* out. All you eventually get back from him are directions to his house. You can follow these directions without caring how he produced them.

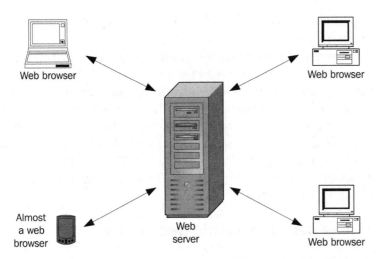

Figure 1.1 The client/server model of computing is, for the most part, an overblown name for a simple idea: place a server on a network and let multiple client machines access it. This is how the Web works: web browsers are the clients, and web servers provide data for them.

The Web works the same way. When a browser asks for a web page, it doesn't need to know how the web server produced the page. Maybe the page is a simple text file, but perhaps it's produced by a program written 20 years ago in COBOL. Maybe it's produced using JSTL. Whatever creates the page, the browser displays it the same way. The browser just sees familiar HTML tags—perhaps an <html> tag, then a <head>, then a <body>, and so on. It uses these tags to print convenient graphical output without regard for how the content was produced.

This simple point implies quite a bit. It means that all the different server-side web languages have the same goal: to produce familiar web pages. A widely diverse array of technologies all have the same purpose. Java's JavaServer Pages (JSP), Microsoft Active Server Pages (ASP), PHP (which recursively stands for *PHP: Hypertext Preprocessor*), ColdFusion, mod_perl, Common Gateway Interface (CGI) scripts—they're all designed to automatically create web pages, just as you manually create them using a text editor or an HTML editor like Macromedia Dreamweaver. The end products are the same.

To put it another way, if you've designed HTML pages, you're probably familiar with a feature most browsers have that lets you see the underlying HTML for a web page. Internet Explorer calls this feature View Source. When you view the source for a web page that a web server sends you, you still see plain HTML, because that's all the browser sees. This HTML might include JavaScript, just as a static page can include JavaScript. But the fact that it was produced by a dynamic process on the server doesn't matter; it ends up as a regular web page.

It's worth pointing out that not all content on the Web is HTML. The Extensible Markup Language (XML) is now used as the basis for some web content. For instance, web servers can communicate with wireless devices using a language called the Wireless Markup Language (WML). XML also supports a stricter successor to HTML called XHTML. At any rate, the final form of content—whether it's HTML, XHTML, WML, or something else—usually doesn't matter to the server-side web language. For instance, with JSTL (and ASP, PHP, ColdFusion, and others) it's as easy to produce WML as it is to produce HTML. You just need to know the target language you want to produce.

1.2 *The simple ideas behind dynamic web content*

In the early days of the Web, the only way to produce dynamic content was to write programs in traditional programming languages. These programs, while nominally deserving of the term *web applications*, were really just conventional programs that printed HTML instead of displaying text like

```
Please enter "yes" or "no" at the prompt:
```

Early web programs also knew how to read information that you entered in HTML forms, figure out what kind of browser you were using, and so on.

After this first generation of web programming—which saw the rise to prominence of the Perl programming language—a different model for producing web pages became popular. Languages sometimes called *template systems* became common. For the most part, a template system is based on the same idea as a feature of many word processors: *mail merge.*

A word processor that supports mail merge lets you write a single letter or document—a *master* or *template*—and then use this single copy to produce customized output for a number of individuals. For instance, you might write something like this:

```
Dear [NAME]:
My records show that you owe me $[DOLLARS].
I need this money now to buy myself a big
[PRESENT]. If I don't get it, I will break
your [APPENDAGE].
```

This letter has two parts. Mostly, it's made up of static *template text*—unchanging text that gets printed for each copy of the letter. In other words, every time you print a letter, it starts with the word *Dear* and contains the text *My records show that you owe me.* Sprinkled within this template text are a few placeholders, like [NAME] and [DOLLARS].

To conduct a mail merge and print a customized letter, you supply the information missing from this single master copy of the letter—perhaps at the prompting of your word processor, or as a preformatted, comma-separated text file. To be complete, each letter needs four pieces of information: NAME, DOLLARS, PRESENT, and APPENDAGE. Like the old *Mad-Libs* games, producing a customized letter simply involves filling in these placeholders. One set of legitimate values might be

```
Jack, 20, tuna sandwich, finger
```

Another might be

```
Leonard, 1200, television, arm
```

You'd use the mail merge in the first place because doing so is simpler than typing each letter manually—or even using a word processor to edit the letter yourself each time you need a new, customized copy.

Believe it or not, template languages for the Web work almost exactly the same way. Starting with a web-development language is no harder than using mail merge. The major difference is that instead of printing simple text letters or documents, the goal of a web-design language is usually to print HTML. For instance, here's what our sample mail-merge letter might look like in JSTL:

```
<html>
<head>
  <title>Nasty letter</title>
</head>
<body>
<h1>Dear <c:out value="${name}"/>:</h1>

<p>
  My records show that you owe me $<c:out value="${dollars}"/>.
  I need this money now to buy myself a big
  <c:out value="${present}"/>. If I don't get it,
  I will break your <c:out value="${appendage}"/>.
</p>
</body>
</html>
```

NOTE   In this example, and throughout the rest of this book, I use **bold** type to highlight JSTL tags that occur within HTML text. This formatting makes it easier to differentiate the dynamic parts of a page from its static, template text.

Other than converting the letter to HTML, all we've done to modify the original mail-merge letter is to use a special syntax to introduce placeholders into the page. Instead of [NAME], we wrote

```
<c:out value="${name}"/>
```

Don't worry about the details of this placeholder's syntax yet. As a first step toward learning JSTL, we'll begin looking at its syntax more closely in chapter 2, and we'll cover it completely in chapter 3. For now, you just need to realize a few important things. First, instead of using an arbitrary, made-up pattern like [NAME], the place-holders used in JSTL look a little like HTML tags. That is, they start with <, end with >, and have attributes like value="${name}", just like familiar HTML tags. This similarity is intentional; it's one of the features that make JSTL easy to work with when you come from an HTML background.

For the most part, learning JSTL is as easy as learning how these placeholders work. The placeholders are called *tags*—like HTML tags—and that's why JSTL is called a *tag library*. It's just a collection of placeholders.

JSTL's various placeholders help you gain more control over your pages than a single, simple placeholder would allow. For instance, in our sample letter, we use the following tag to print out a number:

```
<c:out value="${dollars}"/>
```

However, suppose we want to be precise and format the number as currency, making sure it has an appropriate currency symbol, the right number of decimal points, and so on. JSTL lets us do this using a slightly different placeholder:

```
<fmt:formatNumber value="${dollars}" type="currency"/>
```

JSTL also lets you retrieve the number from a database, an XML document, or even another page on the Web. In all cases, though, the tags look very similar: they're still like familiar HTML tags. They just have different names and accept different attributes.

Not all JSTL tags are designed to output simple values, like words and numbers. Some tags actually make decisions in the middle of your pages. For instance, a tag can decide to print something out, or to remain quiet, based on some data that it checks. A JSTL tag can even decide to repeat part of your page a number of times, which can be useful when you want to build lists or tables of data.

There's one more major difference between a mail merge and a dynamic web page. When you work with a mail merge, you're typically sitting at a single computer. Web languages, however, are designed to transmit data over the Internet.

Communication over the Web

Whenever information is transmitted over a network, both sides need to agree on a *protocol*—a way of communicating. The Web uses a protocol called *HTTP*, the Hypertext Transfer Protocol. HTTP outlines specific rules for how web browsers must talk to web servers. One of HTTP's most important rules is that the Web must work using a style of communication called *request/response*. That is, every operation on the Web has two parts: an attempt to load data (the *request*) and an answer to that request (the *response*). Web browsers and web servers don't work like chat rooms, where multiple parties might stay connected for hours and transmit data whenever they want to.

Therefore, web pages (even dynamic ones) are reactive in nature. They sit around waiting for a web browser to request them. When this happens, they begin to run (or *execute*), printing static template text and filling in placeholders when necessary. A page that uses JSTL never runs on its own; it always runs in response to a web request.

1.3 What you need to run JSTL

Not all word processors support mail merge; and, similarly, not all web servers support JSTL. You can't necessarily take a page with JSTL placeholders (tags) and stick it on a simple web server; not everything that vends your HTML pages can also vend JSTL pages.

As we'll discuss more in chapter 2, JSTL is built on a server-side technology called JavaServer Pages (JSP), which in turn is built on top of Java (see figure 1.2). JSP is a powerful template system, but with its power comes complexity. For instance, a JSP placeholder inside an HTML file can look like this:

```
<%= ((User) session.getAttribute("user")).getLastName() %>
```

This placeholder, like much of JSP, is based on the Java programming language, and it's hard to use unless you're a programmer. By contrast, JSTL lets you write a similarly functioning placeholder like this:

```
<c:out value="${user.lastName}"/>
```

It's still not completely trivial to read and understand, but it's much easier than its JSP counterpart. By the end of chapter 3, you'll be an expert on how to write tags like this.

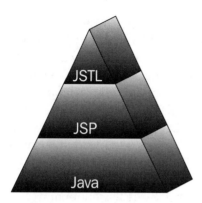

Figure 1.2
Java is a flexible, general-purpose programming language. JavaServer Pages (JSP) depends on Java but hides some of the hard details of writing full-fledged programs. The JSP Standard Tag Library (JSTL) builds on top of JSP, making it even easier to use.

1.3.1 JSP containers

Because JSTL uses JSP, you need a software product called a *JSP container* to use JSTL tags. A JSP container is a web server that also knows how to interpret JSP pages and JSTL tags. Instead of simply sending HTML files out to browsers, it can process JSTL tags and produce appropriate text in their place.

JSTL works with JSP versions 1.2 and higher. If your working environment already includes a JSP 1.2 container, then you can jump right in and start to use the tags we begin to discuss in chapter 3. If you don't already have a JSP container to use, you'll need to set one up. For a few reasons, this book doesn't include instructions for installing a JSP container. For one thing, there's a good chance you won't need them—JSTL is targeted at web-page authors who, in many cases, are supported by back-end Java programmers and system administrators. So, it might not be your responsibility to set up Java server software.

But more important, freely downloadable software products are a moving target: it's usually not worth describing how to install them in books, because the instructions keep changing. Therefore, I've written an introduction to a JSP container called Jakarta Tomcat and posted it on Manning Publications's web site. (See appendix D for this article's URL.) This way, the instructions don't clutter the book, and they can stay up to date. The online instructions, by the way, also cover how to install JSTL into Tomcat; they teach you everything you need to know to get up and running quickly.

It's worth mentioning a few quick mechanical details about the way JSP pages work. JSP pages can be called anything, but just as it's common to store HTML in files whose names end with .html or .htm, you'll usually save JSP files in names that end in .jsp. For instance, index.jsp might be the main page for your application, and we might have named our page from section 1.2 letter.jsp.

Other than that, JSP pages are designed to behave as much like HTML files as possible. For instance, when you make a change to a JSP page, you just need to reload your browser window in order to see your changes. As a result, you don't have to learn how to use any of the traditional programmer's tools like compilers, debuggers, and so on. JSTL inherits all these benefits from JSP.

1.4 *Real-world web applications*

Earlier in this chapter, I compared the Web to a situation in which you call a friend and ask for directions on the phone. Figure 1.3 shows this arrangement graphically. You ask your friend a question, he consults with whatever back-end resources he has, and then he responds to you. The important point is that once you've asked your question, you don't know what's happening on his end.

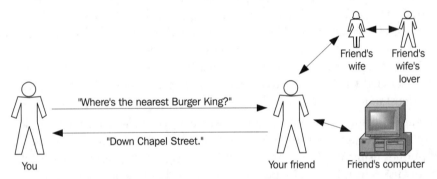

"Where's the nearest Burger King?"

"Down Chapel Street."

You   Your friend   Friend's computer

Friend's wife   Friend's wife's lover

Figure 1.3 **When you ask your friend a question over the phone and he says, "Give me a second," and puts you on hold, you don't know what back-end resources he's using. He might consult with his computer or his spouse.**

Now, to make a new point, let's extend this analogy. Imagine that when your friend talks on the telephone, he uses a device he bought through a spy magazine to disguise his voice. Suddenly, you're shielded from even more of what's happening on the other side of the phone call. For example, your friend could put his wife on the phone in the middle of a sentence, and you might not be able to tell the difference. You began speaking with him when you called, but his wife ended up answering your question without your ever knowing. Many large, real-world Java web applications—often called *enterprise* applications—work like this; secretive hand-offs between components of the application occur without the web browser's ever knowing.

First, consider the way a small, relatively simple web site might work. In figure 1.4, the web browser interacts directly with a JSTL page. In this simple

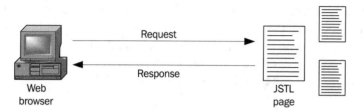

Figure 1.4 Small applications can be designed entirely using JSTL pages. Web browsers load the pages directly, and the pages know how to find all the information that they need to print.

design, the JSTL page does all the work. That is, it knows how to find all the data it needs to print, without any help from back-end Java code.

In contrast with figure 1.4's simple design, consider figure 1.5. The web browser makes a request for a web page, but this request is handled by a *servlet*, which is a web program written in the Java programming language. In order to handle this request, the servlet can interact with other Java code, as well as databases, directories, XML files, messaging systems, and nearly anything else. Finally, once the servlet has decided what it wants to display to the user, it *forwards*—that is, hands off— the request to a JSTL page, which decides how to print out the information.

One key principle of this model is that each JSTL page is designed to do a different thing. For example, one JSTL page might be written to print a shopping cart to cell phones using WML. Another would be designed to present a registration page for new users in HTML. The pages themselves don't decide what task to perform; they only decide what to display. The servlet takes care of all the behind-the-scenes action, which might include determining what kind of device the user's using (cell phone versus web browser) and what the user is asking for (shopping cart or registration page).

Organizing an application as shown in figure 1.5 has a number of benefits. Doing so supports division of labor in your organization, much like traditional division of labor in a factory assembly line. If you work for a large organization, you probably have a number of different kinds of colleagues: programmers, web-page authors, graphics designers, database administrators, and so on. Separating the pieces of your application into different blocks—a servlet, plain Java code, a database, JSTL pages—means that all the people in your organization can focus on what they do best.

This division of labor also makes a site more maintainable. Before template systems, it was common to include HTML in the middle of conventional programs, like this:

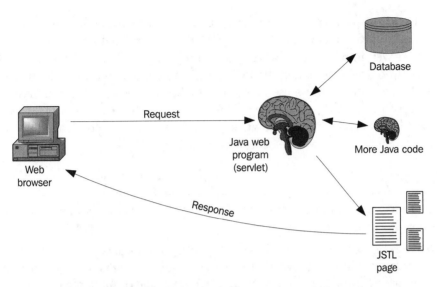

Figure 1.5 **Large web applications are designed using Java, JSTL, and other components like databases. In large applications, it's common for requests from web browsers to be handled by a Java program called a servlet, which interacts with databases and other Java code on the server. The servlet figures out how it wants a response to be printed, and then it forwards the user to the right JSTL page, which takes care of nothing more than presenting information.**

```
if ($FORM{"username"}) {
  print "<b>Congratulations, you're logged in.</b>";
}
```

There's a big problem with code like this: if your site's design undergoes a change, the programs must be modified. Every time a graphic needs to be added to a web site, programmers may have to stop what they're doing and update their code.

With the design from figure 1.5, though, each piece of the puzzle can stand more robustly on its own, making your whole site easier to maintain and update. This design is so popular that many packages and frameworks have grown up around it. You might have heard the term *Model-View-Controller (MVC)* to describe the pattern on which some web sites are based. This term, although originally more specific, has come to be loosely applied to any arrangement that remotely resembles figure 1.5.

The *Struts* framework, from the Apache Jakarta project, is a popular MVC application framework for Java. Many other tools, including *JavaServer Faces*, also rely on back-end Java programming. They're all designed with similar goals: to improve maintainability and to make it easier to write web applications.

JSTL works well with or without these technologies. As you saw in figure 1.4, you can use it for small, stand-alone web sites. But probably more important, it integrates well into situations where back-end Java programmers manage and support the web application, and the JSTL page's only job is to present information to web browsers. JSTL will be useful to you whether you use Struts, JavaServer Faces, a different framework, or nothing. This book doesn't describe how to use these frameworks specifically, but the principles and techniques you learn here will be useful to you no matter where or how you use JSTL.

1.5 Summary

If you're new to dynamic web sites, keep the following points in mind as you read the next few chapters:

- Web browsers don't care how web pages are produced. To a web browser, it makes no difference whether the page it's displaying is static (unchanging) or dynamic (produced by a programming language or template system).

- Template systems like JSP and JSTL are similar to a word-processing feature called mail merge. In a web template system, template text is mixed with a number of placeholders. These placeholders are filled in every time the page needs to respond to a web request.

- JSTL is a template system whose placeholders look like familiar HTML tags.

- JSTL is built on JSP technology, which means you need a JSP container to use JSTL's tags. See appendix D for a pointer to online instructions for installing a JSP container.

- In many large, real-world applications, JSTL pages are just one piece of the puzzle. One popular model lets Java servlets handle every web request. The servlet can decide what it wants to print to the user and then pass the user off to a JSTL page, which formats the data using markup languages like HTML.

Foundation:
XML and JSP

2

This chapter covers...

- The basics of XML syntax
- An introduction to JSP
- JSTL's tag libraries in context
- JSP scoped variables

Before we start looking at JSTL more closely, we need to discuss some of the basics of XML and JSP. XML is important, for now, because JSTL's syntax is based on it. That is, when you use JSTL tags, you're using them according to XML's rules. Similarly, JSTL is a technology that's built on top of JSP, and you'll be a more effective JSTL author if you understand JSP basics.

You're probably familiar with XML even if you've avoided reading a tedious, formal description of it. If you haven't familiarized yourself with XML yet, you might be pleasantly surprised by how easily you'll pick it up. In fact, if you know HTML, you're well on your way to understanding XML. In this chapter, we'll look at these principles—what XML is, how it works, and why we care.

After that, we'll shift gears and introduce JSP. You might be less familiar with JSP than with HTML, but that's fine. One of JSTL's major goals is to simplify JSP and shield web-page authors from unnecessary JSP implementation details. Still, it's important for us to consider a few JSP basics, and we'll do that in the second half of this chapter.

2.1 Introduction to XML

If you've ever written or designed a web page, you probably know HTML, the Hypertext Markup Language. But it's worth a moment to consider what "knowing HTML" means. When you picture HTML, you may have a set of particular markup tags in mind—`<p>`, `<img>`, and so on. HTML is more than just these tags, however. Authors of HTML know how to use tag modifiers, or *attributes*—for example, `src="/picture.jpg"` in an `<img>` tag, or `align="left"` in a `<p>` tag. They also know that HTML tags have a particular structure. For instance, a `<td>` doesn't make sense unless it appears inside a `<table>` element. Tags like `<body>` don't come before tags like `<head>`. And each page has just one `<title>`—having 17 titles wouldn't make sense.

The point is that HTML is a collection of tags and attributes—*and* rules for their usage. HTML also describes the purpose of each individual tag. The `<img>` tag refers to images, `<table>` represents tabular information, and so on. In doing all this, HTML is essentially a specific application of a more general technology known as the Extensible Markup Language (XML). (It is only "essentially" an application—and not actually one—because HTML's rules are looser than XML's, as you'll see in section 2.1.2.)

Here's the simplest way to begin to look at XML: it's what you've got when you have certain kinds of markup tags. These markup tags can be of the familiar HTML kind, like `<p>` and `<html>`, and they can also have names and attributes that are less familiar or even downright strange, like

```
<beef status="rare" contaminated="true">
```

XML is an approach for using these tags to mark off information within a document.

XML, unlike HTML, does not describe a particular set of tags (`<p>`, `<b>`, and so forth) or relationships between such tags. Instead, it describes the rules for using tags in a document in the first place. To draw a loose analogy, XML is a general-purpose mechanism, like Arabic numerals—1, 2, 3, and so on. Receiving a group of Arabic numerals in isolation doesn't tell you much; for example, seeing "79" on a blank page doesn't convey any useful information without a context. However, you know that "79" is a valid string containing just Arabic numerals, and that "g", "49E", and "©" are not.

Similarly, the `<beef>` tag in the previous code snippet doesn't mean anything in isolation. In fact, neither does a tag like `<img src="ugly-man.jpg"/>`. This latter tag has a meaning when it appears in an HTML document, but alone, it is simply an arbitrary tag, just as "79" is an arbitrary string of digits. Nonetheless, it follows XML's rules, so it is a well-formed, recognizable XML tag, whereas

```
[am-I-an-XML-tag?]
```

is not. In a moment, we'll look more at XML's rules.

If you've browsed discussion groups online or exchanged email with enough people, you've probably seen informal uses of tags beyond HTML. For instance, I've often seen people mark off a particularly vibrant part of an email message with tags like `<rant>` and `</rant>`, or introduce a long, rambling section with a `<ramble>` tag. This pseudo-HTML markup, insofar as it technically adds structure to a document, represents the essential goal of XML: tags are used to mark a document in ways that help people and programs identify the purpose of each part of that document.

Jumping right in, we'll first look at some of the jargon used to describe XML tags and their relationships. Then we'll follow up with some syntactic rules of XML.

2.1.1 *A dose of tag terminology*

When we talk about JSTL, it's important to make sure we're on the same page (so to speak). To ensure this, one of the less glamorous things we need to do is cover some XML terminology. We'll also explain the terms and idioms that are used most commonly by JSP and JSTL users.

As you probably know from your experience with HTML, tags often come in pairs: one tag, which might look like `<p>`, starts a block; and a corresponding tag, such as `</p>`, ends it. Figure 2.1 shows an example of an XML *element*—a block of XML between, and including, corresponding start and end tags. The element begins with a *start tag*, optionally contains a *body* (some inner text, tags, or both), and wraps up with an *end tag*.

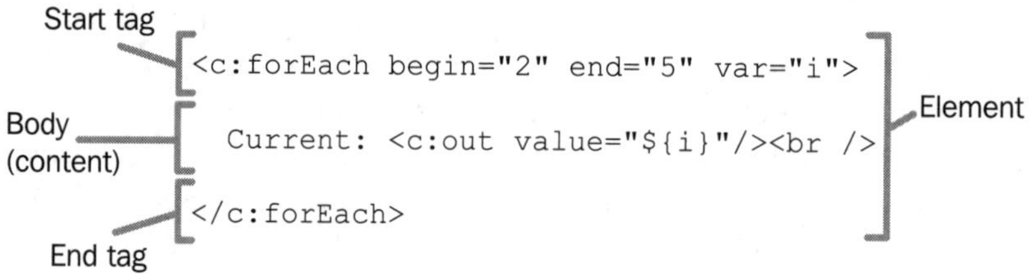

```
Start tag
            <c:forEach begin="2" end="5" var="i">
                                                          Element
Body
                Current: <c:out value="${i}"/><br />
(content)

            </c:forEach>
End tag
```

Figure 2.1   The basic composition of an XML element

MINOR WARNING   The formal XML standard, and some books that focus on XML more heavily than this one, use slightly different terminology. Tags that begin an element are known as *start-tags* (note the hyphen); similarly, tags completing an element are called *end-tags*. The stuff inside the tags is typically called the element's *content*. In this book, however, I've decided to use the terminology more common among JSP and JSTL users.

An element thus consists of a start tag, an optional body, and an end tag. Sometimes, XML users confuse the terms *element* and *tag*. When speaking formally, it is best not to do this. A tag is the text between and including the < and > characters; an element is the combination of a start tag, and end tag, and whatever's in between them.

However, JSP users do not always speak formally; when discussing JSP, the term *tag* is used consistently, in many cases, to refer to what XML people call *elements*. This book adopts this usage, at least in cases where it isn't ambiguous. XML purists might complain, but it makes no sense at this point to buck the trend. Therefore, if a later chapter were describing figure 2.1, it might discuss the "`<c:forEach>` tag's body." This usage is the best way to keep the text simple and straightforward. (We'll discuss more JSP jargon later.)

Empty elements

As I've said, the body of an XML element is optional. The following element is perfectly valid:

```
<lonely></lonely>
```

The start and end tags are touching each other, with nothing in between. That is, the element is said to be *empty*. (Less formally, the element is said to have an empty *body*.) As it turns out, this case is so common in XML that a special, abbreviated syntax is often used for empty elements:

```
<lonely/>
```

This single *empty-element tag* is equivalent to the adjacent start and end tags. You can use either form to represent an empty element, but the latter is far more common and idiomatic (and it saves typing, too). From this point forward, this book uses the shorter form exclusively.

In accepted—or at least widespread—informal usage, empty elements are often referred to as *empty tags.*

Attributes

Start tags and empty-element tags—but not end tags—can have attributes. An *attribute* looks like `name="value"`, where `name` is the *attribute name* and `value` is the *attribute value.* A tag can have as many attributes as you want it to have, but no attribute can be repeated in the same tag. That is,

```
<manager indecisive="true" indecisive="false"/>
```

is not legal—*well-formed*—XML. See figure 2.2 for an example of an attribute.

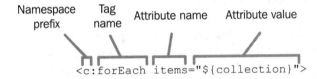

Figure 2.2
An XML start tag, with an XML namespace prefix and an attribute. The attribute is made up of a name and a value.

Just as in HTML, it doesn't matter to XML what order a tag's attributes appear in. For instance, the following two tags are equivalent:

```
<pants fly="zipped" button="fastened" />
<pants button="fastened" fly="zipped" />
```

Namespaces

So far, you're probably familiar with most of the tag syntax and terminology we've discussed. XML, however, introduces a new feature that HTML doesn't have: *namespaces.*

Think of XML namespaces as a way to organize tag names (and attribute names) into groups. In HTML, all tags have simple, bare names like `table`. In XML, however, names can be *qualified.* That is, instead of being a simple word, they can have a *namespace prefix* attached to them. Namespace prefixes are joined to names using a colon (:), so that instead of seeing just `<table>`, you might run into `<coffee:table>` or `<periodic:table>`.

You might want to qualify names like this if a single document needs to use a variety of tags that come from different places. For example, you might have one set of tags that's used to describe home appliances, and another that's used for roles within a restaurant. A tag named <dishwasher> might be used by both sets, for the word *dishwasher* can refer to a person or an appliance. Thus, there might be some confusion if the same document (for whatever reason) needed to contain both tags. For instance, which set would the following tag belong to?

```
<dishwasher gallons="4.5" noiseLevel="50"/>
```

To you, it's probably clear that an entity described by gallons and noiseLevel is a machine, not a person. But a program would not necessarily be able to recognize this difference with absolute certainty, and it might therefore confuse this tag with the other kind of <dishwasher> tag. (Besides, there are indeed people who are best described in terms of gallons and noiseLevel. In many cases, attribute names might not establish a useful distinction.)

XML namespaces let you avoid this kind of clash between names. Instead of just specifying <dishwasher>, you would qualify the name. You might write <appliance:dishwasher> and <job:dishwasher>, for instance—where appliance refers to one namespace and job refers to another.

To use JSTL, you don't need to know much about namespaces. However, JSTL tags all use namespace prefixes when they appear in a page. As figure 2.2 shows, a JSTL tag might use the qualified name c:forEach, where c refers to a namespace and forEach denotes a specific tag within that space. Later in this chapter, you'll see the different namespace prefixes that JSTL tags generally use.

Relationships among elements

As you saw earlier, an element can contain other elements. As shown in figure 2.3, the outer element in such a relationship is called the *parent*, and the inner is called the *child*. (The only other common scenario I can think of where children exist within their parents is, incidentally, mammalian pregnancy.) As usual, we often talk about parent and child *tags*, not *elements*.

```
Parent tag ──⎡<c:forEach items="${collection}" var="c">

Child tag ────⎡<c:out value="${c}"/>

            </c:forEach>
```

Figure 2.3   Parent and child tags

Because of the way an XML document is structured, a child element can't have more than one parent, but a parent element can have any number of children. JSTL tags, like many other XML tags, are frequently parent tags, child tags, or both. The terms *grandparent* and *grandchildren* are rarely used, but we do sometimes speak of *ancestor* and *descendent* tags. For instance, in the following XML fragment, `<a>` is said to be an ancestor of `<c>`:

```
<a>
  <b>
    <c/>
  </b>
</a>
```

Miscellaneous jargon

Start and end tags are occasionally called opening and closing tags. Similarly, it is common to hear an end tag's function described as "closing" the element or start tag. For instance, you might hear someone say, "This `</li>` tag closes the `<li>` tag from the previous line."

Occasionally, child tags are referred to as being "within" or "underneath" their parent tag. Tags within one another are sometimes called *nested* tags.

2.1.2 *The relevant rules of XML*

As you saw earlier in this chapter, XML is, for the most part, a set of rules for using tags within a document. Just as Arabic numerals have rules—a list of valid digits, a convention that initial 0s can be removed, and so on—XML has policies and conventions that are important to us. In this section, we'll discuss some of the syntactic rules of XML that are important to JSTL. Note that this isn't a complete guide to XML, because we don't need to spend time discussing it in much detail. Instead, my goal is to describe the general syntax that XML and JSTL tags share.

It is important to realize that HTML's rules are looser than XML's. Because you are likely already familiar with HTML, let's jump right in and compare HTML with XML. Table 2.1 makes this comparison for several rules, providing examples in both loose HTML and well-formed XHTML (an XML version of HTML that ensures compliance with XML's dictates).

Table 2.1 Some relevant rules of XML syntax, with examples of violating and compliant markup

Rule	HTML example (violating rule)	XHTML example (following rule)
Attribute values must have quotation marks	`<p align=left>`	`<p align="left">`
Case matters	`<P ALIGN="left">`	`<p align="left">`
Start tags must be closed	`<p>thy eternal summer shall not fade`	`<p>summer's lease hath all too short a date</p>`

Table 2.1   Some relevant rules of XML syntax, with examples of violating and compliant markup *(continued)*

Rule	HTML example (violating rule)	XHTML example (following rule)
Empty elements must be closed	` `	` `

A few straightforward rules

Most of these rules are self-explanatory. When writing plain HTML, you can be somewhat sloppy without causing any problems. When constructing a list, you can start a list item with `<li>` but neglect to end it with `</li>`. You can mix uppercase and lowercase freely. And, you can leave off quotation marks in tag attributes (modifiers within a tag) in most cases.

You can still do all these things when you use JSTL, as long as you're just trying to produce HTML pages and not strict XML pages. However, no matter how you use JSTL tags, you need to introduce them into your page following the rules in table 2.1. For instance, your document's `<a>` tags can be written as `<A>`, and you don't need to explicitly end all your HTML tags—but your JSTL tags must have their attributes quoted and must appear in the proper case.

Empty tags must be closed

The final rule in table 2.1 is one of the more confusing to HTML authors starting out with XML or JSTL. In well-formed XML, every tag that's meant to be empty must be closed immediately, using either the longhand form shown earlier (`<br></br>`) or the vastly more common shorthand (`<br/>`). Again, if you're producing loose HTML with your JSTL pages, you don't have to worry about your `<br>` tags. But if you introduce an empty JSTL tag—for instance, `<c:out>`—into your page, you need to close it or use the shorthand empty-tag syntax.

TIP   If you are trying to produce well-formed XHTML pages, instead of loosely structured HTML documents, you might run into a problem. Some older browsers aren't smart enough to recognize empty tags like `<br/>` or `<hr/>`. They expect the loose form of HTML, where the tag is not necessarily closed. In such cases, you can use the expanded form (`<br></br>`). Often, to avoid this cumbersome syntax, you can simply insert a space between the `<br` and the `/>`; many browsers (even the older ones) can handle this correctly. Thus, tags end up looking like `<br />` or `<img src="uglier-man.jpg" />`—note the spaces before the `/>`.

Quotation marks and attributes

In XML, attribute values must be surrounded by quotation marks. They can be either single quotes (') or double quotes ("). In general, it doesn't matter which you use, although if your attribute value has quotes of one type, it is generally sensible to use quotation marks of the other type. For example, in the following tag the value `12"` (presumably referring to "12 inches") is most easily surrounded by single quotes because it contains a double quote of its own:

```
<ruler length='12"'/>
```

If an attribute value needs to contain both single quotes and double quotes, you can represent single quotation marks by typing `&apos;` and double quotes with `&quot;`. These unusual-looking strings are called *entity references* (or often just *entities* informally), but you can safely ignore their details. Just think of `&quot;` as a way of representing, or *escaping,* a double quotation mark within an XML document. Similarly, you can escape the left bracket character (<) with `&lt;`, the ampersand (&) itself with `&amp;`, and the right bracket character (>) with `&gt;`.

XML provides other rules for escaping characters, but they are less important for our purposes. Remember, our goal is to cover just enough XML syntax that you can understand how to use JSTL tags in web pages.

Tags must not overlap

XML tags may not overlap one another. That is, a tag cannot be closed until all of its children tags are closed as well. For example, the following is not legal XML:

```
<a>
 <b>
</a>
 </b>
```

Once the start tag for `<b>` appears, `<b>` must be closed (with `</b>`) before `<a>`'s end tag can appear.

2.2 Introduction to JSP

Moving right along, let's shift our attention to JSP. JSTL depends on JSP: every JSTL page you write is also a JSP page. However, although JSP has a host of features that allow for powerful, general-purpose programming, you only need to know a few things about JSP to be an effective JSTL author.

As you saw in chapter 1, template systems like JSP work by letting you mix program logic and unchanging text in the same document. The major difference among template systems involves how such program logic is introduced to the page.

In JSP, one way (in fact, the most important mechanism for our purposes) to add program logic to a page is to use XML-like tags. When a JSP engine processes a JSP page, it looks to see if it recognizes any tags; if so, it treats them specially. When a JSP engine encounters an HTML tag or any other sequence of characters it doesn't recognize, it simply passes them through to the web browser. However, when it encounters a tag it does recognize, it takes action behind the scenes and dynamically determines what to output.

For this reason, tags with special meaning to JSP are formally called *actions*. But although this term is used by the JSP specification, it doesn't come up much in informal usage. Because of the popularity of the term *tag library*, which refers to a collection of JSP actions, actions are generally called *JSP tags*. This book sticks to the familiar, informal term *tag* to avoid being unnecessarily pedantic. (Even the JSP specification occasionally lapses into this popular terminology.)

2.2.1 *JSP tag syntax*

JSP tags, including all of JSTL's tags, follow the basic rules of XML syntax we outlined in section 2.1. For example, any JSP tag must be closed, is case sensitive, can't overlap another tag, and so on. However, JSP pages can produce any sorts of documents; they don't need to produce well-formed XML documents. For instance, you're allowed to produce the following non-XML HTML with JSP:

```
<ol>
  <li>one
  <li>two
</ol>
```

You can mix HTML fragments like this with JSP tags all you want. JSP couldn't care less about what your HTML looks like; it's all arbitrary template text as far as JSP is concerned. However, your JSP tags need to follow XML rules. For instance, if you have two JSP tags, `<tag:one>` and `<tag:two>`, then you can't write the following legally because the tags overlap each other:

```
<tag:one>
  <tag:two>
</tag:one>
  </tag:two>
```

These tags aren't closed properly.

An interesting subtlety about JSP tags and HTML tags is worth highlighting: you can use JSP tags inside HTML tags, because these HTML tags are just arbitrary template text. For instance, you can write:

```
<a href="<tag:one/>">
```

If `<tag:one>`'s purpose is to print a URL, then this tag might be replaced with

```
<a href="http://your/url">
```

and it works fine.

However, JSP tags cannot appear inside another JSP tag's attributes. For instance, if `<tag:one>` and `<tag:two>` are both JSP tags, then you can't write

```
<tag:one attribute="<tag:two/>"/>
```

and expect `<tag:two>` to run.

Clearly, JSP tags work differently from static, template text. You might wonder, however, what causes a tag like `<tag:one>` to become a JSP tag, whereas something like `<p>` or `<foo:bar>` is considered static, template text.

One criterion is simple: every JSP tag's name has a namespace prefix. A tag like `<p>` can never be a JSP tag, but `<tag:one>` can. But what decides whether it *is* treated as a JSP tag, or whether it's relegated to the uninteresting life of template text? Sections 2.2.2 and 2.2.3 answer this question.

2.2.2 *Standard JSP tags*

Some JSP tags are built into JSP; they're effectively hard-wired into the JSP standard. These tags are often called *standard tags*, although the term is somewhat confusing. This group of "standard" tags doesn't include JSTL tags; instead, it includes core JSP tags that predate JSTL by several years. JSTL's tags are also "standard," but they fall into a separate group of tags that we'll discuss in section 2.2.3. Figure 2.4 demonstrates this double standard.

The first group of standard tags—that is, the core JSP tags—uses the namespace prefix `jsp`. When you see a tag like `<jsp:include>` or `<jsp:forward>`, you know it's

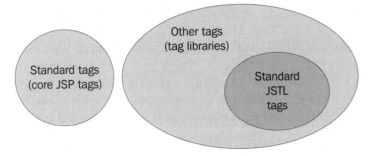

Figure 2.4   The classification of JSP tags. Note that the term "standard tag" has two unrelated meanings.

a standard tag because its name starts with jsp:. Other tags, whether part of JSTL or not, use different prefixes. (We'll look at the usual JSTL prefixes in section 2.2.3.)

Let's look at two of the standard JSP tags, <jsp:include> and <jsp:forward>. Our primary goal is simply to show a few simple standard JSP tags in use; if the details seem intimidating, do not worry about them too much for now.

Including other pages with <jsp:include>

One standard tag, <jsp:include>, lets you include one JSP page from within another, as suggested by figure 2.5. The <jsp:include> tag also lets you include a large chunk of static content, which is useful when you have header or footer text that applies to more than a single page.

Figure 2.5
<jsp:include> lets one page appear as if it is embedded in another. When a <jsp:include> tag appears in your page, it gets replaced by the entire contents of another page.

For our purposes, this tag takes a single important attribute, page, which specifies the location of the page to include. This location is relative to the current page, so this tag works similarly to HTML tags like <img> and <a>. That is, if you are editing page a.jsp and you specify page="b.jsp", the page named b.jsp from the same directory as a.jsp will be included. The target page—in this case, b.jsp—will execute just as if a web browser requested it, and its output will be included in place of the <jsp:include> tag. For instance, suppose you have a file named a.jsp that contains the following text:

```
Welcome to a.jsp.
Now including b.jsp . . .
<jsp:include page="b.jsp"/>
```

Now, suppose b.jsp contains the following text:

```
Welcome to b.jsp.
```

Then a.jsp will output the following:

```
Welcome to a.jsp.
Now including b.jsp . . .
Welcome to b.jsp.
```

The contents of b.jsp have replaced the `<jsp:include>` tag in page a.jsp.

Note that, because the `<jsp:include>` tag (as used here) does not contain a body, it is closed by placing a forward slash before the closing angle bracket. As we described earlier, JSP tags—which follow XML syntax—need to be closed in this fashion if they are empty.

The `<jsp:include>` tag can only include local files—files from the same JSP engine servicing the page in which `<jsp:include>` appears. Either static or dynamic files can be included. That is, the tag can include a simple text file, another JSP page, or even a servlet or other arbitrary resource on the local server.

WARNING If you are an experienced designer of web applications, you might have used the HTML `<base>` tag. This tag allows you to specify a location that all tags like `<a>` and `<img>` will use as their base. That is, if you specify a new base with

```
<base href="http://www.jstlbook.com/"/>
```

then a tag like `<img src="image.jpg"/>` will cause the browser to try to load http://www.jstlbook.com/image.jpg, not the local image.jpg file in the same directory as the web page.

The `<base>` tag, however, does not affect the way that JSP tags like `<jsp:include>` operate. To a JSP engine, the `<base>` tag is arbitrary HTML. `<base>` has its effect because the browser interprets it and uses it to modify the way the rest of the page loads. But JSP engines do not interpret HTML tags; they simply pass them through to the browser. Therefore, although it makes sense to think of `<jsp:include>` as finding files in a manner similar to `<a>` and `<img>`, the analogy is not perfect. `<jsp:include>` always looks for files on the local server.

A typical pattern is to use `<jsp:include>` to include header and footer text in multiple pages. For instance:

```
<jsp:include page="header.jsp"/>
Page contents
<jsp:include page="footer.jsp"/>
```

This fragment causes the contents of header.jsp to be displayed, followed by the page's own custom contents, followed by those of footer.jsp. In many cases, using a few simple `<jsp:include>` tags can help you support a common look and feel for an entire web application.

Even if one page includes another, that second page can include some more pages. For instance, there would be no problem if header.jsp, from the previous example, looked like this:

```
<jsp:include page="header-part1.jsp"/>
<br />
<jsp:include page="header-part2.jsp"/>
```

Forwarding to other pages with <jsp:forward>

A second standard JSP tag, `<jsp:forward>`, lets you cancel the operation of the current page and jump to a new page. The new page is located using the same attribute, `page`, and the same rules for finding files as `<jsp:include>`.

When a JSP engine encounters a `<jsp:forward>` tag, it stops processing the current page and begins processing the page referred to by `<jsp:forward>`. As shown in figure 2.6, the browser doesn't see the contents of the first page; it simply sees the second.

Just as with `<jsp:include>`, there is no problem if the target page of a `<jsp:forward>` tag also uses `<jsp:forward>`. Page A may forward to page B, and page B may forward to page C. Of course, setting up a forwarding loop is generally undesirable: if page A forwards to page B, then page B shouldn't forward back to page A!

Forwarding from one page to another is useful when you have a single page that might act as a dispatcher to other pages. For instance, your application might have a page that determines whether the user is a new or returning customer, and forwards to a specific page appropriate for one case or the other. (Because we haven't yet looked at how JSTL lets you make decisions like this in your pages, we can't easily look at a useful example of `<jsp:forward>` at this point.)

Other standard JSP tags

JSP comes with a few other tags, but for the most part, they are made obsolete by JSTL. You may see pages with tags like `<jsp:useBean>` (discussed in detail in chapter 14) or `<jsp:setProperty>` but you will rarely need these tags when you use JSTL. For more information on older, advanced tags like these, see *Web Development with JavaServerPages.*[1]

---

[1] Duane Fields, Mark Kolb, and Shawn Bayern; 2nd ed. (Manning Publications, 2001).

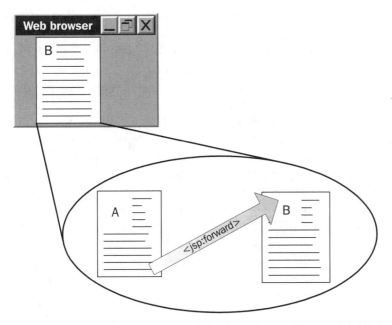

Figure 2.6 `<jsp:forward>` allows one page to abort its processing and jump to another page. If the user tries to load page A, and page A forwards to page B, then the browser sees only the contents of page B. The browser gets no indication that page A's content ever existed.

2.2.3 *JSP tag libraries*

In contrast with the core JSP tags, other tags can be provided by you, vendors—and, of course, JSTL. Such tags come in packages called *tag libraries*: groups of individual tags that are usually designed to work together, or at least to serve a common function. JSTL is a collection of such tag libraries. Of course, it is distinguished by being the *standard* tag library—the one that is found everywhere, and the one you can learn once and reuse wherever JSP containers are found.

The <%@ taglib %> directive

Tag libraries use prefixes other than jsp, and they must be explicitly imported into pages before they can be used. Thus, whereas the jsp: tags can be used in any JSP page without fanfare or preparation, you need to introduce others (including JSTL's) using a special pseudo-tag known as a *directive*. Think of JSP directives as being somewhat like the HTML <head> tag: their function is not specifically to display anything in the browser, but instead to describe some information about the page itself.

Directives are one JSP feature that doesn't strictly follow an XML-like syntax. Instead, a directive begins with `<%@` and ends with `%>`. One such directive, `<%@ taglib %>`, is used to import a tag library into a page. Even though they begin with `<%@` and end with `%>`, directives are similar to XML tags in that they accept attributes. The `<%@ taglib %>` directive requires two attributes: `uri` and `prefix`.

Every tag library has something called a Universal Resource Identifier (URI) associated with it. For our purposes, think of a URI as a Uniform Resource Locator (URL), although in this case, it is not used to load anything over the Web. Instead, it simply acts as a way of differentiating one tag library from another.

To use a tag library in a JSP page, you should know its URI, which you can usually determine from the author or provider of the library. For instance, if you work with Java developers who write tag libraries, they will need to give you the URI for these libraries. If you use JSTL, then the JSTL specification—and, of course, this book—will tell you the appropriate URIs for the JSTL libraries.

Knowing a library's URI or file path, you can use the `<%@ taglib %>` directive to register it and, at the same time, assign it an XML-like namespace prefix for use within the page. For instance, the directive

```
<%@ taglib uri="http://www.acme.com/custom.tld" prefix="acme" %>
```

imports the tag library identified by the URI http://www.acme.com/custom.tld into the page, using the prefix `acme`. After this directive appears in a page, tags from the library can be used with the `acme` prefix. For instance, if the library contains two tags named `create` and `destroy`, the tags could appear in the page as `<acme:create>` and `<acme:destroy>`.

Note that the prefix assigned to the tag library is under your control. When documentation, or this book, describes tags as having certain prefixes, those prefixes are just suggestions. It's usually best to follow the recommendations to make it easy for others to read your pages, but if you're more comfortable with a custom prefix, you can certainly use it.

JSTL's tag libraries

JSTL is provided as a collection of tag libraries designed to meet particular needs. JSTL includes the libraries and recommends the prefixes listed in table 2.2.

Table 2.2 Although JSTL is officially named the JavaServer Pages Standard Tag Library, it divides its tags into four groups and makes them available as separate tag libraries. This table lists the different libraries, along with their URIs and suggested prefixes.

JSTL tag library	Suggested prefix	URI	Example tag
Core library (iteration, conditions, and so forth)	c	`http://java.sun.com/jstl/core`	`<c:forEach>`
XML processing library	x	`http://java.sun.com/jstl/xml`	`<x:forEach>`
Internationalization (i18n) and formatting	fmt	`http://java.sun.com/jstl/fmt`	`<fmt:formatDate>`
Database (SQL) access	sql	`http://java.sun.com/jstl/sql`	`<sql:query>`

The core library includes tags for the following uses:

- Accessing and modifying data in memory
- Making decisions in your pages
- Looping over data

The XML library includes tags for the following purposes:

- Parsing (that is, reading) XML documents
- Printing parts of XML documents
- Making decisions in your page based on the contents of an XML document

The formatting and internationalization library includes tags for these uses:

- Reading and printing numbers
- Reading and printing dates (with support for time zones)
- Helping your application work with more than one language

The SQL library helps you read and write data from databases. Part 2 of this book describes all of these tag libraries in detail.

Using JSTL's tag libraries in your pages

As I mentioned earlier, you need to use the `<%@ taglib %>` directive to import all tag libraries—even JSTL's—into your pages. The four libraries can be imported into your pages using the directives shown in table 2.3.

Table 2.3   Before you can use a tag library, you need to import it. You can use the following lines to import each JSTL library into your page. For each page, you only need to import the libraries you actually use, although there's no harm in importing all of them.

JSTL tag library	`<%@ taglib %>` directive
Core	`<%@ taglib prefix="c" uri="http://java.sun.com/jstl/core" %>`
XML	`<%@ taglib prefix="x" uri="http://java.sun.com/jstl/xml" %>`
Formatting	`<%@ taglib prefix="fmt" uri="http://java.sun.com/jstl/fmt" %>`
Database	`<%@ taglib prefix="sql" uri="http://java.sun.com/jstl/sql" %>`

In this book, I won't always show the `<%@ taglib %>` directive every time I give you a short example of a JSTL tag. However, you'll need to include these directives if you plan to run the tag. (All source code available from the Manning web site includes the appropriate directives, as do this book's longer examples.)

2.2.4   *Other JSP directives*

In addition to `<%@ taglib %>`, JSP has two other directives that are worth looking at quickly. As you just saw, directives are pseudo-tags that have special meaning to the container; they are not passed through to the browser but, instead, are processed by the JSP engine. This section is, by necessity, somewhat technical; you will not miss much if you skip it and come back to it later.

The <%@ include %> directive

Earlier in this chapter, you saw how to include other pages using the `<jsp:include>` tag. JSP also has a directive that lets you include other files: `<%@ include %>`. It takes a `file` attribute corresponding to a relative path, similar to the `<jsp:include>` tag. For instance, to include b.jsp from a.jsp, you could use a directive like

```
<%@ include file="b.jsp" %>
```

Why have two mechanisms to include data? The difference between the two is somewhat subtle and technical, but it boils down to this: the `<%@ include %>` directive works by finding the target file and inserting it into your JSP page, just as if you had cut and pasted it using a text editor. By contrast, `<jsp:include>` locates the target page while your JSP page is executing. This difference in operation implies the following differences in behavior:

- If a file included with `<%@ include %>` changes, its changes will not be noticed until the page containing the `<%@ include %>` directive also changes. Recall from chapter 1 that the JSP engine notices when files are changed and processes them automatically. However, the container doesn't keep track of which pages include `<%@ include %>` directives. When page A uses `<%@ include %>` to include page B, page B's data is simply included in page A every time it is compiled. Therefore, page A must be changed—and recompiled—for any changes in B to take effect. By contrast, `<jsp:include>` notices changes immediately.

- Because `<%@ include %>` works as if you had inserted the target file using a text editor, it only works for basic text, JSP fragments, and so on. If your application also has a Java servlet, you cannot include it with `<%@ include %>`. Instead, you need to refer to it with `<jsp:include>`. (Java servlets are an advanced topic more for programmers than page designers; do not be concerned if you have no experience with them.)

- The `<%@ include %>` directive is, in many cases, more efficient than `<jsp:include>`, but it also uses much more disk space when large files are included. Either way, the differences in efficiency between the two approaches usually are not too important.

- With `<jsp:include>`, the two pages involved—call them page A and page B—are two entirely separate pages. They can use the same names for different variables, or they can use different prefixes for the same tag library. With `<%@ include %>`, because page A and page B are essentially merged before being compiled, there might be clashes between names within the two pages.

Again, these differences are technical, and in most cases, they are not particularly important. I cover them here because you might be interested in them, and we won't have much chance to talk about them later.

The <%@ page %> directive

A third directive, `<%@ page %>`, lets you modify some properties of a JSP page. For this directive, the analogy with HTML's `<head>` tag is even stronger than for the other directives: this directive's goal is to provide meta-information about how to process the page.

With one exception (`errorPage`, which we'll look at in chapter 11), the default configuration for a JSP page is usually fine for our purposes. If you need a complete guide to the nuances of the `<%@ page %>` directive, references like *Manning's Web Development with Java Server Pages* provide all the information you will require.

2.2.5 JSP comments

It's often useful to add text to a page for no other reason than to describe what you were thinking when you wrote it. Such notes are typically called *comments*. They don't have an effect on what the page outputs; instead, they're there just for you and other people who work with the pages you write.

In JSP, anything between the characters `<%--` and `--%>` counts as a comment. For example:

```
<%-- I don't like my users very much. So there! --%>
```

Fortunately, your users will never see this comment; that is, it will never get sent to web browsers. (This fact highlights the point I made in chapter 1: web browsers don't know what goes on behind the curtains in your web application.)

Of course, if you're using JSP to produce HTML, you can include HTML comments too:

```
<!-- I love my users! -->
```

2.2.6 *How JSP organizes data*

When your web pages run, they'll often need to save and retrieve information, or to ask questions about their environment. For instance, they might want to know what a user typed in an `<input type="text">` box, or they might need to retrieve information provided by back-end Java developers. In chapter 4, we'll begin to look at how you save and retrieve data, and how you can write pages that ask questions about their environment. For now, let's look at how JSP pages organize their data.

To help you store and retrieve data, JSP gives you a handful of containers or "boxes" for information. These are formally called *scopes*, and they're JSP's way of letting you manage your data easily. Scopes let you decide two important things: how long your data stays around, and how your data should be shared among different web pages in your application.

Sometimes, it's convenient to think of JSP scopes as receptacles for data, just like the organized mailboxes that some United States post offices have. For instance, at a downtown New Haven post office, there are two mail receptacles: one for mail within the 06520 ZIP code, and one for mail heading anywhere else. Depending on how widely I want my mail to travel, I choose the right mailbox for it.

It might also be convenient to think of scopes not as boxes or containers, but just as extra pieces of information about your data. For instance, suppose that my apartment is infested with rodents, but that some of these rodents are more capable than others. Some simply wander around aimlessly on my carpet, but others have located my building's elevator shaft and move freely from floor to floor. Then (to stretch this dubious analogy to its breaking point), imagine that several flying rats can travel between nearby buildings in my city. Considering these three groups, it is clear that the rodents traveling around my floor have an obviously more limited range—or *scope*—than the ones that can move from floor to floor; these, in turn, have a smaller scope than the flying rats. Any particular rat is described by a particular "scope"; one rat could be called an "apartment rat," whereas another is a "building rat," and yet another is a "city rat."

Returning to reality, different groups of JSP data can have contrasting scopes, just like the hypothetical rodents. Some data can be accessed only from a single JSP page; it's called *page data* or *page-scoped data*. This data is available to any part of a single page, but not to any other page. Other data, by contrast, moves freely throughout a web application—it can be accessed from anywhere in the application, and is *application-scoped*. We'll discuss all the different scopes that JSP provides in a moment.

Scoped variables

A little more formally, all variables in JSP applications have two characteristics: a name and a scope. The name identifies the data, and the scope determines which parts of your application can access the data. Technically, pieces of data stored in the various scopes are referred to as *attributes*, but because these attributes have nothing to do with the XML tag attributes we discussed earlier, this term is confusing. Instead, JSTL refers to objects stored in scopes as *scoped variables*—or, often, simply *variables*.

Why would you want to assign a variable to a particular scope? It all depends on how you want to organize your data and how long you want it to last. You could, technically, just let all your data range freely throughout your application, but such a disorganized approach doesn't usually make sense. For example, imagine a situation where you look up the current user's customer number from a database. It probably wouldn't make sense to store this customer number in a variable named customerNumber that is accessible to the entire application, because more than one user might want to use your application. As soon as a second user logged in, the first user's customer number would be overwritten.

Using the application-wide name customerNumber would not be a good idea. However, you can use a different scope that is tied specifically to the user—in which case you can simply call the customer's number customerNumber and let the JSP container manage the association between users and numbers. Thus, it becomes convenient to associate some data with scopes narrower than the entire application.

JSP has four scopes: page, request, application, and session. As shown in figure 2.7, three of these scopes—page, request, and application—work just like the rodents described in my analogy earlier. They are simply subsets of one another. In particular, page scope is a subset of request scope, which is a subset of application scope. In other words, a particular page has access to its own data, to its request's data, and to its application's data. (I'll define the boundaries of "request" and

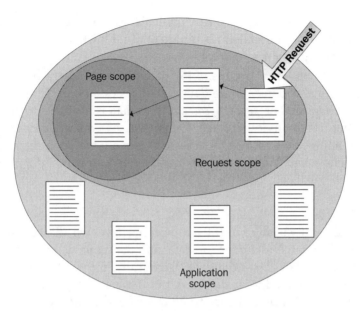

Figure 2.7   **Page scope is more specific than request scope, which is more specific than application scope. Page scope is limited to a single page. Request scope is associated with the processing of a single web request, which might include multiple pages if one page forwards to, or includes, another. Application scope covers an entire web application.**

"application" shortly.) But one page does not have access to data in another page's page-level scope.

The remaining scope, session, is tied to a particular user, regardless of pages and requests.

For now, this discussion is admittedly somewhat abstract; the goal is simply to describe how JSP organizes data logically. Chapter 4 describes how to store and retrieve data using these scopes.

Page scope

Page scope is simple: it lets variables be stored by a single page and retrieved later, as shown in figure 2.8. Data stored in page scope cannot be accessed outside that page (unless it is explicitly stored somewhere else as well). Page scope is useful for variables that you need to store temporarily and for data that is only useful for a single page. You'll see examples of this kind of data in chapter 5.

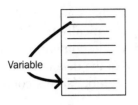

Figure 2.8
Page scope lets one part of a page share data with another part.

Request scope

Earlier in this chapter, we looked at the `<jsp:include>` and `<jsp:forward>` tags. These tags have something in common: they tie together multiple pages.

To access web pages, a web browser makes a *request* for data from a web server. If this request hits a JSP page that uses a `<jsp:include>` or `<jsp:forward>` tag, then multiple JSP pages can be used to service a single request. All of the pages that are used to respond to a single request have access to a common *request scope*. For instance, as suggested by figure 2.9, a page that uses `<jsp:include>` can use the request scope to transfer data to or from the pages it includes. Request scope is useful if the target page needs to act differently depending on an event that occurred in the page that includes it. Or perhaps the target page wants to set a variable that the page using `<jsp:include>` needs to access. Either way, request scope—which is broader than page scope—can be appropriate.

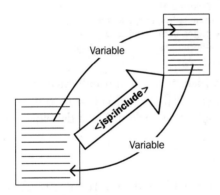

Figure 2.9
Request scope lets pages linked by `<jsp:include>` or `<jsp:forward>` communicate among themselves.

Application scope

In the world of server-side Java programming, the term *web application* has a specific meaning. A web application is a collection of JSP pages and other resources, like servlets and HTML pages. Typically, a web application is located under a common directory on the web server, and it represents a cohesive unit of functionality. For instance, an entire online store or auction site is a good candidate for a web application.

Application scope, as suggested by figure 2.10, allows all the pages in a web application to exchange information. Application scope is typically used for either application-wide constants or status. For instance, it might contain information about where the application's database is located, or what the default locale is (for internationalized applications). It also might contain a global access counter, or other information collected from multiple pages.

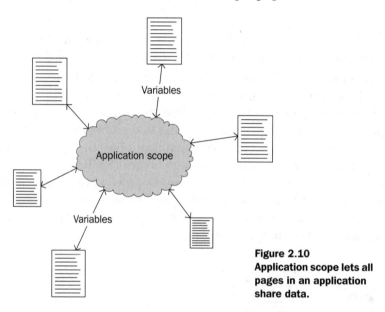

Figure 2.10
Application scope lets all pages in an application share data.

Application scope is the broadest scope, which means you usually need to be careful when writing to it. In many environments, JSP pages don't write to the application scope at all; they simply read from it, allowing back-end Java developers to use it to establish information.

Session scope

Session scope is unlike the others, because it isn't tied to particular pages and it doesn't depend on whether a page is included (or forwarded to) from other pages. Instead, session scope is tied to the user. When a new user connects to a JSP application, the container notices the user and assigns him or her a *session*. This session represents the user's activity in the web application, usually until the user logs out or walks away from the browser.

Think of *session scope* as "user scope"—when you store data to the session scope, it applies to the particular user, and it goes away when the user leaves. As figure 2.11 loosely suggests, session scope is broader than page and request scopes; it allows access data to move between pages, even if they're not part of the same request. But session scope is strictly contained by the web application: a session does not include data from multiple applications. If a user accesses two different web applications, he or she will have two different sessions, one for each of the applications; these sessions will not be related to each other in any way.

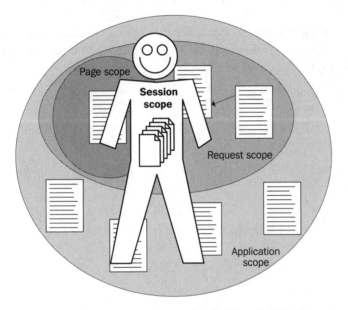

Figure 2.11   Session scope is associated with an individual user: it is broader than page and request scopes, but is contained by the web application.

2.3   *Summary*

Key points to remember about XML and JSP basics are:

- XML is like HTML, but it isn't limited to a particular set of tags. HTML has a specific collection of tags; XML is just a system for using tags in general.
- XML has stricter rules about closing tags, quoting attributes, and case sensitivity. XML also has namespaces, or collections of tags referred to by unique prefixes within a page.
- JSP tags—both "standard" core tags and others, including JSTL's—must use XML syntax when they appear in JSP pages.

- Other than the core tags, all JSP tags come in tag libraries (loose collections of tags). Tag libraries need to be explicitly imported into a JSP page and assigned a namespace prefix.

- Tag libraries are imported using the `<%@ taglib %>` directive. JSP has a handful of other directives, each of which is similar to—but not quite the same as—an XML tag.

- JSP organizes data in scopes, so that different data can be accessed from different places, depending on where it is appropriate. The four scopes are page, request, application, and session.

Part 2

Learning JSTL

Now that you've seen the tip of the iceberg, it's time to focus on the details and principles of JSTL. We've discussed what JSTL's supposed to do; now you get to see how it works.

Part 2 introduces and demonstrates nearly every JSTL tag. (We'll leave two tags until later.) We start with the most fundamental ones: those that handle simple decisions and loops in your pages. Then, we explore all the features JSTL has to offer, from databases to powerful XML support.

Although part 2 is designed as a tutorial and reference, we do (when appropriate) take a step back and look at useful examples of JSTL in action. For more in-depth examples, see part 3.

The expression language 3

This chapter covers...

- JSTL's expression language syntax
- Printing dynamic content
- Storing and retrieving scoped variables
- Producing and reading HTML forms

Part of what makes a dynamic web page dynamic is its ability to gather data from its environment. Dynamic web pages aren't much better than static pages if they can't adapt to changing circumstances. For example, a dynamic page can figure out which check boxes a user checked on your HTML form. Or it can retrieve data from a database or XML file and store it for later use.

JSTL uses a simple language called an *expression language* to make it easy for you to access information. Before JSTL, you really had to know Java to produce an effective JSP page. Even if you wanted to do something simple, like figure out what a user entered in an `<input type="text">` HTML box, you'd have to write code like

```
<%= request.getParameter("username") %>
```

JSTL makes writing pages easier. Its expression language is much simpler than Java; in fact, it's even simpler than JavaScript.

In this chapter, we'll look at some of the things you can do with the expression language. If you haven't read chapter 2 yet, you might want to do so now, because scoped variables—which we introduced in chapter 2—are one of the things that JSTL's expression language makes particularly easy to access.

3.1 Expressions and the <c:out> tag

Before you can use the expression language, we need to look at one basic JSTL tag: `<c:out>`. It's appropriate that `<c:out>` is the first JSTL tag we'll discuss in detail, because it's the most fundamental one, and you'll probably use it more often than any other tag in JSTL.

The `<c:out>` tag lets you print out the result of an expression. For instance, if you want to output—as part of your page—some data that the user entered on a prior HTML form, you can use `<c:out>`. You can also use it to print data that a back-end Java developer exposes to you, and even to print the results of a database query.

TIP   If you've worked with other dynamic languages for producing web pages, you'll find that the `<c:out>` tag is a little like JSP's and ASP's `<%= %>` expressions, ColdFusion's `<cfoutput>` tag, and PHP code that looks like `<?php echo … ?>`.

Remember how JSTL tags work: when they appear in a page, they aren't sent directly to the browser. Instead, they read their tag attributes and cause the JSP container to take action behind the scenes. In `<c:out>`'s case, the behind-the-scenes action is simply to print some custom text.

Let's look at `<c:out>` more closely. Table 3.1 shows the tag attributes it can take. (Note the tag icon next to the table. In this book, all tables that show a JSTL tag's attributes use this icon.)

Table 3.1   `<c:out>` **tag attributes**

Attribute	Description	Required	Default
value	The expression (in JSTL's expression language) to compute	Yes	*None*
default	The expression to compute if `value` fails	No	*None*
escapeXml	Whether to *escape* characters; for example, to print the character & as `&amp;` instead	No	true

By default, `<c:out>` simply prints out whatever it finds in its `value` attribute. For example, if you were to write

```
<c:out value="Hi, there!"/>
```

the `<c:out>` tag would print the text, "Hi there!" Of course, there's normally no reason to do this, because if you just want to include the text "Hi there!" in your web page, you don't need to use JSTL; you can type the text in your web page, and it will get printed as template text. The `<c:out>` tag becomes useful only when the `value` attribute contains an *expression* in JSTL's expression language.

3.1.1 *What expressions look like*

Expressions in JSTL look like this:

```
${expression}
```

They start with `${` and end with `}`; whatever comes between these two markers is treated as an expression. Expressions are like placeholders. In contrast with text like "Hi there!", they aren't simply printed when they appear. Instead, they're computed by the expression language (see figure 3.1), and the results of this computation are printed. For example, consider the following simple expression:

```
<c:out value="${1 + 2}"/>
```

Instead of causing the `<c:out>` tag to print the literal text `${1 + 2}`, the expression in the `value` attribute causes the tag to print out 3.

All JSTL tags work like this. In most cases, when an expression appears in a JSTL tag's attribute, that expression gets computed, or *evaluated.* The result of this evaluation is fed to the tag, which then goes about its business.

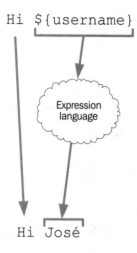

Figure 3.1
Expressions act like placeholders.
When an expression appears, it gets
computed—or *evaluated*—**by the**
expression language. Therefore,
unlike simple text like "Hi", an
expression can produce a different
result every time it runs. In this case,
it adapts to the name of a user.

3.1.2 Where expressions work

In JSTL 1.0, expressions have special meaning only inside JSTL tag attributes. Specifically, they don't work in template text. You can't simply write

```
<p>Hi ${username}</p>
```

in your JSP page and expect the result to be dynamic. Like all template text, this text is printed literally; if you include it in your page, the output of your page will contain the text `<p>Hi ${username}</p>`, and the user will see a paragraph with the text `Hi ${username}`.

JSTL expressions also have no special meaning inside an HTML tag's attribute. In an HTML tag like

```
<a href="${link}"/>
```

the text `${link}` is simply—and in this case, probably erroneously—part of the template text. It's not interpreted as a JSTL expression.

However, when you include an expression in a JSTL tag, it takes on its special meaning, and the expression language comes into play. We'll discuss the exact meaning of expressions like `${username}` later in this chapter. For now, it's just important to notice how `<c:out>` and expressions work in general.

3.1.3 Default values in `<c:out>`

If the expression in the `value` attribute fails for any reason—for instance, in this example, suppose that the expression is `${username}` but the expression language can't find a variable named `username`—then the tag will print nothing out. Sometimes, instead of printing nothing, you want to print an error message, placeholder, or other default value. For cases like these, <c:out> takes a parameter called default. If value's expression fails for any reason, default runs instead. For instance, look at this tag:

```
<c:out value="${username}" default="Nobody"/>
```

This tag works just like the first <c:out> tag we presented; but if ${username} doesn't produce a sensible value, then the tag simply prints out the static text Nobody. The <c:out> tag can also accept a body, which you can use as another way of specifying a default value. Thus, the following tag is equivalent to the last one:

```
<c:out value="${username}">
  Nothing
</c:out>
```

This tag can be useful if your default value is too long to fit conveniently inside an attribute. Or, you can stick other JSTL tags in the body, and they'll be used as the default if ${username} doesn't produce a sensible value.

3.1.4 *Special characters and* *<c:out>*

You should know one more useful thing about <c:out>. By default, it makes sure that any characters with special meaning to HTML or XML are escaped using the *entity references* we discussed briefly in chapter 2. This feature lets you use <c:out> without worrying that your data will get in the way of the HTML or XML output you're producing.

Imagine that a scoped variable contains the text AT&T, or <o>, or another string that has one or more characters with special meaning to XML. (The following characters are special to XML: &, <, >, ', and ".) By default, if you print such a variable with <c:out>, any special characters that it contains will be escaped as &, <, and so forth. This escaping causes HTML browsers to display the characters to the user instead of treating them as part of HTML or XML tags. For example, if the variable eye contains the text <o>, then

```
<c:out value="${eye}"/>
```

will output

```
&lt;o&gt;
```

where < stands in for < and > stands in for >. Thus, an HTML browser will display the text <o>—the original value of ${eye}—to the user. If <c:out> were instead to output <o> unescaped, then the browser would see an unrecognized HTML tag, and the user wouldn't see the information at all.

Normally, `<c:out>`'s escaping is exactly what you want, and you don't have to worry about it. Since `<c:out>`'s escaping covers quotation marks (`"` and `'`), you can even safely use `<c:out>` in the middle of an HTML tag's attribute, as follows:

```
<input type="text"
  name="username"
  value="<c:out value="${param.username}"/>"/>
```

If `<c:out>` didn't escape quotation marks, then a value for `${param.username}` that contained quotes could break your `<input>` tag, potentially causing it to end prematurely. By contrast, the escaped values are safe.

In rare cases, you may want to shut off `<c:out>`'s escaping. You can do this by setting `<c:out>`'s `escapeXml` attribute to `false`, as follows:

```
<c:out value="${quotation}" escapeXml="false"/>
```

This can be useful if you want to allow a variable to contain its own HTML formatting (such as `<b>` or `<i>` tags). With `escapeXml="false"`, the formatting tags will be sent to the browser and will have an effect on the way text is displayed. Otherwise, the user will see the formatting tags as literal text (e.g., `<b>` will show up in the browser window), and the browser will not interpret them.

If this seems confusing, don't worry. You can normally ignore the `escapeXml` attribute.

3.2 Scoped variables and the expression language

Now that we've looked briefly at `<c:out>`, we can discuss the expression language in more detail.

The major goal of the JSTL expression language is to make data easy to access. This data can fall into a number of categories. For instance, you might find the data you need in *scoped variables*, which you initially saw in chapter 2. In addition, you will probably often need to read data from *request parameters*—the mechanism JSP uses to read HTML forms. For now, we'll focus on scoped variables, and we'll look at other kinds of data later in this chapter.

Scoped variables typically are created in one of two ways: either you establish them yourself, or, if your pages are supported by some back-end Java code (written by you or another member of your team), this back-end code can set them. Either way, you can use the expression language to easily access the variables.

3.2.1 Basic syntax to access scoped variables

In some ways, the JSTL expression language centers on scoped variables. An expression like `${username}` simply means "the scoped variable named `username`." That is, an expression that contains just a single name, or *identifier*, points to the scoped variable with that name.

When the name of a scoped variable appears alone in an expression—as in ${username}—it causes the expression language to search all the JSP scopes for a variable. The *page* scope is searched first, followed by *request*, then *session*, and finally *application.* So, the expression ${username} will return the value of the page-scoped variable named username if one exists. If not, then it will return the request-scoped variable named username, and so on. If none of the scopes has a variable named username, then the expression returns nothing.[1]

Sometimes, you want to retrieve a variable from a particular scope. For instance, you might not want some data unless it comes from session or application scope, perhaps because that's where someone else working on your application has told you it exists, or because you know that's where you put it. Either way, you can name specific scopes inside your expression. To do this, begin the expression with the name of the scope, followed by the word Scope, followed by a period (.). For example, consider the expressions in table 3.2.

Table 3.2 In addition to letting the expression language search all scopes automatically, you can point to data in specific scopes using expressions like those in this table.

Sample expression	Meaning
${pageScope.username}	username variable in page scope
${requestScope.username}	username variable in request scope
${sessionScope.username}	username variable in session scope
${applicationScope.username}	username variable in application scope

For example, consider a scoped variable set by a back-end Java developer. I often provide some data about an authenticated user to page authors I work with. I tell them something like, "The session-scoped variable named user contains the user's identification." Then, if the page needs to print the user's identification, the author of that page can write

```
<c:out value="${sessionScope.user}"/>
```

---

[1] This nothingness is formally called null. You may see or hear the term null when you talk with others about Java or JSTL, but you don't usually need to use the null keyword in JSTL's expression language. Instead, see the empty operator in section 3.4.3.

JSTL pages can store data in scoped variables themselves; scopes aren't just for back-end Java developers. As you'll see later in this chapter and in the rest of this book, many JSTL tags let you create and store scoped variables.

3.2.2 *Different types of scoped data*

Scoped variables can come in many different varieties, which are formally called *types* (or *data types*) in Java applications. The expression language supports many types of data. Normally, data types are the sorts of things programmers deal with, and JSTL, for the most part, hides the unpleasant details of types from web pages. Much of the time, you can use a scoped variable without worrying about its type.

However, you'll sometimes need to think about the data type of a scoped variable. For instance, as you'll see in chapter 4, some tags have attributes that need yes or no values, which are represented by a particular data type. In chapter 5, we'll look at the `<c:forEach>` tag, which is useful only when one of its attributes receives a scoped variable that stores a collection or container of other variables; as you'll see soon, you can't sensibly treat all variables as if they're collections of data.

Strings and numbers

You might already be familiar with the term *string*. A string is series of characters that forms some arbitrary text: a word, a sentence, a paragraph, or even a whole book. Strings can contain more than letters; they can also have numbers, punctuation, special characters like "¢", foreign characters like "_", and so on. People typically use strings to store simple textual information, like users' names, email addresses, phone numbers, and so on. Strings are particularly useful for information that will eventually be printed out to a web page.

When a tag like `<c:out>` is pointed to a string, it prints out that string. For instance, if the scoped variable username holds the string José, then the tag

```
<c:out value="${username}"/>
```

will print out the string José.

What happens if the `<c:out>` tag points to a scoped variable that isn't a string? In such cases, JSTL's ability to hide the details of data types comes into play. If the `<c:out>` tag's value attribute resolves to some data type other than a string, it will simply convert the data into a string and print it. (In Java, every piece of data—whether or not a string—has some way of being printed out as a string. As we look at data types in the following sections, we'll discuss how they're converted to strings when necessary.)

Scoped variables can also store numbers. These numbers can be either *integers* (familiar, whole numbers like 6 and –94) or *floating-point numbers* (like –25.77 or 3.14). Numbers are formally a different data type from strings, but with JSTL, you usually don't have to worry about the difference. If a tag ever needs a number, you can provide a string that represents that number (like 5, which is a valid string even though it represents a number). Similarly, if you ever have a number and need to print it out in your web page, JSTL automatically prints it out for you in a default, sensible format. (However, you might want to choose a particular format for your numbers—for instance, you might want to display them as currencies, or with no more than three decimal places. Chapter 10 shows you how you can change the formatting of numbers in your pages.)

When you have two numbers, you can use the expression language to perform simple arithmetic on them. You saw a trivial example earlier: the expression ${1 + 2} results in the number 3. The JSTL expression language supports the mathematical operators listed in table 3.3.

Table 3.3 JSTL supports these mathematical operators in expressions. You can use these operators to write expressions like ${3 + 1} and ${height * width}. The operators / and div are interchangeable, as are % and mod.

Operator	Description	Sample expression	Result
+	Addition	${10 + 2}	12
–	Subtraction	${10 – 2}	8
*	Multiplication	${10 * 2}	20
/div	Division	${10 / 2}	5
%mod	Remainder	${10 % 2}	0

In addition to these operators, you can precede a single number with a minus sign (-) to switch it from positive to negative, or vice versa. For example, if the scoped variable price held the integer 50, the expression

```
${-price}
```

would evaluate to

```
-50
```

Booleans

Programmers often speak of *boolean* data, named after George Boole, a nineteenth-century mathematician who invented symbolic logic. (Symbolic logic is a mathematical way of expressing statements like, "If I took my wristwatch off, it must be on the nightstand. But it isn't on the nightstand, so I must not have taken it off. Or maybe I'm just growing senile.")

A boolean variable has two possible values: `true` and `false`. These values can also be interpreted as "yes" and "no." Whereas strings and numbers can take on virtually unlimited values, a boolean variable can store only these two values.

This limitation makes boolean variables particularly useful for yes-or-no questions. For example, the `escapeXml` attribute for `<c:out>` that we discussed in section 3.1 is a boolean attribute: it needs a boolean variable. Our earlier example showed `escapeXml` being used as follows:

```
<c:out value="${username}" escapeXml="false"/>
```

In this case, `escapeXml` was given the static value `false`. But just as `<c:out>`'s value attribute can accept expressions, so can `escapeXml`. If the scoped variable `status` has a boolean value, you can write this:

```
<c:out value="${username}" escapeXml="${status}"/>
```

This `<c:out>` tag will decide whether to escape special characters depending on the value of the scoped attribute `status`. In chapter 4, you'll see how to set scoped boolean variables.

If you print a boolean value using `<c:out>`, it will be printed as `"true"` or `"false"`, as appropriate.

NOTE   Java has two different boolean data types: `boolean` and `Boolean`. (Java is case-sensitive, so these represent different types.) For our purposes, they are nearly identical, so you don't have to worry about the differences between them.

Collections

When a scoped variable is a string, number, or boolean, it stores exactly one thing: a piece of text, a number, or a truth value. Sometimes, however, a single scoped variable can store an entire collection of objects. The most obvious example, in our mercenary world, is a shopping cart. An application might make a shopping-cart variable accessible as

```
${sessionScope.shoppingCart}
```

Such a variable refers to an entire collection of objects, organized under a single name: `shoppingCart`.

There are two kinds of collections, which are accessed by somewhat different syntax. To visualize the differences, you may want to follow along with figure 3.2.

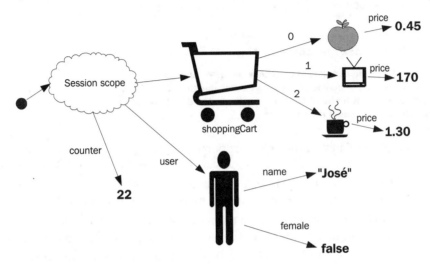

Figure 3.2 A sample session that stores a variety of data. The `counter` variable stores a simple number, but `shoppingCart` and `user` both refer to collections of data. Note how all the collections ultimately lead to simple data like strings, numbers, and boolean values.

One kind of collection stores lists of items, arranged in order. This collection is similar to an *array* in programming languages (in case you've encountered that term before). In figure 3.2, the `shoppingCart` variable is a numeric, ordered collection that stores three items. You can refer to them as `${sessionScope.shopping-Cart[0]}` (the apple), `${sessionScope.shoppingCart[1]}` (the television), and `${sessionScope.shoppingCart[2]}` (the cup of java). You'll see in chapter 5 how to cycle over each of these items automatically in turn. The point, for now, is that you can access them individually using square brackets: `[` and `]`. See figure 3.3.[2]

The second type of collection stores groups of items, organized by name.[3] In figure 3.2, the `user` variable is a collection that has items organized by name. In this example, it has two items: `name` and `female`. Suppose that the `name` item—or *property*—

---

[2] If you're familiar with Java data types, you might wonder what types of ordered data you can access using the `[]` notation in the expression language. The answer is simple: any Java array, and also any `List` object.

[3] The JSTL expression language can access either JavaBeans or `Map` objects as unordered collections, though you don't need to know this if you're not a Java programmer. If you do know Java, chapter 14 will show you how to expose data that the expression language can access.

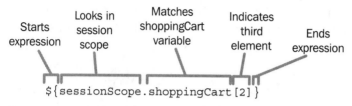

Figure 3.3   A sample expression to access an array, or ordered collection of items. The item is accessed as usual, and then it's followed by square brackets with a number, indicating the ordered item to match. In this case, the third item is selected.

contains the user's first name. This property is a string, and it can take on a value like `Reginald`, `Martha`, or, in figure 3.2, `José`. The second property is boolean, and it describes whether the user is female. In figure 3.2's case, the `female` property is `false`. (What could be less feminine than a men's-room icon named José?)

These items don't have any particular order; they're just grouped for convenience. Therefore, accessing them with `[]` and a number doesn't work. Instead, you can point to an item by using a period (.) followed by the name of the item. For instance, to figure out the user's name, we can write `${sessionScope.user.name}`. To figure out whether the user is female, we can write `${sessionScope.user.female}`.

Any item in a collection can be a collection itself. This fact is demonstrated by the `shoppingCart` variable in figure 3.2. Each item is a collection; it might contain properties like `inStock` (whether the item is in stock) and `freeShipping` (whether the item qualifies for free shipping). Figure 3.2 shows one such potential property: `price`. If we want to figure out the price of the second item in the shopping cart, we can write the following:

```
${sessionScope.shoppingCart[1].price}
```

In figure 3.2's case, such an expression ultimately points to a floating-point number, like 0.45 or 170, representing the number of dollars in the price of the object. Because this object is a number, we can use it with the arithmetic operators we discussed earlier and write an expression like

```
${sessionScope.shoppingCart[1].price - 10}
```

that might represent the price of the second item with a $10 discount. If the data in figure 3.2 were accessible to our page, then the following tag

```
<c:out value="${sessionScope.shoppingCart[1].price - 10}"/>
```

would output 170.0. (This isn't the best way to output a dollar value, but we'll have to wait until chapter 10 to discuss how to print currency more cleanly.)

Miscellaneous types

Java has data types for all sorts of things. Later in this book, we'll encounter scoped variables that store dates, XML documents, database connections, and more. You can print the string interpretation of all these data types using `<c:out>`, but some JSTL tags let you use particular types specially. For instance, a tag like `<sql:query>`, which lets you retrieve data from a database, has a `dataSource` attribute that accepts various kinds of objects that represent database connections. This attribute lets you tell the tag what database you want to connect to. You'll learn more about database tags in chapter 9.

3.3 *Request parameters and the expression language*

JSP pages use scoped variables to manage their own data. But pages can also receive input from the outside world—for instance, from a user entering information into an HTML form. This information is made available to your web page through *request parameters.*

In this section, we'll demonstrate how you can use JSTL to receive input from HTML forms.

| TIP | If you're already familiar with request parameters, there are just two things you need to know, and you can quickly skim the rest of this section. First, to point to a request parameter using the expression language, you simply write `${param.name}`, where *name* is the name of the parameter you want. Second, if a request parameter has multiple values, you need to use `${paramValues.name}` instead of `${param.name}`. Using `paramValues` lets you retrieve a collection of all the parameters with a given name. |

3.3.1 *HTML forms*

As you might know if you've designed dynamic web pages before, HTML forms are a common way to let users enter data into your web application. When you use HTML `<form>`, `<input>`, and similar tags in your page, the user's web browser displays a form that looks a little like a paper form (see figure 3.4).

We don't have the space here to go over every attribute to every HTML form tag in detail; because many attributes for HTML form tags concern graphical layout, a book specifically about HTML is better suited for their details. (Or see appendix D for some excellent online HTML references.)

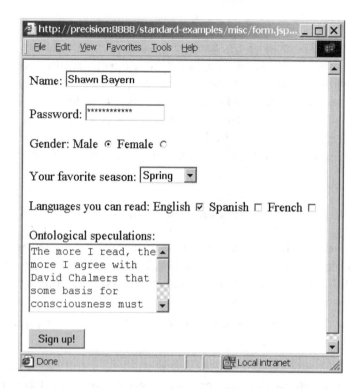

Figure 3.4
**A sample HTML form, which
is built from tags like
`<form>`, `<input>`,
`<select>`, and
`<textarea>`. Forms like
this aren't specific to JSTL,
but you can easily handle
input from them using the
JSTL expression language.**

However, let's look quickly at the way HTML form tags work. If you haven't used
HTML forms before, the examples here should be enough to get you started. Take a
look at listing 3.1, which shows the HTML source used to produce figure 3.4.

Listing 3.1   A simple HTML form

```
<form method="post" action="formHandler.jsp">

  <p>Name:
    <input type="text" name="username" size="20" /></p>

  <p>Password:
     <input type="password" name="pw" size="14" /></p>

  <p>Gender:
    Male <input type="radio" name="gender" value="male" />
    Female <input type="radio" name="gender" value="female" />
  </p>

  <p>Your favorite season:
      <select name="season">
        <option value="winter">Winter</option>
        <option value="spring">Spring</option>
```

```
          <option value="summer">Summer</option>
          <option value="fall">Fall</option>
      </select>
  </p>

  <p>Languages you can read:
    English
      <input type="checkbox" name="language" value="english" />
    Spanish
      <input type="checkbox" name="language" value="spanish" />
    French
      <input type="checkbox" name="language" value="french" />
  </p>

  <p>Ontological speculations:<br />
    <textarea rows="5" columns="40" name="philosophy" />
  </p>

  <input type="submit" value="Sign up!" />

</form>
```

It should be easy to see how the individual tags in listing 3.1 line up with the various parts of the form shown in figure 3.4. Let's look at each piece of the form in turn.

The <form> tag

An HTML form begins with <form> and ends with </form>. Between these two tags come tags for the various form elements, such as <input>, <select>, and <tex-tarea>. We'll look at these individual tags in a moment; for now, I want to draw your attention to the start tag for <form>:

```
<form method="post" action="formHandler.jsp">
```

This tag has two attributes, method and action. The action attribute is more important for us. It functions basically like href in <a> or src in <img>—that is, it lets you enter a link. For our purposes, this link will typically be a relative URL and point to a JSP file in the current directory. The action attribute means, "When the user submits this form, what page should I load, and where should I send the input?" For example, the <form> tag we just looked at causes a page named formHandler.jsp to run and receive the form's input when the user submits the form. (You'll see in a moment how the user submits a form.)

The value of the method parameter doesn't matter much for now, but you can think of it this way: by default, or if method="get", all of the form's input will show up encoded into the URL. (You'll see more about the way this data is structured in chapters 5 and 6.) By contrast, when method="post", this data is hidden from the casual observer and is instead sent to the target page using a different behind-the-scenes mechanism. But JSTL tags don't care whether the `method` attribute is set to `"get"` or `"post"`; in either case, they read the input the same way. In general, if you have to pick one, `"post"` is widely considered to be preferable and more elegant.

Text and password boxes

The most straightforward piece of an HTML form is a simple text box for input. This is a one-line box that lets the user enter a string of text—for instance, a name or email address. The tag looks like this:

```
<input type="text" name="username" size="20" />
```

To create a text box, use an `<input>` tag that has an attribute of `type="text"`. I've also included in listing 3.1 an example of the `size` attribute, which adjusts the width of a text box—the approximate number of characters the user will be able to enter into that box before it scrolls.

The important attribute of all input tags, for our purposes, is `name`. The value of the `name` attribute is the name we'll use to access the data the user enters, once the form is submitted. It is the name of the *request parameter* the browser will submit.

The expression language makes it easy to access request parameters. Recall from table 3.2 that you can use expressions like `${pageScope.variable}` and `${sessionScope.variable}` to access scoped variables. The syntax for accessing request parameters is similar. Instead of beginning your expression with `pageScope` or `sessionScope`, you start it with `param`. For instance, the following example lets you access the value of the request parameter from the `<input>` tag you just saw:

```
${param.username}
```

In the page that handles the form, `${param.username}` will equal whatever the user typed in this text box.

Every request parameter is a string. This is true even if the user enters a number into a particular input field. However, as I said earlier, JSTL doesn't force you to worry about the difference between strings and numbers. If the user enters a proper number, you can treat it as a number if you ever need to. (Chapter 10 discusses in more detail how to handle cases where users input numbers—and even dates.)

A password box is just like a plain text box, but it has the attribute `type="password"` instead of `type="text"`:

```
<input type="password" name="pw" size="14" />
```

The major difference between a password box and a plain text box is that browsers usually print stars (∗∗∗) or other characters to hide the value the user types in the box, because they presume it's something sensitive like a password. Notice that in figure 3.4 you can't see the password I chose, although you can see my name. (You'll have to buy my next book if you want to learn my password too.)

A password box, like a text box, causes a request parameter to be set based on its name attribute. For the sample tag we just looked at, we'll be able to read the user's password using the expression ${param.pw}.

Selection boxes

Selection boxes are a little more complicated than text boxes. Instead of presenting the user with blank box to type in, a selection box displays a list of choices and lets the user select one. Rather than being introduced into your page with a single tag, such boxes begin with a <select> tag and include a number of <option> tags that delineate the options the user can choose from; they end with a closing </select> tag. A select tag starts like this:

```
<select name="season">
```

In this sample <select>, the only thing we need to specify is the name of the tag's request parameter. Because the tag has the attribute name="season", whichever value the user chooses will be available to us using ${param.season}.

You can tell the browser what options to show the user by using <option> tags. The body of each option tag is the option that will be displayed in the user's browser. Option tags have an optional attribute, value, that gives you control over the request parameter that will be sent back to you. For many options, it's common to show the user one thing, but to receive a different chosen string back as the request parameter. For instance, in listing 3.1, we use option tags like this:

```
<option value="winter">Winter</option>
```

This tag displays the choice Winter (with a capital letter) to the user but records the choice as winter (lowercase) if the user chooses this option. There isn't much difference between the two in this case, although if you're storing the information to a database managed by someone else, you might need to make sure you use a lowercase instead of a capital letter (or vice versa). It's common to use <option> tags to convert between numbers and letters so that you don't have to bother doing this conversion in your JSP page. For instance, the following tags display month names, but send you back month numbers instead:

```
<option value="1">January</option>
<option value="2">February</option>
...
```

(These numbers are really strings containing numbers, but again, this difference doesn't matter much in JSTL.) Just because you need numbers doesn't mean the user should have to see an unfriendly prompt; these tags let you choose what the user sees but give you control over the data you receive back.

Nothing prevents you from having multiple options map to the same value. For instance, one application I designed for Yale University asked students to choose their dormitory. Because my application treated some dorms the same as others, several `<option>` tags had the same value. But the user didn't need to know which dorms were treated identically; the `<option>` tags took care of this behavior behind the scenes. As an example, consider a tag like this:

```
Do you love me?
<select name="love">
  <option value="yes">Yes!</option>
  <option value="yes">No!</option>
</select>
```

This example probably isn't useful in your web pages, but it might ease the burden of romantic rejection; no matter which option the user chooses, the box's parameter is set to `yes`.

Select boxes can be arranged to let users select multiple values instead of just a single value. To do this, add the attribute `multiple="multiple"` to the `<select>` tag. When we discuss check boxes in the next section, you'll see what happens when a browser sends multiple values for the same request parameter.

Radio buttons and check boxes

Radio buttons and *check boxes* are two different kinds of fields that a user can click to provide input. Radio buttons usually appear as circles in web browsers, and a user can click only one of them at once. They're appropriate for fields like gender or religion, where a user typically chooses only one out of many potential values. For this reason, radio buttons are a lot like simple `<select>` boxes. The major difference between selection boxes and radio buttons is their visual appearance on your web page. It's common to see radio buttons when an input field has only a few choices, whereas `<select>` boxes are often used when a field has a large number of choices. This makes sense: by default, `<select>` shows only one choice at a time, so it saves space on the user's screen when there are lots of choices.

To use radio buttons, you insert a tag for each button into your page. Unlike the `<option>` tag for selection boxes, any descriptive text (such as "Male" or "Female") isn't part of the tag itself; it just appears near the tag to give the user a hint about which button to click. Here are the two radio buttons from listing 3.1:

```
<input type="radio" name="gender" value="male" />
<input type="radio" name="gender" value="female" />
```

The interesting thing to note about these tags is that they have the same value for the `name` attribute. This is how the browser knows to let the user click only one button. It doesn't matter whether the buttons are near each other (although they usually are); the only thing that connects two different radio buttons is the fact that they share a `name`. When a user submits a form, the browser determines which button the user has clicked and sends its `value` as the appropriate parameter (based on the radio-button group's `name`). In this example, if the user clicks the first button, the expression `${param.gender}` will equal `male`.

Check boxes work just like radio buttons, but users can check as many of them as they want. You can add them to your pages with tags like this:

```
<input type="checkbox" name="language" value="english" />
```

You might wonder what happens when a user selects multiple check boxes and submits a form. If all request parameters are simple strings, what would `${param.language}` equal in our sample form from listing 3.1 if the user clicks the check boxes for both English and Spanish?

The answer is somewhat disappointing: because every `param` expression is a string and not a collection, the parameter can store only one value. In this case, the first one from the form is used. The others are stored in a collection that you can access by starting your expression with `paramValues` instead of `param`. The collection is ordered, so you can use the `[]` syntax to access individual values. For instance, `${paramValues.language[0]}` indicates the first language the user chose from the form, and `${paramValues.language[1]}` indicates the second one (assuming the user chose two). In chapter 11, you'll see how to handle checkbox parameters conveniently.

By the way, I mentioned multiselect boxes—`<select multiple="multiple">`— in the section about selection boxes earlier. When a user chooses multiple values out of a multiselect box, they're handled the same way check boxes with multiple values are handled.

Text areas

The last HTML input type we'll look at for now is the `<textarea>` box. Text areas are useful when you want to give the user an opportunity to type in a long block of prose (or poetry, for that matter). For instance, they'd be useful for resumés, customer feedback, messages in a chat room, and so on. The sample form in figure 3.4 shows a box asking for the user's philosophical thoughts, to demonstrate the broad, flexible nature of these boxes.

When we discussed strings earlier, I mentioned that strings can contain sentences or even paragraphs. With `<textarea>` boxes, strings get to prove their mettle. The entire block of text the user types into a `<textarea>` comes back to your JSP page as a single parameter. For example, the entire box created by

```
<textarea rows="5" columns="40" name="philosophy" />
```

comes back as a single parameter: `${param.philosophy}`.

Submitting a form

To add a submission button to a form, you add an `<input>` tag with the attribute `type="submit"`:

```
<input type="submit" value="Sign up!" />
```

This tag adds a button to the form (labeled with whatever's inside the `value` attribute); when the user clicks it, the form is sent to the page named in the `action` attribute of the original `<form>` tag.

TIP   Submission buttons created with `<input type="submit">` can also have `name` attributes. That is, they can also create request parameters. For instance, a button like

```
<input type="submit" value="Register" name="choice" />
```

will set a request parameter `${param.choice}` equal to the string `Register`. This functionality is particularly useful if you want your form to have multiple submission buttons, and you want to figure out which button the user clicked to submit the form.

3.3.2 A page that reads request parameters

We've spent quite a bit of time discussing HTML forms and individual request parameters. Let's look, at last, at a dynamic page that reads some parameters. As an example, we'll write a page called formHandler.jsp that handles the form in figure 3.4 (and listing 3.1). To get this page to work, simply add it to the same directory as the page that produced the form. Listing 3.2 shows an example of such a page.

> **Listing 3.2   formHandler.jsp: a page that prints out the results of a form**

```
<%@ taglib prefix="c" uri="http://java.sun.com/jstl/core" %>

<p>Wow, I know a lot about you...</p>

<p>Your name is <c:out value="${param.username}"/>.</p>

<p>Your password (sssssh!) is '<c:out value="${param.pw}"/>'.</p>

<p>You are <c:out value="${param.gender}"/>.</p>
```

```
<p>Your favorite season is <c:out value="${param.season}"/>.</p>
<p>One language you can read is
   <c:out value="${param.language}"/>.</p>
<p>Some of your philosophical thoughts include:</p>
      <blockquote><c:out value="${param.philosophy}"/></blockquote>
```

Figure 3.5 shows what this page outputs for the input from figure 3.4.

Figure 3.5
Output of the formHandler.jsp page from listing 3.2. This page prints out different values depending on what the user (in this case, me) entered in an HTML form. Later chapters show how to take advantage of this information more usefully.

In later chapters, we'll look at other things you can do with form input. For instance, you can store it in a long-term database, or ask questions about what the user entered.

3.4 *More powerful expressions*

JSTL's expression language was designed to be easy to use, so although the expressions we've covered so far are all pretty simple, they'll meet your needs in many pages you write. However, the expression language is a little more powerful than we've given it credit for so far. The good news is that it's not too difficult to use the expression language's more advanced features. In this section, we discuss two broad topics. First, in section 3.4.1, we look at how you can use the expression language to access data other than scoped variables and request parameters. Then, in the remaining sections, we introduce some of the expression language's advanced syntax; it lets you write expressions that combine more than one expression, such as `${weight gt IQ}` ("is the `weight` variable greater than the `IQ` variable?") or `${cute and single}` ("are *both* the `cute` and `single` boolean variables equal to `true`?").

3.4.1 *Different ways to access properties*

In section 3.2.2, you saw that you can use a period (.) to access a member of an unordered collection. For example, to get the `phone` property of the `user` variable, you can write `${user.phone}`.

You can also access properties of unordered collections using the `[]` syntax, just as with ordered collections. However, when a collection isn't ordered, you can't use numbers inside the brackets; instead, you need to use a string. For instance, the expression `${sessionScope.user["name"]}` is equivalent to `${sessionScope.user.name}`

You might wonder why JSTL supports two syntaxes to do the same thing. One major reason is historical: JavaScript does this, so JSTL does too in order to be familiar to as many users as possible. But in addition, if a property name contains a special character—like . or - or just about anything that isn't a number or a letter,[4] you can't use the dot (.) notation with it; you need to use brackets (`[]`) instead. For example, if a property is named `My-Address`, you'd want to access it like this: `${user["My-Address"]}`. Note that we used quotes around the name of the property.

TIP   If you don't use quotes, brackets also let you use a variable to decide dynamically which property you want to access. For instance, the expression `${user.phone}` always retrieves the `phone` property of `user`. But consider an expression like this: `${user[data]}`. This expression first looks up the `data` variable, and then uses its value to get a property of `user`. For instance, if `data` equals `phone`, this expression is equivalent to `${user.phone}`; but if `data` equals `address`, the expression means the same thing as `${user.address}`. This is an advanced pattern, so don't worry if it seems confusing. You'll rarely need it, but it's a powerful technique that you should experiment with.

---

[4] Technically, any name that can be used for a variable in Java can be used with the period (.) operator. I'm not going to discuss the details of which names are valid and which aren't because I've never liked books that spend pages and pages discussing what valid identifiers look like—whether or not they, and so on.

3.4.2 *Accessing other data with the expression language*

So far, you've seen six different ways to start an expression: `pageScope`, `request-Scope`, `sessionScope`, `applicationScope`, `param`, and `paramValues`. In addition, you can simply use the name of any scoped variable as an expression unto itself, as in `${username}`.

The interesting thing about each of the six ways you can start an expression is that they're all collections of their own. Remember how a variable like `shoppingCart` (see figure 3.2) could contain items you access by name, simply by typing a period (.) and the name of the item? This is exactly how the core collections—known officially as *implicit objects*—work. The expression `${pageScope}` points to a collection of all the variables in page scope; `${params}` points to your page's request parameters.

We haven't yet discussed a few more core (implicit) objects. Table 3.4 lists them.

Table 3.4 JSTL offers several implicit objects that let you access data other than scoped variables and parameters.

Implicit object	Description
`cookie`	The value of a cookie sent by the web browser
`header`	A header sent by the web browser
`headerValues`	All values of a header sent by the web browser
`initParam`	A context-initialization parameter
`pageContext`	Detailed information about the current page

Let's briefly look at each of these objects.

Cookies

A *cookie* is a way for a web server to send the user some information that the web browser keeps track of persistently—for a few minutes or a few years. Cookies are like the hand stamps that clubs and amusement parks use to record the fact that they've seen you before.

JSTL doesn't give you any way to set cookies, because that's the job of back-end Java code. However, if you're told that a cookie called `colorPreference` is available, you can access it with an expression like `${cookie.colorPreference}`.

Headers

Headers are data that web servers and web browsers use to communicate with each other behind the scenes. When a web page is loaded, it has the opportunity to send header information that describes the request. Headers contain things like the browser type, localization information about the client machine, and other details.

Most of these details aren't important, but using headers to access the browser type is useful when you want to decide what to display based on the user's web browser. Web browsers send information about their make and model to servers using a header called User-Agent. For instance, you can use an expression like

```
${header["User-Agent"]}
```

Rarely, you might need headerValues if a browser sends two headers with the same name. The headers you typically access are available through header instead of headerValues in most cases.

Initialization parameters

As with scoped variables, back-end Java programmers can set information called *context initialization parameters*. If you're told to access an initialization parameter, or if you want to access one that you set yourself, you can do so with initParam—for example, ${initParam.headerUrl}. Initialization parameters are useful when the same application is deployed to multiple servers at once and needs to be configured for each of its environments.

PageContext

The variable that's accessible as ${pageContext} lets you access some detailed information about your page. Most of the time, you won't need this information, and you won't have to use expressions starting with pageContext. Some of these expressions are beyond the scope of the book, and they're listed in table 3.5 only for completeness. But we'll touch on a few of them later in this book, so table 3.5 will be useful for future reference.

Table 3.5 JSTL expressions involving pageContext. These somewhat involved expressions are useful if you need detailed information about the current page's environment. Normally, you won't need to use such expressions, but they come in handy on occasion.

Expression	Description	Sample value
${pageContext.request.authType}	The type of authentication the page used, if applicable	BASIC
${pageContext.request.remoteUser}	The user's ID, if the server manages authentication	djdavies
${pageContext.request.contextPath}	The name of your web application (context)	/examples
${pageContext.request.cookies}	An ordered collection (array) of all your page's cookies	n/a
${pageContext.request.method}	The HTTP method used to access your page	GET

Table 3.5 JSTL expressions involving `pageContext`. These somewhat involved expressions are useful if you need detailed information about the current page's environment. Normally, you won't need to use such expressions, but they come in handy on occasion. *(continued)*

Expression	Description	Sample value
`${pageContext.request.queryString}`	Your page's entire query string	`p1=value1&p2=value2`
`${pageContext.request.requestURL}`	The URL used to access your page	`http://server/app/page.jsp`
`${pageContext.session.new}`	`true` if the session is new; `false` otherwise	`true`
`${pageContext.servlet-Context.serverInfo}`	Information about your JSP container	`Apache Tomcat/5.0.0`
`${pageContext.exception.message}`	For a page marked as an `errorPage`, a description of the error that occurred	`"Something very, very bad happened"`

3.4.3 Comparisons

You can use the expression language to produce boolean values even when your inputs aren't boolean. For instance, the expression `${2 == 2}` results in `true`. Note the use of two equal signs (`==`) as a way of comparing two values. Many programming languages, including Java and JavaScript, use similar syntax, so it might look familiar.

Table 3.6 lists the JSTL expression language's comparison and equality operators.

Table 3.6 JSTL supports these comparison and equality operators in expressions. You can use these operators to write expressions like `${2 == 2}` or `${user.weight gt user.IQ}`. Every comparison operator has a symbolic version (`==`) and a textual one (`eq`).

Operator	Description	Sample expression	Result
`==` `eq`	Equals	`${5 == 5}`	`true`
`!=` `ne`	Not equals	`${5 != 5}`	`false`
`<` `lt`	Less than	`${5 < 7}`	`true`
`>` `gt`	Greater than	`${5 > 7}`	`false`
`<=` `le`	Less than or equal to	`${5 le 5}`	`true`
`>=` `ge`	Greater than or equal to	`${5 ge 6}`	`false`

> **NOTE**   Every comparison operator has two different versions: one that's symbolic
> and one that's textual. For instance, `==` means the same thing as `eq`, and `!=`
> means the same thing as `ne`. You can use whichever version you're more
> comfortable with. Keep in mind, however, that `<` must be written as `&lt;`
> in an XML document.

You can use these operators to compare any two numbers that are accessible to the
expression language. Suppose you have two expressions, `${user.weight}` (representing the user's weight in pounds) and `${user.IQ}` (representing the user's IQ, or
intelligence quotient). You could compare these values (in order to see if the user
has more brains or brawn) by writing this expression:

```
${user.weight gt user.IQ}
```

This expression is `true` if `${user.weight}` has a higher value than `${user.IQ}`; it is
`false` otherwise.

> **NOTE**   It's important to realize that the `${` and `}` delimiters cover the entire expression, not just each component of it. Thus we do *not* write
>
> ```
> ${user.weight} gt ${user.IQ}
> ```
>
> or
>
> ```
> ${ ${user.weight} gt ${user.IQ} }
> ```
>
> Neither of these expressions is valid. Instead, a single set of `${` and `}` is sufficient for the whole expression:
>
> ```
> ${user.weight gt user.IQ}
> ```

Comparisons are particularly useful when you want to check a request parameter
again a specific value. For instance, you could use the expression

```
${param.month == "May"}
```

to determine whether the user chose month 5 from a list of months. If the `month`
parameter corresponds to a `<select>` box, and the user chooses an option like

```
<option>May</option>
```

then `${param.month == "May"}` will be `true`.

   We'll look more at how you can use boolean values—such as those you create
using comparison operators like `==` or `le`—in chapter 5.

The JSTL expression language lets you compare more than just strings. You can compare any two expressions as long as it makes sense to compare them. (The data types of the objects decide what makes sense.) For instance, if you have two dates (see chapter 10 for information on how to get a date), you can compare them to determine which comes earlier or later.

Checking to see if a variable exists

In section 3.2.1, I mentioned that sometimes a variable points to nothingness. Moreover, a collection or string can be empty. You can use the word `empty` to determine if a particular variable or parameter exists or not. For example

```
${empty param.choice}
```

is `true` only if the `choice` parameter wasn't specified on a form. (This might be the case if the form had no input field named `choice`, or—with a set of check boxes—if the user didn't specify any checkbox in the group named `choice`.) Similarly,

```
${empty sessionScope.userName}
```

is `true` if there's no session-scoped variable named `userName`, or if the name is an empty string or some sort of empty collection. If this variable exists and isn't empty, the expression will be `false`.[5]

3.4.4 Boolean operations and parentheses

When you have two boolean values—either because you retrieved them from scoped variables or because you built them using the operators we discussed in the last section—you can use the words `and`, `or`, and `not` to join them. For instance, the expression

```
${2==2 and 3==3}
```

is `true` because 2 equals 2 and 3 equals 3. Similarly, the expression

```
${param.month == 5 and param.day == 25}
```

is `true` only if the request parameter `month` equals 5 *and* the parameter `day` equals 25.

> **NOTE** In addition to `and`, `or`, and `not`, you can use `&&`, `||`, and `!`. You can use whichever style of boolean operator you're more comfortable with, but keep in mind that (as we discussed in chapter 2) the `&` character must be

---

[5] You can also compare a value directly to `null`, as in `${param.choice == null}`. For our purposes, however, the `empty` operator is easier and less prone to errors.

written as `&amp;` in an XML document. This requirement makes `&&` less useful than `and`.

Expressions that use `or` are `true` if *any* of their components is true. For instance,

```
${param.month == 5 or param.month == 6}
```

is true if the `month` parameter equals 5 *or* 6.

Just as in mathematical expressions, you can use parentheses to force a particular grouping for your expression. For instance, the meaning of an expression like

```
${param.month == 5 or param.month == 6 and param.day == 25}
```

might not be immediately clear. But you can add parentheses to group different parts of the expression together. For instance, if you wrote this:

```
${ (param.month == 5 or param.month == 6) and (param.day == 25) }
```

it would be `true` when the month was equal to 5 or 6, and the day was equal to 25. Exactly two days would match the expression: May 25 and June 25. But if you wrote this:

```
${ (param.month == 5) or (param.month == 6 and param.day == 25) }
```

then the expression would be `true` for all of May, and for June 25. Thus, it would match 32 days in total, not just 2 (like the previous expression).

The `not` operator converts `true` into `false`, and vice versa. For instance, to check whether the parameter `choice` is *not* empty or missing, you could write

```
${not empty param.choice}
```

You can mix `and`, `or`, and `not` to your heart's content. The result is always a boolean value—`true` or `false`. You'll see how to use boolean values in chapter 5.

3.4.5 *Multiple expressions*

Wherever you can use a single expression, you can use multiple expressions. You can also mix text freely with expressions. For example, the following is perfectly valid:

```
<c:out value="Hi ${user.first} ${user.last}" />
```

This code isn't too useful in `<c:out>`, because you could accomplish the same thing with a combination of simple template text and multiple `<c:out>` tags, like this:

```
Hi <c:out value="${user.first}"/> <c:out value="${user.last}"/>
```

But for tags that do more than simply print out their expressions—and all JSTL tags other than `<c:out>` do more—it might be useful to keep this ability in mind.

3.5 *Saving data with <c:set>*

So far, we've looked quite a bit at how to read scoped variables, but we haven't yet shown how to create them. Many JSTL tags let you create scoped variables; the most basic is <c:set>.

The function of <c:set> is simple: it takes either an expression or its body, evaluates it, and saves the result. Let's look a little more closely at how <c:set> works. Table 3.7 lists its tag attributes.[6]

Table 3.7 Basic <c:set> tag attributes

Attribute	Description	Required	Default
value	The expression (in JSTL's expression language) to compute	No	*Use body*
var	The name of the scoped variable to save	Yes	*None*
scope	The scope of the variable to save	No	page

The var attribute tells <c:set> the name of the scoped variable to set. The var attribute and its companion attribute scope are used across many different JSTL tags. They mean the same thing in all JSTL tags in which they appear. The var attribute is always used to let you decide the name of a variable to set.

The scope attribute tells the tag what scope to use when setting the variable. It takes four possible values: page, request, session, and application. If you want the data you're about to set to last for the duration of the user's session, you write scope="session". The scope attribute is always optional; its default is page.

The var and scope attributes have something else in common: they are the only JSTL tag attributes you can't use expressions with. You can't write var="${username}", for instance, and expect the expression ${username} to be evaluated. (Instead, var="${username}" creates a scoped variable named, literally, ${username}. This result is almost never what you want.) The reasons for this limitation are complicated and have to do with error checking and page-authoring tools, but it shouldn't get in your way.

Using the value attribute

For our purposes, there are two broad ways you can use the <c:set> tag: with or without a value attribute. When you specify a value attribute, the <c:set> tag will

---

[6] The <c:set> tag has a few advanced attributes that we'll examine in chapter 14. The var attribute is not required for these advanced uses, but it's required for the way we use the tag here.

take the result of this attribute—which may, of course, contain expressions—and save it to the variable indicated by var and scope.

For instance, consider the following tag:

```
<c:set var="four" value="${3 + 1}"/>
```

This tag stores the value 4 in a scoped variable named four. The scoped variable named four is given page scope. If you wanted to store it in the session, you'd instead write

```
<c:set var="four" scope="session" value="${3 + 1}"/>
```

The <c:set> tag can take any kind of JSTL expression in the value attribute; it can result in a string, number, boolean, collection, or anything else.

Using the tag's body

If you write a <c:set> tag without a value attribute, then <c:set> will take whatever appears in its body and save it to the scoped variable indicated by var and scope. It's important to realize that if other tags appear within <c:set>'s body, these tags will be evaluated; like the browser itself, <c:set> only sees their output.

This process might seem unusual, and it's the first time we've encountered a concept that will keep coming up in JSTL. JSP lets every tag have access to the output of its body. Normally, everything in your page simply gets printed to the browser; either it's template text and gets printed directly, or it's a tag and can produce dynamic output (see figure 3.6). But when template text and tags appear inside another tag, the inner text and tags don't get a chance to send their output directly to the browser. Instead, the parent tag collects the output from its body and then decides what to do with it. It can decide to send it on to the browser, to save it to a scope variable, or to ignore it completely; it's the tag's choice (see figure 3.7). In

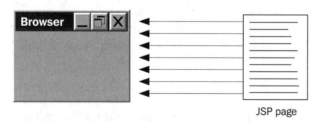

JSP page

Figure 3.6 Normally, all template text and JSTL tags in your page get the opportunity to output directly to a web browser. The template text goes right through (as itself), and the JSTL tags (like <c:out>) have a chance to produce dynamic output that, by default, gets sent to a web browser.

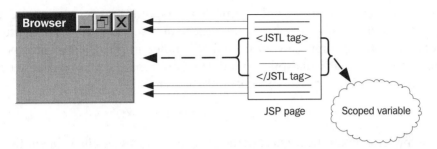

Figure 3.7 In contrast with figure 3.6, JSTL tags can "capture" all the output their bodies produce, whether these bodies contain template text, JSTL tags, or a mixture of the two. The body of a JSTL tag doesn't get a chance to send its output directly to a browser; it sends the output to its parent tag, which decides what to do with it. The parent tag can decide to send the output to the browser after all, to save the output as a scoped variable, or to do something else. The choice is entirely up the tag.

<c:set>'s case, the body is never output to the browser. Instead, it's always saved to a scoped variable.

As an example of this usage, consider the following:

```
<c:set var="eight">
  <c:out value="${4 * 2}"/>
</c:set>
```

This tag creates a page-scoped variable named eight and sets it to the string 8, which is the result of the <c:out> tag. This inner tag didn't have to be a single <c:out> tag; it could have been multiple <c:out> tags, template text, other JSTL tags, or any mixture of these.

NOTE The <c:set> tag will remove all white space at the beginning and end of its body. As a result, you can format the tags however you'd like without worrying about spacing. Because you don't have to consider white space in HTML, it's convenient that JSTL also lets you ignore it.

Using <c:set> with a body is particularly useful if you want to take the output from a custom tag and store it as a scoped variable.

When is <c:set> useful?

The <c:set> tag is helpful primarily when you want to evaluate something once and use it multiple times. It's useful if you have to print out the same thing multiple times but want to avoid repeating large blocks of template text and JSTL tags. It's also handy if you want to take the result of an expression—perhaps containing a request parameter or a variable from a particular scope—and save it in a new scope. For instance, suppose your page that handles an HTML form isn't the only page that needs a particular piece of information from that form. It can set a session-scoped variable to preserve something the user typed:

```
<c:set var="email" scope="session" value="${param.email}"/>
```

This expression takes the request parameter `email` and saves its value in the variable `email`, in session scope. Other pages in the user's session could then use the expression

```
${sessionScope.email}
```

to access the email address a user entered in the HTML form.

3.6 *Deleting data with* <c:remove >

The `<c:remove>` tag is the opposite of `<c:set>`. Instead of creating a scoped variable, it removes the variable. You probably won't need to do this often, and it's certainly not a technique you'll need right away. But in case you ever need to remove a variable, we'll examine how you do it.

Table 3.8 shows the attributes that `<c:remove>` accepts.

Table 3.8 `<c:remove>` **tag attributes**

Attribute	Description	Required	Default
var	The name of the scoped variable to delete	Yes	*None*
scope	The scope of the variable to delete	No	*Any*

The `var` attribute behaves as you might expect: it accepts the name of the variable to remove. The `scope` attribute works a little differently from the conventions described in the last section. It accepts the name of a scope from which to remove the `var` variable, but instead of defaulting to page scope—as `scope` usually does in JSTL—it defaults to each of the scopes, in turn, until a variable with the right name is found.

For instance, the tag

```
<c:remove var="doomed" scope="session"/>
```

deletes the variable `doomed` from session scope. But

```
<c:remove var="doomed"/>
```

doesn't simply remove `doomed` from page scope. Instead, it looks in all the scopes— page, followed by request, then session, and finally application—until it finds a variable named `doomed`, at which point it deletes that variable.

Either way, if the `doomed` variable isn't found, the tag exits quietly, making no change to any other scoped variables.

3.7 *Summary*

You'll soon see lots of expressions in action as we discuss more JSTL tags. When you begin to use the expression language in JSTL tags, remember the following points:

- Expressions can appear in any JSTL tag attributes except `var` and `scope`.
- Expressions start with `${` and end with `}`, and wherever one expression can appear, multiple expressions can appear. For instance, `value="Hi ${user.first} ${user.last}"` is a perfectly valid tag attribute.
- By default, expressions refer to scoped variables, starting with page scope and progressing through request, session, and application scopes until the named variable is found. You can also easily force a variable to come from a particular scope by using expressions like `${pageScope.name}` and `${sessionScope.name}` (where *name* is the name of the variable you're looking for).
- You can use expressions to refer to request parameters: `${param.name}` and `${paramValues.name}`, the latter of which is particularly useful when you have a form with check boxes or some other reason a parameter might have multiple values. The expression language supports easy access to a few other types of data, like cookies and request headers.
- Expressions can perform basic arithmetic on numbers (`+ - * / %`), make comparisons (`== eq != ne < lt > gt <= le >= gt`), compound boolean variables together (`and or not`), and use parentheses to organize the pieces of each expression appropriately. They can also help you decide whether a variable is missing or not (`empty`).
- The `<c:out>` tag prints out the value of an expression, converting it to a string if necessary.
- The `<c:set>` tag sets a scoped variable, either using an expression or using its body.
- The `<c:remove>` tag deletes a scoped variable.

- JSTL tags use the attributes `var` and `scope` to indicate scoped variables. These are the only JSTL attributes that don't accept expressions. The `scope` attribute typically defaults to `page`.

Controlling flow
with conditions

4

This chapter covers...

- Simple conditions
- Mutually exclusive conditions
- Nesting condition tags
- Syntactic rules for JSTL conditions

When you see an HTML `<table>`, you can figure out how many rows it has just by looking at it and counting its `<tr>` tags. In a static page that uses nothing more than HTML, the table's size can't vary: the same layout is displayed each time a web browser loads the page. Every tag has a predictable outcome.

JSP pages work differently. Every time a JSP page is loaded, it can decide what it will send to the user's browser. For a JSP page to print an HTML table with a dynamic number of rows, it simply needs to decide how many times to print out the HTML `<tr>` and `</tr>` tags. Therefore, you can't necessarily expect the same answer each time you ask, "How many rows does this JSP page's `<table>` have?" The answer might be, "One row for each product in the shopping cart." The answer might even be, "No rows at all! The `<table>` won't be printed unless the user is the king of France, and France doesn't have a king anymore." The point is, the page's text and layout can change every time it runs.

When programmers use the term *flow control*, they mean a program's ability to make decisions about what code to run. In a JSP page, flow control is similar: it involves decisions about what tags to process.

JSTL's flow control comes in two forms:

- *Conditional logic, or conditions*

  Lets your application decide whether to take a particular action (like printing out an error message) or skip that action. For example, if your application stores information about users' ages, you might want to check in the middle of the page to see if the current user is older than 18 before displaying suggestive images (or even an obscene joke).

- *Looping, or iteration*

  Lets you repeat a part of your page, usually with minor variations, over and over (although usually not forever!). Looping is useful when you want to build dynamic tables and lists, although it has many other uses. You might loop to print out all the items in a user's shopping cart, or to retrieve all the data the user asked for.

Flow control is one reason the term *template system* (discussed in chapter 1) applies only loosely to languages like JSTL. JSTL is much more powerful than a simple mail-merge engine: it lets you do more than simply insert dynamic content into a lifeless template. When you use JSTL, both the data and the very style and structure of your page are under your dynamic control.

This chapter and the next explore the JSTL tags for flow control. This chapter focuses on conditions, and chapter 5 covers loops.

4.1 Different kinds of decisions

Some questions have a simple yes or no answer. For instance, if you ask, "Did any-one see me bump into that car while I was parallel parking?" there can be only two possible answers: *yes* and *no.* In this sense, the question has a lot in common with the boolean variables you learned about in chapter 3. In fact, if I phrase a yes-or-no question as a statement—such as, "Someone saw me bump into the car"—then just like a boolean variable, it has two possible states: true and false. Simple two-way questions are the most basic kinds of decisions a program can make when it runs.

Some decisions, though, are more complex; they can't easily be satisfied by a yes or no answer. For example, what if I ask, "Should I be driving in the left lane, the middle lane, or the right lane right now?" This question has more than two choices, but it still needs a single answer. (Unless I'm like the drivers on New Haven's Q-Bridge, I can't drive in two lanes at once.) Similarly, a JSP page may be presented with a situation in which it needs to pick one—and exactly one—of many alternatives. Such decisions are said to involve *mutually exclusive* pathways: picking one choice prevents, or excludes, me from picking another, at least until the next time I get to make the choice.

To make this discussion more concrete, let's consider two possible situations faced by a JSP page. Suppose you want to print the title "Dr." before a user's name if you know that user has a Ph.D. This problem can be solved by asking a single yes-or-no question: does this user have a doctorate? But suppose, instead, that you need to print "Dr.", "Mr.", or "Ms.", depending on multiple criteria: the user's gender and education. Because you want to print one title out of three candidates, you should use a mutually exclusive conditional tag.

As you're about to see, JSTL makes it easy to write both types of conditional logic.

4.2 Yes-or-no conditions with <c:if>

Two-way decisions come up all the time in web pages. For example, no matter how clear, productive, and polite an error message is, you probably want to display it only when there's actually an error to report. With a simple error message, you have two choices: your page needs to either display it or not display it. JSTL supports such two-way conditions via the `<c:if>` tag.

4.2.1 The basic syntax of <c:if>

The attributes that `<c:if>` accepts are shown in table 4.1.

Table 4.1 `<c:if>` tag attributes

Attribute	Description	Required	Default
test	Condition to evaluate. If `true`, process the body; if `false`, ignore the body.	Yes	*None*
var	Name of the attribute to expose a boolean value	No	*None*
scope	Scope of the attribute to expose a boolean value	No	page

We'll discuss the `var` and `scope` attributes in section 4.2.5. The `test` attribute specifies a *conditional*—or *boolean*—expression to evaluate. Recall from chapter 3 that expressions in JSTL's expression language can evaluate to boolean values: `true` or `false`. For example, the expression `${param.firstName=='Mildred'}` is `true` if the request parameter `firstName` is equal to `Mildred`; it's `false` otherwise.

> **NOTE** For a review of tag syntax, including how tag attributes work, see chapter 2. The `<c:if>` tag comes from JSTL's core package; so, to use any examples in this chapter, your page should include the following directive at the top:
>
> ```
> <%@ taglib prefix="c" uri="http://java.sun.com/jstl/core" %>
> ```

The `<c:if>` tag's `test` attribute accepts any boolean expression. For example:

```
<c:if test="${user.education == 'doctorate'}">
  Dr.
</c:if>
<c:out value="${user.name}"/>
```

The boolean expression used in this example is `${user.education == 'doctorate'}`. From chapter 3's discussion of JSTL's expression language, you know that this expression will be `true` if the `education` property of the current scoped variable named `user` equals the text `doctorate`; otherwise, the expression will be `false`. (Imagine that our `user.education` property can contain such values as `highschool`, `bachelor`, `master`, and `doctorate`.)

As shown in figure 4.1, the `<c:if>` tag evaluates its `test` attribute, and if this expression evaluates to `false`, the page skips the body of the `<c:if>` tag. On the other hand, as suggested by figure 4.2, if the expression ends up being true, the body is processed normally. This body can contain any valid JSP code, including text, HTML tags, or other JSP tags.

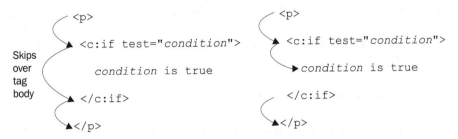

Figure 4.1 `<c:if>`'s body is skipped when its test attribute is `false`.

Figure 4.2 `<c:if>`'s body is processed when its test attribute is `true`.

Think of the `<c:if>` tag as obeying the following two rules:

If the test attribute's condition evaluates to...	Then...
false	The JSP page acts as if the entire `<c:if>` tag, including its contents, never appeared in the first place.
true	The JSP page acts as if just the `<c:if>` and `</c:if>` tags weren't present, but as if the text between these start and end tags appeared unaltered in the page.

Thus, in the example of the last `<c:if>` tag, if `user.education` does not equal doctorate, the example outputs the same thing as the simple line

```
<c:out value="${user.name}"/>
```

If, however, `user.education` does equal `doctorate`, then the example effectively becomes equivalent to

```
Dr. <c:out value="${user.name}"/>
```

The final effect is that the example prints the text `Dr.` before the user's name, but only if the user is a doctor. The name is printed either way, using the `<c:out>` tag that we looked at in chapter 3.

4.2.2 Using <c:if> within HTML tags

Because JSP doesn't draw any distinction between plain text and HTML tags, you can use <c:if> tags anywhere in your page—even in the middle of an HTML tag. For instance, consider this use of a <c:if> tag:

```
<font size="2"
  <c:if test="${user.education == 'doctorate'}">
    color="red"
  </c:if>
>
    <c:out value="${user.name}"/>
</font>
```

This code prints the user's name in red if the user is a doctor. The code checks the user.education property and, if it is equal to doctorate, outputs the following (ignoring white space) where *name* is the user's name, as output by the <c:out> tag:

```
<font size="2" color="red">
    name
</font>
```

If user.education is different from doctorate, we instead get

```
<font size="2">
    name
</font>
```

In the first case, the HTML <font> tag explicitly sets the text color to red, whereas the latter case uses the default color. Recall from chapter 1 that the browser doesn't care how an HTML markup tag was generated—whether it was template text, the output of a JSTL tag, or both. Thus, JSTL tags, like <c:if>, can easily be used to produce HTML tags or parts of them.

4.2.3 Multiple <c:if> tags

When <c:if> tags appear next to one another, they act independently:

```
<ul>
<c:if test="${error1}">
    <li>Error 1 has occurred.</li>
</c:if>
<c:if test="${error2}">
    <li>Error 2 has occurred.</li>
</c:if>
</ul>
```

This example assumes that when certain errors have occurred, your page (or back-end Java code) has stored the value true in page-scoped boolean variables called error1, error2, and so on. (You'll see how to create such variables in section 4.2.5.)

This example uses these error flags to print zero, one, or two error messages, as appropriate. If `error1` is true, then the first error message is printed; if `error2` is true, then the second is printed. Importantly, the outcome of the first `<c:if>` tag doesn't affect the outcome from the second, and vice versa. If you remember high-school probability, you can think of these tags like two independent flips of a coin; they don't affect one another. The two tags are simply next to, not related to, each other.

TIP   Adjacent, unrelated `<c:if>` tags are useful when you want to display independent errors simultaneously. In many applications I've written, I've found it useful to show users all outstanding error messages at once, instead of displaying them one at a time.

Note that, in the previous example, the body of each `<c:if>` tag begins with `<li>` and ends with `</li>`. These tags cause any error messages that are printed to appear as items in an HTML list. The `<ul>` and `</ul>` tags in the example are printed unconditionally, because they don't occur within any `<c:if>` tags. Therefore, if neither `error1` nor `error2` is true, the page will simply output an empty list (ignoring white space):

```
<ul></ul>
```

(Although this empty list gets the job done, it isn't ideal; HTML's `<ul>` tag shouldn't really be empty. You'll see in the next section how to avoid this situation.) On the other hand, if one error message is displayed, we see a list with a single item, like the following:

```
<ul>
  <li>Error 2 has occurred.</li>
</ul>
```

If both error messages are displayed, we see a list with two items:

```
<ul>
  <li>Error 1 has occurred.</li>
  <li>Error 2 has occurred.</li>
</ul>
```

Placing opening and closing tags—like `<li>` and `</li>`—in the body of a single `<c:if>` tag is an easy way to construct HTML lists that grow as needed to accommodate the information you want to display. The strategy is not limited to lists. For instance, a `<c:if>` tag's body could start with `<tr>` and end with `</tr>`, in which case the `<c:if>` tag would represent an optional row in a table. (Whatever layout you're printing, make sure the opening and closing HTML tags match up; you don't want to have an application print a `<ul>` tag and never close it with a `</ul>` tag.)

4.2.4 *Nested <c:if> tags*

`<c:if>` tags can also be *nested*, which means they can appear inside other `<c:if>` tags. When this happens, the outside tag decides whether the inside tag gets a chance to be processed. Only if the outside tag succeeds does the inner tag even evaluate its `test` attribute.

We can use nested tags to prevent the empty `<ul></ul>` from the previous section from being displayed. For instance, consider the following tags:

```
<c:if test="${error1 or error2}">
  <ul>
  <c:if test="${error1}">
     <li>Error 1 has occurred.</li>
  </c:if>
  <c:if test="${error2}">
     <li>Error 2 has occurred.</li>
  </c:if>
  </ul>
</c:if>
```

Here, if neither `error1` nor `error2` is `true`, the expression `${error1 or error2}` will be `false`, and the entire tag will be skipped. This technique will prevent the `<ul>` tag from being empty, which is an error in HTML (even though it will probably display correctly in most browsers).

Let's look at a new example in more detail. Consider the following:

```
<c:if test="${fatalError}">
  I'm sorry,
  <c:if test="${user.education=='doctorate'}">
    Dr.
  </c:if>
  <c:out value="${user.name}"/>,
  but you have committed a fatal error.
</c:if>
```

This example displays an error message if the page-scoped `fatalError` variable is `true`. The error message is interesting, because it contains a `<c:if>` tag of its own.

The individual pieces of this example work just as you'd expect. The outer `<c:if>` tag checks for a flag called `fatalError` and decides whether the error message (its body) will be processed. If this body gets processed, then the inner `<c:if>` tag is reached; this tag simply decides whether or not to display `Dr.`, just as our first example did.

The end result is an optional error message that, when printed, varies depending on the educational status of the user. If a fatal error occurs and the user is a doctor, the following text is printed:

```
I'm sorry, Dr. name, but you have committed a fatal error.
```

In this output, `name` is the user's name as it is printed by the `<c:out>` tag. (In this case, the user who committed the fatal error is a doctor, so we should probably consider printing some information about malpractice insurance.)

Otherwise, if a fatal error occurs but the user is not a doctor, the text

```
I'm sorry, name, but you have committed a fatal error.
```

is printed. Note that the message doesn't contain the `Dr.` title, because the user doesn't deserve it.

Finally, if no fatal error has been recorded in the `fatalError` flag, then no error message is printed.

You can nest `<c:if>` tags as deeply as you'd like; for instance, the following example is perfectly valid:

```
<c:if test="${a}">
  <c:if test="${b}">
    <c:if test="${c}">
      <c:if test="${d}">
        <c:if test="${e}">
           Lots of things are true!  Hooray!
        </c:if>
      </c:if>
    </c:if>
  </c:if>
</c:if>
```

In this example, the `<c:if>` tags are processed like layers in an onion: the first `<c:if>` tag is checked, and if it decides to include its body because the `${a}` expression is true, then the second `<c:if>` tag is evaluated, and so on. The tags are peeled away, so to speak, one by one. Therefore, the final, inner text (Lots of things are true! Hooray!) is printed only if all the tags have let their contents be printed—in this case, only if all of `${a}`, `${b}`, `${c}`, `${d}`, and `${e}` are true.

Nesting `<c:if>` tags is a useful technique, but if you nest them too deeply and use too many `<c:if>` tags, your pages may become hard to manage. For instance, we could have written the last example much more simply like this:

```
<c:if test="${a and b and c and d and e}">
  Lots of things are true!  Hooray!
</c:if>
```

In other cases, though, nesting can be more convenient than the `and` operator; it may let you avoid repeating an expression throughout your page.

4.2.5 *The var and scope attributes*

The `test` attribute isn't the only one that `<c:if>` accepts. The tag lets you enter two more attributes: `var` and `scope`. By and large, these attributes do the same thing they do in the `<c:set>` tag from chapter 3: they create and expose a scoped variable that other tags can access.

Here, however, the variable that gets exposed is boolean—either `true` or `false`. Its value corresponds to the end result of the `test` expression. Normally, the `<c:if>` tag just checks `test` expression's result and uses it to decide whether to let its body be included. The `var` attribute, however, lets you save `test`'s result—either `true` or `false`—and read it back later on the page. You can even store it for the benefit of other pages by setting the `scope` attribute to `request`, `session`, or `application`.

Recording a boolean value is helpful primarily in three situations:

- Making pages cleaner by avoiding repetitive conditional expressions
- Speeding up your pages by computing a conditional expression only once
- Taking a snapshot of a condition because you're afraid it might change

For the first situation, suppose you have a condition like this:

```
${result.limitedByMaxRows and maxRows < 25 and maxRows > 10
  and result.rows[0].userName=='bob'
  and cart.empty}
```

Say that three parts of your page, far apart from each other, need to use this expression. Having to type it once is enough busy-work; there's no reason to type it multiple times. Even if your editor supports cut-and-paste operations, the long expression clutters your page.

In the second case, the condition might be time-consuming. Imagine, for example, that a page-scoped variable has a boolean property called `isPrime`, and that accessing this property computes whether a particular number is prime. The calculations might take a while to complete, so if you run them only once instead of multiple times, you can make your page load faster.

Third, `var` is useful if you want to take a snapshot of a particular conditional expression because you think it might change. For instance, consider the (admittedly unlikely) possibility that the user receives a doctoral degree *while* our JSP page is being processed. And, of course, suppose that the appropriate property—say, `user.education`—is updated accordingly, perhaps by behind-the-scenes Java code. If this happens but we have used multiple tags that look like

```
<c:if test="${user.education=='doctorate'}">
 Dr.
</c:if>
```

then the page might appear inconsistent to the user. After a certain point in the page, the `Dr.` title will appear; but at the beginning, it won't. This difference might not matter; but if consistency is important, we should record the value—whatever it happened to be at a particular point—and then use it for the rest of the page. The `var` attribute allows us to do this.

Consider the following example:

```
<c:if test="${sessionScope.flags.errors.serious.error1}"
    var="error1">    <─── Saves variable
  A serious error has occurred.
</c:if>
```

```
[… large page body …]
```

```
<c:if test="${error1}">    <─── Uses variable
  Since a serious error occurred, your data has not been saved.
</c:if>
```

In this example, when the first tag is reached, the expression in its `test` attribute is evaluated, and the result is saved into a page-scoped variable called `error1`. From this point forward, even if the value of `flags.errors.serious.error1` in the session scope changes, the local `error1` variable will stay the same. Thus, even if the session-scoped `flags.errors.serious.error1` flag changes for any reason, the user will be given a message at the bottom of the page that is consistent with the one displayed at the top. (Note also that in the second `<c:if>` tag, we save some typing by using our own shorter variable name.)

Although most `<c:if>` tags have a body, JSTL's don't require them to. So, you can use `<c:if>` to write a tag whose only purpose is to expose a scoped variable. For example, the following empty tag exposes a boolean variable named `error1`:

```
<c:if test="${sessionScope.flags.errors.serious.error1}"
  var="error1"/>
```

This tag isn't used to make a decision during execution of the page; later tags on the page, however, can use the `error1` variable that this tag creates.

4.3 *Mutually exclusive conditions with <c:choose>, <c:when>, and <c:otherwise>*

As I mentioned earlier, JSTL supports tags that let you introduce into your pages conditions that are more complex than `<c:if>` allows. These *complex conditional* tags support the mutually exclusive conditions we discussed in section 4.1.

4.3.1 *Why JSTL has complex conditional tags*

In section 4.1, I drew a contrast between two-way conditions and multiway conditions. However, given enough opportunities to ask two-way questions, you can easily ask a multiway question. (This principle lies behind the common childhood game Twenty Questions, where one player asks the other multiple yes-or-no questions in an attempt to narrow a general question.) Because the `<c:if>` tag in JSTL can be nested, it can be used to build complex conditional control flow.

As an example, I raised a common three-way question earlier: on a highway, should I drive in the left lane, the middle lane, or the right lane? Instead of asking the question this way, I could have posed it as two yes-or-no questions: should I drive in the left lane? If not, should I drive in the middle lane? Answering these two yes-or-no questions is enough to answer the overall three-way question and, therefore, to distinguish between three mutually exclusive alternatives.

Consider the contrasting examples in figure 4.3. Like an example you saw earlier, the code on the left displays up to three error messages, depending on how many are relevant. The code on the right, however, displays at most a single error message—the first one it finds. The code on the right implements a decision among three mutually exclusive choices, just like the three-lane highway question.

The example on the left in figure 4.3 should be familiar from our earlier discussion of the `<c:if>` tag. On the right, nested `<c:if>` tags are structured in a way that ensures only one error message will be displayed. Think of the example like this, reading from top to bottom: first, if `error1` is `true`, print out a message for error 1. Then, if `error2` is `true`, *but only if* `error1` *is* `false`, print out a message for error 2. Finally, if `error3` is `true`, *but neither* `error1` *nor* `error2` *is* `true`, print out a message for error 3. Remember that text within two or more `<c:if>` tags is printed only when all the nested `<c:if>` tags decide to process their bodies; this is why the text `Error 3 has occurred` is printed only when `error3` is `true` but `error2` and `error1` are `false`.

However, the code on the right side of figure 4.3 has a problem: in each successive `<c:if>` tag, we need to keep track of all the preceding conditional expressions manually. Note how each new message uses extra tags. To decide whether to display the first message, we need one `<c:if>` tag, but the second message uses two

```
<c:if test="${error1}">              <c:if test="${error1}">
   <li>Error 1 has occurred.</li>      <li>Error 1 has occurred.</li>
</c:if>                               </c:if>


<c:if test="${error2}">              <c:if test="${error2}">
   <li>Error 2 has occurred.</li>      <c:if test="${not error1}">
</c:if>                                  <li>Error 2 has occurred.</li>
                                       </c:if>
                                     </c:if>


<c:if test="${error3}">              <c:if test="${error3}">
   <li>Error 3 has occurred.</li>      <c:if test="${not error2}">
</c:if>                                  <c:if test="${not error1}">
                                         <li>Error 3 has occurred.</li>
                                       </c:if>
                                     </c:if>
                                     </c:if>
```

Figure 4.3   On the left, three simple `<c:if>` tags appear next to each other. These tags are unrelated; whether one runs has no effect on whether the others run. Zero, one, two, or three error messages might be displayed, depending on how many errors have occurred. On the right, nested conditions achieve exclusivity; no more than one error message will appear.

and the third uses three. This extra structure—which you have to keep track of yourself—eventually becomes tedious and prone to errors.

NOTE   The example on the right in figure 4.3 has a subtler problem, as well. It does not really guarantee that only one error message will print, because the values of `error1`, `error2`, and `error3` might change while the example executes, causing two or more messages to be displayed. Remember that expressions like `${error1}` can find information in any scope—including session scope, where another page might change it while our page accesses it.

Because mutually exclusive pathways are so common, JSTL provides an easier way to express them in your pages; the following section explains.

4.3.2 *How the complex conditional tags work*

JSTL's support for mutually exclusive conditions comes in the form of three cooperating tags: `<c:choose>`, `<c:when>`, and `<c:otherwise>`. If you've used other programming or web-design languages, you might be familiar with *switch* statements, sometimes called *case* statements. In JSTL, <c:choose> and <c:when> work similarly to the switch and case keywords in languages like C and Java.[1]

The <c:choose> tag is simple: it takes no attributes and serves only as a container for <c:when> and <c:otherwise> tags. Just as HTML's <td> tag makes no sense outside a <table>, <c:when> and <c:otherwise> make no sense outside a <c:choose>. Think of <c:choose> as somewhat like HTML's <form> tag: its major purpose is to contain other, related tags.

The <c:when> tag is similar to <c:if>: it takes a single test attribute (see table 4.2) and lets its body be processed only if its condition, which is specified by test, is true. There's one major difference between <c:if> and <c:when>, though. For each <c:choose> tag, no more than one child <c:when> tag can succeed. If a <c:when> tag decides that its body should be processed, then all other <c:when> tags with the same parent <c:choose> tag will be ignored. (They won't even bother to evaluate their own test attributes; they'll simply be skipped.) To bring back the terminology we used earlier, child <c:when> tags are *mutually exclusive* with one another inside a <c:choose> tag. See figure 4.4.

Table 4.2   <c:when> tag attribute

Attribute	Description	Required	Default
test	Condition to evaluate if no sibling <c:when> tag has already succeeded	Yes	*None*

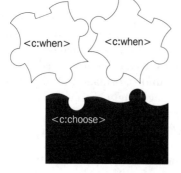

Figure 4.4
This is either an overhead shot of cattle attempting to nurse from a mother cow, or it's a figurative representation of how only one <c:when> tag can succeed within any <c:choose>.

---

[1] If you're familiar with XSLT, you might notice that JSTL's names for mutually exclusive conditional tags follow the names that XSLT uses. This naming is not accidental; the designers of JSTL chose these names to illustrate that the purpose and behavior of these JSTL tags is very similar to their counterparts in XSLT.

Although `<c:when>` tags are mutually exclusive of one another, there's never a guarantee that any particular `<c:when>` tag will be chosen. If all the `<c:when>` tags under a `<c:choose>` have conditions that evaluate to `false`, then none of them will succeed.

This is where `<c:otherwise>` comes in. The `<c:otherwise>` tag participates in the same mutual-exclusivity scheme as `<c:when>` tags, but it takes no attributes, so it has no condition of its own to evaluate. Instead, it succeeds only if all its sibling `<c:when>` tags (those with the same parent `<c:choose>` tag) have failed. (It's like the kid on a little-league team who hopes his friends will strike out because he wasn't chosen to bat.) The behavior of `<c:otherwise>` is useful if you want to have a default condition that applies to a `<c:choose>` tag.

Example 1

Let's look at a few examples of the `<c:choose>` tag in action. The following code behaves similarly to the example on the right side of figure 4.3, which uses `<c:if>` instead of `<c:choose>`, `<c:when>`, and `<c:otherwise>`:

```
<c:choose>
  <c:when test="${error1}">
    <li>Error 1 has occurred.</li>      Only one of these
  </c:when>                             <c:when> tags
  <c:when test="${error2}">             can succeed
    <li>Error 2 has occurred.</li>
  </c:when>
  <c:when test="${error3}">
    <li>Error 3 has occurred.</li>
  </c:when>
</c:choose>
```

Only one of the three `<c:when>` tags can succeed. Because the mutual exclusivity is built into the `<c:choose>` and `<c:when>` tags, the code is much simpler than in figure 4.3, where we had to spell out the exclusivity manually, keeping track of each condition one by one.

Example 2

Suppose we want to modify the previous example to print out a message of reassurance to the user if no errors have occurred. This kind of default behavior calls for a `<c:otherwise>` tag. Thus, we could modify the example as follows:

```
<c:choose>
  <c:when test="${error1}">
    <li>Error 1 has occurred.</li>
  </c:when>
  <c:when test="${error2}">
    <li>Error 2 has occurred.</li>
  </c:when>
  <c:when test="${error3}">
```

```
   <li>Error 3 has occurred.</li>
 </c:when>
 <c:otherwise>
   <li>Everything is fine.</li>
 </c:otherwise>
</c:choose>
```

| Addition of <c:otherwise>
| to display the default message

The example now prints out a reassuring message—by way of the optional <c:oth-erwise> tag—if ${error1}, ${error2}, and ${error3} are all *not* true.

Example 3

Let's consider a slightly more involved example. In the first example in this chapter, we discussed a <c:if> tag used to print the text Dr. if user.education indicated that the user had a doctorate. In that example, Dr. would either appear or it wouldn't; there was no third choice. Instead of this simple yes-or-no choice, let's look at an example that prints one of three choices—Dr., Ms., or Mr.—as appropriate. To do this, we have our tags check both a user.education property and another property, user.gender:

```
<c:choose>
  <c:when test="${user.education=='doctorate'}">
    Dr.
  </c:when>
  <c:when test="${user.gender=='female'}">
    Ms.
  </c:when>
  <c:when test="${user.gender=='male'}">
    Mr.
  </c:when>
</c:choose>
<c:out value="${user.name}"/>
```

We use two different properties of the user variable, but all our tests are grouped under a single <c:choose> tag. The result is that an appropriate title (Dr., Ms., or Mr.) is displayed in all cases. Note that the check for Dr. appears first because it transcends gender. If we checked for a particular gender first, we would miss all the members of that gender who were also doctors. Instead, we want to check gender only if the user is not a doctor.

This example demonstrates that JSTL strictly adheres to the order of your <c:when> tags. If the first <c:when> tag succeeds, then the second (and remaining) tags won't be evaluated; if the second succeeds, then the third (and remaining) tags won't be evaluated; and so on.

The <c:when> tag does not accept a var attribute, but it can use boolean variables exposed by earlier <c:if> tags.

WARNING   `<c:when>` tags only exclude other `<c:when>` tags with the same parent `<c:choose>` tag from running. Tags later on the page (or within a nested `<c:choose>` beneath the successful `<c:when>`) are not affected. For example, in tags structured like the following the two `<c:when>` tags work like nested `<c:if>` tags, not like exclusive sibling `<c:when>` tags:

```
<c:choose>
 <c:when>
   <c:choose>
     <c:when> … </c:when>
   </c:choose>
 </c:when>
</c:choose>
```

4.3.3 *Rules for using the complex conditional tags*

Some combinations of `<c:choose>`, `<c:when>`, and `<c:otherwise>` don't make sense, and JSTL outlaws these combinations. For example, as we already discussed, `<c:when>` and `<c:otherwise>` tags cannot appear outside a `<c:choose>` tag. There's a flip side to this rule: a `<c:choose>` tag cannot have any direct children (or non-white space text) except `<c:when>` or `<c:otherwise>` tags. Furthermore, if `<c:otherwise>` occurs, it must follow all the `<c:when>` tags; it may not come before any of them. Finally, every `<c:choose>` must have at least one `<c:when>` and no more than one `<c:otherwise>`.

To demonstrate these rules, consider the following illegal fragments:

```
<c:choose>
  <p>Here is a choice:</p>
  <c:when> … </c:when>
  <c:otherwise> … </c:otherwise>
</c:choose>
```

This example is illegal because only `<c:when>` and `<c:otherwise>`—no text or other JSP tags—may occur directly beneath a `<c:choose>` tag. Such text outside a `<c:when>` or `<c:otherwise>` tag never needs to be located inside a `<c:choose>`; simply place it before or after the `<c:choose>` tag, depending on where you'd like it to appear.

Similarly, the following fragment is illegal:

```
<c:choose>
  <c:when test="${a}">
    <c:when test="${b}">
      …
    </c:when>
  </c:when>
</c:choose>
```

The inner `<c:when>` tag in this example is not valid; it is the child of a `<c:when>`, not of a `<c:choose>`. It doesn't matter that the inner `<c:when>` tag is inside a `<c:choose>`; all `<c:when>` tags must have a `<c:choose>` as their *immediate* parent tag. Note that the nesting alone doesn't invalidate the inner `<c:when>` tag; `<c:choose>` tags can be nested in a manner similar to `<c:if>` tags. However, no matter where `<c:when>` appears, it must have `<c:choose>` as its parent.

Finally, consider one more illegal example:

```
<c:choose>
  <c:otherwise> … </c:otherwise>
  <c:when> … </c:when>
</c:choose>
```

This example is invalid because the `<c:otherwise>` tag, when it appears, must be the final tag within a `<c:choose>` group; it can never appear before a sibling `<c:when>` tag. This rule is designed to help ensure that you haven't made a mistake when constructing a `<c:choose>` block. If a `<c:otherwise>` tag came before a `<c:when>` tag, the `<c:when>` tag could never succeed; the `<c:otherwise>` tag would always run, preventing the later `<c:when>` tag from doing so. Because the `<c:when>` tag in the last example could never succeed, JSTL declares it to be illegal and prevents the error before the page runs.

4.4 Summary

When using JSTL's conditional tags, keep the following points in mind:

- `<c:if>` supports a simple yes-or-no condition. Adjacent `<c:if>` tags are independent of each other, but nested `<c:if>` tags must all succeed for the innermost body to be printed.

- `<c:choose>`, `<c:when>`, and `<c:otherwise>` support multiway exclusive conditions. They can be nested just like `<c:if>`, although too much nesting of `<c:choose>` tags can lead to confusing code.

We'll look at a few more concrete examples of JSTL's conditional tags in the next chapter.

Controlling flow
with loops

5

Looping involves repeatedly executing the same block of your JSTL page, over and over. It sounds mind-numbingly boring—and if you were a web server, you'd probably agree. But for us, loops are anything but boring. They're a powerful feature that works as the cornerstone for many, if not most, dynamic web pages.

Looping is often called *iteration*. As the word suggests, iteration involves repetition. Figure 5.1 illustrates the way JSTL lets you take any valid JSP fragment—including tags, template text, or both—and cause it to be processed repeatedly. If your repeated JSP fragment depends on scoped variables that change during the looping process, then each repetition can produce slightly different text or HTML. During each loop (that is, during each single pass through the iteration), the static template text stays the same, but the tags each get another chance to run and produce new dynamic output. Because of this behavior, looping is very useful for building dynamic tables and lists.

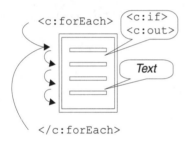

Figure 5.1
Text, other JSTL tags, and even arbitrary JSP can appear in the body of `<c:forEach>` tags.

In the core JSTL library, two tags handle looping: `<c:forEach>` and `<c:forTokens>`. These two tags have a lot in common; they mainly differ in the type of data they *loop over*—that is, the type of data they consider, item by item. In this chapter, we'll look first at simple uses of `<c:forEach>` and `<c:forTokens>` separately, and then we'll move to more complex iterations using tag attributes that are common to both `<c:forEach>` and `<c:forTokens>`.

5.1 *General-purpose looping with* `<c:forEach>`

The `<c:forEach>` tag is JSTL's general-purpose looping tag. As you saw in chapter 4, the expression language can return a *collection* of items. The `<c:forEach>` tag lets you loop over nearly any sensible collection of items that the expression language returns. For instance, recall the picture of a shopping cart from figure 4.2 in chapter 4. The shopping cart contained three items: an apple, a TV, and a cup of coffee. If we looped over the shopping cart with `<c:forEach>`, then `<c:forEach>` would consider each of these items in turn.[1]

The basic function of `<c:forEach>` is to consider every item in the collection specified by its `items` attribute. For each item in the collection, the body of the `<c:forEach>` tag will be processed once, with the current item being exposed as a page-scoped variable whose name is specified by `<c:forEach>`'s var attribute. Because this variable takes a different value for each loop, the body of the `<c:forEach>` tag can print different text each time it is evaluated.

Let's make this behavior concrete. Consider the following use of `<c:forEach>`:

```
<c:forEach items="${user.medicalConditions}" var="ailment">
    <c:out value="${ailment}"/>
</c:forEach>
```

This `<c:forEach>` tag loops over every item in the `medicalConditions` property of the `user` variable. If this property contains a list of medical conditions, like `gingivitis`, `myopia`, and `dehydration`, then the example will print a string for each of these items.

You can also include static template text inside a `<c:forEach>` tag's body, in which case it will appear unchanged for each loop that `<c:forEach>` makes. For example:

```
<p>Sorry, you are afflicted with the following
minor medical conditions:</p>
<ul>
<c:forEach items="${user.medicalConditions}" var="ailment">
    <li><c:out value="${ailment}"/></li>
</c:forEach>
</ul>
```

If `${user.medicalConditions}` contains the three conditions I mentioned earlier, this fragment will output the following HTML (ignoring white space):

```
<p>Sorry, you are afflicted with the following
minor medical conditions:</p>
<ul>
    <li>gingivitis</li>
    <li>myopia</li>
    <li>dehydration</li>
</ul>
```

The template text outside the `<c:forEach>` tag is, of course, included only once. For instance, this example prints only one `<ul>` tag. But text within the

---

[1] In case you encounter specific Java types when talking with Java programmers—or in case you're a developer yourself—you might be interested to know the names of the data types `<c:forEach>` accepts. They include arrays, `Collection` variables (including `Lists` and `Sets`), `Maps`, `Iterators`, and `Enumerations`. As you'll see in section 5.2, it can also accept simple strings.

<c:forEach> tag—in this case, the opening and closing <li> tags—is included once each time the body of the tag is evaluated. The <c:out> tag prints a different value for each round of iteration because it refers to the ailment variable, which <c:forEach> sets to a new value for every loop. The <c:forEach> tag sets the ailment variable (and not some other variable with a different name) because that identifier appears in its var attribute.

The basic attributes of <c:forEach> are shown in table 5.1.

Table 5.1   <c:forEach> tag attributes for basic iteration

Attribute	Description	Required	Default
items	Collection over which to iterate	No	*None*
var	Name of the attribute to expose the current item	No	*None*

NOTE   Even though the items attribute represents the core functionality of the <c:forEach> tag, you can use <c:forEach> without it. See section 5.3.2 for more information on when you might want to do this.

5.2 *Iterating over strings with <c:forTokens>*

Sometimes, data is not structured into a formal collection. If you are communicating with a so-called legacy application, accessing user input directly, or simply dealing with an application that has chosen to represent data as simple strings, you may need a tag that breaks a string into its constituent items. For instance, suppose you are writing an email-related web application, and the user has entered a list of email addresses in the following form:

```
shawn.bayern@yale.edu,david.davies@yale.edu,peter.peters@yale.edu
```

You might wish to analyze the string by breaking it into individual email addresses separated by commas and performing some action on each of them. (For instance, you might save them into your database of addresses so you can send unwanted junk mail to the entire world. Most web sites today seem to do this.) Analyzing a string is known as *parsing*.

When a string is broken into constituent items, these items are often called *tokens*. A token is a single, discrete unit within a larger string. The <c:forTokens> tag iterates over such tokens, which it parses from an input string. Table 5.2 shows the basic attributes that <c:forTokens> uses to retrieve tokens from within strings.

Table 5.2 `<c:forTokens>` **tag attributes for basic iteration**

Attribute	Description	Required	Default
items	Input string over which to iterate	Yes	*None*
delims	Delimiter characters that separate tokens	Yes	*None*
var	Name of the attribute to expose the current token	No	*None*

In short, `<c:forTokens>` uses the `items` and `delims` attributes to generate tokens, which it then exposes as the variable named by `var`. The `items` attribute refers to a string—either a simple, literal string typed directly into the tag, or an expression referring to a string. For instance, you could literally write

```
items="a,b,c"
```

or you could use the expression language

```
items="${emailAddresses}"
```

The `delims` attribute is a string that contains the characters you want to use to separate tokens inside the string. These separators are called *delimiters*. For instance, your string might be divided with a comma (,), but it could instead use another character, like a semicolon (;) or even the letter q. Each individual character in the `delims` attribute is treated, by itself, as a delimiter. Therefore, if `delims` is specified as

```
delims=".,;:"
```

then the four characters specified—period (.), comma (,), semicolon (;), and colon (:)—can separate tokens. For example, these `delims` separate the string

```
a,b.c;d:e:f.g
```

into the following tokens: a, b, c, d, e, f, and g.

Let's look at a few examples of `<c:forTokens>` in action. First, consider the case where you specify the `items` attribute's value directly inside the tag:

```
<c:forTokens items="a;b;c;d" delims=";" var="current">
    <li><c:out value="${current}"/></li>
</c:forTokens>
```

This example uses semicolons to separate the string a;b;c;d into four tokens: a, b, c, and d. It then prints the following output:

```
<li>a</li>
<li>b</li>
<li>c</li>
<li>d</li>
```

Now, suppose that instead of specifying a string directly in the `items` attribute, we use an expression. Imagine that a variable called `user` contains a `phone` property that stores a phone number. If `${user.phone}` returns the value 203-432-6687, the following `<c:forTokens>` tag will break this string into three sets of numbers, each separated by a hyphen (-):

```
<c:forTokens items="${user.phone}" delims="-" var="current">
   <td><c:out value="${current}"/></td>
</c:forTokens>
```

This example prints the following output:

```
<td>203</td>
<td>432</td>
<td>6687</td>
```

Such output might be useful if you wanted to print a tabular list of numbers or separate the area code from the phone number.

Like `items`, the `delims` attribute accepts expressions. However, you'll use expressions in `items` much more commonly than in `delims`. (It's reasonable to assume that you'll just about always use an expression in `items` and rarely use one for `delims`.)

5.2.1 *How JSTL parses strings*

In an `items` string, delimiter characters that appear consecutively are treated as a single delimiter. Therefore, in a case like

```
<c:forTokens items="a,,b,,c" delims=",">
```

the `<c:forTokens>` tag finds three tokens: a, b, and c.

This rule applies even if there are different kinds of delimiters. For example, the following tag has the same effect as the last tag:

```
<c:forTokens items="a,;,b,;,c" delims=",;">
```

Similarly, delimiters that appear at the beginning or at the end of `items` are ignored; they do not produce blank or empty tokens. Therefore, this tag has the same effect as the last two:

```
<c:forTokens items=",;,a,;,b,;,c,;," delims=",;">
```

The tag still finds just three tokens: a, b, and c.

Earlier, I mentioned that `<c:forEach>` can accept a simple string value for its own `items` attribute. In cases where this occurs, it is equivalent to `<c:forTokens>` with only the comma character as a delimiter (`delims=","`). This capability lets the `<c:forEach>` tag iterate over the tokens a, b, and c like this:

```
<c:forEach items="a,b,c">
```

Thus, think of `<c:forEach>` as supporting simple string tokenization and `<c:forTo-kens>` as providing more elaborate tokenization.

5.3 Advanced iteration with <c:forEach> and <c:forTokens>

So far, you've seen simple examples using `<c:forEach>` and `<c:forTokens>`. We've fed them collections of items and watched them run their bodies multiple times, producing different output each time.

But iteration in JSTL doesn't stop there. Using other tag attributes, you can customize the behavior of these tags. For instance, you can determine information about the current item's position within the overall loop: is it first, last, or somewhere in the middle? This ability is valuable in helping you construct visually appealing tables—for example, HTML tables whose rows alternate between two colors, or lists that treat the first item or last item specially. You can also use optional attributes of `<c:forEach>` and `<c:forTokens>` to decide to iterate over only part of the collection at hand: for instance, you might want to display the first 10 items only, leaving the rest for other pages (or a later portion of the same page). Or, you might want to print a table that uses only every second, or third, item in a collection (imagine, for instance, that a collection alternates between dates and times, and you want to print just dates).

We'll first consider JSTL's *subsetting* functionality: the ability of `<c:forEach>` and `<c:forTokens>` to use only part of the collection of items they have been given. Following that, we'll explore the use of *iteration status* (information about the current loop in the iteration) and how this status interacts with the features related to subsetting.

5.3.1 Looping over part of a collection

Sometimes, you simply have too much information, and you need to focus on just one part of it. For instance, consider again the `${user.medicalConditions}` expression we used in section 5.1. Imagine a situation where users are unfortunate enough to have developed so many ailments that the list won't manageably fit on a single page. (Of course, this example is somewhat outlandish, but it is not a difficult leap from this problem to one that most real-life search engines face.) In such situations, results are so numerous that they need to be spread over multiple pages. Therefore, an individual `<c:forEach>` or `<c:forTokens>` loop must deal with only part of the entire collection. Such a limited part is often called a *subset*.

Both `<c:forEach>` and `<c:forTokens>` accept three optional attributes in support of subsetting, as shown in table 5.3.

Table 5.3   Subsetting attributes for `<c:forEach>` and `<c:forTokens>`

Attribute	Description	Required	Default
begin	Item to start the loop (inclusive; `0`=first item, `1`=second item).	No	0
end	Item to end the loop (inclusive; `0`=first item; `1`=second item).	No	Last item
step	Iteration will process every *step*th element (`1`=every element, `2`=every second element).	No	1

JSTL assigns an *index* to every item in a collection; this index represents the item's place in the overall collection. For each collection, the index begins with 0, which—interestingly enough—corresponds to the first item. Each successive element takes the next index number: the second element has an index of 1, the third element has an index of 2, and so on.

The `begin` and `end` attributes accept numbers corresponding to these indexes. By default, `<c:forEach>` and `<c:forTokens>` process the entire collection available to them; like dutiful cogs in a machine, they start at the beginning and finish at the end. The `begin` and `end` attributes override this default behavior by identifying particular start and end indexes. The `begin` attribute directs the tag to start with the item at a particular index, and `end` causes iteration to end with a particular index. For example, `begin="0"` and `end="4"` together instruct that a `<c:forEach>` or `<c:forTokens>` tag should begin with the first element and end with the fifth. Similarly, when a `<c:forEach>` or `<c:forToken>` tag is given the attributes `begin="5"` and `end="9"`, only the indexes 5, 6, 7, 8, and 9 will be included (that is, the sixth through tenth elements).

WARNING   Be careful! Because 0 represents the first element, `end="4"` will cause iteration to proceed through the fifth element. Zero-based indexes can be confusing, but many programming languages adhere to them for consistency. If you have worked with JavaScript or Java before, you probably are familiar with zero-based indexes. (Zero-based indexes are not limited to programming languages. Not too far from where I live, a highway mile marker labeled 0 indicates the beginning of the highway. As a programmer, it warms my heart.)

As an example of simple uses of begin and end, let's look at a <c:forTokens> tag that iterates over letters of the alphabet. Without a begin or end attribute, the following tag iterates over the letters from a through f:

```
<c:forTokens items="a,b,c,d,e,f" delims="," var="letter">
    <c:out value="${letter}"/>
</c:forTokens>
```

Suppose we add just the begin attribute:

```
<c:forTokens items="a,b,c,d,e,f" delims="," var="letter" begin="4">
    <c:out value="${letter}"/>
</c:forTokens>
```

This invocation of the tag will print out only the letters e and f. Similarly, we can use only end:

```
<c:forTokens items="a,b,c,d,e,f" delims="," var="letter" end="4">
    <c:out value="${letter}"/>
</c:forTokens>
```

This tag outputs a, b, c, d, and e, but not f, because the index of e in this collection is 4.

Of course, begin and end can be combined, as in tags like the following:

```
<c:forTokens items="a,b,c,d,e,f" delims="," var="letter"
    begin="2" end="4">
    <c:out value="${letter}"/>
</c:forTokens>
```

This loop outputs c, d, and e—the tokens with indexes 2, 3, and 4.

Only indexes that actually exist in the underlying collection can be included in the iteration. If begin has a value that is greater than any item's index—for instance, if you type begin="20" but there are only four items in your collection—then your <c:forEach> or <c:forTokens> tag won't iterate over anything. Its body will never be processed. If end is higher than the highest index—for instance, end="50" with a 47-element collection—then end has no effect.

The step attribute lets you filter the list further by skipping elements. The default behavior for <c:forEach> and <c:forTokens> is to include every element, but step="2" overrides this behavior and causes the tags to process only every second element. A value of 3 for step includes only every third element in the tag's iteration, and so on. If step does not line up evenly with end, or with the natural end of the collection, then some items at the end of the collection may be skipped. For instance, if 10 is the highest index in a collection, begin is 5, and step is 2, then only the indexes 5, 7, and 9 will be included.

Table 5.4 shows some examples of `begin`, `end`, and `step` operating together, assuming an underlying collection with 11 items (with indexes of 0 through 10). A hyphen indicates that the attribute was not specified.

Table 5.4 Examples of the effect of the `begin`, `end`, and `step` attributes in iteration tags. This table shows which values will be included in an iteration for various permutations of attributes.

Begin	End	Step	Included items (by index: 0=first item, 1=second item, and so forth)
-	-	-	0 1 2 3 4 5 6 7 8 9 10
3	-	-	3 4 5 6 7 8 9 10
-	3	-	0 1 2 3
-	-	3	0 3 6 9
3	3	-	3
3	3	3	3
0	9	2	0 2 4 6 8
0	9	3	0 3 6 9
0	9	4	0 4 8
0	9	5	0 5
0	9	6	0 6
0	9	20	0
20	30	1	*none (begin exceeds greatest index)*

5.3.2 *Looping over numbers*

I mentioned earlier that the `items` attribute is optional in `<c:forEach>`. If you don't specify `items`, then `begin` and `end` must be present. When this happens, a collection containing the numeric values specified with the `begin` and `end` attributes is the basis for the iteration. The following example

```
<c:forEach begin="1" end="5" var="current">
    <c:out value="${current}"/>
</c:forEach>
```

outputs the following, ignoring white space:

```
1 2 3 4 5
```

In `<c:forEach>` tags that lack an `items` attribute, `step` is still permissible and has the expected effect. This example

```
<c:forEach begin="2" end="10" step="2" var="current">
    <c:out value="${current}"/>
</c:forEach>
```

has the following output:

```
2  4  6  8  10
```

In `<c:forTokens>`, the `items` attribute is mandatory. If you want to iterate over numbers, just use `<c:forEach>`.

In the examples so far, we've typed the `begin`, `end`, and `step` attributes' values inside the tag. But like most other attributes in JSTL tags, these attributes accept expressions. If you have a scoped variable called `loopBoundary`, you could write

```
end="${loopBoundary}"
```

TIP   The primary use for iterating directly over numbers is to repeat the loop body a specific number of times. Sometimes, you just need to print a big list of numbers, but this is rare. Instead, looping over numbers is useful when you want to use `<c:forEach>` to repeat static content, but you want to decide how many times to print that content.

For example, many HTML pages manage white space manually using the ` ` HTML entity reference. Although there are often better approaches than using this entity to handle white space, it is more manageable to write

```
<c:forEach begin="1" end="50"> </c:forEach>
```

than to type or paste ` ` 50 times. For example, you might find it easier to experiment with different numbers of spaces, or change the number quickly and in a well-defined manner, if you use the `<c:forEach>` tag. And, of course, you can vary the number dynamically. If `end="50"` in the previous example were instead `end="${width}"`, where `${width}` changed as appropriate, then the number of printed ` ` occurrences could grow or shrink as appropriate.

Although it feels like a dirty HTML hack, I have used a similar approach to produce table cells filled with dynamically generated ` ` entity references—for example, to represent data such as poll results or application progress graphically:

```
<table>
 <tr>
   <td bgcolor="#00aa00">
     <c:forEach begin="1" end="${width}"> </c:forEach>
   </td>
```

```
    </tr>
    </table>
```

This code prints a bar of variable width across the screen. You'll see this technique in practice in chapter 12.

5.3.3 *Loop status*

The `<c:forEach>` and `<c:forTokens>` tags also have a varStatus attribute that you can use to expose information about the iteration that is taking place. This information is useful when you want to exercise specialized control over a loop. Suppose, for instance, that you need to treat a collection's first or last item differently from the rest.

Like the var attribute in `<c:forEach>` and `<c:forTokens>`, varStatus lets you create a scoped variable that can be accessed inside the loop. If var="current", the current item is exposed inside the loop as a page-scoped variable named current. Similarly, if varStatus="s", then a variable that contains information about the current round of iteration is exposed as a variable named s. Table 5.5 shows the most useful properties of this status variable.

Table 5.5 The loop status variable (exposed by the varStatus attribute) includes properties for determining information about the current loop, such as whether it's the first or last iteration. You can also use it to determine the position of the current item in its original collection.

Property	Type	Description
index	number	The index of the current item in the underlying collection
count	number	The position of the current round of iteration, starting with 1
first	boolean	Whether the current round of iteration is the first
last	boolean	Whether the current round of iteration is the last

As you saw earlier, every item in a collection has an index number. These indexes start with 0 and increase by one for each element. The index property of varStatus's variable holds the index of the current item in the loop. For instance, in a round of iteration for the first element in a collection, index will equal 0. For the second, index will equal 1. Whatever the value of the step attribute (the default 1 or a value greater than 1), index will jump by step for each round of iteration. As another example, if you use the attribute begin="10", then for the first loop where `<c:forEach>` enters its body, index will equal 10.

The count property, on the other hand, starts with 1 and reflects the current loop's position among the items for which <c:forEach> runs its body. No matter what, count always increases by one for each loop. For any <c:forEach> or <c:forToken> tag, count will be 1 the first time the body is processed, 2 the second time, and so on. The first and last properties are boolean properties indicating whether the current loop is the tag's first or last, respectively. (The first property is just a convenient way of checking to see whether count currently equals 1.) The count attribute's behavior isn't affected by the begin, end, or step attribute.

Figure 5.2 shows the values of these properties for a sample iteration.[2]

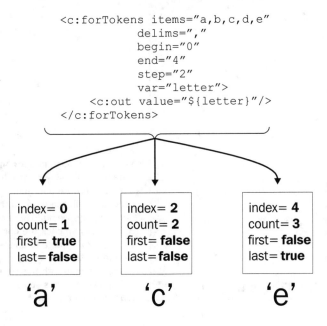

```
<c:forTokens items="a,b,c,d,e"
             delims=","
             begin="0"
             end="4"
             step="2"
             var="letter">
    <c:out value="${letter}"/>
</c:forTokens>
```

index= **0**	index= **2**	index= **4**
count= **1**	count= **2**	count= **3**
first= **true**	first= **false**	first= **false**
last=**false**	last=**false**	last= **true**

'a'   'c'   'e'

Figure 5.2
Values of the varStatus variable's properties during a sample iteration. The tag in this figure iterates three times, producing the letters a, c, and e. The boxes above each letter show the values of the varStatus variable for that letter's loop.

5.4 *Loop example: scrolling through results*

Earlier, we discussed how you can use the begin and end attributes to display only part of a collection, in cases where the collection is too big to fit reasonably on a single screen. Many applications, when they have too much information for a single page, let users pick the information to view. For instance, the user can decide whether to display results 0 through 19, 20 through 39, and so on.

---

[2] The variable that varStatus creates has some other properties, but they are intended more for developers of custom tags than for page authors. If you're a Java developer and are interested in these extra properties, see the LoopTagStatus interface in appendix B.

Let's write a sample page that that allows the user to scroll, or *page*, through information. The page's output should look like figure 5.3: the top prints ranges of data the user can click, and the bottom prints the data.

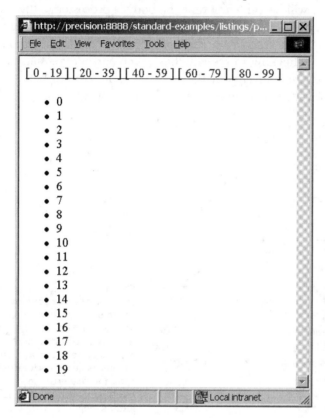

Figure 5.3
When a web page has too much data to fit on a single screen, it's useful to let the user jump around within the data. In the sample page we build in section 5.4, users can click the links at the top of the page to choose what data to view. You can produce pages with this feature using only the tags you've learned about so far.

We can accomplish this result with just the iteration and conditional tags you've seen so far, using the expression language and the `<c:out>` tag to assist us. Of course, for a page to be useful, it needs real data to display. Because we haven't yet looked at how to retrieve information from XML files and databases, we can't yet display real data. So, we'll use `<c:forEach>`'s ability to generate numbers for us automatically when we use the `begin` and `end` attributes without `items`. Thus, we'll be able to experiment with a simple page that lets us scroll over numbers. (As soon as you have real data, you can insert this data into `<c:forEach>`'s `items` attribute, and the page will then let you loop over interesting information, not just numbers.)

Without further ado, let's look at the code (see listing 5.1).

Listing 5.1 scroll.jsp: Using JSTL to let the user scroll through results

```
<%@ taglib prefix="c" uri="http://java.sun.com/jstl/core" %>

<c:set var="totalCount" scope="session" value="100"/>        ❶  Configuration
<c:set var="perPage" scope="session" value="20"/>

<c:forEach
    var="boundaryStart"
    begin="0"
    end="${totalCount - 1}"
    step="${perPage}">

    <a href="?start=<c:out value="${boundaryStart}"/>">
      [
        <c:out value="${boundaryStart}"/>            ❷  Prints
                                                          ranges
          -
        <c:out value="${boundaryStart + perPage - 1}"/>
      ]
    </a>
</c:forEach>

<c:forEach
    var="current"
    varStatus="status"
    begin="${param.start}"
    end="${param.start + perPage - 1}">
  <c:if test="${status.first}">
    <ul>
  </c:if>
  <li><c:out value="${current}"/></li>       ❸  Prints data
  <c:if test="${status.last}">                    items
    </ul>
  </c:if>
</c:forEach>
```

5.4.1 Understanding the example

This is our first real-world example of a full JSTL page, so let's go through it carefully. Overall, the example can be broken into three sections.

❶ We use two `<c:set>` tags to configure our page's behavior. The tags are here only for demonstrative purposes; the two values they set could easily come from anywhere else—for instance, back-end Java code, request parameters, and so on. The rest of the example depends on the two variables these tags create:

- `totalCount`—The total number of items we'd like to let the user scroll through. For instance, if we retrieved 100 items from the database, we'd want `totalCount` to equal `100`. That's the sample value we use here.

- perPage—The number of results we want to show the user on each page. Here, we set this value to 20, which seems like a reasonable number: it's not so small that it's irritating, but it's not so large that it overwhelms people.

❷ With these variables set, we can print out our page's top section (see figure 5.3). This section will look the same no matter which data the user has chosen. (As an exercise, think about how you could highlight or otherwise draw attention to the range the data is currently displaying.) This data depends only on the two variables that configure our page's behavior: totalCount and perPage.

The goal of this section is to produce links of the form

```
[ 0 - 19 ]
```

that let the user choose which results will be displayed.

To produce these links, we loop over our data from the first item (begin="0") to the last one (end="${totalCount - 1}"). We set the step attribute to perPage so that we loop only once for each range we want to print. For instance, if we start with 0 and perPage is 20, we want the current item—which we call boundaryStart—to be 0, then 20, then 40, then 60, and so on. Within each loop, we print out the starting and ending numbers of the range. The starting number is simple: it's boundaryStart (the current item). To get the ending number of the range, we add perPage to boundaryStart using the expression language. Note that we subtract 1 from this sum, because we don't want this boundary to spill over into the next one. We want to print [0 - 19], [20 - 39], and so on, not [0 - 20] and then [20 - 40]. (We begin with 0 to demonstrate that our data starts with item 0, as is usually the case as far as <c:forEach> is concerned. However, if we were printing real data instead of numbers, we could add 1 to the expressions in both the begin and end attributes to make the numbers friendlier to the user: [1 - 20], [21 - 40], and so on.)

We use one trick that needs to be explained. The block of JSTL used to begin each link looks like this:

```
<a href="?start=<c:out value="${boundaryStart}"/>">
```

We're using a <c:out> tag in the middle of an HTML <a> tag: no problem there! Our trick involves the <a> tag itself. Once the <c:out> placeholder gets filled in, the tag will look like this:

```
<a href="?start=20">
```

20 could just as easily have been any other number printed by the <c:out> tag. This <a> tag means, "Link back to the current page, sending a request parameter named start that equals 20." Thus, when our user chooses a specific range, a start parameter will indicate the start of the range the user asked for. We can access this parameter using the expression ${param.start}.

TIP   In general, you can send request parameters as part of a URL in the form `param1=value1&param2=value2`. In chapter 6, we'll look at a much friendlier way to send parameters as part of an HTML `<a>` link. But it's useful to have seen this manual style in action at least once.

---

❸ The final section of our page displays the selected results. If no results have been selected—that is, if the `start` parameter is empty—we begin with the number 0. We do so because `begin="${param.start}"` is the same as `begin="0"` if the `start` parameter doesn't exist. In the page's second loop, we begin at the start of the range and loop over `perPage` elements: `end="${param.start + perPage - 1}"`, which means, "End the iteration with the item `perPage` items away from `param.start`." We subtract 1 because the `end` attribute causes the loop to include the final value, but we want to make sure our ranges don't overlap. Subtracting 1 from the `end` attribute is a fairly common pattern in JSTL pages when you work with ranges.

5.4.2 *Using varStatus in the example*

In the loop at the bottom of the page in our example, notice that we use `varStatus` to expose a variable named `status`. Instead of printing the beginning `<ul>` and the ending `</ul>` outside the `<c:forEach>` tag, we've moved those tags inside and placed `<c:if>` tags around them. This way, we can be sure the `<ul>` element will print only if there are `<li>` items to fill it. That is, we print `<ul>` only when we encounter our first piece of data, and we print the closing `</ul>` tag for the last item. (Recall from the previous chapter that although empty lists—`<ul></ul>`—display fine in most browsers, they're technically an error.) The empty list is not a possibility in our example; because we're just iterating over numbers, they can't be missing! But a real-life collection might not be as big as we expect it to be, in which case these defensive checks are appropriate.

Because we expose this `status` variable, we can also use it to modify the loop's behavior in other ways. For instance, suppose we wanted to treat alternating rows differently. Normally, we might use different colors, but because colors don't show up well in a black-and-white book, we'll instead use different font sizes. Let's make every second row print in a small font:

```
<c:forEach
    var="current"
    varStatus="status"
    begin="${param.start}"
    end="${param.start + perPage - 1}">
  <c:if test="${status.first}">
    <ul>
```

```
    </c:if>
    <c:if test="${status.count % 2 == 0}">
      <font size="-2">
    </c:if>
    <li><c:out value="${current}"/></li>
    <c:if test="${status.count % 2 == 0}">
      </font>
    </c:if>
    <c:if test="${status.last}">
      </ul>
    </c:if>
</c:forEach>
```

To pick out every second row, we use the expression ${status.count % 2 == 0}. Recall from chapter 3 that % in JSTL's expression language is a *remainder* operator. Thus, status.count % 2 means, "Divide status.count by 2 and take the remainder." This remainder will be 0 only for the even rows. Thus, only these rows print in a smaller font in figure 5.4. Note that we use the same condition twice: once to open a <font> tag, and once to close it with </font>.

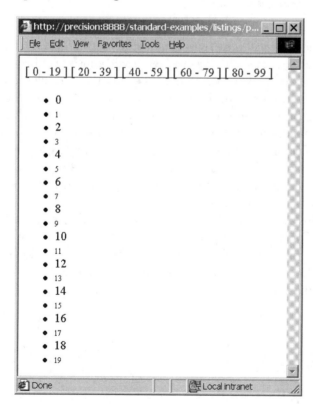

Figure 5.4
Many web sites display alternating rows in different colors. Because colors don't show up well in a black-and-white book, our example of handling alternate rows uses font size instead of color. Here, every second row prints using small text.

5.5 *Summary*

When using JSTL's iteration (loop) tags, keep the following points in mind:

- The `<c:forEach>` tag is JSTL's general-purpose looping tag. It lets you loop over nearly any kind of collection.
- The `<c:forTokens>` tag breaks apart strings and loops over these string fragments, called *tokens*.
- When you iterate, you'll usually want to expose a variable using the iteration tag's `var` attribute. Doing so lets you access each individual item, one by one, in the body of your iteration tag.
- The iteration tags support a `varStatus` attribute that lets you recover information about where you are in the overall iteration. The tags also support `begin`, `end`, and `step` attributes to let you write underachieving `<c:forEach>` and `<c:forToken>` tags that iterate over only parts of a collection.

Importing text

6

115

"Including data," says the JSP specification, "is a significant part of the tasks in a JSP page." It might sound boring, but JSP pages often simply need to include text that comes from elsewhere.

There are many reasons to write a JSP page that includes content from other pages. For instance, most professional web sites have common headers and footers—that is, they all start and end the same way in order to achieve a uniform look and feel. If you create one file called header.jsp and another called footer.jsp, it's easy to establish a consistent layout and design for your site by including them at the top and bottom of all your pages.

But text reuse doesn't stop there. JSP pages can act as a convenient switching mechanism, routing the right information to the right users based on their preferences, roles, or actions, and perhaps personalizing the text for users individually along the way. Pages can also include and merge content from a variety of sources, much as web portals do. (In chapter 13, we'll look at an example of how to aggregate content into a single, coherent web site.)

In chapter 2, we discussed two ways to include text in a JSP page: the `<jsp:include>` tag and the `<%@ include %>` directive. JSTL introduces a third mechanism: the `<c:import>` tag. Think of `<c:import>` as *`<jsp:include>`: The Next Generation.* The `<c:import>` tag supercedes `<jsp:include>`, providing all the functionality of the core JSP tag but also adding new features. For example, whereas `<jsp:include>` only lets you include files from the current web application, `<c:import>` lets you include content from other web servers (see figure 6.1).

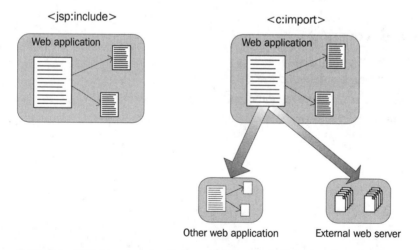

Figure 6.1 Whereas `<jsp:include>` supports simple inclusion of content from within the same web application, `<c:import>` lets you retrieve text from the entire local JSP container, as well as from web servers accessible over the network.

Another important task you'll need to handle when you write dynamic web pages is managing Uniform Resource Locators (URLs). You need to use URLs when you import content with <c:import>, but URLs show up in other places as well. For example, every time your pages display hyperlinks (HTML <a> tags) to other pages, they use URLs.

In this chapter, we look at <c:import> and other tags that help you manage and use URLs. We'll also show how you can communicate with the pages you include, in order to customize their output.

6.1 Including text with the <c:import> tag

To retrieve content from a local JSP page or from another server, you can use the <c:import> tag. Sometimes you'll just want to print the information that you retrieve, but <c:import> also lets you store the retrieved text in a scoped variable instead of printing it.

Table 6.1 shows the <c:import> tag's attributes.

Table 6.1 Basic <c:import> tag attributes

Attribute	Description	Required	Default
url	URL to retrieve and import into the page	Yes	*None*
context	/ followed by the name of a local web application	No	*Current context*
var	Name of the attribute to expose the String contents of the URL	No	*None*
scope	Scope of the attribute to expose the String contents of the URL	No	*page*

The crucial attribute is url, which specifies the URL of the content to retrieve. The other attributes let you modify the way the tag handles its URL.[1]

Often, a page that uses <c:import> is called a *source page*, and the page whose contents are included with <c:import> is called a *target page*.

6.1.1 Absolute and relative URLs

You're probably familiar with the basics of URLs simply from browsing the Web. A URL, which is often called a *web address* by the sort of person who's captivated by

---

[1] The <c:import> tag has a few advanced attributes that you'll need only if you're performing relatively sophisticated text imports. See chapter 14 for more information about advanced <c:import> techniques.

television commercials for America Online, is a string that describes the location of a particular piece of content on the network. A complete URL has two parts:

- A *scheme*, which is the name of a mechanism for finding data (like `http` or `ftp`)
- Information that follows the scheme and describes where to find the data

These two parts are separated by a colon. For instance, a full HTTP URL might look like this:

```
http://java.sun.com/
```

This URL has a scheme of *http*, followed by a colon, followed by the location *// java.sun.com/*. The URL therefore means, "Use the HTTP protocol to get information from the web server named java.sun.com."

HTTP URLs that have a scheme and a server are called *absolute*, meaning that they refer to the same content no matter where they appear. For instance, the meaning of the following URL doesn't change, regardless of where you see it:

```
http://www.uky.edu/FiscalAffairs/Environmental/hmm/outline.htm
```

Wherever this absolute URL appears, it refers to a specific page on the www.uky.edu server. (When this chapter was written, this particular page offered information on "hazardous waste generator training" for workers at the University of Kentucky. I have no idea why it was one of my laptop's bookmarks.)

Not all URLs are absolute; some are *relative*, meaning they're abbreviated, just as phone numbers can be. For example, if I'm talking to a colleague across the country, telling her that my phone number is 432-6687 won't be enough; I also need to give her my area code (which is 203, in case you're interested in stalking me). However, using a shortened version of my complete telephone number is fine as long as the context is clear—if I'm communicating with a local dry-cleaner or exterminator, for instance. In fact, when I give out my phone number to colleagues within my university, I often leave off more than the area code, giving just an extension of 2-6687.

Similarly, the amount of information missing from a URL can vary. A relative URL might only lack a scheme and a server, or it might leave off part of the path, too. Just as with phone numbers, the meaning of a relative URL depends on the place where it appears. Typically, every web page has its own URL, and when a relative URL appears in the source code for a web page, it picks up its missing pieces based on the location (the server and the path) of the current page.

For our purposes, there are two types of relative URLs: *page-relative* and *context-relative*.

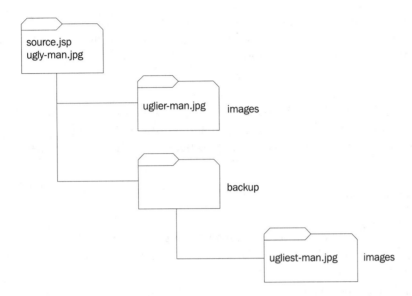

Figure 6.2 Page-relative URLs let you access files based on their relationship to the current page. For instance, from the file source.jsp, it's easy to use a page-relative URL to access files in the same directory (ugly-man.jpg) or in subdirectories (images/uglier-man.jpg, backup/images/ugliest-man.jpg). Page-relative URLs work the same way in HTML and in JSTL.

Page-relative URLs

A URL that simply specifies a filename, or part of a file path, is sometimes called a *page-relative URL*. Page-relative URLs start with any character other than a forward slash (/); for instance, all of the following are page-relative URLs:

```
ugly-man.jpg
images/uglier-man.jpg
backup/images/ugliest-man.jpg
```

Figure 6.2 will help you visualize what these page-relative URLs mean. Assume that these three URLs occur in a JSP page called source.jsp. The first page-relative URL, ugly-man.jpg, refers to the file ugly-man.jpg in the same directory as source.jsp. The second URL in the list refers to the file uglier-man.jpg in the images subdirectory; the third URL points to ugliest-man.jpg in the images directory, which is in a directory called backup.

You may be familiar with page-relative URLs from the `<a>` and `<img>` tags in HTML. For instance, if you wanted to link to outline.html in the current page's directory, you could write

```
<a href="outline.html">Outline</a>
```

The `<c:import>` tag and JSTL's other URL-related tags work the same way. If you wanted to include the file named outline.html from the same directory as the page you're writing, you could simply write

```
<c:import url="outline.html"/>
```

This kind of relative link has the advantage that it doesn't need to be changed when your application moves. You can pick up outline.html and the page that contains a relative URL to it, and then move these two pages anywhere without needing to change the link.

Context-relative URLs

As I mentioned, page-relative URLs work the same way in HTML tags like `<a>` that they do in JSTL tags like `<c:import>`. Relative URLs that start with the / character, however, do not. They have a special meaning to JSTL tags that's different from their meaning in HTML.

In HTML, if we use the tag

```
<img src="/images/ugly-man.jpg"/>
```

then the file ugly-man.jpg comes from the images directory at the root of our entire web server. This directory might store images that are shared by both static and dynamic pages; pages written in Perl, JSP, or any other language can all use the same relative URL as long as they run on the same server.

By contrast, if we use the URL

```
/images/ugly-man.jpg
```

as input to a JSTL tag, the tag doesn't look for the images directory at the root of our web server. Instead, the images directory is found at the root of our JSP page's web application. Recall from chapter 2 that the term *web application* has a specific meaning when describing sites built using JSP: a web application is an organized collection of pages and other resources, typically grouped under a single directory. A single web server might run many different web applications at the same time. The term *context-relative* arises because a web application is sometimes called a *context*.

| **NOTE** | I've written and posted instructions for setting up Tomcat, a free JSP container, on Manning Publications's web site. These instructions also describe web applications (contexts) in more detail. See appendix D for the URL of these instructions. |

Note that the same relative URL might have two different meanings within your page if it starts with /. If it's sent directly to the browser as part of an HTML tag, it takes on its familiar meaning in HTML (server-relative). But if it's used as one of the attributes to `<c:import>` or another JSTL tag, its JSP-specific meaning applies (context-relative). This usage can be confusing, but don't worry about it for now. Later in this chapter, we'll encounter the `<c:url>` tag, which helps you manage URLs and which removes some of the confusion.

6.1.2 *Retrieving data from URLs*

Let's look at a few examples. Suppose we're writing a page called source.jsp, and we want to include the text from a file named target.jsp that exists in the same directory as source.jsp. To do this, we could just write

```
<c:import url="target.jsp"/>
```

Suppose, however, that source.jsp is in a directory called source and target.jsp is in a directory called target, both directories being at the root of our web application. In this case, we could import the target page as follows:

```
<c:import url="/target/target.jsp"/>
```

Now, suppose target.jsp is located on a different web server. In that case, the only way to retrieve the file using `<c:import>` is be to use its full URL:

```
<c:import url="http://www.far-away.net/directory/target.jsp"/>
```

You are not limited to including JSP pages or other resources from a JSP container. You can specify any valid URL. For instance, we can include the entire CNN home page:

```
<c:import url="http://www.cnn.com"/>
```

We can even use the File Transfer Protocol (FTP):

```
<c:import url="ftp://ftp.cs.yale.edu/banner.msg"/>
```

Importing from another web application

Between absolute URLs and those relative to the current web application lies a middle ground. Sometimes, you want to refer to a JSP page (or other resource) from a different web application on the same server as yours. For example, maybe an old application has images, information, or other resources that you want to use. You can retrieve files from another web application by specifying that web application's name using the `<c:import>` tag's context attribute.

The `context` attribute names another web application on the same server as the page you're writing. This name needs to start with a forward slash (/). For instance, consider the following tag:

```
<c:import context="/other" url="/directory/target.jsp"/>
```

This tag imports the page /directory/target.jsp from the web application named "other" in the same JSP container as our source page. Thus, the URL that appears in the `url` attribute is treated as if it is relative to the root of this other web application (that is, the other *context*).

Using expressions

Of course, you're not limited to using URLs that you type literally into the `<c:import>` tag's `url` attribute. The `<c:import>` tag supports the full range of JSTL expressions. For instance, the target URL can come from an expression, as follows:

```
<c:import url="${applicationScope.target}"/>
```

This tag looks up the `target` attribute in the application scope, treats it as a URL, and retrieves information from this URL. The `context` attribute can also come from an expression:

```
<c:import url="${applicationScope.target}"
  context=" ${applicationScope.targetContext} "/>
```

6.1.3 Saving information for later

By default, `<c:import>` retrieves information from a URL and then immediately prints it to your page. This is exactly what `<jsp:include>` does, and in most cases, it's also what you want.

However, suppose you don't want to immediately print the data you retrieve. Sometimes, for instance, you want to import a page and then include its text multiple times in your page. (As an example, imagine a file that contains nothing but some HTML formatting to produce a stylized, horizontal line.) Or you might want to retrieve some text every time the user logs in, and then store this text in the user's session scope for use during the user's session. Saving data from `<c:import>` lets you avoid having to retrieve the contents of a URL multiple times, which can sometimes take a long time and slow your pages.

To save the result of `<c:import>` instead of printing it out, you can use the `var` attribute. Specifying a `var` attribute to the `<c:import>` tag causes the tag to not output anything. Instead, the tag will simply retrieve text and save it to a scoped variable. As with other JSTL tags, you can also use a `scope` attribute to set the scope of the variable you create. (As usual, when you use `var` and `scope`, you need to specify the name and scope manually; you can't use expressions in these two attributes.)

For example, consider the following block of JSP text:

```
<c:import url="http://legal.com/copyright-notice.html"/>
<p>
Welcome to Joe's Legal Services site.
We're not lawyers, but we try real hard.
Been arrested for assault?  Larceny?
Indecent exposure?  Let us help!
</p>
<c:import url="http://legal.com/copyright-notice.html"/>
```

This page displays a copyright notice at the top and bottom of the page by importing a URL that contains the copyright notice. However, this page imports the file twice, and doing so isn't efficient. Importing a URL can be expensive, so the following code, which uses the var attribute, will probably run faster:

```
<c:import
    url="http://legal.com/copyright-notice.html"
    var="copyright"/>
<c:out value="${copyright}"/>
<p>
Welcome to Joe's Legal Services site.
We're not lawyers, but we try real hard.
Been arrested for assault?  Larceny?
Indecent exposure?  Let us help!
</p>
<c:out value="${copyright}"/>
```

In some situations, you might need to pass imported text from the <c:import> tag to another tag. If a tag reads from its body, you can include the <c:import> tag inside it:

```
<string:lowerCase>
  <c:import url="target.jsp"/>
</string:lowerCase>
```

In this example, we're importing the target.jsp page and passing it to a hypothetical, third-party tag called <string:lowerCase>.[2] You can also use the var attribute to communicate between a <c:import> tag and another tag that needs input. Consider the following two tags:

```
<c:import url="/target.xml" context="/other" var="doc"/>
<x:parse xml="${doc}"/>
```

Here, we import a page from another context and then feed it to the JSTL <x:parse> tag, which we'll encounter in chapter 8.

---

[2] The open-source Jakarta Taglibs project contains a String Taglib, written by Henri Yandell. This library includes a <string:lowerCase> tag that's designed to convert its body into lowercase. See appendix D for pointers to more tag libraries that are available online.

6.1.4 *Communicating with imported pages*

Sometimes it isn't enough just to retrieve a page. If the page is dynamic, you may want to customize its output. JSTL gives you two easy ways to communicate with your target pages, and doing so gives those pages an opportunity to tailor their output to your needs.

First, you can use the `<c:param>` tag, which we'll introduce in this section. The `<c:param>` tag lets you send a request parameter to your target page.

Second, if you're importing a relative URL for a page in your web application, you can use the request, session, and application scopes to communicate with your target. (Page scope is the only scope that isn't shared.) Also, when you import a page from the same JSP container, all of your source page's request parameters are passed automatically to the target page.

The *<c:param>* tag

The `<c:param>` tag is an optional child tag for `<c:import>` (and some other JSTL tags we'll encounter later in this chapter). When it appears, it tells `<c:import>` to send a request parameter to the page it's loading. You can access request parameters, as you saw in chapter 3, by using expressions like `${param.user}`. Technically, `<c:param>` works with any URL that appears in `<c:import>`, but the idea of request parameters applies most commonly for HTTP URLs.

Table 6.2 lists the attributes for `<c:param>`.

Table 6.2   `<c:param>` tag attributes

Attribute	Description	Required	Default
name	Parameter name	Yes	*None*
value	Parameter value	No	*Body*

As you saw in chapter 3, every HTTP request parameter has a name and a value. The `name` and `value` attributes are used to specify these, respectively.

For example, suppose we use this tag:

```
<c:param name="quarter" value="25"/>
```

Then if our target page uses JSTL, it can retrieve the value 25 using the expression `${param.quarter}`.

To send parameters to a page that you want to retrieve, simply insert the `<c:param>` tag within `<c:import>`, as the following example demonstrates:

```
<c:import url="http://www.base.net">
  <c:param name="first" value="one"/>
```

```
  <c:param name="second" value="two"/>
</c:import>
```

This code causes the URL http://www.base.net to be retrieved with two parameters (`first` and `second`) just as if the full URL were really the following:

```
http://www.base.net?first=one&second=two
```

The result is also the same as if someone had just filled out an HTML form that looked like this:

```
<form action="http://www.base.net">
  <input type="hidden" name="first" value="one"/>
  <input type="hidden" name="second" value="two"/>
</form>
```

Like other JSTL tags, `<c:param>` accepts expressions; both name and value work with the expression language.

For instance, consider the following tag:

```
<c:param name="user" value="${sessionScope.user}"/>
```

This tag retrieves a variable from the session scope and sends it as a request parameter to a URL.

WARNING   The `<c:param>` tag is just an easy-to-use front end to the manual technique for cramming parameters into a URL that you saw at the end of chapter 5. This approach is fine for most purposes, but it's not a universal way to emulate all web forms. Some web forms use a mechanism called *HTTP POST* that does not encode request parameters in the URL. If a page is written in a language other than JSP, it's not guaranteed to automatically check the URL for parameters. Thus, if you want to use `<c:param>` to emulate HTML forms for arbitrary applications, you'll need to test the application first to make sure it reads the parameters you send.

The <c:set> tag and implicit communication with relative URLs

When you use `<c:import>` with a relative URL, you can use more than just `<c:param>` to communicate with your target page. If your target page is in the same web application as your source page, then your two pages share the same request, session, and application scopes. Even if the page is in a different web application (and you're accessing it using `<c:import>`'s `context` attribute), the two pages share their request scope.

Using `<c:import>` to load another page from your web application lets the two pages communicate as if the user's browser had accessed them separately. For instance, suppose we have two pages, cart.jsp and wishList.jsp, and they both use the expression `${sessionScope.user}` to identify the current user. If the user's browser accesses these two pages, they can both identify the user because the session is shared between them. Similarly, if cart.jsp uses `<c:import>` to include some data from wishList.jsp, then the two pages still share the same session; JSTL automatically ensures that they do. Therefore, if the wishList.jsp page needs to know the name of the current user, it can still retrieve this information using the expression `${sessionScope.user}` even when it's imported with `<c:import>` and not accessed directly by a web browser.

When scopes are shared, source pages can simply use the `<c:set>` tag (which you first saw in chapter 3) to communicate with their targets. When using `<c:set>` to communicate between pages, you need to use a `scope` attribute value of `request`, `session`, or `application`. Request scope is useful if you want to communicate with the target page without modifying the session or application scope. (Recall from chapter 2 that a major reason for request scope's existence is to support communication with included data. This applies to `<c:import>` the same way it applies to `<jsp:include>`.) But if you're planning to modify the session or application scope anyway, you can count on this information's traveling through a `<c:import>` to a target page in your web application. You'll see an example in the next section, to make this concept more concrete.

Why not simply use request parameters, as long as the convenient `<c:param>` tag exists? Broadly speaking, you might want to use `<c:set>` instead for three reasons:

- Sometimes you'll need to import a page that has already been designed. If it looks in the session for some data, you can't simply send it a request parameter and hope that it notices. In some situations, you need to accommodate the target page's existing mode of communication.

- `<c:param>`—and request parameters in general—can use only simple strings of text. When a request parameter is a word, or even a long sentence, this limitation is not an issue. But if you want to communicate an entire bean or other data to a page that you import, you can't always easily flatten it into a request parameter. Instead, you will probably want to use a scoped variable: the source page uses `<c:set>` to store the information, and the target page retrieves it using the expression language.

- Scoped variables allow two-way communication, whereas request parameters let you send data only from the source page to the target.

Figures 6.3 and 6.4 contrast request parameters with other forms of communication.

Despite the advantages of scoped variables, sometimes the explicit nature of `<c:param>`'s parameters leads to cleaner design. When you're maintaining a large

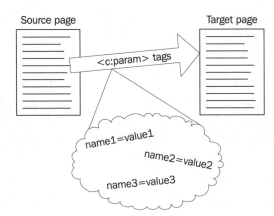

Figure 6.3
`<c:param>` lets you communicate simple request parameters, which take the form `name=value`. Request parameters are flexible, but they can only consist of simple text strings, and they only support one-way communication (from the source page to the target).

web site, you might appreciate the simplicity of `<c:param>` and the fact that, when you use `<c:param>` within `<c:import>`, you can immediately see what data two pages share. If you want to understand two pages that use scoped variables, you may need to spend more time looking at the source code for both the source and the target.

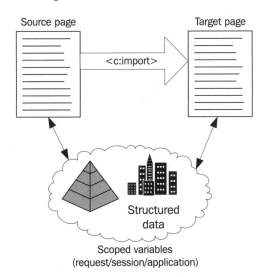

Figure 6.4
In contrast with request parameters, scoped variables—which can be accessed by both the source and target pages of a `<c:import>` tag—can include arbitrarily structured data. They support two-way communication as well. However, they only work for target pages within your web application.

6.1.5 *Import example: a customized header*

Let's look at a concrete example of pages communicating with one another using `<c:import>`. Many web applications need to standardize the appearance of a header throughout the application. We'll throw in a twist, however: in our example, the header will display a customized title that the source page (the one using

`<c:import>`) determines. The header has a few static characteristics that provide a standard look for the web application, but each page needs to insert its own title into this static template.

Example 1: customization with <c:param>

We'll first look at the simplest case: communication using a request parameter and the `<c:param>` tag. As we discussed in the previous section, this tag can be used only to send simple text strings from one page to another. Our example uses three pages:

- *page1.jsp*—A first sample application page
- *page2.jsp*—A second sample application page
- *header.jsp*—A JSP file that prints header information for use by both page1.jsp and page2.jsp

Listing 6.1 contains the code for the header page.

Listing 6.1 Import example application: header.jsp

```
<%@ taglib prefix="c" uri="http://java.sun.com/jstl/core" %>
<table width="100%">
  <tr>
    <td align="left" bgcolor="#888888">
      <big><font color="#FFFFFF">
        <c:out value="${param.title}"/>        ◁── Retrieves the title
      </font></big>                                 parameter
    </td>
    <td align="right">
      <small>
        Import example application
      </small>
    </td>
  </tr>
</table>
<hr />
```

This header represents nothing spectacular; the goal is just to display some dynamic text using the `<c:out>` tag we discussed in chapter 3. The rest of the page is simply static template text. The `<c:out>` tag in listing 6.1 retrieves the request parameter named `title` and prints it in the middle of a table that the tag constructs. This table establishes the header's structure, and it includes some static template text (Import example application.) Figure 6.5 shows how the header page might appear in a browser.

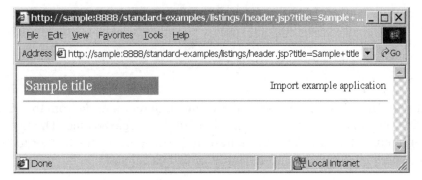

Figure 6.5 Our bare-bones header page, displayed directly in a browser. The URL for this page includes a sample title.

Let's now look at two pages that import this header: page1.jsp and page2.jsp, shown in listings 6.2 and 6.3, respectively.

Listing 6.2 Import example application: page1.jsp

```
<%@ taglib prefix="c" uri="http://java.sun.com/jstl/core" %>
<html>
<body>
<c:import url="header.jsp">
  <c:param name="title" value="Welcome to Page 1"/>
</c:import>

<h4>Page 1 information</h4>

We're pleased to introduce <b>Page 1</b>, our newest,
most cost-effective product.

</body>
</html>
```

Listing 6.3 Import example application: page2.jsp

```
<%@ taglib prefix="c" uri="http://java.sun.com/jstl/core" %>

<html>
<body>
<c:import url="header.jsp">
  <c:param name="title" value="Welcome to Page 2"/>
</c:import>

<h4>Page 2 information</h4>

<b>Page 2</b> is our luxury version of page 1,
```

```
complete with leather interior and a caviar
dispenser.

</body>
</html>
```

Page 1 and Page 2 are nearly identical; the only difference, aside from the different static text they display, is the `value` attribute of the `<c:param>` tag. The two pages send different values for the `title` parameter, which causes the header to be displayed differently for each page, as shown in figures 6.6 and 6.7.

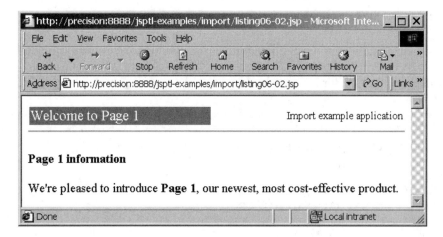

Figure 6.6   A web browser's display of page1.jsp, which supplies the text "Welcome to Page 1" to the header page.

The point of this short example was to demonstrate a simple header that accepts a variety of input. Clearly, the HTML used in this header is not extravagant; but from this example, it should be clear how you can supply custom text into an arbitrarily complex HTML header that can be used across multiple pages.

Example 2: customization without `<c:param>`

As you saw in section 6.1.4, a page that retrieves another page using `<c:import>` can communicate with its target using scoped variables. Here's a brief example of this type of communication—which, as we discussed earlier, can let your source page pass information both to and from your target page.

Consider the following pages: source.jsp and target.jsp. The former page imports the latter, and it both sends and receives data from the page that it includes. The code for source.jsp is as follows:

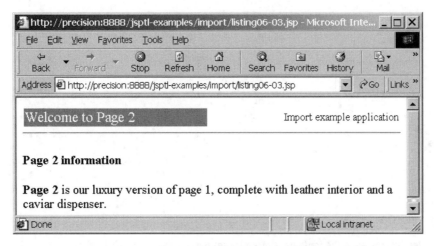

Figure 6.7   A web browser's display of page2.jsp, which supplies the text "Welcome to Page 2" to the header page. Note how the static text and form of the header are unchanged from page1.jsp; only the parameterized text differs.

```
<%@ taglib prefix="c" uri="http://java.sun.com/jstl/core" %>
<c:set var="input" scope="request" value="INPUT TEXT" />
Calling target.jsp...
<hr />
<c:import url="target.jsp" />
<hr />
source.jsp received back: <c:out value="${requestScope.output}" />
```

And here's the code for target.jsp:

```
<%@ taglib prefix="c" uri="http://java.sun.com/jstl/core" %>
target.jsp received: <c:out value="${requestScope.input}" />
<c:set var="output" scope="request" value="OUTPUT TEXT" />
```

These two pages work in a coordinated fashion: source.jsp is meant to be loaded first. It sets a request-scoped variable and gives it the value INPUT TEXT. Then it calls target.jsp, which reads this variable, prints it, and sets its own variable with a different name. When target.jsp is finished, source.jsp prints this new variable. Figure 6.8 demonstrates graphically the flow of these two pages, and figure 6.9 shows the output when source.jsp is called.

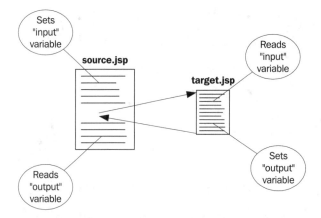

Figure 6.8 source.jsp sets a variable and then imports target.jsp, which reads the variable. Before target.jsp finishes, it sets its own variable, which source.jsp later reads.

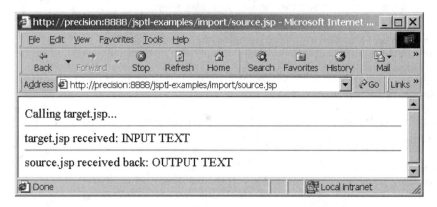

Figure 6.9 source.jsp displays output that looks like this when loaded by a web browser.

6.2 *Redirecting with* <c:redirect>

In some situations, your web pages need to act like seasoned bureaucrats and refer you elsewhere. Fortunately, web browsers tend to have more patience than most people do. Normally, when a browser sends a request for a web page, it receives back an HTML file, image, or other content in response. Sometimes, however, it gets *redirected* to another page. Essentially, the server says, "I don't have what you want; go look *here* instead," where *here* is a particular URL the browser needs to follow. The browser then loads this URL and displays its content—or perhaps it's redirected to yet another URL.

Redirections on the Web serve many purposes. Sometimes they act as forwarding addresses, indicating things like "My collection of illegal MP3 files doesn't live here any more; please find it at the following URL...." Such redirection might be necessary if the owner of a page needed to move it to a new server (which, given most ISPs' policies, might happen with some regularity to a collection of illegal MP3 files).

In dynamic applications like JSP pages, redirections have another use: they can simplify the overall flow of your application. For instance, imagine you have a single page called master.jsp that routes requests to the appropriate place depending on the value of a request parameter:

```
<c:choose>
  <c:when test="${param.action == 'buy'}">
    ... send the user to the buy.jsp page ...
  </c:when>
  <c:when test="${param.action == 'sell'}">
    ... send the user to the sell.jsp page ...
  </c:when>
</c:choose>
```

To perform redirections like this from your JSP pages, you can use the <c:redirect> tag. Its attributes are listed in table 6.3.

Table 6.3 `<c:redirect>` tag attributes

Attribute	Description	Required	Default
url	URL to redirect to	Yes	*None*
context	/ followed by the name of a local web application	No	*Current context*

When <c:redirect> executes, it forwards the browser to a new page, and then your page immediately stops running. For instance, consider the following two tags:

```
<c:redirect url="newPage.jsp"/>
<bank:addMoney dollars="40,000,000" user="${sessionScope.user}" />
```

In this case, the <bank:addMoney> tag will never run; <c:redirect> aborts the page as soon as it runs, meaning that the user will stay poor—or, at least, not gain $40,000,000 for doing nothing. (It's too bad; making money on the Internet used to be easier.)

The simplest use of <c:redirect> bounces the user to a new relative or absolute URL. For instance, to fill in the missing code from our last example, we might write

```
<c:when test="${param.action == 'buy'}">
  <c:redirect url="buy.jsp"/>
</c:when>
```

This `<c:redirect>` tag sends the user to the buy.jsp page in the same directory as the page where the `<c:redirect>` tag appears.

You can also use the `context` attribute to bounce the user to a page in a different web application, or context, in your JSP container:

```
<c:redirect context="/brokerage" url="/buy.jsp"/>
```

As with the `<c:import>` tag, when you use the `context` attribute, the values of both it and the `url` attribute must begin with /.

Like `<c:import>`, the `<c:redirect>` tag lets you use `<c:param>` within it if you want to send request parameters to the page to which you're redirecting the user. For instance, consider the following tags:

```
<c:redirect context="/brokerage" url="/buy.jsp">
  <c:param name="stock" value="IBM"/>
</c:redirect>
```

These tags work like the last tag, but now a single request parameter (whose name is stock and whose value is IBM) is passed to the buy.jsp page when the user is redirected.

6.3 Formatting URLs with `<c:url>`

It's extremely common to write web pages that link to one another. In fact, you might say that links are the essence of the Web. After all, the *HT* in both *HTML* and *HTTP* stands for *hypertext*, which means text with links (or *hyperlinks*).

6.3.1 How to use `<c:url>`

JSTL provides a `<c:url>` tag whose sole job is to print out a URL (or to store one in a scoped variable). Table 6.4 lists its attributes.

Table 6.4 `<c:url>` tag attributes

Attribute	Description	Required	Default
value	Base URL to print or store	Yes	*None*
context	/ followed by the name of a local web application	No	*Current context*
var	Name of the attribute to expose the final URL	No	*None*
scope	Scope of the attribute to expose the final URL	No	page

Just as with `<c:import>` and `<c:redirect>`, you can include `<c:param>` tags within the body of a `<c:url>` tag. For instance, the following tag prints out a URL that embeds a request parameter:

```
<c:url value="buy.jsp">
  <c:param name="stock" value="IBM"/>
</c:url>
```

It's simple to use <c:url>. Simply insert it into your page whenever you want to print a URL. Often, you'll want to insert <c:url> in the middle of an HTML tag, such as <a>. For example:

```
<a href="<c:url value="buy.jsp">
          <c:param name="stock" value="IBM"/>
        </c:url>">Buy IBM's stock</a>
```

Here, we embed <c:url> in the href attribute of an <a> tag in order to create a link to a JSP page. This link transfers a request parameter because of the <c:param> tag beneath <c:url>; thus, it's a simpler way to pass parameters than the relatively convoluted approach we had to use in the example at the end of chapter 5.

6.3.2 *Why to use <c:url>*

You've already seen one reason to use <c:url>: it makes it easy to construct a link that, when followed, passes a request parameter to a page. But when you're not passing parameters, you might wonder why you should use <c:url>. After all, you can introduce links into your page without JSTL's help; to create a link to the page menu.jsp, you could just write

```
<a href="menu.jsp">Return to the main menu</a>
```

However, the <c:url> tag is useful even in such simple cases, and I encourage you to use it whenever you need to create a relative link in your pages. The <c:url> tag is useful for two primary reasons:

- URLs sometimes need to be modified to preserve the user's session across various pages. The <c:url> tag takes care of this modification automatically.
- You might want to adjust context-relative URLs so that they point to the root of your web application, not to your entire server. The <c:url> tag makes this adjustment for you.

These reasons are both somewhat technical, but they're worth exploring briefly—if for no other reason than to justify the use of <c:url>.

Session preservation

This first reason to use <c:url> is fairly interesting. Throughout this book, we discuss session scope as if it exists magically. A user hits your pages and is automatically assigned a session, which stays around until the user goes away. But behind the scenes, both the server and the browser must do some work to ensure that the right session is associated with the right user. Normally, this work can be handled using a browser feature called *cookies*, which we discussed briefly in chapter 3.

Cookies let the user's browser and your JSP container manage the details of user sessions without your having to get involved. But not all browsers support cookies—and some users, concerned more with personal privacy than with learning how technology works, have refused to let their browsers accept cookies. Therefore, if your application is designed to work with browsers that don't use cookies—and most public applications should try to accommodate as many users and browsers as possible—then you need to help the JSP container by adding some information to URLs that lets the JSP container identify users appropriately. The `<c:url>` tag does this for you automatically.

Adjusting relative URLs

The second reason to use `<c:url>` is somewhat less interesting, but it's just as important. In addition to helping sessions work, `<c:url>` also makes sure that if your URL begins with /, it's mapped to the root directory of your web application, not to your entire web server. Earlier in this chapter, we talked about the difference between the way relative URLs are handled in JSP tags and they way they work in plain HTML tags. When a URL starts with /, it points to the root directory of your entire web server in HTML tags, but it refers to the root directory of your web application in JSP tags like `<c:import>` and `<c:redirect>`. Thus a URL like the following can refer to two separate files, even when it appears multiple times in the same page:

```
/info/copyright.txt
```

In HTML tags like the following, the URL refers to the info directory at your server's root directory:

```
<a href="/info/copyright.txt">Read the copyright notice</a>
```

But in a JSTL tag like the one shown here, the URL points to the info directory beneath your web application's root directory:

```
<c:import url="/info/copyright.txt">
```

For instance, if your web application comes with a directory named images that contains the application's logos and other graphics, you can't simply refer to a file in that directory as

```
/images/logo.gif
```

The application's images directory doesn't necessarily contain the same files as the web server's images directory. To use such an image in your page, you could write

```
<img src="<c:url value="/images/logo.gif"/>"/>
```

Here, the `<c:url>` tag is embedded within the `<img>` tag's `src` attribute; it causes the URL to be transformed appropriately so that the user's browser can understand it.

You can use `<c:url>`'s `context` attribute to create a URL to a page in another web application in your JSP container.

The `<c:url>` tag is also useful if you want to save a URL (using the `var` and `scope` attributes) and use it multiple times in your application.

6.4 *Summary*

In this chapter, we looked at tags that support text retrieval, redirection, and URL management. Key points to remember include the following:

- `<c:import>` works like `<jsp:include>`, but it lets you retrieve data from absolute URLs, as well as pages from different web applications on the same JSP server. It also lets you save data instead of printing it out immediately.

- If the source and target pages are in the same web application, then they can share variables in request, session, and application scope. Doing so allows two-way transmission of whatever data you'd like (including, of course, simple strings).

- `<c:redirect>` lets you bounce the user to a new page, using either an absolute or relative URL.

- Whenever you write out a relative URL to a page, you should use `<c:url>` instead of printing the URL directly. Doing so makes sure sessions work even in browsers that don't support cookies, and it also simplifies use of context-relative URLs (those that begin with /).

- `<c:param>` lets you pass simple text strings from the source page to the target page. It works with `<c:import>`, `<c:redirect>`, and `<c:url>`.

Selecting XML fragments

This chapter covers...

- Basic syntax of XPath (the XML Path Language)
- XPath's vision of an XML document
- JSTL's use of XPath variables
- XML namespaces and XPath in JSTL

It's probably safe to say that no web-related standard released in 2002 would be complete without accommodating XML. Failing to work with XML is, in some circles, tantamount to being unpatriotic or antisocial.

JSTL indeed supports XML—and it does so with flying colors. In fact, JSTL introduces a new and very convenient way to use XML in your dynamic pages.

You might have heard of other technologies that let you produce dynamic pages with XML, such as Extensible Stylesheet Language Transformations (XSLT), so you may wonder why JSTL bothers to introduce a new way of working with XML. The answer is simple: JSTL's support will be easier for many page authors to use than XSLT. If you've struggled with XSLT, JSTL might solve your problems with a much gentler learning curve.

Before we look at JSTL's features, though, we'll need to examine the main thing XSLT and JSTL share: the language called XPath (the XML Path Language). This language is the standard way to refer to parts of an XML document. Unless you don't care what's inside an XML document and just want to print it out wholesale, you'll usually need to identify the particular fragments you care about within a document. XPath gives you a convenient way to do this.

In this chapter, we'll introduce and explore XPath. By and large, this is the same XPath language that XSLT uses, so once you learn it here, you'll have learned a core XSLT skill. If you're already familiar with XPath, you can skim the beginning of this chapter quickly; but toward the end, I discuss some important details about how XPath and JSTL interact.

In the next chapter, we'll look at all of JSTL's tags for XML manipulation.

NOTE   If you don't yet feel comfortable with XML, reviewing chapter 2 will probably help.

7.1 XPath's vision of an XML document

XPath lets you specify parts of XML documents. For instance, you might be interested only in the document's `<customer>` tags, or in those `<product>` tags that are inside `<inventory>` tags. XPath is an extremely expressive language that is somewhat complex in its full form. Therefore, we won't discuss all of XPath's details here. Instead, my goal is simply to provide a gentle tutorial for XPath's core features. For a more complete look at XPath, many excellent references exist, including Bob DuCharme's *XSLT Quickly* and several online tutorials, listed in appendix D.

In chapter 2, we discussed some potential relationships between XML tags. For example, one tag that appears inside another tag is known as a *child tag*. When you work with XML documents using JSTL tags, these relationships become important.[1]

If your experience with markup languages comes primarily from HTML, you might be used to thinking of a document as linear—an ordered, one-dimensional collection of tags. An HTML document, for instance, starts with an `<html>` tag; later comes `<body>`, and after that, you'll typically see a few `<p>`, `<img>`, `<a>`, and `<table>` tags, followed by a closing `</body>` tag and, eventually, the final closing `</html>` tag. This is a useful, coherent way to think of (or describe) a web page.

XPath, however, takes a slightly different approach. The relationships between tags—for instance, the fact that one tag appears inside another—become critical. XPath sees the entire document as a tree: parents have children, and these children have their own children, just as in a family tree or organizational chart. Every well-formed XML document has a single element that contains all other elements; this *root element* (for example, the `<html>` element in an HTML document) has children, and these children can have their own children. As an example of a tree view of a document, consider the following HTML:

```
<html>
 <head>
  <title>Poem</title>
 </head>
 <body>
  <h1>Poem</h1>
  <p>I think that I shall never see</p>
  <p>an HTML document lovely as a <b>tree</b>.</p>
 </body>
</html>
```

Figure 7.1 shows this document's basic structure in tree form. Although it's natural to think of the `<head>` and `<body>` tags as being so-called children of the `<html>` element, you might find it stranger to describe the `<b>` element as a child of the `<p>` element in which it appears. Nonetheless, this structure is clear: `<b>` is a child tag of `<p>`, given the rules we discussed in chapter 2.

---

[1] As I mentioned in chapter 2, this book often uses the loose XML vocabulary common to JSP authors and others. For instance, I say *tags* instead of *elements* when the intent is clear. By and large, there's little value in sticking too closely with XML's formal vocabulary, except to be pedantic.

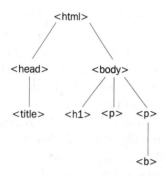

Figure 7.1
The tree structure of a sample HTML document. When an element like <h1> occurs inside <body>, you can think of it as a child of that <body> element.

7.2 XPath's basic syntax

XPath operates on documents using the type of tree structure you just saw. As you probably know, trees are commonly seen on computers. On nearly all modern operating systems, for example, a disk is organized into *directories* (or *folders*), each of which can contain other directories. This kind of organization naturally arranges itself into a tree, and we often speak of *child directories* or *subdirectories* when we discuss disks.

XPath takes advantage of our familiarity with traditional filenames, applying a similar syntax to the tree representing an XML document. If you have three directories on your disk—a, b, and c—and you are running Windows, you can refer to these directories as follows:

```
c:\a\b\c
```

Note how the backslash character (\) is used to separate the directory names. Unix systems use the regular slash (/) character in a similar capacity:

```
/a/b/c
```

XPath adopts this Unix convention, using the slash character to separate the name of one XML element from another. For example, in the tree from figure 7.1, the <b> element could be described by the following path:

```
/html/body/p/b
```

This XPath expression matches the highlighted part of our sample document:

```
<html>
 <head>
  <title>Poem</title>
 </head>
 <body>
  <h1>Poem</h1>
```

```
 <p>I think that I shall never see</p>
 <p>an HTML document lovely as a <b>tree</b> .</p>        <— /html/body/p/b
 <p>an HTML document lovely as a <b>tree</b>.</p>
 </body>
</html>
```

7.2.1 *Deep descendants*

XPath introduces a new syntax to meet a need seen often in XML documents but rarely in file systems. On a disk, you hardly ever want to find all files named autoexec.bat or inetd.conf; if you do, you probably need to use a tool that is specifically designed to let you search the disk. By contrast, when manipulating XML documents, you may often need to perform an operation on all elements that descend from a particular point in a document, no matter how deeply those tags appear. For example, it's relatively common to iterate over "all the <p> elements underneath <body>," all <customer> tags, and so on.

XPath simplifies this type of search by letting you use two adjacent slashes (//) to refer to *any* descendent of an element, no matter how deeply it appears. For instance, the <b> element from figure 7.1 could also be described by the following XPath expression

```
/html/body//b
```

or even simply

```
//b
```

Just as file paths on a disk can refer to more than one file (for instance, b* matches all files beginning with *b* in a directory), XPath expressions can match more than one element. For instance, the XPath expression

```
//p
```

matches both of the <p> elements from figure 7.1:

```
<html>
 <head>
  <title>Poem</title>
 </head>
 <body>
  <h1>Poem</h1>
  <p>I think that I shall never see</p>                    //p
  <p>an HTML document lovely as a <b>tree</b>.</p>
 </body>
</html>
```

7.2.2 *Attributes*

Another simple feature of XPath syntax lets you refer to tag attributes. This capability, just like //, has no direct analog to disk-based file paths. For instance, even though files on disk have characteristics (like modification dates) other than their filenames, file paths always refer to filenames alone. When prompted for a filename, you can't enter something like

```
c:\[date=Jan 1 2004 07:02:47 a.m.]
```

By contrast, XPath lets you identify elements using attributes and other characteristics; this is a convenient and commonly used feature.

As an example, suppose you had the following XML document:

```
<customers>
  <customer id="555" status="regular">
    <name>Jim Heinz</name>
  </customer>
  <customer id="556" status="preferred">
    <name>Roberto del Monte</name>
  </customer>
  <customer id="557" status="preferred">
    <name>Richard Hunt</name>
  </customer>
</customers>
```

Now, suppose you're interested only in preferred customers—those that have status="preferred" as an attribute. XPath (somewhat cutely) lets you use the @ ("at") symbol to represent tag attributes. The preferred customers in this document can be identified by the following XPath expression:

```
//customer[@status="preferred"]
```

This expression matches all <customer> tags in the document that have a status attribute with a value of preferred. Thus, it would match the parts of our document highlighted here:

```
<customers>
  <customer id="555" status="regular">
    <name>Jim Heinz</name>
  </customer>
  <customer id="556" status="preferred">          //customer[@status=
    <name>Roberto del Monte</name>                "preferred"]
  </customer>
  <customer id="557" status="preferred">
    <name>Richard Hunt</name>
  </customer>
</customers>
```

You can easily combine /, //, and @ in the same expression, as in this example:

```
//customer[@id="555"]/name
```

In our sample document, this expression refers to the `<name>` element containing the text `Jim Heinz`, because that element is the only one called `<name>` beneath a `<customer>` tag with the attribute `id="555"`:

```
<customers>
  <customer id="555" status="regular">
    <name>Jim Heinz</name>              ←— //customer[@id="555"]/name
  </customer>
  <customer id="556" status="preferred">
    <name>Roberto del Monte</name>
  </customer>
  <customer id="557" status="preferred">
    <name>Richard Hunt</name>
  </customer>
</customers>
```

7.2.3 *Predicates and element order*

The previous example presupposes a fact about XPath expressions that I have skipped until now: brackets (`[]`) introduce a type of conditional expression that's formally called a *predicate*. Predicates act as filters; when they appear, they serve as additional criteria that must be satisfied for the XPath expression to match an element. So, whereas the expression

```
//customer/name
```

would match three elements in our previous sample document (the `<name>` elements beneath all three `<customer>` tags), adding the predicate `@id="555"` after `customer` causes the expression to match only one element (the `<name>` element beneath the `<customer>` tag that has the attribute `id="555"`).

Predicates let you filter XML documents based on more than just tag attributes. For instance, you can use a predicate to filter elements by the order in which they appear. Thus, in the tree from figure 7.1, we can use an XPath expression to differentiate the first `<p>` element from the second one. A predicate that consists of a sole integer matches elements based on position. For example, `p[2]` means "the second `<p>` element." To refer to the second `<p>` element in figure 7.1's tree, we can use the following XPath expression:

```
/html/body/p[2]
```

NOTE   In XPath, numeric predicates start with 1. This numbering is different from situations where indices start with 0, as in the `<c:forEach>` tag's `begin` and `end` attributes.

In such XPath expressions, order doesn't apply to the entire document; it applies only to the part of the document that an expression already matches. For example, the previous expression wouldn't be affected by the presence of a `<p>` element that somehow occurred outside `<body>`; it would still match the second `<p>` element within `<body>`.

7.2.4 *Strings and booleans*

You might wonder what these XPath expressions refer to. Do they address the start tag specifically, the whole element, the text inside the element, or something else? The answer depends on how the XPath expression is used: where it appears, and what, broadly speaking, is expected from it. JSTL uses XPath a few different ways.

In the simplest case, an XPath expression like

```
/html/body//p
```

refers to a collection of one or more elements. Specifically, the expression points to the entire element. As you'll see in chapter 8, this approach is useful if you want to use an XPath expression to iterate over elements in a document.

XPath expressions are more flexible than this, however. XPath assigns a *string value* to every part of an XML document, so XPath expressions can be used to produce strings of text. The string value for an XML element is, loosely speaking, all the text that appears inside that element, as if no XML markup were present. For instance, consider the following document fragment:

```
<p>
   Fortune favors the <b>bold</b> and <i>Italic</i>.
</p>
```

In this fragment, the string value of the `<p>` element is

```
Fortune favors the bold and Italic.
```

In addition, XPath expressions are sometimes important for their boolean values. An XPath expression may appear in a situation where only the values "true" and "false" are sensible. For example, the following XPath expression will be considered `true` if at least one element is matched; it will be `false` if no elements are matched:

```
//p
```

Therefore, `//p` is `true` if it is applied to a document that has at least one `<p>` element, and it's `false` if the document has no `<p>` elements.

NOTE XPath expressions are more flexible than I've shown here. For instance, they can also call functions that directly return numeric values, boolean values, and so on. XPath also provides general rules for converting between numbers, booleans, and other types of data. Details about XPath data types are beyond the scope of this book because they're not needed to use JSTL; see appendix D for references to more information.

7.3 *XPath variables and JSTL*

Like many languages, XPath supports variables. Just as in JavaScript, Java, and other languages, XPath variables are evaluated and replaced with actual values, which might be different every time an XPath expression executes.

JSTL depends on XPath variables in a somewhat novel way: it maps them to dynamic scopes that resemble JSTL's expression language. Therefore, XPath variables can refer to things that are similar to those the familiar expression language can refer to (see chapter 3).

Broadly speaking, an XPath variable is simply a qualified name (see chapter 2) introduced with a dollar sign ($). That is, it's a dollar sign followed by either a name without a colon, like `stomach`, or a name with a colon, like `large:intestine`.

The XPath expressions we've presented until now haven't used variables; they simply contained text, as in

`/a/b/c`

You can introduce a variable into this static XPath expression. This variable can have a different value each time an XPath expression is evaluated. Variables can refer to data from a variety of sources. For instance, the expression

`$pageScope:document/b/c/d`

contains the variable `$pageScope:document`. Recall from chapter 2 that in the name `pageScope:document`, `pageScope` is a namespace prefix, and `document` is a specific, local name. JSTL recognizes the namespace prefixes listed in table 7.1.

These prefixes have the same behavior as the *implicit objects* described in chapter 3 for the general-purpose expression language. Furthermore, just as in JSTL's language, the default behavior when searching for a variable (the behavior when no namespace prefix is specified) is to search first in the page scope, and then

Table 7.1 JSTL recognizes these namespace prefixes in its XML manipulation tags' XPath expressions. Using variables with these prefixes (such as $pageScope:customerName or $param:status) lets you access familiar JSTL data from within an XPath expression.

Prefix	Meaning
pageScope	Page scope
requestScope	Request scope
sessionScope	Session scope
applicationScope	Application scope
param	Request parameter
initParam	Context initialization parameter
cookie	Cookie value
header	Request header

in the request, session, and application scopes, in that order. For instance, the variable $doc in a JSTL XPath tag means the same thing as ${doc} in JSTL's language.

In chapter 8, we'll look at how to use XPath variables practically.

7.4 JSTL, XPath, and namespaces

Imagine you have a document that looks like this:

```
<fax:call>
  <fax:dial number="203-432-6687"/>
  <fax:send>
    <myData:picture/>
  </fax:send>
</fax:call>
```

This document has tags that use XML namespace prefixes. Think about how you might access the inner `<myData:picture/>` tag using XPath. Could you write

```
/fax:call/fax:send/myData:picture
```

to match the tag? Or would a simpler expression like the following do the job?

```
/call/send/picture
```

The answer, in JSTL 1.0, is somewhat unfortunate: neither expression works. In fact, in JSTL 1.0, you can't use simple XPath expressions like /a/b/c to access tags that use namespaces. This is the case because a namespace prefix is just a shortcut for the namespace's real, behind-the-scenes identifier: a Universal Resource Identifier (URI). So, `myData:picture` doesn't have a way to match the right namespace, and `picture` is incomplete, because the tag uses a namespace.

If the mechanics of namespaces aren't entirely clear, don't worry; you don't need to understand them to use JSTL effectively. But if you want to use JSTL's XPath tags to access a document that uses namespaces, you need to use a workaround. Instead of simple XPath expressions that are based on the tag's names, you must use predicates to refer to the correct tags.

For example, the following expression refers to the inner `<myData:picture/>` tag in the last sample document:

```
//*[name()='picture']
```

It means "match all tags whose name is `picture`" regardless of namespace or namespace prefix. You can build XPath expressions out of these kinds of predicates similarly to the way you build simple XPath expressions. For example, the following expression also matches the inner `<myData:picture>` tag:

```
//*[name()='send']/*[name()='picture']
```

You can use the `namespace-uri()` function if you know an XML tag's namespace URI and want to match it specifically. Otherwise, stick with `name()` when you have a document that uses namespaces.

7.5 *More advanced XPath*

So far, you've seen only the most basic uses of XPath. These basic uses—even though they're simple to use—cover quite a bit of functionality. They let you pick out relevant elements from an XML document based on parent/child relationships, attributes, and the order of elements. Nonetheless, XPath supports a far richer syntax.

> **NOTE** You can skip this section if you're eager to start using JSTL's XML manipulation tags right away. However, this information will be helpful if you ever need to use the more advanced features of JSTL's XPath support.

7.5.1 *Nodes and axes*

The discussion so far has broken XML documents entirely into elements (as defined in chapter 2). But XPath sees XML documents as a collection of *nodes*. All elements are nodes, but not all nodes are elements. For example, attributes, comments, and even the text in a document are represented by nodes.

An XPath expression can refer to any node. For instance, an XPath expression might not simply use attributes to help select a set of elements; the expression might, instead, refer to the attribute nodes themselves. Similarly, you might write an XPath expression that directly refers to text within an XML document—not to an element or attribute.

Also central to XPath is the concept of an *axis*. An XPath axis is essentially a direction you can move in from any given node in an XML document. For instance, "attribute" is an axis, referring to all the attributes of a node. Another axis is "ancestor," which refers to all the ancestors (parent, parent's parent, and so on) of a node. The syntax we've covered so far includes a handful of the more commonly used axes, using XPath-supported abbreviations like @ and // to invoke particular axes.

To tie this general information together, consider the following document:

```
<p>
  <span class="first">$1000</span>
  <span class="business">$800</span>
  <span class="economy">$200</span>
</p>
```

Suppose we want to print the name of the `class` attribute used in the first `<span>` tag: we're interested in the attribute itself, not the element or the element's text. To point to this attribute, we can use the following expression:

```
/p/span[1]/@class
```

Read this expression as "The `class` attribute of the first `<span>` child of `<p>`." Again, the expression refers directly to an attribute—the "@" syntax appears outside a predicate. Here's what it matches:

```
<p>
  <span class="first">$1000</span>          <— /p/span[l]/@class
  <span class="business">$800</span>
  <span class="economy">$200</span>
</p>
```

Just as elements all have a string value, other kinds of nodes have string values as well. For instance, an attribute's string value is simply the attribute's value; so, the string value of the XPath expression we just saw is

```
first
```

because this is the value of the relevant `class` attribute.

7.5.2 *Contexts*

Also important to a full understanding of XPath is the recognition that XPath expressions always have a *context*—a term that means roughly what it does in informal usage. Most XPath expressions make no sense without the particular environment in which they're rooted. This environment can contain a number of things, but it most importantly contains a *context node*—a node in the XML tree that represents a jumping-off point for the XPath expression. Axes make the most sense when you think of them in terms of a context node: axes are a direction to go from a particular context node. All the examples in this chapter have assumed that the root of the example document is the context node.

The notion of context might seem abstract or novel, but it's no more complicated than the corresponding principle in filesystems. Programs on Windows and Unix all have a *current working directory*; when people say that programs are "in" a particular directory at any given time, they're referring to this directory. When a program encounters a relative file path—one that doesn't begin with a drive letter on Windows (such as c:\) or / on Unix—this file path will be interpreted using the program's current directory as a base, or context. For example, the unadorned filename chapter7.doc refers to the file named chapter7.doc in the current directory. (This might remind you of chapter 6's discussion of relative URLs.) Similarly, the filename images/ugly-man.jpg refers to the file named ugly-man.jpg in the directory images, which in turn can be found in the current directory. Compare it with the filename c:\images\ugly-man.jpg, which means "the file ugly-man.jpg in the images directory, which exists directly under the *root* directory on the c: drive."

Just as filenames can be relative, XPath expressions also need not begin with /. For instance, the following is a relative XPath expression:

```
body/p
```

It means "<p> children of the <body> node, which in turn exists as a child of the current (context) node." As you'll see in chapter 8, context nodes become important chiefly when you're iterating over a group of XML elements.

7.5.3 *Further reading*

If you printed out the official XPath specification, it would take up about 40 pages—and of course, a full tutorial on a subject is typically longer than the dry specification. (And the XPath specification is indeed dry.)

For this reason, and because this is not a book on XPath or XML, I don't cover the full range of XPath features here. My goal has simply been to cover enough of XPath to let you begin using it productively. Given an understanding of XML as a tree, a familiarity with the basic syntax of XPath, and an introduction to the concepts of axes and predicates, you have all the tools necessary to master XPath if you decide you need features more advanced than those covered here. Appendix D lists some excellent online tutorials that will help you pick up where we leave off.

7.6 Summary

In this chapter we explored XPath's basic syntax, in order to let you use XPath with JSTL. Keep in mind the following points:

- JSTL's support for XML manipulation depends on XPath.
- XPath (the XML Path Language) can be used to select parts of XML documents.
- XPath treats XML documents as trees and accesses individual nodes in the document in a similar manner to the way you access files on a disk.
- You can use XPath to filter documents based on node names, attribute values, and even the order in which nodes appear. But be careful if your documents use namespaces.
- XPath includes many more features than we've discussed here. Appendix D lists resources that will help you learn XPath in more depth, if you want to do so.

8

Working with
XML fragments

Knowing the basics of XPath isn't useful in a vacuum (although it will help you find any XML tags that happen to be in the vacuum with you). In chapter 7, you saw how to select XML fragments using XPath. Now, we'll look at what you can do with these document fragments once you've selected them.

In JSTL, XML support comes in two flavors. First, JSTL lets you select and manipulate XML directly using JSTL tags. For instance, one JSTL tag lets you parse an XML document and prepare it for use later in a page. Once you have parsed a document, you can perform several operations on it: printing part of it, storing part of it for later use on a page, or using it as the basis of flow control (`<if>` and `<forEach>` operations). For example, you could ask the question, "Does the document have any `<customer>` tags with a `location` attribute equal to Númenor?" and perform some operations only if it does.

Second, JSTL lets you incorporate stylesheet logic written in the Extensible Stylesheet Language Transformation (XSLT) language into your JSP pages. If you have an XSLT stylesheet and an XML document, you can use a JSTL tag to combine them and produce a new XML document. Then, you can print this document out, run more transformations on it, or manipulate it with JSTL's other tags.

Because JSTL supports a wide range of features, it lets you integrate XML data into your application in a broader manner than XSLT does. For example, suppose you want to retrieve one XML document out of a database, retrieve another from the Web, and pull relevant text from each of them to display in your web application. You can do this with JSTL without any programming in the traditional sense.

8.1 *Parsing documents with* `<x:parse>`

Before handling an XML document with JSTL, you must acquire it from somewhere—or, at a minimum, enter it manually into your JSP page. However, simply having an XML document as a text string isn't useful. What's to say that your text string is truly an XML document, and not a comma-separated file or a free-verse poem? Before XML can be usefully handled, it needs to be *parsed*. Parsing in general is the process of analyzing the syntax of text and turning it into a useful representation. When you parse an XML document, you convert the raw XML text into a format that can be handled with XSLT, XPath, or other XML-manipulation technologies.

When you have raw XML text, you can parse it using JSTL's `<x:parse>` tag. The goal of this tag is to take the raw text of an XML document and, using the `var` attribute, to produce a scoped variable that stores a parsed version of this document. Table 8.1 lists its attributes.[1]

---

[1] The `<x:parse>` tag has a few advanced attributes that we cover in chapter 14.

Table 8.1 Basic `<x:parse>` tag attributes

Attribute	Description	Required	Default
xml	The raw XML text to parse	No	*Body*
var	Name of the variable to expose the parsed document	Yes	*None*
scope	Scope of the variable to expose the parsed document	No	page

8.1.1 *Sources of XML*

The `<x:parse>` tag accepts raw XML text from two places: its `xml` attribute and its body. For each invocation of the tag, you can use only one or the other of these mechanisms; if `xml` is specified, the tag must be empty, and if not, then the tag must have a body.

Like `<c:set>`, which we first encountered in chapter 3, `<x:parse>` accepts input from both a tag attribute and its body in order to be flexible. Using an attribute is convenient when you know the location of a variable and you want to use the expression language to pass this variable to `<x:parse>`. But sometimes, you'll want to parse a document that another tag produces, or even enter XML manually within your JSP page. In these cases, it is useful for `<x:parse>` to accept XML content from its body.

Any text string can contain valid XML, and any such string may be passed to the `<x:parse>` tag for parsing. You might get such a string from the `<c:import>` tag, from a database, or from a custom tag library.

As an example of both approaches, suppose you want to retrieve the XML content from http://www.cnn.com/cnn.rss, which, at the time this chapter was written, contained a news feed from CNN in Rich Site Summary (RSS) format. (The news was about 10 months old, for some reason, but that didn't make the XML any less valid!)

TIP   RSS is an XML format commonly used by media publications and others that offer sites that can be easily summarized in terms of headlines and links. We'll encounter it again at the end of the chapter and in part 3.

The content from CNN can be introduced to `<x:parse>` using two straightforward patterns. First, we can store a variable in `<c:import>` and pass this variable to `<x:parse>`:

```
<c:import var="cnn" url="http://www.cnn.com/cnn.rss"/>
<x:parse xml="${cnn}" var="cnnXml"/>
```

Alternatively, we can rely on the default behavior of `<c:import>`: to print the content it retrieves where it appears in the page. In this case, if it appears inside an `<x:parse>` tag, it will simply print out its retrieved content, and `<x:parse>` will immediately read this content back in:

```
<x:parse var="cnnXml">
  <c:import url="http://www.cnn.com/cnn.rss"/>
</x:parse>
```

These two approaches are nearly identical, so you should pick the one that seems more straightforward to you. The former appeals to me because it lets me tell the JSP container, "Do an *import*, then do a *parse*." The latter pattern, though, avoids the intermediate cnn variable and is, in many ways, more elegant. Take your pick.

8.2 *Accessing XML with* `<x:out>` *and* `<x:set>`

JSTL's XML library parallels the core library in some ways. Even though JSTL already has core tags that support flow control, saving data, and printing data, the XML library supports the same operations. The major difference is that the XML library lets you use XPath to manipulate XML documents, whereas the core library lets you use an expression language to work with regular variables.

For example, `<c:out>` lets you retrieve a scoped variable and print its value, but `<x:out>` lets you retrieve part of an XML document and print *its* value. The `<c:set>` tag saves a scoped variable representing generic data; `<x:set>` saves a scoped variable representing XML data, or representing data pulled from an XML document.

8.2.1 *Finding a document*

All the XPath expressions in chapter 7 were somewhat isolated. I'd show you a document and then say, "The XPath expression `//a/b/c` refers to the `<c>` tag inside this document." By contrast, in real-life JSTL pages, your XPath expressions need to point explicitly to any documents they want to refer to.

In section 7.3, we discussed how JSTL supports XPath variables, which look like `$sessionScope:userName`. In fact, one of the major uses of XPath variables is to point to an entire XML document that's stored as a scoped attribute.

For example, suppose we've created a scoped variable named doc by using this tag:

```
<x:parse var="doc">
  <c:import url="mydocument.xml"/>
</x:parse>
```

To point to this document, our XPath expression can use the variable `$doc` (or `$pageScope:doc`). For example, instead of simply writing

```
//table
```

we'd write

```
$doc//table
```

This expression tells JSTL to find the `doc` variable, and then find all `<table>` tags within the document it represents.

It's easy to confuse a variable that points to a document with the root element of that document. For instance, consider the following `<x:parse>` tag:

```
<x:parse var="orders">
  <orders>
    <order item="4"/>
  </orders>
<x:parse>
```

To refer to the inner `<order>` element, you could write `$orders/orders/order`, but *not* `$orders/order`. The inner `<order>` element is not a direct child of the document; it is a child of the `<orders>` element.

8.2.2 *The <x:out> tag*

The `<x:out>` tag evaluates and prints out the string value of an XPath expression; the starting node is often retrieved from an XPath variable. (For more information about string values, see section 7.2.) The `<x:out>` tag is one of the most basic ways of introducing an XPath expression into your JSP page. The tag takes the attributes listed in table 8.2.

Table 8.2   `<x:out>` tag attributes

Attribute	Description	Required	Default
select	XPath expression	Yes	*None*
escapeXml	Whether to print characters like & as &	No	true

Let's look at `<x:out>` in action. Suppose our page contains the following `<x:parse>` tag:

```
<x:parse var="simple">
  <a>
    <b>
      <c>C</c>
    </b>
    <d>
      <e>E</e>
    </d>
  </a>
</x:parse>
```

This tag parses a simple XML document specified inline—right in the JSP page, as the body of the tag. The parsed document is exposed as a variable called `simple`. Once this document has been exposed, we can refer to it in subsequent XPath expressions using `<x:out>` and other JSTL XML tags.

For example, consider the following tag:

```
<x:out select="$simple//c"/>
```

This tag would print out the text "c" because that is the string value of the node to which the expression refers. In more detail, the XPath expression first causes the tag to retrieve the document stored by the variable named `simple`; it then matches all nodes named `<c>` descending from the root of this document. This happens to match a single `<c>` node, and this `<c>` node has a string value of "c" because the element contains "c" as its text content. The `<x:out>` tag simply prints out this string value.

As another example, the following tag prints out the value "E":

```
<x:out select="$simple/a/d/e"/>
```

The `escapeXml` attribute in `<x:out>` works just as it does for `<c:out>`. By default, if the `<x:out>` tag is ever about to print a value like "AT&T", it escapes it as "AT&T" so you don't have to worry about escaping it yourself. You can shut off this behavior, in rare cases where it's not what you want, by specifying `escapeXml="false"`.

8.2.3 The `<x:set>` tag

The `<x:set>` tag's syntax is similar to that of `<x:out>`, but its behavior is different. Instead of printing out the value of its XPath expression, it stores the result in a variable named by its `var` attribute. Table 8.3 lists the `<x:set>` tag's attributes.

Table 8.3   `<x:set>` tag attributes

Attribute	Description	Required	Default
select	XPath expression	Yes	*None*
var	Name of the variable to expose the result of the XPath expression	Yes	*None*
scope	Scope of the variable to expose the result of the XPath expression	No	page

The `<x:set>` tag is primarily useful when you want to store a subset of a document, usually for later manipulation. For instance, consider the following tags:

```
<x:parse var="simple">
  <a>
    <b>
```

```
        <c>C</c>
      </b>
      <d>
        <e>E</e>
      </d>
   </a>
</x:parse>
<x:set var="b" select="$simple/a/b"/>
```

First, the `<x:parse>` tag parses its entire document (between and including `<a>` and `</a>`); it stores this document in a variable called `simple`. Then, `<x:set>` stores the following highlighted subset of the document in a variable called `b`:

```
<a>
  <b>
    <c>C</c>        /a/b
  </b>
  <d>
    <e>E</e>
  </d>
</a>
```

There are a few reasons you might want to store part of a document. First, it might be simpler to use a single `<x:set>` before a number of intricate XPath operations in order to simplify the expressions you need to type and maintain. Also, you might have some data that you want to store in the session for access from other pages—and it is both simpler and less costly, from a memory-usage perspective, to store a small document than a larger one.

The kind of variable that `<x:set>` creates is up to the XPath expression in its `select` attribute. For the sorts of XPath expressions that we use in this book, `<x:set>` typically exposes a partial document. (XPath calls this a *node-set*.)

8.3 *Control flow based on XML documents*

Just as with `<x:out>` and `<x:set>`, the JSTL XML library offers tags that are parallel to those in the core JSTL library. It does so by offering two types of control-flow tags:

- Conditional tags that let you make decisions in your JSP pages based on the contents of XML documents

- An iteration tag to loop over nodes in an XML document

When an XML document provides the raw information you need to make a conditional decision in a JSP page, you'll probably find JSTL's conditional XML tags useful. These tags work like the conditional tags we discussed in chapter 4, but they let you use an XML document directly as the basis for your decision. As you'll see, each core conditional tag—<c:if>, <c:when>, and so on—has an analog in the XML library.

Similarly, the XML library provides a straightforward iteration tag—<x:forEach>—that lets you loop over parts of an XML document.

8.3.1 Simple conditions with <x:if>

Let's look at an example of the simple XML conditional tag—<x:if>—in action. Table 8.4 shows its attributes.

Table 8.4   <x:if> tag attributes

Attribute	Description	Required	Default
select	XPath expression to evaluate. If `true`, process the body; if `false`, ignore the body.	Yes	*None*
var	Name of the variable to expose the boolean result.	No	*None*
scope	Scope of the variable to expose the boolean result.	No	page

Imagine that we have an XML document that contains a <customer> element for each one of our customers. Suppose that this <customer> tag always contains the customer's name within a <name> element, and it also contains an <order> element for each order the customer has placed. Thus, if the customer has placed no orders, no <order> elements will appear for that customer's record. Consider the following example:

```
<customers>
  <customer id="525">
    <name>Jim Heinz</name>
    <order>20005</order>
    <order>20127</order>
  </customer>
  <customer id="526">
    <name>Roberto del Monte</name>
  </customer>
</customers>
```

This document shows that Jim Heinz has placed two orders—order numbers #20005 and #20127—but that Roberto del Monte hasn't ordered anything yet.

Now, suppose we want to print a special greeting for repeat customers:

```
Thank you for letting us sell you something.
We hope you enjoyed the experience as much as we did.
```

If Jim hits our page, he should receive the special greeting; Roberto, however, should not.

With a bit of tinkering, we might be able to produce this behavior using a combination of the XML tags we've discussed so far and the core JSTL tags. However, JSTL's XML control flow tags provide a simple way to solve this problem. Displaying a special message to repeat customers, using the criteria I've outlined, is as simple as the following:

```
<x:if
 select="$pageScope:doc/customers/customer
        [@id=$pageScope:customerId]/order">
   Thank you for letting us sell you something.
   We hope you enjoyed the experience as much as we did.
</x:if>
```

This example[2] encompasses quite a few things; let's walk through them in detail.

The example assumes that two variables have already been exposed in page scope: doc, which refers to the XML document containing data about customers and order numbers, and customerId, which holds the user's customer ID number.

The bulk of the example's work is performed by the XPath expression in the select attribute of the <x:if> tag. This expression finds the document stored by the doc variable and then walks through the document, applying the rest of the XPath expression to it. First, all <customers> elements are found; then, the XPath expression considers all children of this element. For the expression to be interested in a child element of <customers>, the child must be named <customer> and must have an id attribute equal to the current value of the customerId variable. For instance, if customerId is currently equal to 824, a child element that begins with

```
<customer id="1117">
```

or

```
<customer>
```

will be ruled out by the expression, but an element beginning with

```
<customer id="824">
```

could still match. Finally, within all these potentially useful children, all <order> children are matched.

That explanation was somewhat detailed, so let's make it concrete. Look back at the original XML document—the one that shows order records for Jim Heinz and Roberto del Monte. Now, suppose the XPath expression we've just dissected is evaluated against this document. If customerId equals 526, then the expression will not

---

[2] Note that white space between tokens in an XPath expression isn't significant.

match any elements. If `customerId` equals `525`, however, then the expression will match the two order records for Jim Heinz.

So, if Jim Heinz is the current customer (the one whose number is stored in `customerId`), we'll match two nodes. For Roberto, we won't match any. Note that we're not interested in *what* the nodes are. For example, we couldn't care less if the order number is 20005. Because we simply want to differentiate customers who have placed orders from those who haven't, the mere presence of `<order>` elements for Jim Heinz (and their absence for Roberto del Monte) is decisive. Recall XPath's boolean conversion rules from section 7.2: an XPath expression that matches one or more nodes is `true`, and one that doesn't match any nodes is `false`. Therefore, our sample XPath expression is `true` for Jim Heinz because he has placed orders, and it's `false` for Roberto del Monte because he hasn't. Jim will therefore receive the special message intended for repeat customers, and Roberto won't. Problem solved!

Storing a boolean result

The `<x:if>` tag, just like `<c:if>`, lets you save the result of a condition to a boolean variable using the `var` and `scope` attributes. As before, this tag has a number of uses:

- To avoid wasteful re-evaluation of a condition.
- To "lock in" a condition if you're afraid it will change.
- To use the result of a condition in a `<c:when>` or `<x:when>` tag that appears later in the page. (We'll look at `<x:when>` in a moment.)

8.3.2 Compound conditions with <x:choose>

Just as the core JSTL library provides `<c:choose>`, `<c:when>`, and `<c:otherwise>` for complex, mutually exclusive conditionals, the XML library offers `<x:choose>`, `<x:when>`, and `<x:otherwise>` for compound XML-based conditions. Their use is identical to the core library's, except that each `<x:when>` tag uses an XPath expression. Table 8.5 shows the attribute for `<x:when>`. (As with the core library, the other mutually exclusive conditional tags don't take attributes.)

Table 8.5   `<x:when>` tag attribute

Attribute	Description	Required	Default
select	XPath expression to evaluate. If `true`, process the tag's body; if `false`, ignore the body.	Yes	*None*

As a simple example of `<x:choose>`, `<x:when>`, and `<x:otherwise>`, consider the following small document, which you first saw in chapter 7:

```
<customers>
  <customer id="555" status="regular">
    <name>Jim Heinz</name>
  </customer>
  <customer id="556" status="preferred">
    <name>Roberto del Monte</name>
  </customer>
  <customer id="557" status="preferred">
    <name>Richard Hunt</name>
  </customer>
</customers>
```

Let's print out the word "Normal" if the user is a regular customer, "Important" if the user is a preferred customer, or "Unknown" otherwise. We can do this with the following tags:

```
<x:choose>
  <x:when
    select="$doc//customer[@id=$customerId]/@status='regular'">
    Normal
  </x:when>
  <x:when
    select="$doc//customer[@id=$customerId]/@status='preferred'">
    Important
  </x:when>
  <x:otherwise>
    Unknown
  </x:otherwise>
</x:choose>
```

Here, we assume that the scoped variable `customerId` stores the current user's customer number. We might have set this value earlier, or the variable could have been set by back-end Java code. We compare this variable to the `id` attribute of the `<customer>` tag and then see whether the `status` attribute of the same tag is equal to `regular`, `preferred`, or something else.

Using XML logic with generic conditionals

Tags like `<c:when>` and `<x:when>` can't be mixed; that is, you can't place a `<c:when>` tag under an `<x:choose>` tag, or vice versa. However, you can construct a mutually exclusive condition that uses both XPath-based logic and the general-purpose expression language by saving boolean variables using the `var` attribute of the `<c:if>` and `<x:if>` tags.

For example, let's extend the code from section 8.3.1 to take into account information other than whether the user has placed an order. Suppose the following expression is a boolean value that tells us whether the user is an especially important customer:

```
${user.vip}
```

Further, suppose that we want to display three potential messages:

- If the user is a VIP, display a polite greeting.
- Otherwise, if the user has placed an order, print the recurring-customer message.
- If neither of the first two cases is true, inform the user that we're losing patience.

We could accomplish this task using the following JSTL code:

```
<x:if
 var="repeatCustomer"                    <— saves repeatCustomer
 select=
  "$pageScope:doc/customers/customer
    [@id=$pageScope:customerId]/order"/>
<c:choose>
  <c:when test="${user.vip}">
    Ooh, it's nice to see <i>you</i>, ma'am!
  </c:when>
  <c:when test="${repeatCustomer}">    <— uses repeatCustomer
    Thank you for letting us sell you something.
    We hope you enjoyed the experience as much as we did.
  </c:when>
  <c:otherwise>
    C'mon, cheapo.  Buy something already.
  </c:otherwise>
</c:choose>
```

The `<x:if>` tag evaluates the same XPath expression that we used in the previous section, but this time, it simply stores the result in a variable called `repeatCustomer`. This boolean can be used later by tags in the core library, allowing the XML library to communicate with the core library in a straightforward manner.

The first `<c:when>` tag checks the user's VIP flag; if the user is a VIP, then she's greeted warmly. The second `<c:when>` tag uses the `repeatCustomer` variable stored earlier by `<x:if>`. Thus, our repeat-customer message is displayed only for non-VIPs who have placed a previous order.

Finally, if neither of the first two conditions applies, the page prints a rude message to the user.

8.3.3 *Looping over parts of a document with `<x:forEach>`*

Just as you can iterate over arrays, lists, and other Java objects, you can also iterate over XML documents. For instance, you might want to loop over every `<order>` record in a document, performing some action for each order—like printing a line in a table with the order number.

Recall from earlier in this chapter that an XPath expression can refer to multiple nodes in an XPath document. For example, the following expression would refer to every `<customer>` element in the document:

```
//customer
```

You can use expressions like this as the basis for iteration—that is, as the collection of items to iterate over.

Table 8.6 shows the attributes that `<x:forEach>` accepts.

Table 8.6   `<x:forEach>` attributes

Attribute	Description	Required	Default
select	XPath expression over whose result to iterate	Yes	*None*
var	Name of the variable to expose the current node	No	*None*

Let's look again at the short document we used as an example in the last section:

```
<customers>
  <customer id="555" status="regular">
    <name>Jim Heinz</name>
  </customer>
  <customer id="556" status="preferred">
    <name>Roberto del Monte</name>
  </customer>
  <customer id="557" status="preferred">
    <name>Richard Hunt</name>
  </customer>
</customers>
```

This document provides a list of customers, all of whom have a unique ID number. Some customers are marked "preferred," whereas others are marked "regular." Each customer also has a name.

To begin, let's use `//customer` as the basis for a simple loop. Assume we've already parsed this document and stored it in a variable called doc. Now, consider the following tag:

```
<x:forEach select="$doc//customer">
  <p>Customer record found.</p>
</x:forEach>
```

This tag's expression will find three customer records, and the tag will evaluate its body for each of them. Because its body contains no dynamic text, the following simple static value will be output three times:

```
<p>Customer record found.</p>
```

Using the context node

Of course, unless your users are spectacularly slow-witted, repeating the same static text multiple times isn't helpful. You normally want to do something different for each iteration. Suppose, for example, that instead of printing a static message for each customer, we want to print the customer's name.

There are a few ways to handle such tasks. The simplest and most elegant solution requires you to recall from section 7.4 that every XPath expression has a *context node* that acts like the current, or starting, node. (As we discussed in section 7.4, this is similar to the *current directory* that every program on a Windows or Unix machine has.) During an <x:forEach> loop, the current node in the iteration becomes the context node. That is, each node referenced by the original XPath expression in <x:forEach> becomes the context node for XPath expressions that occur inside the <x:forEach> tag's body.

Therefore, if we want to print the customer's name, we note that every <customer> element has a <name> child. So, if <customer> is the current node, the XPath expression to print the customer's name is as simple as

```
name
```

This expression simply means, "All <name> children directly under the current node." (This expression could appear more fully as ./name, but just as in file systems, the leading ./ is optional.)

In view of this discussion, consider the following iteration:

```
<x:forEach select="$doc//customer">
  <p><x:out select="name"/></p>
</x:forEach>
```

If doc points to our sample document, then this example will print the following output:

```
<p>Jim Heinz</p>
<p>Roberto del Monte</p>
<p>Richard Hunt</p>
```

Why does it print this output? First, the $doc//customer expression matches each individual <customer> tag in the document. Then, within each loop, the <name> tag under the context node—each successive <customer> tag in turn—is matched and printed by <x:out>.

All the other XML-manipulation tags, including the control flow tags, can take advantage of the same context node. For example, it's easy to add a conditional check that differentiates "preferred" customers from "regular" ones:

```
<x:forEach select="$doc//customer">
  <p>
```

```
<font
    <x:choose>
      <x:when select="@status='preferred'">
        color="#000000"
      </x:when>
      <x:otherwise>
        color="#888888"
      </x:otherwise>
    </x:choose>
  >
   <x:out select="name"/>
  </font>
 </p>
</x:forEach>
```

In this case, preferred customers are printed in a deep black (`color="#000000"`), and regular customers are printed in a lighter gray (`color="#888888"`). Ignoring white space, the example outputs the following HTML text:

```
<p>
  <font color="#888888">Jim Heinz</font>
</p>
<p>
  <font color="#000000">Roberto del Monte</font>
</p>
<p>
  <font color="#000000">Richard Hunt</font>
</p>
```

Note how we use XPath's @ syntax to refer to attributes of the context node. Read the expression "`@status='preferred'`" as "Does the current node's `status` attribute equal `preferred`?"

Nested iteration

If a `<x:forEach>` tag appears inside another `<x:forEach>`, it inherits the outer tag's context node.

Consider the following sample document:

```
<customers>
  <customer id="555">
    <order id="1310">
      <item id="30"/>
      <item id="84"/>
    </order>
    <order id="1340">
      <item id="46"/>
      <item id="84"/>
    </order>
  </customer>
</customers>
```

This document lists individual items that have been ordered from an online store, but it organizes them first by customer and then by order number. You can see that customer 555 placed order 1310, which included two items: 30 and 84. The same customer placed another order: number 1340, again for two items: 46 and 84. (The customer must have really liked item 84, whatever it was.)

Suppose we want to list all the item numbers customer 555 has ordered. Assuming the document has been parsed and stored in a variable called doc, we can print this information using the following JSTL tags:

```
<x:forEach select='$doc/customers/customer[@id="555"]/order'>
  <x:forEach select="item">
    <x:out select="@id"/>
  </x:forEach>
</x:forEach>
```

This example first loops over all `<order>` elements for customer 555, and then, for each one, considers each `<item>` element in turn. For each `<item>` element, the example prints the id attribute. Thus, for this document, ignoring white space, the example will print

```
30 84 46 84
```

Note how we've again used XPath's @ syntax directly, outside a predicate. For this example, we are interested in the attribute value for its own sake, not simply as a basis for including or excluding an element.

You might wonder how this example differs from a simple expression like `//item` or `//customer [@id="555"]/order/item`. The answer is that it lets us handle each level within the tree specially, perhaps printing custom text or formatting as we go. For instance:

```
<table border="1">
<x:forEach select='$doc/customers/customer[@id="555"]/order'>
  <tr>
    <td>
      Order #<x:out select="@id"/>:
    </td>
    <td>
      <x:forEach select="item">
        <x:out select="@id"/>
      </x:forEach>
    </td>
  </tr>
</x:forEach>
</table>
```

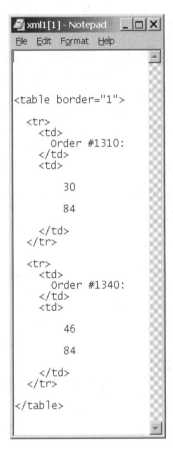

Figure 8.1 Output of a sample <x:forEach> loop that loops over parts of an XML document and prints an HTML table containing some of its data

**Figure 8.2
The HTML source code for figure 8.1**

As figure 8.1 shows, these tags produce an HTML table with one row for each order. The first column lists the order number, and the second column lists the item numbers in each order. Figure 8.2 shows the source HTML that this tag produces.

8.4 *XML transformations using JSTL*

If you frequently need to convert one XML document into another, you may be interested in XSLT. The XSLT language approaches XML manipulation from a different point of view than JSTL. Whereas JSTL's tags tend to be *imperative*—they let you direct the web server to "print this, set that, and then loop over these items"— XSLT's tend to be *functional* and based on pattern matching. Instead of letting you construct a program or a page, step by step, XSLT lets you provide a series of rules for converting one document into another. Broadly speaking, these rules take the form, "When you see input like X, produce output like Y."

When these rules are expressive enough, such an approach can be reasonably powerful. On the other hand, some programmers find them constraining and inconvenient. These programmers might compare programs to driving directions: they want to be told, "Take exit 3 to Trumbull Street, then go a quarter of a mile, and turn left onto Prospect Street." Thus, they might consider XSLT stylesheets analogous to the following disordered jumble:

- If you see Hillhouse Avenue, drive past it.

- If you find yourself on Prospect Street, go south.

- If you happen to be at exit 3 on I-91, get off the highway.

- When no other instructions match, drive straight.

If you're in the right mood, these directions (which are based on pattern matching) can have a certain appeal: no matter where you are, you can simply consult your trusty action/reaction guide and determine what to do. But by and large, I think most web-page authors and programmers find them difficult to read and write. (Even though XSLT enjoys moderate popularity, I have never been among its enthusiastic fans.)

At any rate, JSTL and XSLT aren't mutually exclusive; you can easily use both in your applications, as this section describes. We'll discuss the basic syntax of the JSTL tags that support XSLT transformations, go over a few examples, and consider briefly—from my admittedly biased point of view—how using JSTL with XSLT is more useful than using XSLT alone.

NOTE   This section assumes that you already know XSLT and that you want to use JSTL to invoke a stylesheet from within your JSP page. I don't have the space to discuss XSLT here. (And even if I did, I'm not sure I'd want to!) See appendix D for some references that will help you learn XSLT.

8.4.1 *Simple transformations with <x:transform>*

JSTL provides a simple tag—`<x:transform>`—that should handle most of your XSLT-transformation needs. Table 8.7 shows its attributes.

The `<x:transform>` tag's two most basic attributes are `xml` and `xslt`. Given a source XML document (`xml`) and an XSLT stylesheet (`xslt`), the tag's default behavior is to apply the stylesheet to the source and output the result into the page. Consider:

```
<c:import var="xmlDocument" url="${documentUrl}"/>
<c:import var="xsltStylesheet" url="${stylesheetUrl}"/>
<x:transform xml="${xmlDocument}" xslt="${xsltStylesheet}"/>
```

Table 8.7 Basic `<x:transform>` attributes

Attribute	Description	Required	Default
xml	The XML document to transform	No	*Body*
xslt	The XSLT stylesheet to apply	Yes	*None*
var	Name of the variable to expose the resulting document	No	*None*
scope	Scope of the variable to expose the resulting document	No	page

This simple use of the `<x:transform>` tag accepts a source document and a stylesheet, both of which are exposed by `<c:import>` tags. The tag then applies the XSLT stylesheet to the document and outputs the result.

Let's look at a more specific example in order to make the tag's behavior concrete. One typical application of XSLT is to replace tags from one kind of markup language (such as RSS) with tags from another (perhaps HTML). Let's use `<x:transform>` to replace custom markup with more familiar HTML. Listing 8.1 shows an entire JSP page demonstrating this use.

Listing 8.1   transform.jsp: sample XSLT transformation

```
<%@ taglib prefix="c" uri="http://java.sun.com/jstl/core" %>
<%@ taglib prefix="x" uri="http://java.sun.com/jstl/xml" %>

<c:set var="xml">    <—— Sets xml variable
  <paragraph>
     This document uses <bold>unusual</bold> markup,
     which we want to replace with <bold>HTML</bold>.
  </paragraph>
</c:set>

<c:set var="xsl">        <—— Sets xsl variable
  <?xml version="1.0"?>
  <xsl:stylesheet
    xmlns:xsl="http://www.w3.org/1999/XSL/Transform" version="1.0">

  <xsl:template match="paragraph">
    <p><xsl:apply-templates/></p>
  </xsl:template>

  <xsl:template match="bold">
    <b><xsl:value-of select="."/></b>
  </xsl:template>

  </xsl:stylesheet>
</c:set>

<x:transform xml="${xml}" xslt="${xsl}"/>    <—— Uses xml and xsl
```

Could be replaced by `<c:import>` tag

The JSP page in listing 8.1 is an archetypal example of how to use XSLT from JSTL. First, a `<c:set>` tag sets the `xml` variable with body content that appears directly in the page. (Of course, this inline content could easily be replaced with a `<c:import>` tag to fetch a document from elsewhere). Next, another `<c:set>` tag sets the `xsl` variable using a simple, typed-in stylesheet. (Again, this stylesheet could reside elsewhere, and the page could retrieve it using `<c:import>`.) Finally, the `<x:transform>` applies the XSLT stylesheet to the XML document and outputs the result. The page therefore outputs the following, ignoring white space:[3]

```
<?xml version="1.0" encoding="UTF-8"?>
<p>
    This document uses <b>unusual</b> markup,
    which we want to replace with <b>HTML</b>.
</p>
```

For information on how the XSLT stylesheet works, see the references listed in appendix D.

8.4.2 Using the var attribute

If you specify a `var` attribute for `<x:transform>`, the document that results from the `<x:transform>` tag's transformation is saved in a variable instead of being output to the page. This result can be useful in a number of situations. For instance, once you've stored the output of a transformation using `var`, the output can be used as input to another `<x:transform>` tag. Or, you can select portions from the resulting document using XPath and `<x:out>`.

For example, the final line of listing 8.1 is a simple `<x:transform>` tag that outputs its result to the page:

```
<x:transform xml="${xml}" xslt="${xsl}"/>
```

Suppose we replaced this tag with one that stores the document in a variable and uses it in an `<x:out>` tag, as follows:

```
<x:transform var="doc2" xml="${xml}" xslt="${xsl}"/>
<x:out select="$doc2//b[2]"/>
```

If these two lines replace the final line in listing 8.1, the listing's JSP page then outputs simply HTML—the string value of the second `<b>` tag in the resulting document.

Instead of passing `$doc2` to the `<x:out>` tag, we could have passed it to another `<x:transform>` tag. Chaining XSLT transformations—applying them successively, using the output of one transformation as input to another—is a flexible technique

---

[3] In this example, the XML declaration (beginning `<?xml`) is added by the XSLT processor that's used behind the scenes to perform the transformation.

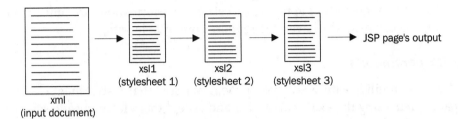

Figure 8.3   In our two examples, the same series of transformations is conducted on an input document. Three stylesheets (xsl1, xsl2, and xsl3) are applied to the input document, and the final result is output by the JSP page.

used by technologies like Cocoon, from the Apache Software Foundation, and uPortal, from JA-SIG. You have direct access to this technique using JSTL and the `<x:transform>` tag. You can chain transformations two ways: by using temporary var variables, or by nesting the `<x:transform>` tags.

Consider the following two contrasting examples; as suggested by figure 8.3, they both apply three transformations to a base document called xml using three stylesheets, xsl1, xsl2, and xsl3. The first example uses three parallel `<x:trans-form>` tags and two temporary variables:

```
<x:transform var="tmp1" xml="${xml}" xslt="${xsl1}"/>
<x:transform var="tmp2" xml="${tmp1}" xslt="${xsl2}"/>
<x:transform xml="${tmp2}" xslt="${xsl3}"/>
```

In this code, the first transformation processes xml with xsl1, producing tmp1. Then, tmp1 and xsl2 are used to produce tmp2. Finally, xsl3 is applied to tmp2, and the result is output to the page.

The following code does the same thing as the previous code, but it avoids the use of temporary variables by simply placing one `<x:transform>` tag inside another:

```
<x:transform xslt="${xsl3}">
  <x:transform xslt="${xsl2}">
    <x:transform xslt="${xsl1}" xml="${xml}"/>
  </x:transform>
</x:transform>
```

Recall from earlier in this section that the `<x:transform>` tag uses its body as its source XML document when no xml attribute is specified. Therefore, this example uses the output of the innermost `<x:transform>` tag as the input to the middle `<x:transform>` tag, and uses this middle tag's output as input to the outer `<x:transform>` tag. Finally, because this outer tag isn't contained by any other `<x:transform>` tag, its output can appear in the JSP page's output.

These two methods of applying successive transformations are functionally the same; you can pick whichever you're more comfortable with.

8.4.3 *XSLT parameters*

If you're familiar with XSLT, you probably know that a stylesheet can declare parameters using the `<xsl:param>` tag and accept them from outside sources. For stylesheets that take advantage of this ability, JSTL provides the `<x:param>` tag, whose attributes are listed in table 8.8.

Table 8.8   `<x:param>` tag attributes

Attribute	Description	Required	Default
name	Name of the parameter to set	Yes	*None*
value	Value of the parameter to set	No	*Body*

The `<x:param>` tag sets the XSLT parameter called `name` to the value of `value`. For instance, the following tag sets the `color` parameter to the value `green`:

```
<x:param name="color" value="green"/>
```

If no `value` attribute is specified, then `<x:param>` can obtain its parameter value from its body. Therefore, the following tag also sets the `color` parameter to `green`:

```
<x:param name="color">green</x:param>
```

Of course, instead of the literal, typed-in text `green`, other tags (like `<c:out>` or `<x:out>`) can appear in the `<x:param>` tag's body.

The `<x:param>` tag always applies to its immediate parent tag, which must be `<x:transform>`.

8.4.4 *Advantages of using XSLT within JSTL*

The examples of applying multiple XSLT transformations from section 8.4.2 demonstrate the flexibility of JSTL's XSLT support. Instead of requiring that all modifications to a document be implemented in terms of a single XSLT stylesheet, JSTL lets you integrate XSLT logic into your page whenever it's appropriate but avoid using it when it isn't. You're not limited to applying XSLT transformations successively. For instance, you can use JSTL to retrieve an XML document from the Web, parse a particular URL from this document using XPath, and then perform an XSLT transformation on the document you retrieve from this second URL. You can easily mix XML-manipulation tags with database tags, text-formatting tags, and so on. Thus, as you'll see in chapter 13, it's easy to use JSTL to tie together multiple pages, aggregating the portions of each that are relevant to your site.

Generally speaking, when you use JSTL to invoke XSLT, you get the familiar benefit of JSTL: you need only be comfortable with JSP tags, not Java code. Even if your application depends heavily on XSLT, something needs to invoke the transformation processor. With JSTL, you don't have to learn Java APIs or rely on back-end Java programmers to fit together your XSLT stylesheets.

8.5 An XML example: reading RSS files

Earlier in this chapter, I mentioned RSS files. Like HTML, RSS is an application of XML; it's a set of tags with rules about how these tags work and what they mean. RSS has become popular for syndicating content on the Web. It's a simple way to provide pointers to articles or other kinds of information on your site. RSS lets you provide a list of links, each of which has a headline, a description, and other characteristics.

Figure 8.4 shows part of an RSS file, as displayed by Internet Explorer. An RSS file begins with information describing the channel, or feed, that it represents.

```
- <rss version="0.91">
  - <channel>
      <title>CNET News.com</title>
      <link>http://news.cnet.com/?tag=pt.rss..feed.fd</link>
      <description>Tech News First</description>
      <language>en-us</language>
    - <image>
        <title>CNET News.com</title>
        <url>http://www.cnet.com/i/ne/gr/newslogo.gif</url>
        <link>http://www.news.com/</link>
        <width>88</width>
        <height>31</height>
      </image>
    - <item>
        <title>Yipes files for Chapter 11 bankruptcy</title>
        <link>http://news.cnet.com/news/0-1004-200-9453338.html?
          tag=pt.rss..feed.ne_9453338</link>
        <description>The start-up, a competitor of traditional phone
          companies like AT&T that offers cheap, fast Internet service to
          businesses, files for bankruptcy protection.</description>
      </item>
    - <item>
        <title>Movie studios tout first DVD bust in U.S.</title>
        <link>http://news.cnet.com/news/0-1005-200-9453346.html?
          tag=pt.rss..feed.ne_9453346</link>
        <description>A rogue DVD-burning lab is shut down by law
          enforcement in New York. But the retrieved booty is a relatively
          small win for the movie industry.</description>
      </item>
```

Figure 8.4 Part of an RSS file, as displayed by Internet Explorer. The `<item>` elements are most useful to us; they signify individual links, or articles. For instance, in this RSS file, one article has the headline, "Movie studios tout first DVD bust in U.S."

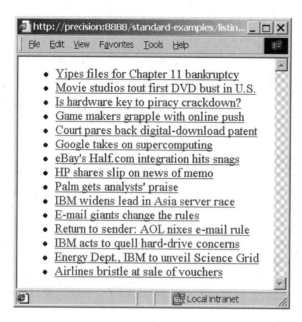

Figure 8.5
RSS files are meant to convey information to programs, not people. To be useful to users, the RSS file must be converted into something they can use—for instance, a bulleted list of headlines and HTML hyperlinks.

Eventually, the RSS begins to list individual articles, or items. Each item is each represented by an `<item>` tag, which has a number of different children describing the article. For our purposes, we're interested in two of these children:

- The `<title>` element, which contains the headline for the article
- The `<link>` element, which tells us the URL for the article

RSS files are designed primarily to communicate information to programs; they're not convenient for users to read. A user might want to see a simple bulleted list of headlines, each of which is an HTML `<a>` hyperlink to an article; for instance, see figure 8.5. Let's look at how we can use JSTL to reformat an RSS file. Listing 8.2 shows our first attempt.

Listing 8.2   simpleRss.jsp: converts an RSS channel into a list of hyperlinks

```
<%@ taglib prefix="c" uri="http://java.sun.com/jstl/core" %>
<%@ taglib prefix="x" uri="http://java.sun.com/jstl/xml" %>

<c:import var="xml" url="${param.rssUrl}" />
<x:parse var="rss" xml="${xml}" />

<ul>
<x:forEach select="$rss//item">
  <li>
    <a href="<x:out select="link"/>">
      <x:out select="title"/>
```

```
    </a>
   </li>
</x:forEach>
</ul>
```

This surprisingly short example is all we need to handle simple RSS files. We start by loading and parsing the RSS file from a URL specified by one of our request parameters, rssUrl. To pass the simpleRss.jsp page this parameter, we might use an HTML form like this:

```
<form method="post" action="simpleRss.jsp">
  Enter the URL for an RSS feed:
  <input type="text" name="rssUrl" />
  <input type="submit" />
</form>
```

Once simpleRss.jsp has retrieved its RSS file over the Web, it loops over each <item> tag in the RSS file and prints out its <link> and <title> children. We insert the contents of the <link> item into an <a> tag's href attribute, and we print the headline (<title>) as the body of the hyperlink. A sample result is shown in figure 8.5. (This example uses a news feed from CNet, which was available at the following URL at the time this chapter was written: http://export.cnet.com/export/feeds/news/rss/1,11176,,00.xml. See appendix D for more examples of RSS feeds.)

Dealing with namespaces

The simpleRss.jsp example is short and sweet, and it works for many RSS files, but it has a problem: it doesn't work for newer types of RSS files that use XML namespaces. This limitation arises because, as you saw in chapter 7, XPath expressions like //item and link don't match elements that use namespaces. To match these items in all RSS files, you need to use a slightly different syntax. Instead of writing

```
//item
```

to match all <item> tags, we'll need to use an XPath expression like this:

```
//*[name()='item']
```

This expression matches all tags whose name is equal to item, regardless of the RSS document's use of namespaces. Listing 8.3 shows a more general page that parses and prints out RSS documents.

> **Listing 8.3 rss.jsp: converts an RSS channel (with namespaces) into a list of hyperlinks**

```
<%@ taglib prefix="c" uri="http://java.sun.com/jstl/core" %>
<%@ taglib prefix="x" uri="http://java.sun.com/jstl/xml" %>
```

```
<c:import var="xml" url="${param.rssUrl}"/>
<x:parse var="rss" xml="${xml}" />

<ul>
<x:forEach select="$rss//*[name()='item']">
  <li>
    <a href="<x:out select="./*[name()='link']"/>">
      <x:out select="./*[name()='title']" />
    </a>
  </li>
</x:forEach>
</ul>
```

Listing 8.3 is identical to listing 8.2 except for its use of slightly more complicated expressions that ensure compatibility with RSS files that uses XML namespaces. Review section 7.4 for more information.

The great thing about JSTL is that you aren't limited to transforming the RSS document, as you would be with XSLT. Instead, you can perform real-world operations on the data you parse out of RSS files. For instance, instead of simply printing a URL for one of the RSS document's articles, you could follow this URL: you could import it using `<c:import>` and print it out. If this file was an XML document, you could even parse it using `<x:parse>` and continue to retrieve XML data.

As an example of this powerful technique, look at listing 8.4.

Listing 8.4 rssFollow.jsp: converts an RSS channel (with namespaces) into a list of hyperlinks

```
<%@ taglib prefix="c" uri="http://java.sun.com/jstl/core" %>
<%@ taglib prefix="x" uri="http://java.sun.com/jstl/xml" %>

<c:import var="xml" url="${param.rssUrl}"/>
<x:parse var="rss" xml="${xml}" />

<ul>
<x:forEach select="$rss//*[name()='item']">
  <li>
    <a href="<x:out select="./*[name()='link']"/>">
      <x:out select="./*[name()='title']" />
    </a>
    <blockquote>
      <x:set var="newUrl" select="string(./*[name()='link'])" />
      <c:import url="${newUrl}"/>
    </blockquote>
  </li>
</x:forEach>
</ul>
```

The highlighted section of listing 8.4 retrieves the URL of each article in the RSS file, and then follows this URL—it retrieves the target and prints out its data. Note that this result won't look very pretty if each article uses its own formatting. If the target of the hyperlink expects to be printed as a full page, then we probably shouldn't include it wholesale in our own page. But this technique is a good starting place if your target links are printable fragments (instead of whole HTML pages), XML documents that you can parse with `<x:parse>`, or some other manageable format.

The XPath expression that we use in `<x:set>` needs an explanation. When an XPath expression uses the XPath `string()` function, the subexpression within `string()` is converted to a string. Otherwise, expressions like

```
/item
```

or

```
./*[name()='link']
```

represent XPath nodes, not strings. We use a string here because `<c:import>` doesn't know anything about XML nodes; it accepts only a string for its `url` attribute.

8.6 *Summary*

As you manipulate XML with JSTL, keep in mind the following points:

- Before you work with an XML document, you must parse it. The `<x:parse>` tag lets you parse a document and expose it to your page.
- The XML-support library in JSTL contains tags that correspond in scope and function to the following tags:

```
<c:if>
<c:choose>
<c:when>
<c:otherwise>
<c:out>
<c:set>
<c:forEach>
```

- These tags work just like the ones in the core library, but they use XPath instead of the normal expression language.
- You can use JSTL's support for XPath variables to refer to a parsed document in the XPath expressions that you feed to `<x:if>`, `<x:out>`, and the other XML-manipulation tags.
- JSTL lets you run XSLT transformations using the `<x:transform>` tag. It's easy to conduct multiple transformations or even string transformations together, using output from one as input to another.

Database-driven pages

9

This chapter covers...

- When to use JSTL's database support
- How to perform database queries and updates
- Ways to access data you've retrieved
- Why and how to use database transactions

When you need a user's information to last for an entire session, you can store it in JSP's session scope. However, some information needs to last longer than the session scope allows.

For instance, you probably don't want to make your visitors enter their preferences each time they come to your site. Most users would prefer to enter their information once and have your site remember it. Some information—like a customer's full name, address, and phone number—might not even have anything to do with the user's session or web experience; you might simply need to gather this information for use offline, after the user has left, to process orders or conduct other business operations.

To store data for long periods of time, you can use a software product called a *relational database management system*—abbreviated RDBMS but often, these days, described by the more general term *database*. Database packages include Oracle, Microsoft SQL Server, PostgreSQL, MySQL.

Of course, simple files on disk can also store information for a long time. You might wonder why you should use a database when you can store data in straightforward text files.

The answer is that using databases is safer, and in many cases more convenient, than managing arbitrary files on a disk. Databases are designed to store structured information. When you write to files, you must devise a way to represent your data manually. For instance, you can separate names and phone numbers with commas, and then store each user's record on a different line in the file. But this process is as error-prone as it is tedious, and it makes your file idiosyncratic. A missing comma might cause you to greet a user as "Dear Mr. 203-432-6687." If other people or applications need to read your data, they must learn the format you personally devised and implemented. By contrast, databases provide standard interfaces to your data, and they help you organize it.

Databases also help keep your data safe and consistent. A database can be set up to ensure that every entry for a customer comes with a phone number and birthdate, so you don't accidentally end up with partial data. When databases guarantee the consistency—or *integrity*—of data, they let you focus on other considerations. You can set up a database once (or have a database administrator set one up) and then read and write data to it, confident in its ability to handle the data quickly and accurately.

All the tags we introduce in this chapter come from JSTL's sql tag library. (See chapter 2 for more information on JSTL's various tag libraries.) To use any of the examples in this chapter, you'll need to use a directive like the following at the top of your pages:

```
<%@ taglib prefix="sql" uri="http://java.sun.com/jstl/sql" %>
```

9.1 *When to use JSTL's database support*

Even with the advantages that they provide, databases are not appropriate for all web applications. Furthermore, even if your application uses a database, you might want to avoid JSTL's database tags. This is not because of any limitation in JSTL's tags, but simply because JSP pages should, in some cases, avoid directly accessing databases.

9.1.1 *When to use databases*

Broadly speaking, your application will need to use databases in two situations. The first is clear-cut: you're working in an environment where databases are already used. For instance, your application might need to access a centralized database that stores customers or product information. In cases like this, back-end Java programmers will often take care of managing database connections for you. You'll simply be given instructions about how to access the database.

The second situation is more ambiguous: your application might need some long-term data for its own, internal purposes. For example, suppose you want to let your visitors decide between a flashy interface and a simple one and remember their decision—or store a username and password used specifically to access your web site. In such cases, the data is your application's responsibility. Therefore, if you are responsible for designing the application, you will need to decide where information like this is stored.

No catch-all rule lets you decide when databases are appropriate, but a few guidelines are useful. As I mentioned in this chapter's introduction, when data needs to persist longer than the user's session, JSP's session scope is insufficient, and you will need to find a longer-term alternative. The application scope in JSP can store data even after an individual user's session expires, but data stored in this scope—like any other scope—is transient. (For instance, depending on which JSP container you use, all data in application scope might go away if a single server crashes or is rebooted.) Therefore, you should consider using databases for important information that needs to last for a long time—preferences, credentials, user profiles, orders, and so on. Think of databases as analogous to human long-term memory, whereas JSP scopes are like short-term memory.

9.1.2 *Direct access from JSP pages*

As you saw in chapter 1, most large Java web applications are not made up entirely of JSP pages. Many applications also contain servlets that handle requests from the user. Servlets can directly invoke whatever logic the application requires, and then they can pass the user's web request to a JSP page. In such an environ-

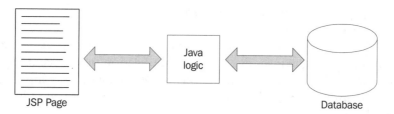

Figure 9.1 In large applications, JSP pages do not access databases directly. Instead, they rely on intermediate Java code to access databases.

ment, JSP pages handle nothing more than the display of formatted information; they are not responsible for answering any questions other than, "How should the data be displayed?"

If an application uses JSP pages just to present information, and not to handle any application logic, then the JSP pages do not need to access databases. Instead, as figure 9.1 suggests, they rely on Java code to manage information retrieval and storage behind the scenes. If you are working on a project where Java programmers handle all database access, you may have no use for JSTL's database tags. Instead, you'll probably use JavaBeans or custom tags that your Java-developer colleagues provide—or that you, wearing a different hat, create.

However, for small applications, prototypes, or projects where you're the only developer, JSTL's database tags may come in handy. As figure 9.2 suggests, these tags allow you to access databases directly from JSP pages. This more direct approach is useful when nobody's around to write intermediate Java code to access databases, or when you don't want to go to the trouble of separating out the logic. Even large applications can contain JSP pages that access databases directly, but many developers feel that such applications become cumbersome. Why, they ask, should a component of the application's presentation need to know where the database is kept? Why should the JSP pages need to change if the data model changes? And isn't it dangerous for a JSP page to modify data permanently in a database?

These developers have a good point, which explains the popularity of servlet-based application frameworks. But there are contrasting opinions that are sometimes forgotten in the debate over application design. Because this is not a book

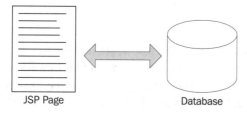

**Figure 9.2
JSP pages can access databases directly. Doing so might be useful in small applications, prototypes, or when you don't want to bother with intermediate logic.**

about application design, I will not address the advantages of the various approaches here. Other books, like *Web Development with JavaServer Pages,*[1] discuss application architectures in some detail. For more information, see that book and appendix D. For our purposes, it's just important to note that it makes sense to use JSTL's database-access tags in at least some situations—perhaps many.

9.2 *Setting up a database connection with <sql:setDataSource>*

JSTL's database tags need to know what database to use, and the `<sql:setData-Source>` tag is one way of telling them. It's important to emphasize that `<sql:set-DataSource>` is just one way to prepare a database for use in your pages. In many large applications, `<sql:setDataSource>` is not necessary, because back-end Java developers manage all database connections. These developers can set up a default database behind the scenes so that you never have to worry about the issue. Or, they can give you a scoped variable that represents a database, and you can use this scoped variable as input to JSTL's database tags. If you can rely on such a variable or default database being available, then you can skip this section.[2]

However, for smaller applications, or those where all database management is handled by JSP pages instead of by back-end Java code, `<sql:setDataSource>` is a useful crutch. It accepts as attributes all the information required to connect to a database. With this information, it lets you do two things. First, you can decide to expose a scoped variable that represents the database; you can then use this scoped variable as input to other JSTL database tags. Second, you can change the default database for your pages. For instance, you can set up a database each time the user logs in, declare this database as the default for your user's session, and then never worry about it again.

Table 9.1 lists the attributes for `<sql:setDataSource>`.

Table 9.1 `<sql:setDataSource>` tag attributes

Attribute	Description	Required	Default
dataSource	Existing database to use	No	*None*
driver	JDBC driver class name	No	*None*
url	JDBC database URL	No	*None*

---

[1] Duane Fields, Mark Kolb, and Shawn Bayern, 2nd ed. (Manning Publications, 2001)

[2] If you're a Java developer, chapter 14 tells you how to set up a default database for JSTL tags.

Table 9.1 `<sql:setDataSource>` tag attributes *(continued)*

Attribute	Description	Required	Default
user	Database username	No	*None*
password	Database password	No	*None*
var	Name of the variable that represents the database	No	*None*
scope	Scope of the variable or new default	No	page

The `<sql:setDataSource>` tag depends on a Java standard known as JDBC, which would stand for Java Database Connectivity if it weren't actually just an opaque product name used for marketing purposes. JDBC is Java's package for connecting to databases. To use JDBC to connect to a database, you need up to four pieces of information:

- The URL for the database connection
- The username for the database connection
- The password for the database connection
- The name of a JDBC driver to load so that you can connect successfully

You need to get this information from whoever manages your database. When you install a database yourself, you need to figure out these four pieces of information on your own by consulting the database's documentation.

TIP In case your organization doesn't have a database for you to use, I've posted instructions at Manning's web site that describe how to set up a small, free database system called hsqldb. (See appendix D for the URL for these instructions.) Using the directions in that online document, you'll be able to experiment with JSTL's `<sql:setDataSource>` tags. The document also describes what URLs and driver names to use when connecting to an hsqldb database.

Let's look at an example of how the `<sql:setDataSource>` tag works. Suppose we're told the following pieces of information by our database administrator:

- JDBC driver name to load: `org.hsqldb.jdbcDriver`
- JDBC URL: jdbc:hsqldb:
- Username: `sa`
- Password: `donkey`

To prepare connections to this database, we'd use the following tag:

```
<sql:setDataSource
  driver="org.hsqldb.jdbcDriver"
  url="jdbc:hsqldb:."
  user="sa"
  password="donkey"/>
```

Because this `<sql:setDataSource>` tag doesn't have a `var` or a `scope` attribute, it will replace the page's default database. That is, any other database tags that appear later in the same page will use the database identified by this tag's attributes. Suppose we add just a `scope` attribute, as follows:

```
<sql:setDataSource
  driver="org.hsqldb.jdbcDriver"
  url="jdbc:hsqldb:."
  user="sa"
  password="donkey"
  scope="session" />
```

With this new attribute, the `<sql:setDataSource>` tag will set up a new default database for the user's session. We could also specify `scope="request"` or `scope="application"` if we wanted to set a default for the request or application scope.

Setting a default is useful when your application has only—or primarily—one database to use. For instance, you can put an `<sql:setDataSource>` tag in a common header file included with `<c:import>` into your page. If such an `<sql:setDataSource>` tag has a `scope="application"` attribute, then it sets an application-wide default, and you may never have to think about `<sql:setDataSource>` again until you start working on a new application.

When different default databases exist for the page, request, session, and application scopes, then JSTL's database tags use page first, followed by request, session, or application. This sequence lets you set a default for a specific scope without destroying the defaults for more general scopes. For instance, you can use `<sql:setDataSource>` in a single page but rely on a session-scoped default database for other pages.

If your application works with multiple databases, then instead of using `<sql:setDataSource>` to set a default connection, you might instead use it to expose a scoped variable that represents a database. You can do this by adding a `var` attribute:

```
<sql:setDataSource
  driver="org.hsqldb.jdbcDriver"
  url="jdbc:hsqldb:."
  user="sa"
```

```
password="donkey"
var="databaseOne"
var="databaseOne"
scope="session" />
```

This tag exposes a session-scoped variable called `databaseOne`. Another tag might expose a different variable called `databaseTwo`, or even something with a more creative name. Then, using syntax we'll encounter in a moment, you can decide which database to connect to for each database tag that appears in your pages.

If back-end Java code, or an `<sql:setDataSource>` tag you've used, has created a scoped variable that points to a database, you can feed this variable into `<sql:setDataSource>` in order to instruct it to set a new default. For instance, after we've exposed `databaseOne`, we can make it the request scope's default with the following tag:

```
<sql:setDataSource
  dataSource="${databaseOne}"
  scope="request" />
```

Note that when you use the `url`, `driver`, `user`, and `password` attributes, you can leave out any of these four pieces of information except `url`. You might leave out `driver` because sometimes, a back-end Java programmer or system administrator will promise that a driver has already been registered for you, so you don't need to worry about loading it from your pages. You can omit either `user` or `password` or both if your database doesn't require them.

9.2.1 Caution against `<sql:setDataSource>`

Earlier in this chapter, I advised you that JSTL's database tags might not be appropriate for large web applications. This warning is particularly true for the `<sql:set-DataSource>` tag. If you've worked with databases before, you might have heard of the idea of *database connection pooling*. Like carpooling, connection pooling uses a single vehicle (in this case, a database connection) for multiple purposes. Pooling is very important in real-world applications, because just like a drive to New York City during rush hour, opening a database connection is a slow operation (and you don't want to do it too often).

However, the `<sql:setDataSource>` tag does not support connection pooling. It's not designed to do so. Instead, Java programmers who set up default databases for JSP pages have ample opportunity to set up their own pooling strategies. Doing so makes `<sql:setDataSource>` suitable only for applications where high performance isn't crucial. In particular, `<sql:setDataSource>` is great for small applications, proof-of-concept or test pages, and real-world applications that don't need to support a lot of users. But `<sql:setDataSource>` probably won't be efficient enough for pages that handle a large number of requests.

9.3 *Performing queries with <sql:query>*

Databases wouldn't be very useful if you couldn't retrieve information from them. The `<sql:query>` tag is the JSTL tag you use to pull information from databases. Its goal is always to expose a scoped variable that represents the results of a database query.

Table 9.2 lists `<sql:query>`'s attributes.

Table 9.2 `<sql:query>` tag attributes

Attribute	Description	Required	Default
sql	The SQL query to execute (SELECT...)	No	*Body*
dataSource	Provider of database connections	No	*See section 9.3*
startRow	Row of the result to start recording	No	0 *(the first row)*
maxRows	Maximum number of rows to record	No	*See section 9.3.3*
var	Name of the variable to expose the result	Yes	*None*
scope	Scope of the variable to expose the result	No	page

If you supply a scoped variable for the `dataSource` attribute, then `<sql:query>` will connect to the database using the scoped variable you provide. You can expose an appropriate scoped variable for the `dataSource` attribute by using `<sql:setData-Source>`, or you might retrieve a scoped variable from back-end Java code through the request, session, or application scope. For instance, we could use an `<sql:query>` tag that looks like this:

```
<sql:query dataSource="${sessionScope.databaseOne}" …/>
```

If you don't use the `dataSource` attribute, then the `<sql:query>` tag will try to find a default database. As I mentioned in the previous section, `<sql:query>` (or any other JSTL database tag) will first look in the page scope for a default database; it will then search request, session, and application scopes in order. If no default database is found, the tag will cause an error to be triggered. Chapter 11 describes different approaches for handling errors.[3]

---

[3] A default database can also be hard-coded for an application in its *deployment descriptor*. If you're an advanced user, chapter 14 explains how to establish defaults, including how to use the deployment descriptor to configure JSTL's behavior.

9.3.1 *Performing a database query*

To perform a database query, you usually need to use a language called the *Structured Query Language* (SQL). The rest of this chapter assumes you're familiar with the basics of SQL. If you haven't learned SQL yet, appendix C shows you how to use it with JSTL's database tags.

The `<sql:query>` tag can use any valid SQL query to retrieve information from a database. SQL queries can appear either in the `sql` tag attribute or as the body of an `<sql:query>` tag. For instance, if we wanted to retrieve all data from a table named CUSTOMERS, we could use the following tag:

```
<sql:query var="result">
  SELECT * FROM CUSTOMERS
</sql:query>
```

We could also simply write:

```
<sql:query var="result" sql="SELECT * FROM CUSTOMERS"/>
```

These two approaches are nearly identical. Tag attributes, however, let us conveniently use the expression language, so that if the text of the SQL query (that is, the literal text SELECT * FROM CUSTOMERS) were stored in a variable called `query`, we could refer to it as follows:

```
<sql:query var="result" sql="${query}"/>
```

On the other hand, including an SQL command in the tag's body makes it easy to generate the query dynamically using other tags. Imagine, for instance, that our organization maintains a central list of SQL queries in an XML document. We could use the `<x:out>` tag to retrieve a query and then print it inside an `<sql:query>` tag:

```
<sql:query var="result">
  <x:out select="$doc/query/customerQuery"/>
</sql:query>
```

NOTE   These examples of the `<sql:query>` tag, and the rest of the examples in this chapter, assume that a default database is properly set up (see section 9.2). If you haven't set a default database with `<sql:setData-Source>`, and if your pages haven't had a default database installed by a back-end Java programmer, then you'll need to use the `dataSource` attribute for these examples to work.

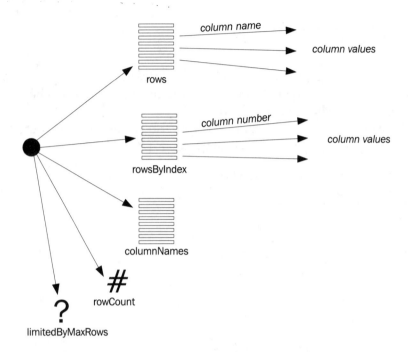

column name

column values

rows

column number

column values

rowsByIndex

columnNames

#
rowCount

?
limitedByMaxRows

Figure 9.3   The <sql:query> tag stores a scoped variable with a few specific properties. The query's data is accessible using the rows and rowsByIndex properties. You can retrieve information about the data—that is, metadata—using the remaining properties.

9.3.2 *Reading a query's results*

The <sql:query> tag doesn't output anything, because there's no single, standard way to output the result of an SQL query. The tag can't guess whether you want to produce a bare-bones HTML table, an elaborate graphical output, or something else. Indeed, you might not even want to print any data immediately.

As I said before, the goal of the <sql:query> tag is just to execute a query and store the resulting data in the variable identified by var and scope. This scoped variable has the structure shown in figure 9.3.

How a database result is organized

When you retrieve information from a database table, that data is presented in rows and columns, just like a table in a spreadsheet. Each row corresponds to a record, and each column is a field within that record. Imagine that one of our pages uses a tag like this:

```
<sql:query var="result">
  SELECT NAME, IQ FROM USERS WHERE IQ > 120
</sql:query>
```

The SQL query in this tag produces a result with exactly two columns: NAME and IQ. The number of rows depends on the data itself—in this case, on the number of people in the USERS table who have IQs above 120.

Table 9.3 shows a sample result for this SQL query. The user named Richard has an IQ of 132, Jonathan weighs in at a less-impressive 121, and so on.

Table 9.3   A sample result from a database, with two columns and five rows

NAME	IQ
Richard	132
Jonathan	121
Liz	140
Michael	162
Rachel	149

The job of `<sql:query>` is to retrieve a result—just like that in table 9.3—and expose it as a scoped variable. Such a scoped variable isn't as simple as a string or number; instead, it's divided into a number of properties. These properties let you access two things about a database result:

- The data in the table
- Information about the data (often called *metadata*)

Figure 9.3 shows all the properties of the variable that each `<sql:query>` exposes. The first two, rows and rowsByIndex, are for accessing data. The remaining properties—columnNames, rowCount, and limitedByMaxRows—just help describe the data.

Accessing metadata

Let's begin by looking at the metadata. Suppose you've used an `<sql:query>` tag to create a variable called result. The simplest property of this result variable is rowCount. The expression `${result.rowCount}` lets you retrieve the number of rows in the result. For instance, for table 9.3, rowCount would be 5, because five pairs of NAME and IQ values are listed.

You can also use the result variable to retrieve the names of the columns in the result. The columnNames property is a list of column names. Recall from chapter 3 that you can access the items in an ordered list using square brackets ([]) and index numbers starting with zero. For instance, to access the name of the first column in a result, you can write an expression like this:

```
${result.columnNames[0]}
```

In the case of our sample, this expression would evaluate to NAME. Similarly,

```
${result.columnNames[1]}
```

would evaluate to IQ.

Because columnNames is a collection, you can also loop over it. Doing so is particularly useful when you want to print a header for an HTML <table>. You'll see an example of how to do this in a moment.

We'll look at the final metadata property, limitedByMaxRows, in section 9.3.3.

Accessing data

Accessing metadata can be useful, but the purpose of most database queries is to retrieve data itself. The <sql:query> tag's variable lets you access data through two properties: rows and rowsByIndex. Both of these properties expose collections; typically, you'll want to loop over these collections to print results. The difference between rows and rowsByIndex is that during each loop, you access the data in rows using column names, and you access the data in rowsByIndex using column numbers. Figure 9.4 compares rows, rowsByIndex, and columnNames.

Let's look at a couple of different ways to access data. The following loop uses the rows collection to loop over data and access column values using the names of columns from table 9.3:

```
<sql:query var="smartUsers">
  SELECT NAME, IQ FROM USERS WHERE IQ > 120
</sql:query>
<table>
<c:forEach items="${smartUsers.rows}" var="row">
  <tr>
    <td><c:out value="${row.NAME}"/></td>
    <td><c:out value="${row.IQ}"/></td>
  </tr>
</c:forEach>
</table>
```

This loop prints a single HTML table row (<tr>) for each row in the database table. Each row in the HTML table contains two columns: the first prints the user's name, and the second prints the user's IQ. (Note that although we wrote ${row.NAME}, we could also have written ${row.name}; it doesn't matter whether the column names we specify are uppercase, lowercase, or any mixture between the two.)

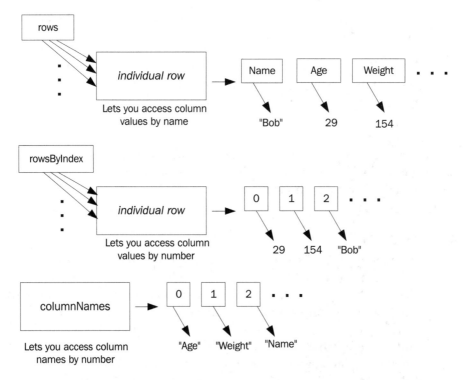

Figure 9.4 When `<sql:query>` exposes a result, its `rows` property lets you access individual column values in each row by name. Its `rowsByIndex` property lets you access values for each row by number. Both of these attributes are collections of collections, but `columnNames` is a simple collection that lets you access column names by number.

For the data in table 9.3, this example would print out the following HTML (ignoring white space):

```
<table>
  <tr>
    <td>Richard</td>
    <td>132</td>
  </tr>
  <tr>
    <td>Jonathan</td>
    <td>121</td>
  </tr>
  <tr>
    <td>Liz</td>
    <td>140</td>
  </tr>
  <tr>
    <td>Michael</td>
```

```
    <td>162</td>
  </tr>
  <tr>
    <td>Rachel</td>
    <td>149</td>
  </tr>
</table>
```

To use rowsByIndex, we'd write a similar loop; but instead of referring to row.NAME and row.IQ, we'd use row[0] and row[1]. This approach can be useful if you don't know the names of the columns, or if the column names might change. For instance, this block would have the same output as the last example, but it uses column numbers instead of column names:

```
<sql:query var="smartUsers">
  SELECT NAME, IQ FROM USERS WHERE IQ > 120
</sql:query>
<table>
<c:forEach items="${smartUsers.rowsByIndex}" var="row">
  <tr>
    <td><c:out value="${row[0]}"/></td>
    <td><c:out value="${row[1]}"/></td>
  </tr>
</c:forEach>
</table>
```

Tying it together

Often, a single loop will combine metadata and data to produce a convenient header. This technique is particularly useful when you want to write a generic page that handles multiple queries, no matter where they come from. For instance, you can write a general printQuery.jsp page and then include this page, sending it the result of an <sql:query> tag using a request-scoped attribute. Such a printQuery.jsp page might look like listing 9.1.

Listing 9.1 printQuery.jsp: general-purpose query formatter

```
<c:forEach
    items="${requestScope.result.rowsByIndex}"
    var="row"
    varStatus="s">
  <c:if test="${s.first}">
    <table>
    <tr>
      <c:forEach
          items="${requestScope.result.columnNames}"
          var="col">
        <th><c:out value="${col}"/></th>
      </c:forEach>
```

```
    </tr>
  </c:if>
  <tr>
    <c:forEach items="${row}" var="value">
      <td><c:out value="${value}"/></td>
    </c:forEach>
  </tr>
  <c:if test="${s.last}">
    </table>
  </c:if>
</c:forEach>
```

This example does a lot, so let's walk through it. We begin by iterating over the rowsByIndex property of an <sql:query> result we retrieve from the request scope. We also use <c:forEach>'s varStatus attribute so that we can print special information at the beginning and at the end of the loop. First, we use the varStatus variable to print <table> at the beginning of the loop and </table> after it. Doing so is better than writing <table> and </table> outside the <c:forEach> loop, because in this case, we don't print <table> and </table> unless we have some results to iterate over. (If we printed <table> and </table> outside the loop, then we'd print those tags even if the result were empty, and it's messy to print an empty table with no data.)

Additionally, within the <c:if test="${s.first}"> check that runs only the first time through the loop, we print a table row (<tr> … </tr>) that will contain a table header. To print header entries, we loop over the columnNames property and print each column name within a <th> element. This step works because the order of the columns in the columnNames collection must match the order of the column data in the rowsByIndex collection.

Finally, in the body of the loop, we loop over the row. The rows and rowsByIndex properties are collections, but each of their elements is a collection, too. (See figure 9.4.) That is, they're collections of collections. Thus, the inner <c:forEach> tag loops over each row—first over rowsByIndex[0], then over rowsByIndex[1], and so on, once for each column in the table.

The result is a completely generic page that can print the result from any SQL query, including a header for the result's column names. As an example of its results, figure 9.5 shows how printQuery.jsp might display the data and metadata in table 9.3. We produce this output by calling printQuery.jsp as follows:

```
<sql:query var="result" scope="request">
  SELECT NAME, IQ FROM USERS WHERE IQ > 120
</sql:query>
<c:import url="printQuery.jsp"/>
```

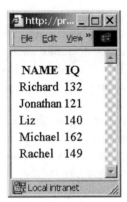

Figure 9.5
Sample output from printQuery.jsp,
using the data shown in table 9.3.
The generic printQuery.jsp page
accepts any result from
`<sql:query>` and formats it as a
simple HTML table.

9.3.3 *Limiting the size of a query's result*

We use databases because they're good at storing large amounts of data. If all applications managed only a small amount of data, a general-purpose, relational database would probably be overkill. The size of databases, though, can lead to a problem: it becomes easy, with a simple query, to retrieve a set of results that is unmanageably large. For example, the documentation for PostgreSQL, a free high-quality database, says that some PostgreSQL installations have databases 60GB in size. (That's more than 64 *billion* characters.)

Imagine that your application has a large database, and you perform a query based on user input. You have a page that prints data for all customers who match the user's keyword. Now, suppose the user enters an uninspired keyword like "Bob" that matches 50,000 rows. JSTL lets you prevent the query from going out of control by using two attributes of the `<sql:query>` tag: maxRows and startRow.

The maxRows attribute

The maxRows attribute is straightforward. When it appears in an `<sql:query>` tag, it ensures that no more than a specific number of rows will be stored by the scoped variable that `<sql:query>` stores. For example, the following tag might produce a very large result named customers:

```
<sql:query var="customers">
  SELECT * FROM CUSTOMERS
</sql:query>
```

However, this tag will never store more than 20 rows in customers:

```
<sql:query var="customers" maxRows="20">
  SELECT * FROM CUSTOMERS
</sql:query>
```

Sometimes, you want to let the user know whether maxRows effectively truncated a query. For instance, you might want to print a message like, "Your query returned more than 20 customers. Please narrow it down next time." To make such a decision, you can use the limitedByMaxRows property of the variable exposed by <sql:query>. As figure 9.3 showed, this is a boolean property. It's true if the result would have contained more than maxRows allowed but was cut short. It's false if the result from the database contained only as many, or fewer, rows than maxRows. For example, in the last example, ${customers.limitedByMaxRows} would equal true if the query returned 21 or more rows; otherwise (if the query returned 20 or fewer rows) it would be false. You can use limitedByMaxRows like this:

```
<c:if test="${customers.limitedByMaxRows}">
  Your query returned too many customers.
  Please be more specific next time.
</c:if>
```

Back-end Java programmers can set a default maxRows for your pages, but you can always override this value by using maxRows yourself. If you want to ensure that the size of your result won't be limited, you can set maxRows equal to -1.

The startRow attribute

In addition to limiting the number of rows an <sql:query> tag stores, JSTL lets you specify a specific starting row with the startRow attribute. Recall the example of *paging* through data in chapter 5. The startRow attribute works like the begin element in <c:forEach>: it ignores all data before the particular element named by startRow. Like begin, it is a zero-based index: the first row is numbered 0, the second is numbered 1, and so on. For example, the following query would return all rows in the CUSTOMERS table except the first two rows (numbered 0 and 1):

```
<sql:query var="customers" startRow="2">
  SELECT * FROM CUSTOMERS
</sql:query>
```

If there were no such rows—for instance, if the table had only two rows—then the customers variable would be empty.

As with maxRows, you can specify any positive integer or 0 for the startRow attribute.

Using maxRows and startRow together

You can use maxRows and startRow in the same tag. When they appear together, each has its usual, independent effect. For example, consider the following query:

```
<sql:query var="customers" startRow="2" maxRows="10">
  SELECT * FROM CUSTOMERS
</sql:query>
```

This query will skip the first two rows (numbered 0 and 1); then, starting with the row numbered 2, it will save up to 10 rows in the `customers` variable. If there aren't 10 rows, then `customers` will contain fewer rows. Therefore, supposing that the `CUSTOMERS` table contains 100 rows, the last example will store rows numbered 2 through 11 in `customers`.

TIP   Some databases support two nonstandard SQL keywords, `LIMIT` and `OFF-SET`, which work similarly to `maxRows` and `startRow`, respectively. JSTL provides the `startRow` and `maxRow` attributes for two reasons. First, not all databases support `LIMIT` and `OFFSET`; they are, after all, not specified by standard ANSI SQL. Second, databases that do support `LIMIT` don't usually provide an easy way to let you know whether the `LIMIT` took effect, the way the result bean's `limitedByMaxRows` property does. For example, if we wrote

```
SELECT * FROM CUSTOMERS LIMIT 20
```

and received 20 customer rows in response, we wouldn't know whether there were exactly 20 customers, or whether the query was stopped abruptly after the twentieth record.

9.4 *Modifying data with <sql:update>*

Just as you can query data using JSTL tags, you can also modify database data from within your JSP pages. You should think twice before doing so, however. Earlier in this chapter, I mentioned that some large applications can be maintained more easily when JSP pages do not access databases directly, leaving this task instead for Java code in JavaBeans or custom JSP tags. This caution is particularly important when it comes to updating data from a JSP page. If the function of JSP pages is to display information, it can be dangerous to throw database updates into the mix.

However, JSTL does provide an `<sql:update>` tag with the hope that it will be useful, at the very least, for relatively small applications. If you don't depend on Java programmers to write JavaBeans or other intermediate code to *read* from your database, why should you suddenly need to do so when *writing* data? Furthermore, other web-scripting languages, such as PHP, provide for this kind of database access with great effect, so it makes sense for JSTL to do so, too.

9.4.1 *Simple uses of the <sql:update> tag*

Because of the nature of database updates, the `<sql:update>` tag is extremely simple to use. Unlike queries, where the `<sql:query>` tag is merely the first in a series of steps for accessing data, database inserts and updates usually stand on their own.

Once you execute an `<sql:update>` tag, you can pretty much forget about it and move on to other tasks.

Like `<sql:query>`, the `<sql:update>` tag uses the SQL language. (If you're not familiar with SQL, see appendix C.)

The `<sql:update>` tag, despite its name, doesn't just support SQL UPDATE commands; it also supports INSERT and DELETE, and in general lets you pass through any SQL command that doesn't produce a result. You can, for example, pass through a CREATE TABLE command from within the `<sql:update>` tag. (Appendix C describes some situations where doing so might be useful.)

Table 9.4 lists `<sql:update>`'s attributes.

Table 9.4 `<sql:update>` **tag attributes**

Attribute	Description	Required	Default
sql	The SQL query to execute (such as UPDATE...)	No	*Body*
dataSource	Provider of the database connections	No	*See section 9.3*
var	Name of the variable to store the row count	No	*None*
scope	Scope of the variable to store the row count	No	page

To figure out what database to connect to, `<sql:update>` uses the same rules as `<sql:query>`, which we discussed in section 9.3. If the dataSource attribute is specified, the tag uses the specific variable you pass to it; otherwise, it uses the default database connection.

In addition, `<sql:update>` accepts SQL statements using both methods that `<sql:query>` supports (see section 9.3.1). Specifically, the SQL statement can appear in the sql attribute or in the tag's body. Thus, both of the following tags are valid; they both send a command to the application's default database:

```
<sql:update>
  INSERT INTO PEOPLE(NAME, AGE, WEIGHT)
  VALUES('John "Fatso" Smith', 34, 540)
</sql:update>
```

and

```
<sql:update sql="DELETE FROM PEOPLE WHERE AGE < 18"/>
```

9.4.2 *Measuring the effect of an* *<sql:update>* *tag*

Every time SQL statements like INSERT, UPDATE, and DELETE run, they affect a specific number of rows. For instance, a single UPDATE command might change 1 row,

12 rows, or some other specific number of rows. Every DELETE command removes a particular number of rows—or even zero rows.

You can use <sql:update>'s var attribute to record the number of rows that <sql:update> affected. For example, for an UPDATE that modifies seven rows, the tag will save the number 7. For SQL statements like CREATE TABLE that don't operate with data directly, this number will always be zero.

Consider the following tag:

```
<sql:update var="n">
  DELETE FROM CUSTOMERS
  WHERE AGE < 18
</sql:update>
```

This tag will delete all rows in CUSTOMERS whose AGE column has a value less than 18, and it will store in the scoped variable named n the number of rows that were deleted. We could then, for instance, report this number back to the user:

```
<p>Our CUSTOMERS table had
<c:out value="${n}"/> minors.
They have all been removed.
Close call; we're lucky the
Feds didn't come after us.</p>
```

We could also use this number in a <c:if> condition:

```
<c:if value="${n == 0}">
  No rows were removed.
</c:if>
```

9.5 *Using <sql:param> with adjustable queries*

When you use SQL, you'll find that it's common for a query to need a small bit of data filled in. For instance, you might write a query that can retrieve any user's full name and birthdate, but the query won't make sense until you have an individual user's customer number. If we were sharing such queries with other people, we might write them as follows:

```
SELECT * FROM TABLE WHERE CUSTOMER_NUMBER=XXX
```

Then, separately, we'd explain what *XXX* means. It's common to have a general-purpose template query that must be customized repeatedly—depending, perhaps, on some information about the current user or about a specific product in a warehouse.

9.5.1   *Template queries*

One way to use queries like this is to customize them with simple JSP, just like you customize an HTML page. After all, JSP is great for adding dynamic content to otherwise static text. For example, we can use JSTL's `<c:out>` tag (see chapter 3) to fill in part of an SQL query:

```
<sql:query var="result">
  SELECT * FROM TABLE
  WHERE CUSTOMER_NUMBER=<c:out value="${customerNumber}"/>
</sql:query>
```

This is a simple way to use JSTL to modify a query. It effectively plugs the value of a scoped variable into an SQL statement. However, this technique is more problematic than it might seem at first. You're not always working with numbers; sometimes you'll use strings. In SQL, strings must be quoted with single quotes. So far, that doesn't sound like a problem; we could just insert the quotes manually, like this:

```
WHERE CUSTOMER_NAME='<c:out value="${customerName}"/>'
```

However, if the customer's name contains a quotation mark, like `David O'Davies`, the result will be the following unfortunate text:

```
WHERE CUSTOMER_NAME='David O&#039;Davies'
```

Because `<c:out>` escapes the quotation mark by default, it yields an incorrect value; SQL does not understand XML escaping.

There's even a security risk in building up queries manually. If you decide to get around `<c:out>`'s escaping problem by using the attribute `escapeXml="false"`, a malicious user could purposely corrupt the query to retrieve private information or even alter your database. For example, suppose the user, instead of a name like `David O'Davies`, enters the following unexpected text:

```
David' OR CUSTOMER_NAME <> 'David
```

In this case, the end of the query becomes

```
WHERE CUSTOMER_NAME='David' OR CUSTOMER_NAME <> 'David'
```

Because every customer name is either equal or not equal to `'David'`, this query will match every row in the table! Therefore, it's not usually a good idea to use `<c:out>` to build up an SQL statement yourself.

9.5.2   *Safe, convenient parameters with <sql:param>*

JSTL lets you avoid these problems by using a special syntax borrowed from JDBC, the Java package that supports database connectivity. Using this syntax, you can write a template query and leave out all unknown pieces, putting question marks (?) in their place. Then, you can fill in these question marks using the `<sql:param>` tag, which you insert as a child tag to `<sql:query>` and `<sql:update>`.

Table 9.5 lists `<sql:param>`'s single attribute, `value`.

Table 9.5   `<sql:param>` tag attribute

Attribute	Description	Required	Default
value	Parameter value (to fill in the placeholder)	No	*Body*

The `value` attribute accepts a value, and `<sql:param>` uses this value to fill in a single question-mark placeholder in its parent `<sql:query>` or `<sql:update>` tag. If multiple `<sql:param>` tags occur in the body of an `<sql:query>` or `<sql:update>` statement, they will match each successive ? placeholder, in order. You need exactly one `<sql:param>` tag for every ? you've used in an SQL command. Figure 9.6 demonstrates the relationship between multiple ? placeholders and `<sql:param>` tags.

```
<sql:query>
   SELECT * FROM CUSTOMERS
      WHERE NAME=?
      AND ADDRESS=?
      AND AGE=?

   <sql:param value="${page.username}"/>

   <sql:param value="${param.address}"/>

   <sql:param value="${age}"/>
</sql:query>
```

Figure 9.6
When a tag uses a query with multiple ? markers, it must have exactly one `<sql:param>` tag for each marker. Each `<sql:param>` tag sets a corresponding ? marker, in order.

Let's look at `<sql:param>` in action. Suppose we want to write a query that looks up a customer's number (from a column named NUMBER) based on the customer's name (NAME)—and that we want this query to work for multiple customers. We can write this query but use a question mark instead of a specific customer name:

```
SELECT NUMBER FROM CUSTOMERS WHERE NAME=?
```

Now, suppose the customer's name is stored in a scoped variable called customer-Name. We can replace the question mark with the value of this variable as follows:

```
<sql:query>
   SELECT NUMBER FROM CUSTOMERS WHERE NAME=?
   <sql:param value="${customerName}"/>
</sql:query>
```

Each time this tag runs, the ? placeholder gets filled in with a new value—the value of the `customerName` variable. For example, if `customerName` equals `David Davies`, then the query will run just as if we had written

```
SELECT NUMBER FROM CUSTOMERS
  WHERE NAME='David Davies'
```

Note how the value is quoted properly, if it needs to be. Therefore, we don't have to worry about whether the variable contains a rogue quotation mark. If the last example runs again, and `customerName` equals `Bob O'Customer` this time, the query will execute correctly; the quotation mark in the middle of Bob's last name is managed automatically.

Question-mark syntax

The ? placeholder can't be used just anywhere within an SQL statement. You can't use it to substitute for a table or column name. For example, you can't write the following:

```
SELECT ? FROM CUSTOMERS WHERE CUSTOMER_NUMBER=3
```

You also can't write this:

```
SELECT * FROM ? WHERE CUSTOMER_NUMBER=3
```

A ? character can only be used to substitute for a value—a string, number, or other data—within an SQL command. So, as in our last example, we can set a column equal to it in a SELECT query (NAME=?). You can also use ? in UPDATE, INSERT, and DELETE statements. Consider the following `<sql:update>` tag, which contains an INSERT statement:

```
<sql:update>
  INSERT INTO PEOPLE(NAME, AGE, WEIGHT)
    VALUES(?,?,?)
    <sql:param value="${userName}"/>
    <sql:param value="${userAge}"/>
    <sql:param value="${userWeight}"/>
</sql:update>
```

In this example, each `<sql:param>` tag in turn fills in one successive ? in the INSERT statement. These placeholders are specified in the middle of the VALUES clause in the statement, which is a valid use of ?. Consider another example:

```
<sql:update>
  UPDATE PEOPLE
  SET AGE=?
  WHERE WEIGHT=?
    <sql:param value="${newAge}"/>
    <sql:param value="${oldPounds}"/>
</sql:update>
```

This time, ? placeholders appear in the SET and WHERE clauses of an UPDATE command. The ? is legitimate in both cases. Note that the first ? is part of the new data being added by UPDATE, and the second ? is part of the old data being matched by the statement's WHERE clause.

<sql:param>'s body

If <sql:param> doesn't contain a value attribute, the tag will use the content of its body as the value to substitute for its corresponding ?. So, you can easily produce a value using other tags. For example, the following would replace a ? placeholder with a value retrieved from an XML document:

```
<sql:param>
  <x:out select="$doc/customers/customer/number"/>
</sql:param>
```

9.5.3 *Date parameters with <sql:dateParam>*

Databases typically have special support for dates. A column in a database that stores a user's birthday really treats it as a date, not just as a string that describes the date. This way, the database can perform date-related operations on the data; for instance, you could compare the user's birthday with a known date to ensure that the user isn't a minor.

Consider an SQL statement like this:

```
SELECT * FROM USERS
 WHERE BIRTHDAY < ?
```

This query finds all users who were born before a given date. But if you have a scoped variable representing a date (see chapter 10 for information on how to create such a scoped variable), you might not be able to use <sql:param>. I say might not because it depends the specific database driver you're using. To make sure you can add dates to any query, JSTL provides an <sql:dateParam> tag, whose attributes are listed in table 9.6.

Table 9.6 <sql:dateParam> tag attributes

Attribute	Description	Required	Default
value	Date value (to fill in the placeholder)	Yes	*None*
type	The value time, date, or timestamp	No	timestamp

The value attribute requires an expression pointing to a scoped-variable that stores a date, and the type attribute lets you describe more precisely how the database should treat the value: does it just store a time of day (time), a calendar date (date), or both a time and a date (timestamp)?

Except for accepting a date, <sql:dateParam> works just like <sql:param>. For instance, to use our previous query, we could write an <sql:query> tag like this:

```
<sql:query>
  SELECT * FROM USERS
    WHERE BIRTHDAY < ?
  <sql:dateParam value="${myBirthday}"/>
</sql:query>
```

9.6 *Managing transactions with* <sql:transaction>

If your application manages any sensitive data, it's a good exercise to consider the following question for every point in your page: "What would happen if lightning struck the web server at precisely *this* point?" Figure 9.7 evokes this kind of reasoning by demonstrating a failure in the middle of a series of <sql:update> tags. Two tags complete successfully, but the remaining three don't.

If these five tags are unrelated, then you have nothing to worry about (other than making sure your server starts back up after the stroke of lightning). But some applications require that groups of database operations either succeed or fail together, in one fell swoop. For example, suppose the first two tags bill a customer for a product and the final three tags ensure that the product is shipped. It isn't acceptable for the first two tags to run without the final three tags running, too; all

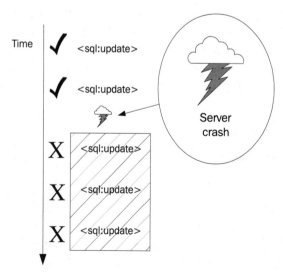

Figure 9.7
Even the best hardware and software can crash or run into other unexpected errors at any point. If an error occurs in the middle of a sensitive series of database updates, the data can be left in an inconsistent state. Here, a five-part series is interrupted after the second step, potentially leaving data in an inconsistent state. JSTL's <sql:transaction> **tag can help prevent your data from getting out of sync.**

five operations must be treated as a single unit. Operations that need to succeed or fail as a single unit are known as *transactions*.

WARNING Although most well-engineered database systems support transactions, not every software product does. Before using the tags in this section, check with your software's documentation or your database administrator to ensure your database supports transactions.

9.6.1 The <sql:transaction> tag

In JSTL, transactions let you treat a series of `<sql:query>` and `<sql:update>` tags as part of a unified whole. All query and update tags within a transaction succeed or fail together; there is no middle ground. If the end of a transaction doesn't complete successfully, the beginning is stricken from the record: the database pretends it never happened. This sort of pretending is formally called *rolling back*, and it involves restoring the database's state to a prior one—specifically, to the way things were before the first `<sql:update>` in the transaction executed.

JSTL supports transactions with a tag called `<sql:transaction>`. This tag acts as a parent tag for `<sql:update>` and `<sql:query>` tags. Each `<sql:transaction>` tag

Figure 9.8
The `<sql:transaction>` tag protects its `<sql:update>` and `<sql:query>` children. It does so by ensuring that these children succeed or fail as a unit. If any of the individual steps under an `<sql:transaction>` fails, the database will be rolled back to a prior state, as if the transaction had never begun.

groups all of its children `<sql:update>` and `<sql:query>` tags into a transaction, as figure 9.8 suggests. All child tags in an `<sql:transaction>` succeed or fail together.

Even though `<sql:query>` tags don't modify data, they might represent necessary steps in a transaction. For instance, you might conduct an update, followed by a query, followed by an update based on the intermediate query. This is why `<sql:transaction>` allows `<sql:query>` tags to participate in a transaction.

Note that any valid text, JSTL tags, or other JSP content can appear inside an `<sql:transaction>` tag. If a fatal error occurs anywhere inside this block—for example, if you decide to retrieve a file with `<c:import>` and this file doesn't exist—then the entire transaction will be stopped immediately and rolled back. This process lets you tie the success of database operations to some non-database actions. (Keep in mind, however, that `<sql:transaction>` can only roll back database operations. It doesn't erase scoped variables that you create or otherwise prevent its body from having a lasting effect. Also note that anything printed from within an `<sql:transaction>` tag—that is, any template text or output from tags like `<c:out>`—will be ignored.)

Table 9.7 lists the attributes for the `<sql:transaction>` tag.

Table 9.7   `<sql:transaction>` **tag attributes**

Attribute	Description	Required	Default
dataSource	Provider of the database connections	No	*See section 9.3*
isolation	Transaction's isolation from others (advanced)	No	*See section 9.6.2*

The `<sql:transaction>` tag determines what database to use in the same manner as `<sql:query>` and `<sql:update>`. It can either use its `dataSource` attribute or, if none is specified, rely on the default database, which can be established by `<sql:setDataSource>` or back-end Java code.

When an `<sql:transaction>` tag occurs in your page, it immediately sets up a database transaction. This transaction uses a database connection, and this connection is supplied by default to all the `<sql:update>` and `<sql:query>` children of the transaction. For example, consider the following tag:

```
<sql:update sql="${command}"/>
```

This tag would normally use the default database, because no `dataSource` attribute is specified. But when this tag appears inside an `<sql:transaction>` tag, it uses whatever database its parent `<sql:transaction>` tag used. As figure 9.9 suggests, `<sql:transaction>` takes a single database and exposes it to all its `<sql:update>` and `<sql:query>` children, making this database the new default within its body.

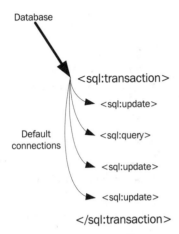

Figure 9.9
The `<sql:transaction>` tag replaces the default connection for all its `<sql:query>` and `<sql:update>` child tags. This step is necessary because database transactions are, by nature, tied to an individual connection; it's important that all the SQL operations beneath a single transaction share the same connection.

Let's look at the `<sql:transaction>` tag in action. The typical example of database transactions—a funds transfer, where money is added to one account and deleted from another—happens to be a good one, so we'll use that. Suppose the following SQL command removes $100 from our first account:

```
UPDATE ACCOUNTS
SET BALANCE=BALANCE-100
WHERE ACCOUNT='Shawn-acct1'
```

The following corresponding statement adds money to our second account:

```
UPDATE ACCOUNTS
SET BALANCE=BALANCE+98
WHERE ACCOUNT='Shawn-acct2'
```

We add back only $98 instead of $100 because we're one of those irritating banks that charges a fee for everything.

If we want to execute a transfer of funds, we'd better make sure that nothing interrupts the transfer and causes it to complete only partially. We can do so with the following `<sql:transaction>` tag:

```
<sql:transaction dataSource="${database}">
  <sql:update>
    UPDATE ACCOUNTS
      SET BALANCE=BALANCE-100
      WHERE ACCOUNT='Shawn-acct1'
  </sql:update>
  <sql:update>
    UPDATE ACCOUNTS
      SET BALANCE=BALANCE+98
      WHERE ACCOUNT='Shawn-acct2'
  </sql:update>
</sql:transaction>
```

This code ensures that both updates execute as a unit; they either both succeed or both fail. If they succeed, then we know the funds (minus the $2 fee) have been transferred safely.

Note that the two `<sql:update>` tags do not specify a `dataSource` attribute. They simply use the default connection that `<sql:transaction>` manages for them. The master `<sql:transaction>` tag, on the other hand, uses the explicitly named `database` variable as its database.

9.6.2 *Transaction isolation*

Parents often tell their kids, "Look both ways before crossing the street." They really mean, "Look both ways *immediately* before crossing the street"; planning ahead doesn't help. If you check for traffic but then stop, turn around, and pick up a dime off the sidewalk, you need to check for traffic again before walking into the middle of the street.

You can think of "checking for traffic" and "crossing the street" as two parts of a transactional operation, where both parts must succeed together. But these operations have an additional requirement: it's important that nothing interrupts, distracts, or confuses you between the two parts of the operation.

Not all database transactions have this requirement; not all transactions care whether the data they're working on gets pulled out from under them in the middle of their work. Consider the example of a funds transfer from the end of the previous section. This transaction might not care if the funds in my bank account change while the transaction is proceeding. For instance, once the first `<sql:update>` tag has withdrawn $100 from our first account, it might not matter if someone else takes out $300 more while the transaction proceeds to redeposit our money into the second account.

However, it's important that some transactions be effectively *isolated* from other transactions. That is, the transaction shouldn't be affected by other things occurring simultaneously in the database.

For instance, imagine that you use an `<sql:query>` tag to determine the average age of all your users. Then, you perform several `<sql:update>` operations based on this average age. Suppose these operations depend on the average user's age not changing during the transaction. If a simultaneous operation outside your transaction adds, modifies, or deletes a user, and if this change shows up to your transaction, then your transaction might not behave correctly.

JDBC supports four transaction modes, and JSTL mirrors JDBC's support by letting you specify one of these four modes (more formally called *isolation levels*) in the `<sql:transaction>` tag. This is the purpose of the `isolation` attribute, which takes the values listed in table 9.8.

Table 9.8 `isolation` attribute values

Transaction isolation level	Dirty reads?	Nonrepeatable reads?	Phantom reads?
`read_uncommitted`	-	-	-
`read_committed`	Prevented	-	-
`repeatable_read`	Prevented	Prevented	-
`serializable`	Prevented	Prevented	Prevented

This table shows the four acceptable isolation levels and what sorts of potentially undesirable reads they prohibit. A *dirty read* is a read (for example, from a SELECT statement) of rows that have not yet been *committed*—confirmed by another transaction. Uncommitted data might only be speculative; it might still be rolled back by the other transaction. Dirty reads let your transaction see only partial data from another transaction; this situation can be dangerous, because the partial data might not be consistent.

A *nonrepeatable read* occurs when the same SELECT statement returns different results when executed within the same transaction. A *phantom read* is like a nonrepeatable read, but it involves new rows added to a table that show up under the second SELECT (whereas, by contrast, a nonrepeatable read may affect existing data).

You might think that the *serializable* mode is thus the best overall isolation level, because it provides the most isolation and protection. However, its extra features come at a potential performance cost, so it is not always wise to use serializable transactions.

Overall, transaction isolation levels are an advanced, technical topic that we can't treat in-depth here. The important point is that JSTL supports them. For instance, to make a transaction serializable, we could use the following tag:

```
<sql:transaction isolation="serializable">
   transaction body
</sql:transaction>
```

For more information on transaction isolation levels, consult the JDBC documentation or a book on databases; see appendix D for pointers to further reading.

9.7 SQL example: a hit counter

Let's look at how to create a simple *hit counter*—a feature that counts how many times users have loaded your pages, and optionally displays the running tally.

To begin, we'll need to create a database table to store the counter information. This table will be simple in structure, because it only needs to keep track of a single number. We can create a suitable table, which we'll call counter, using the following SQL command:

```
create table counter (
    counter integer
)
```

NOTE   You'll need to type this command into your database's text interface. The instructions for doing so vary from database to database, so you'll need to check with your database's manual or administrator to determine how to send it commands manually. (My hsqldb tutorial at Manning Publication's web site describes the procedure for hsqldb. See appendix D for its URL.)

If you have trouble sending commands to your database manually, you can enter the command into an `<sql:update>` tag and run the tag manually by loading its page. This technique is somewhat clumsy, but it's a decent alternative. For instance, the following tag will create the counter table in the default database:

```
<sql:update>
  create table counter (
      counter integer
  )
</sql:update>
```

The counter table has a single column, also called counter, which stores an integer. Our table will contain a single row, and this row's value for the counter column will represent the current tally of web-page hits. Before we use the counter, we'll need to create this row manually. To do so, we can run the following SQL command:

```
insert into counter(counter) values(0)
```

This line initializes our database and sets the counter's starting value to 0.

Now that we've set up the counter table, we're ready to look at a page that uses it. Listing 9.2 shows such a page.[4]

Listing 9.2   counter.jsp: a simple hit counter

```
<%@ taglib prefix="c" uri="http://java.sun.com/jstl/core" %>
<%@ taglib prefix="sql" uri="http://java.sun.com/jstl/sql" %>

<sql:transaction>
```

---

[4] Remember, this chapter's examples, including listing 9.2, assume you have a default database set up. If you don't, you'll need to use the `<sql:setDataSource>` tag and the dataSource attribute for `<sql:transaction>`. See section 9.2.

```
<sql:update>
  update counter set counter = counter + 1
</sql:update>
<sql:query var="result">
  select * from counter
</sql:query>
<c:set var="count" value="${result.rows[0].counter}" />

</sql:transaction>
```

This example begins by setting up an SQL transaction with `<sql:transaction>`. This step is hardly necessary for something as frivolous as a hit counter, but it's useful to experiment with the tag.

The `<sql:update>` tag increments the counter using this SQL statement:

```
update counter set counter = counter + 1
```

After updating the counter, we read in the new count with an SQL SELECT statement inside `<sql:query>`. The `<sql:query>` tag stores its result as a scoped variable named `result`.

Normally, if our table had multiple rows, we'd iterate over them using `<c:forEach>`. In this case, we know that our table has only one row, so we can access this row directly using an expression like `${result.rows[0]}`. (Remember, row numbering starts with 0, so `rows[0]` represents the first row.) In our case, we're interested in the column named `counter` in our single row, so we use the following expression:

```
${result.rows[0].counter}
```

We use a `<c:set>` tag to save this value as a scoped variable named `count`. This way, we can print out the current count later using an expression like this:

```
<c:out value="${count}"/>
```

We'll look at many more examples of JSTL's database tags in part 3.

9.8 *Summary*

Keep the following points about JSTL's database support in mind:

- In large applications, it's often better to access databases using behind-the-scenes Java code rather then JSTL tags. However, JSTL provides database tags for smaller applications and any other situations where you find them convenient.
- JSTL's database access requires that you understand SQL, which we discuss in more detail in appendix C.

- JSTL's database tags work best when a database is set up behind the scenes by Java code. However, you can also set up your own default database using the `<sql:setDataSource>` tag.

- To retrieve information from a database, use the `<sql:query>` tag. This tag exposes a scoped variable that stores the results of the query. You can easily loop over these results using `<c:forEach>`.

- To modify data in a database, use `<sql:update>`. This tag exposes a scoped variable to indicate the number of rows it modified.

- To group database operations so that they succeed or fail as a single unit, place them within an `<sql:transaction>` tag. This tag has an `isolation` attribute to help you ensure the transaction doesn't get confused by other simultaneous operations that occur in the database. In most cases, though, you won't need to worry about transaction isolation.

10

Formatting and internationalization

This chapter covers...

- Printing numbers and dates
- Parsing numbers and dates
- Time zones, locales, and resource bundles
- Internationalizing text messages

215

As a designer of web pages, it's your job to present information. Even when information is straightforward, the best way to display it isn't always obvious. For instance, should your page print the number 52577 as "52577", "52,577" "52,577.00", or some other alternative? If you read the date "July 2, 1947" from a database, should you print it out as "7/2/47", "July 2, 1947", "2 Jul 1947", or as something else entirely?

For some of your web pages, answers to these questions might merely be a matter of preference or spacing. For example, "52,577" might look better to you than "52577", or an HTML <table> that you're printing might only have room for "7/2/47" and not a longhand version of the same date. In such cases, JSTL tags let you specify a single format and then forget about the issue.

But if your pages are targeted to users in different countries, you might need to make sure your page will present appropriate information every time it's loaded. The string "7/2/1947" means "July 2, 1947" in the United States but "February 7, 1947" in France. If your page's target audience is half French and half English, you might want to print dates differently depending on how the user's browser is configured (or on what country users say they're from). JSTL tags can help you make sure users see values that are meaningful to them.

Some applications take *internationalization*—the process of setting up a single application so that it can easily work with multiple languages—a step further. In addition to numbers and dates, they internationalize the words and phrases they print out. JSTL has tags to support this kind of internationalization as well.

In this chapter, we'll first look at a collection of JSTL tags that help you input and output numbers and dates. Then, we'll focus on JSTL's support for internationalizing text messages. All the tags we introduce in this chapter come from JSTL's fmt tag library, which is used for what the JSTL spec calls "internationalization-capable formatting." (See chapter 2 for a list of JSTL's tag libraries.) To use any of the examples in this chapter, you'll need to make sure that a directive like the following appears at the top of your page:

```
<%@ taglib prefix="fmt" uri="http://java.sun.com/jstl/fmt" %>
```

10.1 Printing numbers with <fmt:formatNumber>

In chapter 3, we discussed different data types, like booleans, strings, and numbers. If you have a scoped variable that's a number, you can print it in your page by using the <c:out> tag, because <c:out> lets you print out any kind of data. For instance, if the page-scoped variable netWorth is a number that equals 500000.01, then the tag

```
<c:out value="${netWorth}"/>
```

will output

```
500000.01
```

The `<c:out>` tag prints the number in a simple, default form. Integers, for instance, are presented as a sequence of digits. Floating-point numbers are displayed similarly, but with a decimal point (.) separating some digits from the other digits. This simple format might be okay for many of your pages, but if a page prints out a lot of numbers, or if presenting numbers is a page's main job, then you'll probably want more control over how numbers are printed. That's what `<fmt:formatNumber>` is for.

10.1.1 *Basic usage of <fmt:formatNumber>*

In its simplest form, you can use the `<fmt:formatNumber>` just like `<c:out>`. For example, we can write

```
<fmt:formatNumber value="${netWorth}"/>
```

This usage is similar to `<c:out>`: the tag has an attribute, `value`, that points to the number we want to print out. However, even in this simple form, the `<fmt:format-Number>` tag does something more interesting than `<c:out>`: it prints the number using its best guess about what format the user wants to see. Web browsers can convey information about their *locale*—essentially, their location and preferred formats for numbers, dates, and other data. The `<fmt:formatNumber>` tag can automatically sense this locale and customize its output. So, if `${netWorth}` equals `500000.01`, the simple `<fmt:formatNumber>` we just presented will output the following values for these countries:

Country	Sample numeric format
United States	500,000.01
France	500 000,01
Germany	500.000,01
Switzerland	500'000.01

As this table shows, the format is different for the United States, France, Germany, and (as you might know if you have a Swiss bank account) Switzerland.

TIP   If you're using Windows and Internet Explorer, you can experiment with different locales by going to the Start menu and choosing Settings, then Control Panel, and finally Regional Options. From there, the General tab lets you pick your locale. (These instructions may vary slightly if you use something other than Windows 2000.) This setting can be useful when you're testing JSTL pages; for instance, you can pretend you're coming from France or Germany. The interface might be messy, but it's cheaper than buying a plane ticket.

If you're familiar with localization, you might have realized that I'm being imprecise when I say that number formats are associated with particular countries: they're actually associated with country/language combinations. But this difference won't matter for now. The point is that `<fmt:formatNumber>` will print the right value based, by default, on the browser's configuration.

Let's look at some `<fmt:formatNumber>` attributes that give you more control over how to display numbers (see table 10.1).

Table 10.1   `<fmt:formatNumber>` tag attributes

Attribute	Description	Required	Default
value	The numeric value to format	No	*Body*
type	Whether to print regular numbers, currencies, or percentages	No	number
currencyCode	ISO-4217 currency code	No	*None*
currencySymbol	Currency symbol (such as $)	No	*None*
groupingUsed	Whether to group digits, as in 1,234,567	No	true
maxIntegerDigits	The maximum number of integer digits to print	No	*None*
minIntegerDigits	The minimum number of integer digits to print	No	*None*
maxFractionDigits	The maximum number of fractional digits to print	No	*None*
minFractionDigits	The minimum number of fractional digits to print	No	*None*
pattern	Detailed pattern to use when formatting the number	No	*None*
var	Variable to expose the formatted number (as a string)	No	*None*
scope	Scope in which to expose the formatted number	No	page

10.1.2 *Different ways to specify a value*

Notice in table 10.1 that the `value` attribute is optional. Instead of specifying a `value` attribute, you can use `<fmt:formatNumber>`'s body to feed the tag a value. Doing so is convenient if you have a non-JSTL tag that doesn't easily store scoped variables but instead prints out a number. For instance, suppose our organization produced a tag that outputs a number, like the following:

```
<myCompany:printMinimumShippingCharge/>
```

We could use this tag with `<fmt:formatNumber>` as follows:

```
<fmt:formatNumber>
  <myCompany:printMinimumShippingCharge/>
</fmt:formatNumber>
```

In addition, instead of using an expression or a custom tag, we can feed `<fmt:formatNumber>` a value directly, like this:

```
<fmt:formatNumber value="500000.01"/>
```

When you type in a number or use the tag body, the string that `<fmt:formatNumber>` receives should be printed in Java's default numeric format, which generally looks the way we've shown it here: `500000.01`. It resembles a bare-bones version of the English locale.

The `<fmt:formatNumber>` tag doesn't accept numbers already formatted for a locale. For example, the following tag is invalid:

```
<fmt:formatNumber value="500 000,01"/>
```

In many of this chapter's examples, we'll specify numbers directly, as with `value="500000.01"`. This is just for demonstrative purposes. In most of your pages, you'll use expressions like `value="${user.netWorth}"`.

10.1.3 *Storing a number instead of printing it*

By default, `<fmt:formatNumber>` prints out a formatted version of its input number. If you want to use this formatted value multiple times or share it with another page, you can store it in a scoped variable instead of printing it. The syntax to do so is familiar: you use the `var` and `scope` attributes. For instance, again assuming `${netWorth}` equals `500000.01`, consider the following tag:

```
<fmt:formatNumber value="${netWorth}"
  var="argent" scope="session" />
```

If this page is loaded by a French browser, it saves the formatted value `500 000,01` in a session-scoped variable named `argent`. This variable could later be printed out, for instance, with `<c:out>`:

```
<c:out value="${sessionScope.argent}"/>
```

10.1.4 *Printing different types of numbers: percentages and currencies*

If you've spent time with Microsoft Excel, you know it can format different cells using special rules. If you're working on your taxes, for example, you probably want all numbers to show up as dollar values. In other situations, you want a number like .24 to appear as 24%.

The `<fmt:formatNumber>` tag has a similar feature. Using the `type` attribute, you can instruct the tag to print your numeric value as either a currency or a percentage. Table 10.2 shows the valid values for the `type` attribute.

Table 10.2 Using the `type` attribute, you can tell the `<fmt:formatNumber>` tag to format numbers as percentage values and as currency. The `type` attribute can take the values listed here.

type attribute value	Description	Example (for value .24)
number	General-purpose number (default)	.24
currency	Locale-specific currency	$0.24
percent	Percentage	24%

Percentages

By and large, percentages work the same way as regular numbers, but the number is multiplied by 100 before being printed. Thus, .24 becomes 24%, and the number 24 becomes (in the English locale) 2,400%. As with regular numbers, `<fmt:format-Number>` prints decimal points and other pieces of the number according to locale-specific rules. For instance, consider the following tag:

```
<fmt:formatNumber type="percent" value="24"/>
```

For browsers that are set to the United States's default locale, this tag prints

```
2,400%
```

In French, however, it prints

```
2 400%
```

In principle, different locales can have different percent signs, although this doesn't come up very often. (At least, not in my admittedly parochial experience with different locales.)

Currencies

Currencies are another special case, but they're more complicated than percentages and regular numbers. Currencies have two important extra features:

- A currency symbol, such as $ for U.S. dollars or F for French francs
- A standard number of digits after the decimal point—for example, two for U.S. dollars and French francs, but zero for Italian lira

When the `type` attribute is set to `currency`, the `<fmt:formatNumber>` tag applies these two extra considerations to the numbers it prints. Consider the following tag, which formats the numeric value `78.74901`:

```
<fmt:formatNumber type="currency" value="78.74901"/>
```

For the typical United States locale, `<fmt:formatNumber>` rounds the number to `78.75` and prints it out with a dollar sign:

```
$78.75
```

For Italy, the tag shortens the number further (to `79`) and prints it out with a symbol for the lira:

```
L. 79
```

(Presumably, digits after the decimal point don't make sense when discussing the lira, just as a third digit after the decimal point isn't conventional when referring to U.S. dollars.)

Of course, `<fmt:formatNumber>` doesn't perform any currency conversions. It doesn't convert values between dollars, francs, and euros using any exchange rate. (Wouldn't it be cool if it did?) It simply takes the numeric value that it's given and prints it with the correct symbols and formatting.

Currency codes and symbols

The `<fmt:formatNumber>` tag has two special attributes that work only when `type="currency"`. They're designed to give you more control over how the tag formats currencies. The first attribute, `currencyCode`, accepts a code that you can pick from a specific list of currency codes maintained by a group that cares intensely about such things. You can find a current list as a link from the following URL:

```
http://www.bsi-global.com/iso4217currency
```

This list is updated as countries adopt new currencies, so if your application is particularly sensitive to how it displays currencies, you might want to use this list to override any automatic determination your system makes based on locale.

As an example of currency codes, `EUR` represents the euro, and `USD` represents the dollar. Thus, the following example would display a number formatted correctly for the U.S. dollar (such as `$78.75`), regardless of the browser's preferred locale:

```
<fmt:formatNumber type="currency"
    currencyCode="USD" value="78.74901"/>
```

(Technically, there can be multiple symbols for the dollar; if so, then the browser's preferred one—based on locale—is chosen.)

WARNING   By default, the `currencyCode` attribute works only on JDK 1.4 and later versions. Check with your system administrator if you're not sure what version of the JDK your JSP container runs on. If you use the `currency-Code` attribute on a system that has an older version of Java, the code you use will be printed as a currency symbol. I wouldn't recommend this approach; use the `currencySymbol` attribute instead.

A separate attribute, `currencySymbol`, lets you set a specific currency symbol to use. For instance, you might write `currencySymbol="$"` to indicate the dollar.

10.1.5 *Grouping digits together ... or not*

By default, `<fmt:formatNumber>` arranges digits into groups that are appropriate for the browser's locale. For example, as you saw earlier, the number `500000.01` is printed as `500,000.01` in English. This formatting is used because of the locale's customary rules: groups of three digits are separated by a comma (,). In Switzerland, the style uses groups of three digits separated by an apostrophe (').

You can use the `groupingUsed` attribute to explicitly shut off this grouping, which will cause the number to be printed without any group separator. Figure 10.1 shows an example.

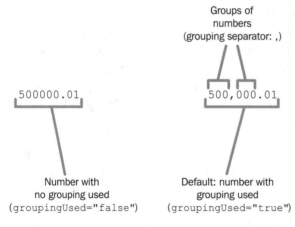

Figure 10.1
By default, the
`<fmt:formatNumber>` tag
arranges numbers into groups
of digits, using a locale-specific
group separator. You can shut
off this behavior with the
`groupingUsed` attribute.

The following two tags are equivalent because `groupingUsed="true"` is the default:

```
<fmt:formatNumber value="500000.01" />
<fmt:formatNumber value="500000.01" groupingUsed="true" />
```

For the English locale, these tags both print

```
500,000.01
```

The following tag is different, however:

```
<fmt:formatNumber value="500000.01" groupingUsed="false" />
```

For the English locale, this tag simply prints

```
500000.01
```

A decimal separator—in English, the period (.)—is still used if appropriate. The separation of numbers into a decimal part and a fractional part doesn't count as grouping for the purposes of the `groupingUsed` attribute.

10.1.6 *Controlling how many digits print*

No fewer than four attributes for `<fmt:formatNumber>` give you fine-grained but convenient control over how many digits print when your numeric value is formatted. These attributes (see table 10.1) are `maxIntegerDigits`, `minIntegerDigits`, `maxFractionDigits`, and `minFractionDigits`.

By default, or when `type="number"`, digits are printed only when necessary. For values like `98.6` (the average human body temperature), three digits are printed because you need exactly three digits to specify the value `98.6` accurately. (When `type="currency"`, some extra fractional digits might be added or removed, but the number of integer digits is still based on the numeric value.) These attributes let you override this default behavior and, instead, make explicit choices about the number of digits that print before and after the decimal point.

The attributes whose names begin with `min` let you specify a minimum number of digits to use when printing the number. For instance, consider the following tag:

```
<fmt:formatNumber value="98.6"
  minIntegerDigits="4"/>
```

In the English locale, this tag prints out the following:

```
0,098.6
```

Four integer digits are used, even though we only need two. This technique is useful for *padding* numbers in tables or lists so that they line up correctly.

However, notice how the leading `0`s are still grouped into sets of three and separated by a comma (,). This looks bizarre to most people; so, if you intend to pad numbers with leading `0`s, you might want to use the `groupingUsed` attribute we discussed in the previous section:

```
<fmt:formatNumber value="98.6"
  minIntegerDigits="4" groupingUsed="false"/>
```

For English, this tag will print the following:

```
0098.6
```

The `minFractionDigits` attribute works similarly: it makes sure that a particular number of digits will follow the decimal point, padding with 0's at the end, if necessary.

The other two attributes—`maxIntegerDigits` and `maxFractionDigits`—truncate or interrupt a number. This action is more commonly appropriate for fractional digits than for integers. For instance, sometimes you just don't have space for (or don't care about) the tenth decimal place of a number. In such cases, you can use tags like this:

```
<fmt:formatNumber value="3.141592653589"
  maxFractionDigits="2"/>
```

This tag prints out the following when loaded by an English browser:

```
3.14
```

It's less common to use `maxIntegerDigits`, but the attribute exists in case the space that numbers take up is more important to your page than printing their values correctly!

Table 10.3 shows a few examples of these four attributes working in concert, for the numeric value `99.2`. (This value has risen from `98.6`, which we used in earlier examples; spending too much time formatting numbers is apt to give you a slight fever.) All examples in this table assume the English locale.

Table 10.3 The four attributes `minIntegerDigits`, `maxIntegerDigits`, `minFractionDigits`, and `maxFractionDigits` give you fine-grained control over how many digits print in each part of your number. This table shows how these values affect the formatting of the value `99.2` in the typical United States (English) locale. If a column contains -, an attribute wasn't specified. For all rows, the `groupingUsed` attribute is set to `false`.

minInteger-Digits	maxInteger-Digits	minFraction-Digits	maxFraction-Digits	Formatted output
-	-	-	-	99.2
1	-	-	-	99.2
2	-	-	-	99.2
3	-	-	-	099.2
4	-	-	-	0099.2
-	0	-	-	.2
-	1	-	-	9.2
-	2	-	-	99.2
-	3	-	-	99.2
-	-	1	-	99.2

Table 10.3 The four attributes `minIntegerDigits`, `maxIntegerDigits`, `minFractionDig-`
`its`, and `maxFractionDigits` give you fine-grained control over how many digits print in each
part of your number. This table shows how these values affect the formatting of the value `99.2` in
the typical United States (English) locale. If a column contains -, an attribute wasn't specified. For all
rows, the `groupingUsed` attribute is set to `false`. *(continued)*

minInteger-Digits	maxInteger-Digits	minFraction-Digits	maxFraction-Digits	Formatted output
-	-	2	-	99.20
-	-	3	-	99.200
-	-	4	-	99.2000
-	-	-	0	99
-	-	-	1	99.2
-	-	-	2	99.2
-	-	-	3	99.2
4	-	4	-	0099.2000
	1	-	1	9.2
2	4	2	4	99.20

Notice how the attributes whose names begin with `max` do not force the output to
have extra digits; they simply specify an upper limit. Similarly, if a number contains more digits than the `min` attributes specify, these attributes have no effect.

Tips for managing digits

Here are a couple of tips for managing digits:

- The `maxIntegerDigits` and `maxFractionDigits` attributes are useful when
  you want to make sure a number can't highjack your page's overall layout.
  For instance, HTML `<table>` elements automatically resize based on their
  contents. If you print an unknown numeric value in such a table, its layout
  might become distorted if the number contains too many integer or fractional
  digits. Therefore, when you're not sure where your numeric values come
  from—perhaps you read them from a user, or a database beyond your control—it makes sense to think about reasonable maximums and specify both
  of these attributes. However, if you specify `maxIntegerDigits`, your numbers
  might be cut off and convey the wrong information to users. Therefore, you
  should choose a number high enough that this happens rarely, if ever. You
  can choose numbers as high as about 300 for the `max` attributes.

- The `minIntegerDigits` and `minFractionDigits` attributes cause your numbers to be padded with zeroes (0) if necessary. Doing so is useful for fractional digits, and it comes up most often when you're printing tables and lists of numbers that should line up. For applications that handle money, it's better to use `type="currency"` than to manage fractional digits yourself, but sometimes you'll need to align nonmonetary numbers. (For instance, suppose you're listing shares of mutual funds, which are typically carried to three decimal places.) In these cases, `minFractionDigits` is useful.

10.1.7 *More control: custom number patterns*

If the four attributes from section 10.1.6 aren't enough for you, and if you want to override locale-specific behavior by deciding on your own how a `<fmt:formatNumber>` tag should display numeric values, you can use the `pattern` attribute. This attribute gives you almost unlimited control over how numbers are displayed.

This attribute will not be useful for most of your pages, and it's more complicated than using the other `<fmt:formatNumber>` attributes. One special case that's difficult to handle without using `pattern`, however, is *scientific notation.* Scientific notation is particularly useful for very large and very small numbers; it shows a core part of a number (formally called a *mantissa*) being raised to an exponent. For instance, the scientific notation `7.89E40` means 7.89×10^{40}. You can tell `<fmt:formatNumber>` to use scientific notation like this:

```
<fmt:formatNumber value="52577" pattern="###.###E0"/>
```

This tag will print out

```
52.577E3
```

The benefits of scientific notation come to the surface when we try to format a particularly large number:

```
<fmt:formatNumber
   value="203787490020343266877275964040"
   pattern="###.###E0" />
```

Instead of wasting lots of space printing the entire number, this tag instead prints

```
203.787E27
```

Without scientific notation, it's hard to both shorten a number and still show how large it really is. Still, scientific notation isn't appropriate for all applications; many web users aren't familiar with it, so for some pages, it might be more harmful than helpful. But if you're printing out reports for statisticians or physicists, scientific notation might be just what you need.

For more information on how patterns work, you can read the Javadoc page for the DecimalFormat class, which (for the version of Java that was current at the time this chapter was written) should be available at http://java.sun.com/j2se/1.4/docs/api/java/text/DecimalFormat.html.

10.2 *Printing dates with <fmt:formatDate>*

Just as JSTL provides support for formatting numbers with <fmt:formatNumber>, it gives you <fmt:formatDate> to help print out dates and times. Table 10.4 lists its attributes.

Table 10.4 <fmt:formatDate> tag attributes

Attribute	Description	Required	Default
value	Date to print	Yes	*None*
type	Whether to print dates, times, or both	No	date
dateStyle	Preformatted style to use for the date	No	default
timeStyle	Preformatted style to use for the time	No	default
timeZone	Time zone to use when formatting the date	No	*See section 10.5*
pattern	Explicit formatting pattern to use	No	*None*
var	Variable to expose the formatted date (as a string)	No	*None*
scope	Scope in which to expose the formatted date	No	page

10.2.1 *Differences from <fmt:formatNumber>*

Besides the obvious difference that <fmt:formatDate> is for printing dates and <fmt:formatNumber> is for printing numbers, a few syntactic differences exist between the two tags. First, <fmt:formatDate> always takes a value attribute; this attribute is required. In addition, it cannot accept data from its body.

The value attribute for <fmt:formatDate> must point to a date variable; it can't simply point to a string that represents a date, like "Jan 1, 2001". There's no good, unambiguous way for <fmt:formatDate> to accept and interpret strings as dates. That job is given to another JSTL tag, <fmt:parseDate>, which we'll encounter later.

You can get real date variables a few ways. You might retrieve one from a database or receive one from back-end Java code. Or, you might use the <fmt:parseDate> tag we just mentioned, which we'll describe in section 10.4, to produce a date variable. You can also produce a date using an advanced tag called <jsp:useBean>. We'll leave this tag's inner workings as magic for now; we'll mention it again in more detail in chapter 14. For now, here's how you can use `<jsp:useBean>` to store a date in a scoped variable:

```
<jsp:useBean id="current" class="java.util.Date"/>
```

This tag creates a scoped variable named `current` that stores the date corresponding to the moment the `<jsp:useBean>` tag ran. You can use `<jsp:useBean>` anywhere you can use a JSTL tag, and you don't need a `<%@ taglib %>` directive to use it.

Otherwise, `<fmt:formatDate>` is similar to `<fmt:formatNumber>`. When you pass a date object to `<fmt:formatDate>`, it prints out a properly localized date by default, automatically sensing the browser's preferences. For instance, if we use the previous `<jsp:useBean>` tag to expose a scoped variable named `current` with the then-current date, then we can use the following tag to print this date in the user's default locale:

```
<fmt:formatDate value="${current}"/>
```

The following table shows some default values for different parts of the world, for the date May 20, 2002:

Country	Sample default date format
United States	May 20, 2002
France	20 mai 2002
Germany	20.05.2002
Netherlands	20-mei-2002
Spain	20-may-2002

Dates are a little more impressive than numbers, because they contain text that JSTL automatically translates for you.

10.2.2 *Printing times, dates, or both*

When a Java variable—like a scoped variable named `birthDate`—stores a date, it also technically stores a time. Sometimes (as with most birthdays, for example) this time isn't significant; it might simply be set to midnight as a reasonable default. Other times, you'll want to print out both a date and a time.

By default, the `<fmt:formatDate>` tag prints only dates. You can use the `type` attribute to print times—either in addition to, or instead of, dates. The following table shows the three possibilities and their corresponding outputs for the familiar English locale. In this case, the scoped variable `d` corresponds to a date/time combination of May 20, 2002 at 7:51:30 in the morning. This table shows what `<fmt:formatDate>` outputs for different values of the `type` attribute:

Tag	Output

`<fmt:formatDate`
`  value="${d}"`
`  type="date"/>`
	`May 20, 2002`

`<fmt:formatDate`
`  value="${d}"`
`  type="time"/>`
	`7:51:30 AM`

`<fmt:formatDate`
`  value="${d}"`
`  type="both"/>`
	`May 20, 2002 7:51:30 AM`

Both the date and time are formatted appropriately for a locale. You saw a few different date formats in the previous table. A locale's preferred format for times can also be different from that of English. For instance, some countries use military time instead of 12-hour time. Others use . instead of : to separate hours from minutes and minutes from seconds, and so on.

10.2.3 *Printing longer or shorter dates and times*

Two more attributes, `dateStyle` and `timeStyle`, let you choose how lengthy and detailed the output of `<fmt:formatDate>` should be. Until this point, you've seen the default output, which is equivalent to a `<fmt:formatDate>` tag with the attributes `dateStyle="default"` and `timeStyle="default"`. Table 10.5 shows the different possibilities for these attributes, along with examples for the English locale.[1]

Table 10.5 The `dateStyle` and `timeStyle` attributes for `<fmt:formatDate>` let you choose an appropriate level of detail for the times and dates your pages print.

Attribute value	Description	Date example	Time example
`default`	Default style	`Jun 20, 2002`	`7:51:30 AM`
`short`	Abbreviated style	`6/20/02`	`7:51 AM`
`medium`	Medium-length style	`Jun 20, 2002`	`7:51:30 AM`
`long`	Longer style	`June 20, 2002`	`7:51:30 AM EDT`
`full`	Full information	`Monday, June 20, 2002`	`7:51:30 AM EDT`

[1] Note that `timeStyle="long"` and `timeStyle="full"` add a time zone. We'll discuss time zones in section 10.5.

From table 10.5, you can see that for the English locale, `default` has the same effect as `medium`. This isn't guaranteed to be the case for every locale.

You can mix `dateStyle` and `timeStyle` attributes however you'd like. For instance, we can write the following:

```
<fmt:formatDate
   type="both"
   timeStyle="short"
   dateStyle="full"
   value="${date}"/>
```

For the English locale, this tag will print out a date that looks like this:

```
Tuesday, January 1, 2002 12:00 AM
```

Note how the time defaulted to midnight, because we only specified a date in the `value` field.

10.2.4 *More control: custom date patterns*

Just like the `<fmt:formatNumber>` tag, `<fmt:formatDate>` has a `pattern` attribute that gives you more control over how to print dates. However, the `pattern` attribute for dates is easier to use—and more useful—than the one for numbers.

The `pattern` attribute lets you specify exactly how a date should appear. To build a pattern, you use letters from a list of special characters to indicate parts of the date you want to print. For instance, `y` represents "year" and `M` represents "month." Table 10.6 shows the most useful characters you can use in a pattern. (Some others exist that don't come up for most applications; you can read about them at http://java.sun.com/j2se/1.4/docs/api/java/text/SimpleDateFormat.html.)

Table 10.6   In `<fmt:formatDate>`, the `pattern` attribute gives you detailed control over how your dates will be printed. You construct a pattern using the characters in this table. When formatting a date, the number of each character that you use is significant: "MMMM" is different from "MM".

Character(s)	Meaning	Example
yy	Shorthand year	02
yyyy	Full year	2002
M	Month number	4
MM	Zero-padded month	04
MMM	Short month name	Apr
MMMM	Long month name	April
d	Day of month	5

Table 10.6 In `<fmt:formatDate>`, the `pattern` attribute gives you detailed control over how your dates will be printed. You construct a pattern using the characters in this table. When formatting a date, the number of each character that you use is significant: "MMMM" is different from "MM". *(continued)*

Character(s)	Meaning	Example
dd	Zero-padded day	05
EE	Short weekday name	Fri
EEEE	Long weekday name	Friday
H	Military-time hour	21
HH	Zero-padded military hour	21
h	Hour (1–12)	9
hh	Zero-padded hour (1–12)	09
m	Minute	4
mm	Zero-padded minute	04
s	Second	6
ss	Zero-padded second	06
S	Millisecond	249
a	AM / PM	PM
zz	Shorthand time zone	EST
zzzz	Full time zone name	Eastern Standard Time
Z	Time zone description	-0500

A pattern can also contain punctuation, which is passed through literally. To insert letters into a pattern, you have to quote them using single quotes (`'`). To print a single quote, you can write `''` (two single quotes). However, you should do so only if you've quoted the attribute value itself with double quotes (`"`).

Suppose `${d}` is the following full date:

```
Friday, April 5, 2002 at 9:04:06 p.m., Eastern Standard Time
```

Consider the following examples:

Patterns are a bit harder to use and read than the `dateStyle` and `timeStyle` attributes, so I recommend those attributes as long as they're suitable for your purposes. But as these examples show, you can achieve some tailored, specific formatting using `pattern`.

Tag	Output
`<fmt:formatDate value="${d}" pattern="d MMM yyyy"/>`	`5 Apr 2002`
`<fmt:formatDate value="${d}" pattern="m 'after' h"/>`	`4 after 9`
`<fmt:formatDate value="${d}" pattern="MMMM ''yy"/>`	`April '02`
`<fmt:formatDate value="${d}" pattern="EEEE 'at' h:mm a"/>`	`Friday at 9:04 PM`

10.3 *Reading numbers with* `<fmt:parseNumber>`

So far in this chapter, we've only discussed outputting data—formatting dates and numbers and then (usually) printing them or (less frequently) saving them to scoped variables. JSTL has two tags that help you handle input: `<fmt:parseNumber>` to help you read numbers, and `<fmt:parseDate>` to help you read dates.

In many cases, you don't need these tags. As you saw in chapter 4, JSTL lets you treat simple numbers as strings, and vice versa. For example, if the request parameter named boundary equals the number 50 because that's what the user entered in an HTML form, we can say

```
<c:forEach … end="${param.boundary}">
```

and the `<c:forEach>` tag will know to stop its iteration after the fifty-first element.

The `<fmt:parseNumber>` tag is specifically for cases in which you need to *parse*—or interpret—more complicated numbers. If the user enters 50,000 (including the comma), or if you read values that contain commas or spaces from an XML file or database, you can't treat these values as numbers; you need to parse them first.

Table 10.7 lists the attributes that `<fmt:parseNumber>` accepts.

Table 10.7   `<fmt:parseNumber>` tag attributes

Attribute	Description	Required	Default
`value`	The string to parse into a number	No	*Body*
`type`	How to parse the number (`number`, `currency`, or `percent`)	No	`number`

Table 10.7 `<fmt:parseNumber>` tag attributes *(continued)*

Attribute	Description	Required	Default
`integerOnly`	Whether to discard any fractional digits	No	`false`
`pattern`	More detailed information about how to parse the number	No	*None*
`parseLocale`	Locale to use instead of default	No	*See section 10.3.2*
`var`	Variable to expose the parsed number (as a number)	No	*None*
`scope`	Scope in which to expose the parsed number	No	`page`

10.3.1 *Why you might want to parse numbers*

Most of your pages probably won't have to parse numbers. The `<fmt:formatNumber>` tag is useful only if you need to retrieve a numeric value from a string. You might want to do this for a few reasons:

- You need to save a numeric value to a database using `<sql:update>` and `<sql:param>`, but all you have is a string like `500 000,00`.
- You want to *normalize* the display of numbers—that is, make sure they all appear similarly. But some of your numbers might come from users or different databases, and appear in different forms. Before you can feed a number to `<fmt:formatNumber>`, you normally need to parse it with `<fmt:parseNumber>`.
- Sometimes (although rarely) you have a string like `500,000` but need a number for tags like `<c:forEach>` (the `begin`, `end`, and `step` attributes), `<sql:query>` (the `startRow` or `maxRows` attribute), and so on.
- You want to perform simple math on a number the user entered (or one you retrieved from a database, XML file, or elsewhere). For instance, suppose you're writing an application that assists the user with taxes, and you want to calculate 27.5% of the user's income.

10.3.2 *How <fmt:parseNumber> works by default*

The `<fmt:parseNumber>` tag receives the number it's supposed to parse either by its `value` attribute or from its body. It then parses this number. The resulting numeric value is either stored to the scoped variable indicated by `var` (and `scope`) or printed out to the page in its simple, unlocalized form—for instance, `500000.01`—with no commas, grouping, extra spaces, or other fancy formatting.

Recall from section 10.1.1 that every locale has a default way to print numbers. The `<fmt:parseNumber>` tag determines, by default, the browser's locale, and it uses this locale's mechanism to parse a number. This is useful if you're accepting input from the user. For instance, if you ask an English-speaking user for his favorite number, he might type `500,000.01`. (Admittedly, this would be a strange number to pick as a favorite, but it's a better example than 7.) A Frenchwoman might, instead, enter `500 000,01`. The `<fmt:parseNumber>` tag assumes by default that users will enter values that are formatted using the customs of their own locales.

For instance, consider the following HTML form:

```
<form method="post" action="parseNumber.jsp">
  What's your favorite number?
  <input type="text" name="favorite" size="10" />
  <input type="submit" value="Enter"/>
</form>
```

Listing 10.1 shows a page that handles this form.

Listing 10.1   parseNumber.jsp: a page that parses the user's number

```
<%@ taglib prefix="c" uri="http://java.sun.com/jstl/core" %>
<%@ taglib prefix="fmt" uri="http://java.sun.com/jstl/fmt" %>

<p>You entered "<c:out value="${param.favorite}"/>". </p>

<fmt:parseNumber var="fav" value="${param.favorite}"/>

<p>As far as I can tell, this corresponds to the
number <c:out value="${fav}"/>.</p>

<p>If you multiply this number by 2 and add 1, you get
<c:out value="${fav * 2 + 1}"/>. I like that number
better.</p>
```
◁── **Parses number and creates fav variable**

Now, suppose my browser is configured for English and I enter `500,000` in the input box. This page correctly parses the user's number, and it displays the output shown in figure 10.2.

If I were instead French and entered `500 000`, this page would not work correctly, by default, unless my browser's locale were set to French. If it were, then parseNumber.jsp from listing 10.1 would adapt to French automatically. This is the key thing to realize about JSTL's parsing and formatting support: by default, pages automatically adapt to the correct locale, and you can forget about the matter and focus on more important things.

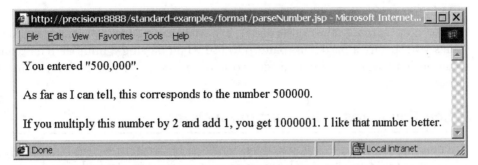

Figure 10.2 Sample output for the page shown in listing 10.1, when the user enters the number "500,000" as the request parameter `favorite`. This output assumes an English locale—or at least one that treats "500,000" as the number 500000.

10.3.3 Changing <fmt:parseNumber>'s parsing rules

The remaining attributes for `<fmt:parseNumber>` let you change the rules by which the number from the `value` attribute (or the tag's body) will be parsed.

Throwing away fractions

The `integerOnly` attribute is useful if you care only about the integer part of a number and you want to throw away its fractional part. Use this attribute if you want to be sure you get an integer back—for instance, because your database, or a tag attribute, accepts only integers. For example, the following tag stores the number 50.05:

```
<fmt:parseNumber
  var="number"
  value="50.05"/>
```

But this one stores the number 50:

```
<fmt:parseNumber
  var="number"
  value="50.05"
  integerOnly="true"/>
```

Changing the locale

Sometimes, you read numbers not from a user but from a database or imported XML file. If the data was imported from another country (would this involve a customs check?), you might know beforehand the locale that was used to format the numbers. In such a case, you don't care about the user's browser's preferred locale; you instead want to parse a number using a specific locale.

The `parseLocale` attribute handles this need. The attribute accepts the name of a specific locale to use. In section 10.6, we'll describe the values this attribute can take.

Using specific patterns

Like `<fmt:formatNumber>`, the `<fmt:parseNumber>` tag has a `pattern` attribute that lets you specify a particular pattern to use when parsing a number. The details of numeric patterns are beyond the scope of this book; see section 10.1.7 for more information.

10.4 Reading dates with `<fmt:parseDate>`

The `<fmt:parseDate>` tag is to dates what `<fmt:parseNumber>` is to numbers. You can use `<fmt:parseDate>` when you need to read a string from the user, a database, or an XML file and treat it as a date, using locale-specific rules.

Table 10.8 shows the attributes for `<fmt:parseDate>`.

Table 10.8 `<fmt:parseDate>` tag attributes

Attribute	Description	Required	Default
`value`	The date string to parse	No	*Body*
`type`	How to parse the date (`time`, `date`, or `both`)	No	`date`
`dateStyle`	How detailed a date to expect to parse	No	`default`
`timeStyle`	How detailed a time to expect to parse	No	`default`
`pattern`	Specific pattern to use when parsing a date	No	*None*
`parseLocale`	Locale to use instead of the default	No	*See section 10.3.2*
`timeZone`	Time zone to apply to the parsed date	No	*See section 10.5*
`var`	Variable to expose the parsed date (as a number)	No	*None*
`scope`	Scope in which to expose the parsed date	No	`page`

The `<fmt:parseDate>` tag is similar to `<fmt:parseNumber>`, but it parses and stores dates instead of numbers. The `value`, `var`, `scope`, and `parseLocale` attributes work exactly like they do in `<fmt:parseNumber>`, so we don't need to discuss them here in detail. Instead, we'll focus on the differences between the two tags.

We'll also wait until section 10.5 to cover the `timeZone` attribute.

10.4.1 How `<fmt:parseDate>` parses dates by default

The `<fmt:parseDate>` tag, like the other formatting and parsing tags, is sensitive to the browser's locale by default. Without any attributes other than `value`, it parses a date the same way that `<fmt:formatDate>` formats a date. The parsing rules are fairly strict. Thus, the tag

```
<fmt:parseDate value="Aug 24, 1981"/>
```

would work for the English locale, but

```
<fmt:parseDate value="Aug 24 1981"/>
```

would lead to an error because it lacks a comma. This behavior makes the default case almost useless for processing input from users, because it's usually inappropriate to force users to be so specific in the values they enter. However, this use of `<fmt:parseDate>` is appropriate in a few situations:

- It's useful if you know you're getting data that was printed with `<fmt:formatDate>`.

- You can also use this simple form of `<fmt:parseDate>` if you're generating a string based on individual fields of user input—for instance, a pull-down menu for month, followed by another one for date, and so on. See chapter 11 for an example of this technique.

If given a `var` attribute, `<fmt:parseDate>` stores a scoped variable that holds a date and time (the time is always midnight in this simple case). Otherwise, it prints the date in a somewhat ugly, unlocalized format:

```
Sat Aug 24 00:00:00 EDT 2002
```

You therefore almost always want to use a `var` attribute with `<fmt:parseDate>` (except, perhaps, if you're just testing your page).

10.4.2 Changing how <fmt:parseDate> parses dates

The `<fmt:parseDate>` tag comes with four attributes that let you change how it parses dates. The first is simple: you can use the `type` attribute to let the tag parse times as well as dates. Just as with `<fmt:formatDate>`, the `type` attribute has three possible values: `date`, `time`, and `both`; `date` is the default. If you specify `type="time"`, then `<fmt:parseDate>` tries to read and parse a time in the locale's default representation (for example, `"07:45:02 PM"`). For `type="both"`, the tag expects a default date/time combination, like

```
Aug 24, 2002 08:52:00 PM
```

The `type` attribute is somewhat limited when used alone. It can be useful when used in conjunction with two more powerful attributes, `timeStyle` and `dateStyle`. They let the `<fmt:parseDate>` tag accept the sorts of values shown in table 10.5, earlier in this chapter.

Using patterns

The `<fmt:parseDate>` tag has a `pattern` attribute, which is typically the most useful way to use the tag. The `pattern` attribute accepts a date pattern—of the same syntax you saw in section 10.2.4—and parses the date according to this pattern. For instance, if you read dates from XML files you import, you might encounter the ISO 8601 date format. Dates that follow this format might look like this:

YYYYMMDDTHHMMSS

The T character separates the date (YYYY = year, MM = month, DD = day) from the time (HH = hour, MM = minute, SS = second). As an example of this format, the date August 24, 2002 at 8:52 p.m. would be written as follows:

20020824T205200

Note that 24-hour military time typically is used, as is a four-digit year.

Suppose we've retrieved a date in this format from an XML file and stored it in the scoped variable ISOdate. We could use the following tag to parse this date:

```
<fmt:parseDate
  value="${ISOdate}"
  pattern="yyyyMMdd'T'HHmmss" />
```

As you can see, using `pattern` with `<fmt:parseDate>` is much more flexible than the other, simpler alternatives.

10.5 Overriding time zones with <fmt:timeZone> and <fmt:setTimeZone>

Saying "May 20th at 7 in the morning" doesn't, by itself, indicate a specific point in time; if you want to be complete, you need to add a time zone. In normal daily conversations, we often leave out time zones because figuring out the correct one is easy. But time zones are still there, lurking beneath the surface.

Conversely, when a scoped variable points to a date, this date is somewhat abstract; no time zone is associated with it. It represents a particular point in time, which might equally well be described as 9:00 p.m. Eastern time, 8:00 p.m. Central time, or 1:00 a.m. Greenwich Mean Time.

Time zones become important when you want to print out a description of this moment in time—that is, when you format dates with `<fmt:formatDate>`. Should the `<fmt:formatDate>` tag display 9:00 p.m. for Eastern Standard Time (EST), 8:00 p.m. for Central Standard Time (CST), 1:00 a.m. for Greenwich Mean Time (GMT), or any of the other equally good alternatives?

Similarly, time zones are important when you parse dates and times with
`<fmt:parseDate>`. If the number you're parsing contains `6:00 AM`, does this mean
6:00 a.m. in EST, CST, GMT, or some other time zone?

10.5.1 *How JSTL figures out time zones by default*

By default, the `<fmt:formatDate>` and `<fmt:parseDate>` tags do their best to figure
out a sensible time zone. If your JSP pages interact with back-end Java code, this
code can manage time zones for you so that you don't have to worry about them.
(This approach might be appropriate if time zones involve calculations or data
retrieval that's beyond the scope of your JSP pages.) If you're a Java programmer,
chapter 14 shows you how to manage time zones from within Java code.

If no back-end Java code manages time zones, then your pages will use the time
zone of your JSP container. This is usually the time zone of the machine that runs
the container, and is therefore also usually the time zone you're in. This time zone
might be appropriate for many applications, but if your users live throughout the
country or the world, you might need to manage time zones yourself. Even if your
application's back-end Java code does manage time zones for you—a fact you can
determine by asking the back-end Java programmers who support your application—you might want to override these time zones in some cases.

10.5.2 *Setting time zones for individual tags*

JSTL gives you three ways to set times zones from within your JSTL pages. First,
and simplest, the `<fmt:formatDate>` and `<fmt:parseDate>` tags both accept a time-
Zone attribute. This attribute lets you set a specific time zone for an individual tag.

The `timeZone` attribute accepts a number of different kinds of identifiers for
time zones. The easiest ones to use are the common abbreviations for North Amer-
ican time zones: EST for Eastern Time, CST for Central Time, MST for Mountain
Time, and PST for Pacific Time. Note that you use the standard-time abbreviation
(E*ST*, P*ST*, and so on), and not the daylight-savings abbreviations (such as E*DT* and
P*DT*). When you specify time zones this way, JSTL automatically takes care of daylight-savings time changes for you.[2]

As an example of time zones in action, consider the following tags and their output:

---

[2] The problem with this syntax is that not every worldwide time zone has an accepted abbreviation (and some abbreviations clash, which can be confusing). Therefore, JSTL supports standard
Java time-zone identifiers, which are based on prominent cities in each time zone. See the Javadoc page for Java's java.util.TimeZone class, which is accessible at http://java.sun.com/j2se/
1.4/docs/api/java/util/TimeZone.html, for more information on the time-zone identifiers supported by JSTL.

Tag	Output

`<fmt:formatDate`
`    value="${d}"`
`    timeZone="EST"`
`    type="time"/>`
	3:04:45 AM

`<fmt:formatDate`
`    value="${d}"`
`    timeZone="CST"`
`    type="time"/>`
	2:04:45 AM

`<fmt:formatDate`
`    value="${d}"`
`    timeZone="MST"`
`    type="time"/>`
	1:04:45 AM

`<fmt:formatDate`
`    value="${d}"`
`    timeZone="PST"`
`    type="time"/>`
	12:04:45 AM

10.5.3 Long-lasting changes with <fmt:setTimeZone>

If you find yourself using the `timeZone` attribute to set the same time zone repeatedly, you can save yourself a little work by using the `<fmt:setTimeZone>` tag. Instead of operating on a tag-by-tag basis, `<fmt:setTimeZone>` lets you set a time zone that is applied repeatedly—for a page or any other scope.

The `<fmt:setTimeZone>` tag takes three attributes, which are listed in table 10.9.

Table 10.9   `<fmt:setTimeZone>` tag attributes

Attribute	Description	Required	Default
`value`	Identifier of the time zone to set	Yes	*None*
`var`	Variable to expose the time zone	No	*None*
`scope`	Scope in which to expose the time zone	No	`page`

You must always specify the `value` attribute, which takes the same sorts of time zone identifiers described in section 10.5.2.

If you use `<fmt:setTimeZone>` without a `var` attribute, then it overrides the default time zone for the given `scope`—or the current page, if no `scope` is specified. For instance, the following tag sets Eastern Standard Time to be the default time zone for your entire application:

```
<fmt:setTimeZone value="EST" scope="application"/>
```

Similarly, this tag sets it for the session:

```
<fmt:setTimeZone value="EST" scope="session"/>
```

This technique is useful if you want to retrieve a time zone for the user from a database and apply it to the user's entire session.

Note that `<fmt:setTimeZone>` just sets a new default time zone; it doesn't mandate one. You can still override the new time zone for individual `<fmt:formatDate>` and `<fmt:parseDate>` tags using their `timeZone` attributes.

You can also use `<fmt:setTimeZone>` to expose a time zone as a scoped variable whose name you choose with `var` (and whose scope you optionally choose with `scope`). This approach is similar to saving the string identifier for a time zone (such as `"EST"`), but it's a little more efficient. This pattern might be useful if you wanted to retrieve a time zone from an HTML form or a database and apply it to particular `<fmt:formatDate>` and `<fmt:parseDate>` tags in your pages. For instance:

```
<fmt:setTimeZone
  value="${param.timezone}"
  var="userTimeZone"
  scope="session"/>
<fmt:parseDate value="${d}" timeZone="${sessionScope.userTimezone}">
```

This example assumes `${param.timezone}` equals something like EST or PST.

By and large, using `var` with `<fmt:setTimeZone>` is inconvenient, and you probably won't need to do so very often.

10.5.4 *Temporary changes with* `<fmt:timeZone>`

JSTL also provides a `<fmt:timeZone>` tag that you can use as a parent tag to wrap some parts of your pages. Doing so is useful when you have a particular set of tags that should all use the same time zone, but you don't want to override your page's default time zone. Table 10.10 shows `<fmt:timeZone>`'s single attribute.

Table 10.10   `<fmt:timeZone>` tag attribute

Attribute	Description	Required	Default
value	The identifier for the time zone to set	Yes	None

Figure 10.3 demonstrates `<fmt:timeZone>`'s behavior.

As before, you can override individual `<fmt:formatDate>` and `<fmt:parseDate>` tags' time zones by specifying a `timeZone` attribute manually for each tag whose zone you want to override.

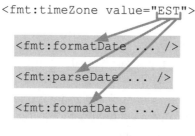

```
<fmt:timeZone value="EST">

    <fmt:formatDate ... />

    <fmt:parseDate ... />

    <fmt:formatDate ... />

</fmt:timeZone>
```

Figure 10.3
When the `<fmt:timeZone>` tag surrounds one or more `<fmt:formatDate>` or `<fmt:parseDate>` tags, the time zone from `<fmt:timeZone>` automatically applies to each of these child tags.

10.6 *Overriding locales with* `<fmt:setLocale>`

Throughout this chapter, I've mentioned that tags use the user's web browser's preferred locale by default. But JSTL page authors and back-end Java programmers can also influence the locale used for the `<fmt:format...>` and `<fmt:parse...>` tags. Doing so can be useful if you want to give users a choice of locale instead of letting the browser automatically speak for them.

Just as with time zones, back-end programmers have control over what locales are used; they can explicitly choose to override the browser's locale. See chapter 14 for information (geared to programmers) about how to do this.

JSTL also lets you control the locale using a tag: `<fmt:setLocale>`. Table 10.11 lists this tag's attributes.

Table 10.11 `<fmt:setTimeZone>` tag attributes

Attribute	Description	Required	Default
value	Name of a locale to use (see section 10.6.1)	Yes	*None*
variant	Specific variety of the chosen local to use (see section 10.6.1)	No	*None*
scope	Scope for which to override the locale	No	page

As table 10.11 shows, `value` is always required. Using `value`, you can specify the name of a locale. This locale will become the new default for the scope identified by the `scope` attribute—or for the current page by default, if you don't specify a `scope` attribute. (The `variant` attribute is beyond the scope of this book.)

10.6.1 *How to identify locales*

The `value` attribute for `<fmt:setLocale>` lets you specify the name for a new default locale. To specify a locale, you need at least one piece of information: a language, such as English, French, or Spanish. You can also qualify this language by a country: for instance, the United States has different conventions than England even though residents of both countries speak English; and Canada and France differ on some formatting rules, even though both countries' residents speak French. In general, currency formatting varies (sensibly) more by country than by language.

The name for a locale has two pieces: a language code and a country code. The language code is lowercase, and the country code is uppercase. They are separated by a hyphen (-) or an underscore (_). You can find the full list of language codes at http://www-old.ics.uci.edu/pub/ietf/http/related/iso639.txt, and a full list of country codes at http://userpage.chemie.fu-berlin.de/diverse/doc/ISO_3166.html. Table 10.12 shows some commonly useful locale codes.

Table 10.12 The `<fmt:setLocale>` tag's `value` attribute, as well as the `parseLocale` attribute in `<fmt:parseNumber>` and `<fmt:parseDate>`, let you specify a specific locale to use. These attributes accept locale codes, which contain a lowercase language code and, optionally, an uppercase country code.

Locale code	Locale description
en	English
fr	French
es	Spanish
de	German
en_US	English (United States)
en_CA	English (Canada)
fr_CA	French (Canada)
fr_FR	French (France)
de_CH	German (Switzerland)
es_ES	Spanish (Spain)
es_CL	Spanish (Chile)

As an example of how the `<fmt:setLocale>` tag works, consider the following tags and their corresponding output, if they occur on a page in order:

Tag	Output	Description of behavior
`<fmt:formatDate value="${d}"/>`	`Mar 17, 2002`	Prints the current date in the default locale
`<fmt:setLocale value="es"/>`		Changes the locale to Spanish
`<fmt:formatDate value="${d}"/>`	`17-mar-2002`	Prints the current date in the Spanish locale
`<fmt:setLocale value="fr"/>`		Changes the locale to French
`<fmt:formatDate value="${d}"/>`	`17 mars 2002`	Prints the current date in the French locale
`<fmt:setLocale value="fr_CA"/>`		Changes the locale to French (Canada)
`<fmt:formatDate value="${d}"/>`	`2002-03-17`	Prints the current date in the French Canadian locale

A tag like the following changes the default locale for the current user's whole session:

```
<fmt:setLocale value="fr" scope="session"/>
```

Of course, the `value` attribute can accept an expression, so we can compute and set a locale dynamically:

```
<fmt:setLocale value="${param.userLocale}" scope="session"/>
```

This tag might be appropriate if we have a form with a `userLocale` parameter that lets the user choose a locale. For instance:

```
What language do you speak?
<select name="userLocale">
  <option value="en">English</option>
  <option value="es">Spanish</option>
  . . .
</select>
```

This selection box lets the user choose a language, which we can use as input to the `<fmt:setLocale>` tag.

10.6.2 *The parseLocale attribute for <fmt:parseNumber> and <fmt:parseDate>*

The `<fmt:parseNumber>` and `<fmt:parseDate>` tags let you override the default locale with one for the tag itself. Doing so is useful if you know that a number or date you need to parse was previously formatted using a specific locale.

You can override the default locale by using these tags' `parseLocale` attribute. This attribute takes the same kind of locale codes that we discussed in section 10.6.1.

10.7 *Internationalizing text messages with `<fmt:message>`, `<fmt:param>`, `<fmt:bundle>`, and `<fmt:setBundle>`*

So far, we've discussed how you can make sure your pages adapt to different locales and formatting styles for numbers and dates. Of course, the world (thankfully) contains more than just numbers and dates; your pages will also need to display text. If your application is truly going to serve users in multiple locales, you'll need to make sure your page can figure out what language to use when printing its text.

Except on *Star Trek*, this translation doesn't come for free; you can't flip a switch and have a JSP container automatically translate your pages to French or German. Java applications, however, support a standard mechanism for plugging in special *resource bundles* that contain translated text. A resource bundle is essentially a file that maps a generic *key*, such as `WelcomeMessage`, to a single translated value, like `Hi there!` A different resource bundle might map `WelcomeMessage` to `Bonjour!` or `Wassup?` Resource bundles come in *families*: groups of different, locale-specific values for the same set of keys.

Creating resource bundles and internationalizing applications from scratch are beyond this book's scope. Our goal here is to briefly discuss JSTL's support for using existing message bundles that are already set up for your application. If you want more information on internationalizing Java applications, see appendix D for references.

10.7.1 *Using `<fmt:message>`*

The `<fmt:message>` tag accepts a key and looks up its translated value in a resource bundle. It takes the attributes listed in table 10.13.

Table 10.13   `<fmt:message>` tag attributes

Attribute	Description	Required	Default
key	Internationalized key to use	No	*Body*
bundle	Family of resource bundles to use	No	*See section 10.7.2*
var	Variable to expose the localized message	No	*None*
scope	Scope in which to expose the localized message	No	page

If you don't use the `key` attribute, the `<fmt:message>` tag looks for a key in its body. A key is, again, something like `WelcomeMessage`. The exact key to use depends on the resource bundles you're using; typically, if your application has been internationalized, you'll be given a list of appropriate keys.

By default, `<fmt:message>` prints out its localized message—the translated message it finds for the value of the `key` attribute. If `var` (and, optionally, `scope`) is specified, the localized message is saved to a scoped variable instead.

Also by default, `<fmt:message>` uses a family of bundles prepared automatically by back-end Java code. The bundles all have the same keys, but they have different values depending on locales. For instance, the following tag will print out the value of the `WelcomeMessage` key in the bundle that matches the current locale:

```
<fmt:message key="WelcomeMessage"/>
```

It therefore might print out `Hello` or `Bonjour`, depending on how the user's browser is configured or on the locale we previously set with `<fmt:setLocale>` (discussed in section 10.6).

Message parameters

Some messages have *parameters*, which work a little like the SQL parameters we discussed in chapter 9. A message might have a placeholder for you to insert the user's name. This feature is important because different languages or dialects might require the user's name (and other parameters) to appear in different places within a localized message. Whoever provides you with message keys should let you know if they need parameters. To specify a parameter, you can use the `<fmt:param>` tag, which takes a single attribute described in table 10.14.

Table 10.14 `<fmt:param>` tag attribute

Attribute	Description	Required	Default
value	Parameter to add	No	*Body*

If you don't specify a `value` attribute, you can insert the value into the tag's body. Doing so is useful if the parameter comes from other tags.

Here's how you'd add the parameter represented by `${user.name}` to a message:

```
<fmt:message key="WelcomeMessage">
  <fmt:param value="${user.name}"/>
</fmt:message>
```

10.7.2 *Loading a bundle family with <fmt:bundle> and <fmt:setBundle>*

If no back-end Java code manages message bundles for your pages, or if you want to override the bundle, you can use the `<fmt:bundle>` and `<fmt:setBundle>` tags.

Table 10.15 lists the attributes for `<fmt:bundle>`.

Table 10.15   `<fmt:bundle>` tag attributes

Attribute	Description	Required	Default
basename	Name of the resource-bundle family to use	Yes	*None*
prefix	String to prepend to each key (for long key names)	No	*None*

Table 10.16 lists the attributes for `<fmt:setBundle>`.

Table 10.16   `<fmt:setBundle>` tag attributes

Attribute	Description	Required	Default
basename	Name of the resource-bundle family to use	Yes	*None*
var	Variable to expose the bundle	No	*None*
scope	Scope in which to expose the bundle	No	page

The difference between `<fmt:bundle>` and `<fmt:setBundle>` is the same as the difference between `<fmt:timeZone>` and `<fmt:setTimeZone>`. The tags with *set* in their names change the defaults for an entire scope, whereas the tags without *set* apply only to their child tags.

JSTL's two bundle-related tags let you describe a group of related bundles using the `basename` attribute. You'll know the *base name* of a bundle if you've internationalized an application yourself; if you're using someone else's bundle, then whoever internationalized the application should tell you the base name.

The `<fmt:bundle>` tag changes the bundle for all the `<fmt:message>` tags in its body. For instance:

```
<fmt:bundle basename="my.bundle">
  <fmt:message key="my.key.Welcome"/>
  <fmt:message key="my.key.Error"/>
</fmt:bundle>
```

When you use the `<fmt:bundle>` tag like this, you can give it a `prefix` attribute. This attribute is a string that is added before every key in each `<fmt:message>` tag within `<fmt:bundle>`, thus saving you typing and making your pages more readable. For instance, this would be equivalent to the previous `<fmt:bundle>` tag:

```
<fmt:bundle basename="my.bundle" prefix="my.key.">
  <fmt:message key="Welcome"/>
  <fmt:message key="Error"/>
</fmt:bundle>
```

With `<fmt:setBundle>`, you cannot specify a `prefix`. Instead, `<fmt:setBundle>` lets you specify a `var` (and, optionally, `scope`) attribute to save the bundle that's created into a scoped variable. Then, you can point individual `<fmt:message>` tags at this bundle by using their `bundle` attribute (see table 10.13). In addition, you can use `<fmt:setBundle>` without specifying a `var` attribute. In this case, just like `<fmt:setLocale>` and `<fmt:setTimeZone>`, `<fmt:setBundle>` changes the default bundle for the given `scope`—or the current page, if you don't specify a `scope`.

10.8 Summary

JSTL's internationalization and formatting (`fmt`) tags help you input and output numbers and dates, and also help you target your page to users around the world. When using the `<fmt:...>` tags, keep the following things in mind:

- The `<fmt:formatNumber>` tag outputs numbers, whereas `<fmt:formatDate>` outputs dates. (You can use both tags to store a formatted value in a scoped variable.)

- The `<fmt:parseNumber>` tag converts strings to numbers, and the `<fmt:parseDate>` tag converts strings to dates. You can normally treat simple strings like `34` as numbers, but if the strings contain commas or other special formatting, you'll need to parse them.

- By default, the four tags just mentioned automatically sense the user's locale (loosely, language and country) by reading information from the user's web browser. You can set a new default locale with the `<fmt:setLocale>` tag.

- The two tags that manage dates are sensitive to time zones. You can set a new default time zone using the `<fmt:setTimeZone>` and `<fmt:timeZone>` tags.

- The date and number formatting and parsing tags aren't just useful for localization; they also help you handle general input and output of information. In particular, the `pattern` attribute of the date tag is useful for reading and printing different kinds of dates.

- The `<fmt:message>`, `<fmt:param>`, `<fmt:bundle>`, and `<fmt:setBundle>` tags help you localize the text messages in your application. See appendix D for references that will help you create message bundles and internationalize your application in general.

Part 3

JSTL in action

So far, we've looked at what JSTL is and how it works. You've seen a few examples of JSTL in action, but now we'll examine more closely how to handle practical tasks using JSTL. In chapter 11, we'll show how you can use JSTL to address some common but small-scale needs. In the chapters after that, we'll discuss more in-depth examples of web development with JSTL.

A minor warning is in order. In some cases, you won't be using JSTL as a stand-alone technology. You might use it with Jakarta Struts, for example, or with tag libraries developed specifically for your site. We can't cover all the technologies that JSTL might interact with in this book; therefore, although most of the material in part 3 is core, nuts-and-bolts stuff that you can use immediately, some of the examples push JSTL to its limits. This is intentional; I think the best way to learn a technology is by trying to use it creatively. So don't be surprised if some of the examples use JSTL for tasks that you might otherwise solve with a custom, local library or with Struts. The examples here aren't designed to demonstrate principles of web-application architecture; books like *Web Development with Java-Server Pages*[1] already address that topic quite well. Instead, my goal is to show you as many uses of JSTL as you could possibly want to see.

My hope is that these "stretches" will serve as a good reference as your knowledge of JSTL progresses. You just might find that JSTL can handle more than you'd expect!

---

[1] Duane Fields, Mark Kolb, and Shawn Bayern, 2nd ed. (Manning Publications, 2001).

Common tasks

This chapter covers...

- Reading check boxes from HTML forms
- Reading dates from HTML forms
- Handling errors
- Validating user input

Some tasks never go away. If I had a dime for every time I had to write a JSP page that signed up new users for a web application, I'd probably have more than $1.50 by now.

However, JSTL makes lots of common tasks easier. In this chapter, we look at how to use JSTL to address some common, specific issues like reading a date from a user, accepting `<input type="checkbox">` parameters, and handling errors. These are all practical, but somewhat isolated, examples.

They're meant to help you generalize about JSTL. For instance, if you ever need to read a date from a user of your web page, section 11.2 is a cookbook-like solution. But even if you don't need to read dates frequently, understanding the examples in section 11.2 will be useful to solidify your knowledge of the `<fmt:parseDate>` and `<fmt:formatDate>` tags. Similarly, the discussion of `paramValues` applies equally well to `headerValues` and other collections; `paramValues` is just more common and practical.

Before leaving this chapter, we get as far as a basic HTML-form handler that validates its input and prepares to register a new user. Chapters 12 and 13 show more complete, application-like examples.

11.1 *Handling checkbox parameters*

When we originally discussed JSTL's expression language in chapter 3, you saw how to use the expression language to handle HTML forms. For instance, an HTML form parameter from a tag like

```
<input type="text" name="username" />
```

shows up to your JSTL tags as the expression `${param.username}`.

In chapter 3, however, I mentioned that checkbox parameters are special because the same name can map to multiple values. Suppose we have an HTML form with the following tags:

```
<input type="checkbox" name="language" value="english" />
<input type="checkbox" name="language" value="spanish" />
<input type="checkbox" name="language" value="french" />
```

If the user checks all three boxes, then the `language` parameter will have three values: `english`, `spanish`, and `french`.

You can access a collection that contains all these values by using the expression `${paramValues.name}`, where *name* is the name of the parameter you're looking for. You can use the `<c:forEach>` tag to loop over the individual parameters in this collection and handle them one at a time.

Figure 11.1
A view of checkboxForm.html from
listing 11.1 in a web browser. Check
boxes typically show up as small boxes,
either empty or checked depending on
whether the user has selected them.
Check boxes differ from radio buttons
(see chapter 3) in that a user can
choose multiple check boxes with the
same name. For this reason, they're a
little harder to handle than text fields
or radio buttons.

11.1.1 *The HTML form*

Let's look at a soup-to-nuts example of how to handle checkbox parameters. Begin
with listing 11.1, which shows an HTML form with several check boxes. The goal of
this particular form is to let the user give feedback to a web site's customer-service
department. Figure 11.1 shows what this form might look like in a browser.

Listing 11.1   checkboxForm.html: a form with checkbox parameters

```
<form method="post" action="checkbox.jsp">
  <p>Please check adjectives you would
  use to describe this web site's
  customer service:</p>

  <p>Atrocious
  <input type="checkbox" name="feedback" value="atrocious"/></p>

  <p>Loathsome
  <input type="checkbox" name="feedback" value="loathsome"/></p>

  <p>Flagitious
  <input type="checkbox" name="feedback" value="flagitious"/></p>

  <p>Satisfactory
  <input type="checkbox" name="feedback" value="satisfactory"/></p>

  <p><input type="submit" value="Submit" /></p>
</form>
```

Note how all the checkbox parameters have the same value for the `name` attribute: `feedback`. Users can choose as many check boxes as they feel are appropriate, and the expression `${paramValues.feedback}` will contain a collection of all the parameters.

11.1.2 A simple checkbox handler

Listing 11.2 shows how we can use this expression to loop over all the `feedback` parameters, one at a time.

Listing 11.2   checkbox.jsp: a page to handle checkbox parameters

```
<%@ taglib prefix="c" uri="http://java.sun.com/jstl/core" %>

<c:choose>
 <c:when test="${not empty paramValues.feedback}">          ◁─┐ Decides if there are
  You described our customer service as                        any feedback params
  <ul>
  <c:forEach items="${paramValues.feedback}" var="adj">
    <li><c:out value="${adj}"/></li>
  </c:forEach>
  </ul>
 </c:when>
 <c:otherwise>
  You didn't choose any feedback checkboxes.
 </c:otherwise>
</c:choose>
```

As figure 11.2 shows, the checkbox.jsp page from listing 11.2 lists each adjective we've chosen in a bulleted list (`<ul>`). It does so by looping over `${paramValues.feedback}` with the `<c:forEach>` tag. The `<c:forEach>` tag exposes each element as a scoped variable named `adj`, which is printed out by a `<c:out>` tag.

Figure 11.2
The checkbox.jsp page figures out which check boxes the user has chosen and prints out the text corresponding to each. It does so with a `<c:forEach>` loop and a `<c:out>` tag.

Note how listing 11.2 prints a special message if the user didn't choose any of the check boxes. We do this by using a `<c:choose>` tag. The first condition—`<c:when>`—makes sure the user has chosen at least one checkbox. It does so using the expression

```
${not empty paramValues.feedback}
```

which is `true` if the user chose at least one `feedback` checkbox, and `false` otherwise.

I included this check to demonstrate a few things. Checks against nonexistent parameters will be useful to you later for form validation, so I wanted to show you a straightforward example of this technique. But in addition, I wanted to avoid looping over nonexistent values.

It's actually not a problem to loop over a collection that doesn't exist. If you say

```
<c:forEach items="${paramValues.nope}" var="item">
  Item!
</c:forEach>
```

and the expression `${paramValues.nope}` refers to a nonexistent parameter, then the `<c:forEach>` tag will simply do nothing. The rationale is that a missing collection is much like a collection with zero elements, so iterating zero times makes sense.

However, we don't rely on this behavior of `<c:forEach>` here, because we don't want to print the trappings of a list—the initial `<ul>` tag and the closing `</ul>` tag—when the list won't have any items. (HTML lists, like `<ul>` and `<ol>`, should all ideally have at least one `<li>` item.)

TIP   There are other ways to ensure that `<ul>` and `</ul>` print only when the list has at least one item, other than wrapping the whole `<c:forEach>` loop with a `<c:if>` or `<c:when>` tag. You can use `<c:forEach>`'s `varStatus` attribute to determine whether to print `<ul>` before the list's first item and `</ul>` after the list's last item, from inside `<c:forEach>`'s body. For example, this set of tags will print out `<ul>` and `</ul>` only if `<c:forEach>` iterates in the first place (if `${paramValues.feedback}` contains at least one parameter):

```
<c:forEach var="adj" items=${paramValues.feedback}" varStatus="s">
  <c:if test="${s.first}">
    <ul>
  </c:if>
  <li><c:out value="${adj}"/></li>
  <c:if test="${s.last}">
    </ul>
  </c:if>
</c:forEach>
```

If you've used languages like XSLT, you might be surprised at this block of JSP code. Your first thought might be, "Wait! The `<ul>` tag doesn't line up with the `</ul>` tag. The tags are crossed: `<ul>` starts, and then another tag—`<c:if>`—is closed." These crossed tags aren't a problem for JSP pages.

11.1.3 *Handling some check boxes specially*

The page from listing 11.2 treats all `feedback` parameters the same; it prints them all out in an undifferentiated list. But within the `<c:forEach>` tag, it's easy to use expressions that refer to the current item—`adj`, in this case—to make decisions about how to handle each item individually. For instance, you might decide to save some data in a database, or to display an otherwise hidden part of your page—but only if a user has chosen a particular checkbox.

Typically, you handle individual checkbox parameters by including a `<c:choose>` tag directly within your `<c:forEach>` tag. Doing so lets you match, and take particular actions for, an individual parameter.

Listing 11.3 shows a somewhat frivolous example, but it should drive home the point. Instead of printing out the customer feedback that has been received, the checkbox2.jsp page from listing 11.3 glorifies more positive remarks by printing them in big letters and diminishes negative comments by making them small. You can see the result in figure 11.3.

Figure 11.3
The checkbox2.jsp page from listing 11.3 looks at individual parameters' values before printing them out. In this case, the page glorifies positive remarks by printing them in large letters; it similarly diminishes negative feedback by making it smaller.

Listing 11.3   checkbox2.jsp: a more interesting checkbox handler

```
<%@ taglib prefix="c" uri="http://java.sun.com/jstl/core" %>

<c:choose>
 <c:when test="${not empty paramValues.feedback}">
```

```
You described our customer service as
<ul>
<c:forEach items="${paramValues.feedback}" var="adj">
  <c:choose>
    <c:when test="${adj == 'satisfactory'}">
        <font size="+2">
    </c:when>
    <c:otherwise>
        <font size="-2">
    </c:otherwise>
  </c:choose>
  <li><c:out value="${adj}"/></li>
  </font>
</c:forEach>
</c:when>
<c:otherwise>
  You didn't choose any feedback checkboxes.
</c:otherwise>
</c:choose>
```

◁── **Checks to see if the current parameter equals a specific word**

Again, this listing's demonstration is somewhat silly, but it demonstrates an important technique: using a `<c:choose>` tag directly below a `<c:forEach>` tag in order to take special action depending on the parameter's value. Instead of the trivial

```
<font size="+2">
```

it's easy to see how you could do something more useful, like

```
<sql:update>
  UPDATE feedback SET satisfactory = satisfactory + 1
</sql:update>
```

This code would update a database when the page was loaded, but only if the box for `satisfactory` customer service had been checked.

11.2 Accepting dates

Although HTML forms are flexible, they don't do a lot of user-interface work for you. HTML lets you choose from a few basic types of input fields—text boxes, selection boxes, radio buttons, and so on—but it doesn't make it easy to accept special kinds of formatted input from the user. For instance, if you need your user to enter a date or time, HTML doesn't give you any tools to handle this input automatically. Instead, you have to construct and interpret individual form fields.

Using JSTL, it's easy to write an HTML form that asks the user for a date or time. Of course, you could always prompt the user for a date by displaying a text box and asking them to type one in. You could then parse the date with the `<fmt:`

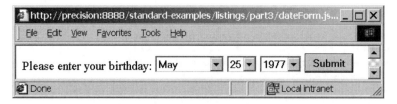

Figure 11.4   A convenient interface for entering a date. Users might appreciate this structured interface more than a simple text box that lets them type in a date—or lets them enter arbitrary text that might not be a date, which would require an irritating extra step for validating the input.

parseDate> tag discussed in chapter 10. But most users would think that such a generic interface is unfriendly. The whole point of <select> boxes and radio buttons is to guide the user toward sensible input, and this guidance is particularly useful when users have to enter structured information like dates. For instance, most users would find the interface shown in figure 11.4 convenient for entering a date. It uses three <select> boxes for the month, day, and year. In contrast with a free-text entry box, any user who uses this form is guaranteed to enter a structurally valid date. (Whether it's the right date is still, of course, up to the user.)

11.2.1   *The HTML form*

Listing 11.4 shows a JSP page that we could use to generate the form from figure 11.4.

Listing 11.4   dateForm.jsp: a JSP page that lets the user enter a date

```
<%@ taglib prefix="c" uri="http://java.sun.com/jstl/core" %>

<form method="post" action="dateHandler.jsp">

   Please enter your birthday:

   <select name="month">
     <option value="Jan">January</option>
     <option value="Feb">February</option>
     <option value="Mar">March</option>
     <option value="Apr">April</option>
     <option value="May">May</option>
     <option value="Jun">June</option>
     <option value="Jul">July</option>
     <option value="Aug">August</option>
     <option value="Sep">September</option>
     <option value="Oct">October</option>
     <option value="Nov">November</option>
     <option value="Dec">December</option>
   </select>
```

❶ Simple, static form field

```
<select name="day">
  <c:forEach begin="1" end="31" var="day">
    <option><c:out value="${day}"/></option>
  </c:forEach>
</select>

<select name="year">
  <c:forEach begin="1930" end="2003" var="year">
    <option><c:out value="${year}"/></option>
  </c:forEach>
</select>

<input type="submit" value="Submit" />

</form>
```

❷ **Dynamically generated fields**

Note that although listing 11.4 generates a simple HTML input form, it's not a static HTML page. JSTL tags, of course, aren't limited to pages that handle forms; as you'll see in a moment, they can be useful to produce forms, too.

❶ The page starts with a simple static form field. This month field lets the user choose a month. Note how we map each month's full name (which we want the user to see) into an abbreviation (which is more convenient for us later).

❷ After this simple month field are two fields that we produce dynamically: day and year. These fields are unchanging lists of numbers, so we could write a static HTML page to produce them. However, when we're listing numbers like 1 to 31—and 1930 to 2003—it's substantially more convenient to produce these lists dynamically. The end result is the same as if we manually wrote out each <option> field, but we've avoided some busy-work.

Of course, you can include fields like these three—month, date, and year—in a form that lets the user enter other information. For now, we're focusing just on a single field because it demonstrates a worthwhile technique.

11.2.2 *Handling the form and reading the date*

Now that we've produced a form, let's look at how to retrieve the information users enter into the form. Note that in the dateForm.jsp page from listing 11.4, the form posts to a page called dateHandler.jsp. Listing 11.5 shows this page.

> **Listing 11.5   dateHandler.jsp: a page that reads a date from dateForm.jsp**

```
<%@ taglib prefix="c" uri="http://java.sun.com/jstl/core" %>
<%@ taglib prefix="fmt" uri="http://java.sun.com/jstl/fmt" %>

<fmt:parseDate
  var="date"
  parseLocale="en_US"
  value="${param.month} ${param.day}, ${param.year}"/>
```

❶ **Parses the date from the form**

```
You were born
<fmt:formatDate
  value="${date}"
  dateStyle="full"/>.
```
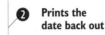 **❷ Prints the
date back out**

This page is deceptively simple. Let's look more closely at what's going on.

❶ The core of the page's function lies in the `<fmt:parseDate>` tag. Our strategy for handling the date the user entered is simple: because the date comes in three separate pieces—month, day, and year—we must combine them into a single string before parsing them. We perform this aggregation inside the `<fmt:parseDate>`'s value attribute, using three different expressions:

```
value="${param.month} ${param.day}, ${param.year}"
```

This expression causes the `month` parameter to be printed first, followed by a space, then the `day` parameter, then a comma, a space, and, finally, the `year` parameter. The result is a formatted string like `"May 25, 1997"` or `"Aug 24, 1981"`. As you might remember from chapter 10, such strings match the familiar U.S. English locale exactly. (Remember how, in dateForm.jsp, we were careful to map each month's name to an abbreviated value in English? This is why.) To force JSTL to parse this date using the U.S. English locale's rules, rather than the browser's current locale or one that the application was configured to use, we set the `<fmt:parseDate>` tag's `parseLocale` attribute equal to `"en_US"`. This way, the tag will parse the date correctly and save it in the scoped variable `date`, which we set using the `var` attribute.

❷ Now, with the user's chosen date saved in the `date` variable, we print out a full representation of it using the `<fmt:formatDate>` tag. (See figure 11.5.) Just to prove that we really parsed the date—and we aren't just spitting back some text the user sent us—we use the `dateStyle="full"` attribute, which causes the tag to print the date in its entirety, including weekday. Note that the system figured out the weekday

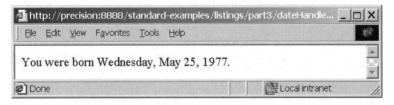

Figure 11.5   We parsed the user's date by printing the different form fields in a single, easy-to-parse format. Once we've done that, it's easy to treat the date as a date—which lets us compute information like the date's weekday, which the user never entered manually.

automatically, based on the date; the user never entered it. This is something we get for free when handling dates in JSTL.

Thus, our parsing strategy was to take all of the users' input and assemble it into an easy-to-parse string. From there, parsing with `<fmt:parseDate>` was straightforward, and printing the date with `<fmt:formatDate>` was simple.

Of course, we could do things with this date other than just printing it. We could save it to a database with tags like this:

```
<sql:update>
  UPDATE user SET birthdate=?
  <sql:param value="${date}"/>
</sql:update>
```

Or we could use the date in a custom tag. Because we parsed it, it's now a full-fledged date variable, not simply a collection of text.

11.3 *Handling errors*

Just as good automobile drivers can still have accidents, well-designed JSP pages can still run into errors or unexpected situations. Users might enter bizarre input, or a URL from which your page imports information might be unavailable. Any public, important page needs to take into account the possibility of errors. In some cases, it's enough to print a kind message to the user: "Something went wrong. Please try again, or call 203-432-6687 for assistance." In other cases, you might be able to recover automatically, without bothering the user. As an example, imagine that your page uses the `<c:import>` tag to fetch and display the weather in the upper-right corner of the browser's window. If the weather's URL was unavailable (perhaps as a result of a thunderstorm that brought down some power lines), you could simply print "Online weather unavailable; go look outside", or you could automatically switch to a different URL. The point is, you don't have to interrupt the entire page for an error that affects only a small piece of it.

When you use JSTL tags, there are basically three things you can do with errors:

- Avoid thinking about them. When you do this, any error that your page encounters causes the page to fail to load, usually with the JSP container providing information about the error in the page's place. This approach is great while you're debugging your pages, but it usually looks unprofessional to users.

- Use the `<c:catch>` tag to handle and even recover from errors within the same page. Doing so gives you flexibility, but it can clutter your pages, and it might not be appropriate if an error is meaningful and shouldn't be discarded.

- Use a facility that JSP gives you known as an *error page* (often written `errorPage`). A JSP `errorPage` is a page you can design and set up to handle your errors from multiple pages. The advantage of such a page is that it lets you easily apply the same behavior to a group of pages; simply point all of them at the same error page, and then figure out what to do in that page. It's an ideal place to say, "Something went wrong. Please try again."

11.3.1 Ignoring the issue

JSP and JSTL don't force you to think about errors. Some web applications' JSP pages don't have to worry about errors, because the application could have been deployed with error handling already set up. Just as back-end Java programmers and application deployers can manage things like default locales, time zones, and databases, they can also manage default error handling.

Separately, if you're reasonably confident that your pages won't encounter any unexpected errors—or if you're happy with the look and feel of your JSP container's default error message—then you can forget about them and move on. (See

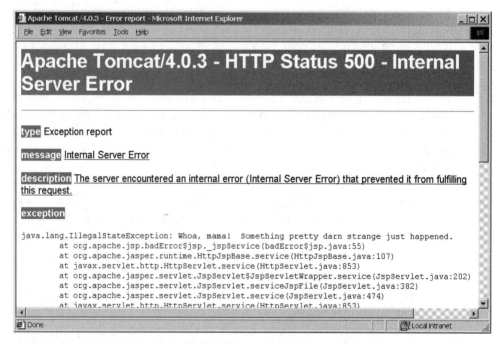

Figure 11.6   By default, errors in your JSP pages result in behavior that might look like this—or different, depending on what your JSP container decides to show. The point is, you probably don't want your important pages to produce such errors. Unless back-end Java programmers supporting your application have promised to take care of errors, you should catch and handle them yourself— or use a JSP errorPage.

figure 11.6 for an example of what a container's default error page might look like—in this case, Jakarta Tomcat's.)

Note that your page immediately aborts when it encounters its first unhandled error. That is, if line 2 of your page produces an error that you ignore, line 3 will never be executed. Instead, the user will see your application's default error behavior immediately.

11.3.2 Catching errors with <c:catch>

On the opposite side of the spectrum from simply forgetting about all errors is another alternative: you can sweep them all under the rug. The <c:catch> tag lets you capture errors and either discard them entirely or record information about them for later study. Table 11.1 shows its single attribute.

Table 11.1 <c:catch> tag attribute

Attribute	Description	Required	Default
var	Variable to expose information about the error	No	*None*

Errors that occur inside the body of a <c:catch> tag do not cause your whole page to abort. Instead, they abort only the rest of the <c:catch> tag's body.

If you use <c:catch> without a var attribute, it ignores all errors that occur in its body and lets your page continue. This approach is useful if you want to try something speculatively but don't really care if it succeeds. For instance, remember the database-driven hit counter from chapter 9? If the database for the counter is down, that's probably not an error serious enough to warrant the failure of your entire page. And there's no need to tell the user about the error, because they couldn't do much. Instead, you could wrap all of the counter's logic in a <c:catch> ... </c:catch> tag.

When you specify a var attribute, <c:catch> saves information about the error in the indicated scoped variable.

Let's look at an example of <c:catch> in action. Recall from chapter 10 that the <fmt:parseNumber> tag helps you read numbers that users enter into a form. In listing 10.1, you saw an example of a page that parses the number a user entered; the page reads the number, and then performs some simple arithmetic on it before printing it out.

Now, let's add some error handling. Listing 11.6 shows how to make the page from listing 10.1 more robust by allowing it to recover gracefully from bad input.

Listing 11.6   parseNumberCarefully.jsp: parsing and error recovery

```
<%@ taglib prefix="c" uri="http://java.sun.com/jstl/core" %>
<%@ taglib prefix="fmt" uri="http://java.sun.com/jstl/fmt" %>

<p>You entered "<c:out value="${param.favorite}"/>". </p>

<c:catch var="parsingError">                        ←❶ Creates a parsingError
                                                          variable for bad input
  <fmt:parseNumber var="fav" value="${param.favorite}"/>

  <p>As far as I can tell, this corresponds to the
  number <c:out value="${fav}"/>.</p>

  <p>If you multiply this number by 2 and add 1, you get
  <c:out value="${fav * 2 + 1}"/>.  I like that number
  better.</p>
</c:catch>

<c:if test="${not empty parsingError}">            ←❷ Checks whether an
  Sorry, this doesn't look like a number to me.          error occurred
  Perhaps you're in the wrong country?
</c:if>
```

❶ To add error handling to this page, we start by inserting a `<c:catch>` tag around it. This tag ensures that any error that occurs won't rise high enough to be noticed by the JSP container. Instead, it will be captured within the page, as suggested by figure 11.7.

Note that if an error occurs during the `<fmt:parseNumber>` tag, the rest of the `<c:catch>` tag's body never executes. This behavior is appropriate: if the number fails to parse, we don't want to start performing arithmetic on it or printing it out.

❷ The most useful thing you can usually do with a new scoped variable is to check if it's `empty`. In this case, because we used the attribute `var="parsingError"` in the earlier `<c:catch>` tag, our scoped variable will be named `parsingError`. If `parsingError` is `empty`, then no parsing error has occurred. Otherwise, we can be sure that some error occurred within the `<c:catch>` block.

We use this fact to make a decision in a `<c:if>` tag. If the `parsingError` variable is `not empty`, then we know an error has occurred, and we print out a custom error message. Thus, when an error occurs during the `<fmt:parseNumber>` tag, we display an error message and nothing else. (Remember, when `<fmt:parseNumber>` runs into an error, the rest of `<c:catch>`'s body—including all the template text beneath `<fmt:parseNumber>`—won't execute. The page picks up right after the closing `</c:catch>` tag.)

So, if we send this page a legitimate value like 500,000 for the parameter `favorite`, this page behaves exactly like listing 10.1; we get a response similar to the one

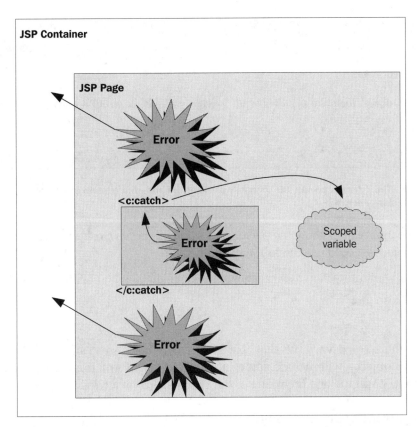

Figure 11.7 Normally, errors that occur in your JSP page are sent immediately to the JSP container. By default, they abort your page and cause the container to print out an error message. But the `<c:catch>` tag lets you capture and handle errors. When you catch an error with `<c:catch>`, you can save information about it in a scoped variable.

in figure 10.2. However, if we enter garbage like `!@#$%^`, we get the graceful error message shown in figure 11.8. Without the `<c:catch>` tag, we'd get a less friendly error message from the JSP container itself (like the one in figure 11.6).

Getting more information about errors

Variables created by `<c:catch>` have at least one useful property: `message`, which contains some information that describes the error that occurred. This property is useful if you want the user to have some sense of what went wrong. For instance, having this information might help the user describe the error to your organization's help desk.

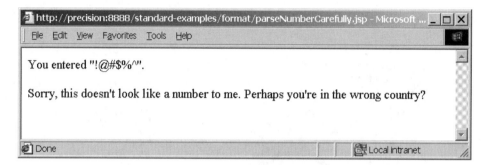

Figure 11.8 The `<c:catch>` tag lets us easily catch errors and print custom error messages like the one shown here.

To include information about the parsing error that might have occurred in listing 11.6, for example, we could use the following tag:

```
<c:out value="${parseError.message}"/>
```

We could also just write

```
<c:out value="${parseError}"/>
```

Printing the scoped variable that stores the error itself—technically, it's a Java `Throwable` object—will include some more technical information about the error. (By default, it will include the name of the `Throwable`'s Java class.)

11.3.3 *Passing errors to an error page*

When an error reaches the JSP container (see figure 11.7), the container will, by default, display its own error message. However, you can change this behavior by using a JSP error page. When your page has an error page, the user is forwarded to this page whenever an error occurs (almost as if you had included a manual `<jsp:forward>` tag in your page).

To declare an error page, you use the `<%@ page %>` directive that JSP provides. Include the following, typically at the top of your page:

```
<%@ page errorPage="target" %>
```

In this directive, `target` is the name of your error page—for instance, myErrorPage.jsp.

This error page is just like any other JSP page; for instance, you can use JSTL tags within it as long as you use the correct `<%@ taglib %>` directives first. The only difference is that you should begin this page with the following line:

```
<%@ page isErrorPage="true" %>
```

This line tells the JSP container that it can use this page as an error page.

Note that you can use an error page and the `<c:catch>` tag from the same page. The error page applies only if an error occurs but isn't captured by a `<c:catch>` tag.

Error pages are particularly useful when you want to provide a single, easily changeable way to handle all your application's errors. If you design an error page that looks like the rest of your site—for instance, with the same headers, footers, fonts, and color scheme—then your site's error handling will look much more professional.

Creating an error page

Listing 11.7 shows a simple error page.

Listing 11.7   errorPage.jsp: a sample JSP error page

```
<%@ page isErrorPage="true" %>
<%@ taglib prefix="c" uri="http://java.sun.com/jstl/core" %>
<%@ taglib prefix="fmt" uri="http://java.sun.com/jstl/fmt" %>

<h4>Error!</h4>

<p>Something bad happened in one of your pages:</p>

<p><c:out value="${pageContext.exception.message}"/></p>
```

Note how we use the expression `${pageContext.exception.message}` to print out information about the error that occurred. The `pageContext.exception` variable is just like the scoped variable that `<c:catch>` stores: you can use its `message` property to get information about the error that occurred, or you can print out the error itself, which usually includes more technical information.[1]

Listing 11.8 shows how to use an error page.

Listing 11.8   useErrorPage.jsp: a page that uses a JSP error page

```
<%@ page errorPage="errorPage.jsp" %>
<%@ taglib prefix="c" uri="http://java.sun.com/jstl/core" %>
<%@ taglib prefix="fmt" uri="http://java.sun.com/jstl/fmt" %>

<fmt:parseDate value="A midsummer night"/>     <— Always an error
```

If we load the page in listing 11.8, we'll always get an error; the string `"A midsummer night"` is not a valid date. Without the first line—`<%@ page errorPage="errorPage.jsp" %>`—we'd get an error much like the one in figure 11.6. But with the

---

[1] Note that the error message's details can vary from one implementation of JSTL to another.

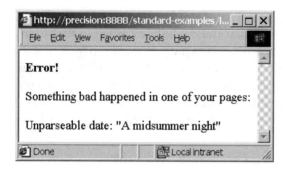

Figure 11.9
In contrast with figure 11.6, error pages let us control what is displayed when an error that's not handled by `<c:catch>` occurs in a page.

error page, we get an error like that shown in figure 11.9. Unlike the default error page, this error page is under our control; in this case, it displays the contents produced by listing 11.7.

11.4 Validating input

Whenever you accept information from the user, you should think about whether you need to validate it—or check to make sure it's sensible and correct—before processing it.

If you use JavaScript, you may already send pages to the browser with embedded JavaScript to validate web forms. For instance, your scripting code might pop open a window saying, "You must enter a username," if the user clicks on your Submit button without entering a username.

Although this *client-side validation* is convenient for the user, it's often not enough if you want to make sure your web application is secure and robust. The user's browser might not support JavaScript—or the user might even purposely be trying to wreak havoc with your web application.

Therefore, for important applications, it's best to think of client-side validation merely as a feature of the user interface. It's a convenience and a good first line of defense, but it's nothing more than that. You should always think about validating information on the server.

11.4.1 Different kinds of form validation

The first thing to realize about input validation is that, in a large web application, it might not be your job. JSP pages—with or without JSTL—might not be the best place to validate user input, especially in applications that use Struts or other frameworks that promote division of labor and implementation. In such applications, the job of your JSP pages might merely be to present some information and forms for the user to fill out; the back-end plumbing takes care of the rest.

JSTL 1.0 isn't intended for complex data validation. For instance, if you want to determine whether the user entered a reasonable phone number (based on the syntax of phone numbers, rules about which area codes your application accepts, and so on), you probably shouldn't use JSTL to do it. Instead, you should use a Java-Bean or other object that's accessible as a scoped variable in your page. (If you're not a Java programmer, then tasks like this currently lie beyond your scope; they'll need to be handled by someone who writes Java.)

However, JSTL is useful for simple kinds of validation. This includes things like:

- Making sure the user entered something in a form field (versus leaving it blank)

- Checking to see that if one form field is filled in, another is too (or isn't)

- Comparing a number that a user entered to a limit or range (such as "is the user's age above 13?")

Not coincidentally, this is often the sort of validation that an application's *presentation tier* (its front-end JSP pages) conducts.

Handling these simple validations is straightforward; as you might expect, you can use the expression language, `<c:if>`, and `<c:choose>`, as appropriate. For example, consider the following tag:

```
<c:if test="${empty param.username}">
  <font color="red">You must enter a username!</font>
</c:if>
```

There's nothing complicated about this validation; we're simply checking to see if a form parameter is empty in order to determine whether the user entered something for it.

There are only two tricky aspects of input validation: precisely where in your pages to check the user's input, and what to do if it isn't valid. The example in this section shows one convenient approach for addressing these issues.

11.4.2 *Tasks involved when validating a form*

Because a good web application needs to make things easy for users, validating input isn't enough. When a user provides bad input, you need to make the user aware of the error so that he or she can correct it. Typically, web applications inform users of errors by printing the original form again, with some additional error messages included. For instance, near a text box where the user was supposed to enter a username, you might print, in bright red letters, "You must enter a username!" Feedback like this is convenient for users; it tells them exactly what they did wrong.

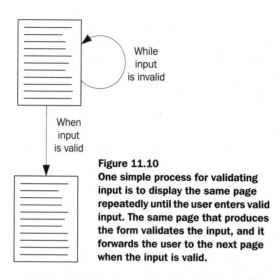

While
input
is invalid

When
input
is valid

Figure 11.10
One simple process for validating
input is to display the same page
repeatedly until the user enters valid
input. The same page that produces
the form validates the input, and it
forwards the user to the next page
when the input is valid.

Fortunately, it's also easy to write pages that follow this pattern. Start by looking at figure 11.10. Our goal is to present a page, and then to keep presenting that page—over and over, if necessary—until the user gets the information right. Only then do we let the user proceed to the next page.

Under a model like this, the same page that produces the form also validates the input. That is, a single JSP page contains tags to display the form, to check the input, and to print error messages. The <form> tag in such a page directs the browser to send the form's data back to the same page. (You can do this by specifying an action attribute that points to the URL for the current page, although it's easier to simply leave out the action attribute to the HTML <form> tag. When no action is specified, the browser defaults to sending information to the current page.)

TIP   Because a page that both displays and validates a form is complex, you can break such pages into smaller sections and include the different pieces with <jsp:include>. However, you might find it easier to keep everything in a single file.

Before we look at a page that both prints and validates, I should point out one subtlety. When you redisplay a form that has multiple fields, it's irritating to users if the form loses all the information they submitted. Unfortunately, this happens by default; when a browser loads the page a second time, the HTML forms will be empty. You'll see how to solve this problem when we examine our sample page.

Note that there are other models for validating input. Instead of cycling the same page repeatedly, you can cycle between two pages: one that displays the form, and another that validates input. I present a single-page cycle here because it demonstrates some JSTL features better than the alternatives.

11.4.3 *A sample form validation*

Listing 11.9 shows a page that displays our sample form, validation logic, and error messages, as appropriate.

Listing 11.9 formCycle.jsp: a page that prints and reprints a form until it's satisfied

```jsp
<%@ taglib prefix="c" uri="http://java.sun.com/jstl/core" %>
<%@ taglib prefix="fmt" uri="http://java.sun.com/jstl/fmt" %>

<h1>Peter's Junk-Mail Service</h1>

<c:if test="${param.submitted}">
  <c:if test="${empty param.name}" var="noName" />
  <c:if test="${empty param.email}" var="noEmail" />
  <c:if test="${empty param.age}" var="noAge" />

  <c:catch var="ageError">
    <fmt:parseNumber var="parsedAge" value="${param.age}" />
    <c:if test="${parsedAge < 13}" var="youngAge" />
  </c:catch>
  <c:if test="${not empty ageError}" var="badAge" />

  <c:if
    test="${not (noName or noEmail or noAge or badAge or youngAge)}">
    <c:set value="${param.name}" var="name" scope="request"/>
    <c:set value="${param.email}" var="email" scope="request"/>
    <c:set value="${param.age}" var="age" scope="request"/>
    <jsp:forward page="spamFormHandler.jsp" />
  </c:if>
</c:if>
<form method="post">
  <p>
  Thanks for signing up for our junk-mail service.
  Once you submit your information on the form below,
  you'll begin to receive all the "spam" you ever wanted.
  </p>

  <input type="hidden" name="submitted" value="true" />

  <p>
  Enter your name:
  <input type="text" name="name"
    value="<c:out value="${param.name}"/>" />
  <br />
  <c:if test="${noName}">
```

❶ Validation logic

❷ Forwards to the next page on success

❸ If we didn't forward, then we display the form

❹ "Hidden" field sets param automatically

❺ Sets the default field value dynamically

```
  <small><font color="red">
    Note: you must enter a name
  </font></small>
</c:if>
</p>

<p>
Enter your email address:
<input type="text" name="email"
  value="<c:out value="${param.email}"/>" />
<br />
<c:if test="${noEmail}">
 <small><font color="red">
   Note: you must enter an email address
 </font></small>
</c:if>
</p>

<p>
Enter your age:
<input type="text" name="age" size="3"
  value="<c:out value="${param.age}"/>" />
<br />
<c:choose>
  <c:when test="${noAge}">
   <small><font color="red">
     Note: you must enter your age
   </font></small>
  </c:when>
  <c:when test="${badAge}">
   <small><font color="red">
     Note: I couldn't decipher the age you typed in
   </font></small>
  </c:when>
  <c:when test="${youngAge}">
   <small><font color="red">
     Note: You're too young to receive adult
     junk mail.  Please grow older and try again.
   </font></small>
  </c:when>
</c:choose>
</p>

<input type="submit" value="Sign up" />

</form>
```

6 Prints an error message if appropriate

7 More complicated error-handling logic

The page begins by looking more like a page that *handles* a form than a page that *displays* one. This page does both, but we start with the validation logic. First, we use a <c:if> tag to determine whether this page is (a) responding to a submitted form or (b) displaying the form for the first time. We'll explain later how the parameter named submitted gets set; for now, it's just important to realize that it will be set (that is, not empty) only when the page is responding to a form submission—not when it's being loaded for the first time.

❶ Inside the `<c:if>` tag that causes the code to run only if it's responding to a submitted form, we validate the form's parameters. Our overall goal is to make sure a few things happened:

- The user entered a name.
- The user entered an email address.
- The user entered an age greater than or equal to 13.

We begin this validation by using a series of `<c:if>` tags that don't have bodies; instead, they're designed only to set a scoped variable with the result of the check. For instance, the tag

```
<c:if test="${empty param.name}" var="noName" />
```

sets a scoped variable named noName to true if param.name doesn't have a meaningful value; if the value is not empty, then noName will be false. Thus, noName functions as an error flag: if it's true, we've got a problem.

When we check the user's age, we do something a little trickier. The age parameter can have a few different problems:

- The user could have left it blank.
- The user could have entered garbage (an unparseable number).
- The age might be too low for our purposes (less than 13).

The first case—a blank age—is easy to address; we treat it like a blank name or email address. But if the field isn't blank, we want to parse it in order to determine what numeric value the user entered. If the user didn't enter a number, this parse will fail. We use a `<c:catch>` tag to account for this possibility. The `<c:catch var="ageError">` tag sets the scoped variable named ageError if there was a parsing error while checking the age. Right after the `<c:catch>` tag, we determine (with another `<c:if>` tag) whether ageError has a value; if it does, we know that the user entered a bad value, and we set the scoped variable badAge. If, instead, the user entered a parseable date, then we compare it with 13 and set the youngAge flag to true if this check fails.

❷ After the validations are complete, we have an immediate use for their result. While still inside the `<c:if>` tag that makes sure the code runs only if it's responding to a form (and not printing it for the first time), we use a big `<c:if>` check to determine whether any error flags are set. This tag uses the following expression:

```
${not (noName or noEmail or noAge or badAge or youngAge)}
```

If this expression succeeds, we know the input is valid, so we `<jsp:forward>` to a new page. Before we forward, however, we do something interesting: we set a few request-scoped attributes. When we use `<jsp:forward>` to forward to a new page, that page will have access to our request parameters; it could say, for instance, `${param.name}`, and retrieve the name parameter the user entered. The problem with this approach, however, is that it gives the user a way to avoid validation. If we let the next page rely on request parameters, it would have to redo the validations to ensure its input makes sense. If the new page didn't check its input, then our checks would become meaningless; the user could contact the next page directly and send bad data. To get around this problem, we manually set the request-scoped variables that we know the next page will need. Request-scoped variables are never directly under the user's control, which makes this mechanism more secure and robust than simple request parameters.

This target page can do whatever it wants with the values. We don't show a sample target page here, although chapter 12 discusses typical things such a target page might do. For instance, if this were really a user-registration application, the page spamForm-Handler.jsp would probably store the user's name and email address in a database.

❸ If we've come as far as the `<form>` tag without forwarding to a new page, then we know that one of two things is true: either this is the first time we're printing the form, or the form has errors. Either way, we must print the `<form>` and give the user a chance (perhaps *another* chance) to enter correct information. We can use the error flags to determine whether to display error messages as appropriate. We can also use `param.submitted` to differentiate between the first and subsequent requests to this page, just as we did earlier in the page. Doing so might be useful if we wanted to print a special message the first time the form loads, but not subsequent times. However, we don't bother with such details in this example.

❹ Earlier, I promised I'd explain how the parameter `submitted` is set. Recall that this parameter will be equal to `true` if we're responding to a form (instead of printing it the first time); otherwise, it won't be set. We create this distinction by making sure that every time the form is submitted, it sets a parameter named `submitted`. Of course, we can't rely on users to do this themselves, so we use a special type of HTML form field: `<input type="hidden">`. Hidden fields, true to their name, don't show up graphically in the form; the user never sees them. But behind the scenes, they force a parameter to be set with a particular value. We could achieve something similar by adding a `name` attribute to our `<input type="submit">` button; but hidden fields are more flexible, and I wanted to demonstrate one here.

❺ In section 11.4.2, I mentioned that we'd need to make sure we supplied the user's old values to a reprinted form. If we don't do so, then the form will be cleared each time we represent it, and the user will need to reenter information. Users hate doing this, so we don't want to make them. Instead, we can force each form field to take a default value. The nature of the default value is simple: it's the parameter the user just entered.

For `<input type="text">` fields, as well as `<input type="password">`, we can use the `value` attribute to seed a value into the form. That's what we do in this listing:

```
<input type="text" name="name"
value="<c:out value="${param.name}"/>" />
```

This code sets the `value` field in the new form to the value of the `name` parameter in the old form.

For other types of input fields—selection boxes, radio buttons, and check boxes—it's trickier to add default values, but doing so is still more-or-less straightforward. For a `<select>` box, you can't simply specify a `value` attribute for the default value. Instead, you must add the attribute `selected="selected"` to the correct `<option>` tag. You can do so by comparing a parameter value with the value of the `<option>` tag you're about to print. For example:

```
<select name="milk">
  <option value="lowfat"
    <c:if test="${param.milk == 'lowfat'}">
      selected="selected"
    </c:if>
  >Low fat</option>
  <option value="skim"
    <c:if test="${param.milk == 'skim'}">
      selected="selected"
    </c:if>
  >Skim milk</option>
</select>
```

The `selected="selected"` attribute will print only for the correct value.

Radio buttons and check boxes work the same way, but instead of adding the attribute `selected="selected"`, you add the attribute `checked="checked"`. For `<textarea>` fields, simply insert your desired default value into the body of the `<textarea>`:

```
<textarea name="prose"><c:out
  value="${param.prose}"/></textarea>
```

TIP   Note how I've avoided putting `<c:out>` on a new line within `<textarea>`, or otherwise using extra white space. It's good to be careful about doing this, because even the white space inside `<textarea>` is included in the text area's default value. The white space (and line break) *within* the `<c:out>` tag—before the `value` attribute—doesn't matter.

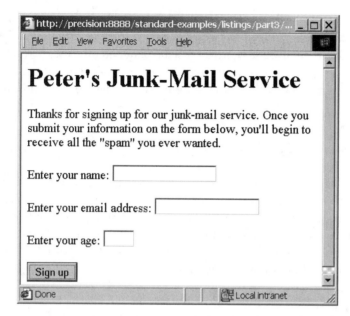

Figure 11.11
The first time our sample page from listing 11.9 loads, it displays a regular HTML form.

❻ At appropriate places in the form, we can use the error flags we created earlier to print out error messages. Remember, these error flags can't be set unless we're re-printing a form; this behavior is appropriate, because we wouldn't want to accuse users of crimes they didn't commit.

❼ We can also use `<c:choose>`, just as easily as `<c:if>`, as a way to make decisions about what error message to print. For instance, in the case of bad ages, we want to choose the most appropriate message to print. Our logic earlier in the page doesn't ensure that only one error flag related to age will be set; instead, we use `<c:choose>` to make sure that only one error based on these flags will print.

That's it. It's a big page, but overall, it works cleanly. The first time it's loaded, it displays the form shown in figure 11.11.

Now, suppose I enter bad input to this page. Let's say I enter a valid name, but I leave out the email address entirely, and I enter the age 6. I'll end up with the form shown in figure 11.12. It's the same form, but it includes error messages. Note also that it includes all the information I entered earlier, saving me the trouble of having to type it again.

Finally, and only when the information is correct, we reach the target page—which, as I mentioned before, could save our information in a database. We don't show such a page; we'll go over thorough examples of pages that use databases in chapters 12 and 13.

Figure 11.12
When the page from listing 11.9 is fed invalid input, it reprints its form with appropriate error messages interspersed. It also explicitly fills in the form with the values the user entered, making it easier for the user to correct them.

11.5 *Summary*

In this chapter, we discussed a few demonstrations of JSTL in action. Take the following pointers from these examples:

- Because checkbox parameters and cookies come in lists, you often need to loop over them with `<c:forEach>`. You can find checkbox parameters with the expression `${paramValues.name}`, where *name* is the name of the parameter you're looking for.

- If you need to let the user enter dates, you can use multiple expressions in the same attribute value to assemble different request parameters (different form fields) into a date that's parseable by `<fmt:parseDate>`.

- The `<c:catch>` tag lets you handle errors within your page.

- JSP's `errorPage` mechanism helps you control errors that aren't handled in your page.

- You can use `<c:if>` tags, `<c:choose>` tags, and the expression language to validate form input. One common strategy for validating input is to present a page that cycles (see figure 11.10) until it receives correct input. Listing 11.9 shows an example of such a page.

- If a user filled out a form incorrectly and you decide to redisplay it, it's important to seed that form with the values the user previously entered; otherwise, the user will have to retype the entire form. The process for setting default values varies for each HTML form element, but it's generally easy to do with either a `<c:out>` or `<c:if>` tag. See ❺ in listing 11.9.

Dynamic features
for web sites

This chapter covers...

- Writing an online survey application
- Building a discussion forum
- Setting up sample applications' databases
- Practical tips and tricks

Now that we've looked at a few individual, isolated tasks, we're ready to plunge into more complicated applications. This chapter presents two applications. The first, an online survey program, lets you add surveys, votes, and polls to your pages. The second, a message-board system, lets you insert discussion forums and guest books into your web site.

These applications have a lot in common. They both use databases, and they're both self-configuring. That is, they don't require any setup or ongoing maintenance, other than a few database tables that must be created before the applications can run. The applications are thus simpler and more interesting than they'd be if they included unnecessary baggage.

If you're like many programmers and learn by example, this chapter is definitely for you.

NOTE   The applications in this chapter assume that your application has a default database set up. If this is not the case, you'll need to use the `<sql:set-DataSource>` tag to set up a default database. See chapter 9 for more information on using the `<sql:setDataSource>` tag. If you don't already have a database you can experiment with, my instructions for installing the hsqldb database, available from Manning Publication's web site, might be useful. See appendix D for the instructions' URL.

12.1 An online survey

You've surely run across an online survey during your web travels. Personally, I don't like these polls. They're often tedious, presenting unimaginative questions and a handful of uninspired choices (and to top it off, they're haphazard and non-scientific, so their results don't tell me much).

Still, lots of web sites like them, and I can see why. Adding a survey to web site is a good way to help build that site's sense of community. To many users, a site feels more dynamic and responsive if it lets people give quick feedback; it gives them a chance to express an opinion and see a sample of what other people are thinking.

An online survey isn't difficult to write, but it involves a number of pieces. If you're going to write a survey, you need to store results, tabulate them, and print them out. Fortunately, JSTL gives you all the tools you need. You can use JSTL's database tags to store and retrieve information; you can apply the formatting tags to help print out results.

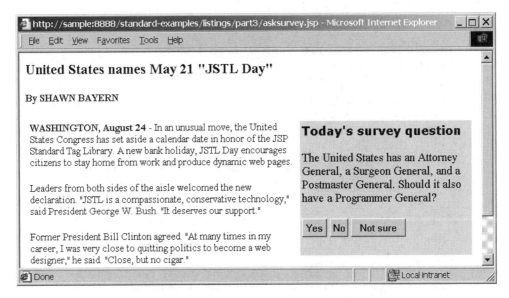

Figure 12.1   A hypothetical newspaper web site that asks a survey question. The user can respond by clicking one of the buttons.

12.1.1 *What our survey looks like*

Let's start by looking at what our completed project looks like. Figure 12.1 shows a page that might be part of a newspaper's web site. Most of the page displays a news article, but on the right side, we include a box with a survey question. In figure 12.1's case, the question has three possible answers: Yes, No, and Not sure.

When the user clicks one of the buttons to answer the survey's question, a new window pops up. This window looks like figure 12.2. It presents some detailed information about the survey's results and a graph of these results. Of course, in a real application, you probably wouldn't need to display detailed information; the graph alone might be enough. Later in this section, we'll explain how to customize the survey's output. For now, I wanted to show what our survey application will be capable of.

12.1.2 *Setting up the survey database*

Our survey results will be stored in a database. We'll save and retrieve users' responses with the `<sql:update>` and `<sql:query>` tags. Whenever you work with a database, a key question is, "What do the database's tables look like?" For our survey application, we need only a single table; let's call it `survey_results`.

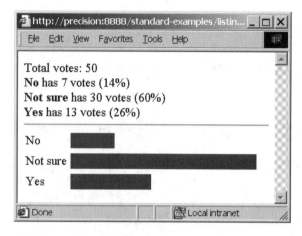

Figure 12.2
Our survey can respond by printing detailed information about the user's choices, or even a graph of the results.

The `survey_results` table has two columns (see table 12.1).

Table 12.1   Our survey application's database table (`survey_results`) has two columns: one that identifies the survey and another that stores the choices users make.

Column name	Type	Purpose
`survey_id`	`INTEGER`	Stores a number that distinguishes each survey question from the others
`choice`	`VARCHAR(30)`	Contains an individual user's choice for the corresponding `survey_id`

The first column in this table, `survey_id`, contains a number that identifies an individual survey question. For instance, survey 2 could be, "Which of your internal organs do you find most appealing?" and survey 3 could be, "Are you a Democrat or a Republican?" The questions don't need to have anything to do with each other; all questions that your site uses can live side-by-side in the `survey_results` table.

Every row in this table stores an individual user's choice. For instance, if a user submits the value `pancreas` for survey 2, we add a row that looks like (2, 'pancreas'). The next user might vote for the choice `liver`, which would lead us to create a new row: (2, 'liver'). The table thus allows duplicate rows, which are fine in a relational database.

> **TIP** We could have structured this table differently. Instead of storing one row for each response, `survey_results` could contain one row for each different choice and could keep a counter that is incremented, much like the counter we used in chapter 9. I decided to use the approach outlined in table 12.1 for two reasons:

- It's more general. If you wanted to add a column that records the user's name or the date the user's choice was made, you could do that. This way, the survey application could easily become a vote-tallying application that prevents users from voting twice. Or, you could add logging and error recovery more easily.

- It demonstrates a way of thinking about databases that many people neglect. Your first instinct might have been to use a count, but as you'll see later in this section, the approach we use here shows a few aspects of databases that you'd otherwise miss.

Our approach has two drawbacks. First, it wastes space in the database, but this isn't a big deal. Perhaps slightly more important, the database doesn't know the potential choices for a survey question until each choice is picked at least once. This behavior might give the first few users of the survey confusing results. (The results won't be incorrect; they'll just leave out choices that haven't yet been chosen.)

To make things concrete, here's what the table could look like after a few votes:

survey_id	Choice
2	liver
2	pancreas
2	pancreas
2	liver
2	pancreas
3	Democrat
3	Democrat
3	independent
3	Republican

For survey 2, the results would tally as follows: 2 liver, 3 pancreas. For survey 3, the results would be 2 Democrat, 1 independent, 1 Republican.

To keep this example simple, we need to keep track of our survey questions manually. For instance, nothing in the database stores the fact that survey 2 concerns body parts or survey 3 concerns political affiliation. We must remember that ourselves; we'll need to use the correct number when we add survey questions to our web pages. (You'll see how to do this in section 12.1.3.) Furthermore, nothing in this database checks to make sure entries are valid. Nothing prevents a user's voting twice (or 100 times), and nothing checks to ensure that the user isn't trying to submit an unacceptable choice to the survey. We could add checks to help, but doing so would divert our attention from more fun matters. So, if you decide that you need more error checking, I leave it as an exercise for you. (Chapter 11 discussed validating input and handling errors.)

With this survey application, multiple surveys can easily be active at once. You can use the `survey_results` table to manage and differentiate between a virtually unlimited number of surveys behind the scenes.

Creating the survey_results table

To create the `survey_results` table, we can use the following SQL statement:

```
create table survey_results (
  survey_id integer,
  choice varchar(30)
)
```

You need to type this command in your database's command-line interface. The procedure differs widely among databases, so consult your database's documentation or administrator. (For the hsqldb database, see my instructions at the Manning web site; the URL is listed in appendix D.)

12.1.3 Adding survey questions to pages

Before users can respond to survey questions, we need to add the questions to our pages. In figure 12.1, we inserted a question inside a table cell on the right side of the screen. To ask the question and give the user a way to respond, here's what we added:

```
The United States has an Attorney General,
a Surgeon General, and a Postmaster General.
Should it also have a Programmer General?

<form method="post" action="survey.jsp" target="_blank">
  <input type="hidden" name="surveyId" value="7" />
  <input type="submit" name="choice" value="Yes" />
  <input type="submit" name="choice" value="No" />
  <input type="submit" name="choice" value="Not sure" />
</form>
```

The rest of the page is simple, static HTML containing a sample news article. The only interesting part is the `<form>` tag. This tag uses a few tricks to enable the look and feel we desire.

We include the `surveyId` for the survey we're asking as a hidden field in the HTML form. As I mentioned earlier in this chapter, nothing manages these numbers for us. Instead, we must pick a number that hasn't been used before every time we write a new survey question. For this question, I picked the number 7 and included the following hidden field:

```
<input type="hidden" name="surveyId" value="7" />
```

To give the user particular choices, we use different `<input type="submit">` buttons. Because each of these buttons has a `name` attribute, clicking one of them will cause the browser to send a request parameter to the page it loads. For instance, if you click on the first button, then `${param.choice}` in the target page will equal `Yes`. If you click on the second button instead, the same parameter will be set to `No`. Either way, the same page will be loaded; the only difference in the three buttons is the value of `${param.choice}` in the target page.

This target page in the example `<form>` you just saw is called survey.jsp. Note that the HTML `<form>` tag has an extra attribute you haven't seen before: `target="_blank"`. It tells the browser to open the form's response in a new window instead of navigating to it in the current window. Therefore, when the user clicks on one of the three `<input type="submit">` buttons, the browser will load survey.jsp in a new window.

12.1.4 *How the survey works*

The survey.jsp page contains the core survey logic. This page accepts the user's survey choice and prints out the survey's results. It needs two parameters: `surveyId` and `choice`. In section 12.1.3, you saw how to write a form that sends these parameters. The first, `surveyId`, contains the number for a survey. The survey.jsp page, just like the database, can handle multiple, active surveys at once; it needs a `surveyId` number to figure out two things:

- How to record the user's response
- Which survey results to display

The `choice` parameter contains the user's choice. For instance, if you use the form from section 12.1.3, the `choice` parameter will equal `Yes`, `No`, or `Not sure`.

With this in mind, let's finally look at how the survey works. Listing 12.1 shows the survey.jsp page.

Listing 12.1   survey.jsp: stores new survey votes and prints results

```
<%@ taglib prefix="c" uri="http://java.sun.com/jstl/core" %>
<%@ taglib prefix="fmt" uri="http://java.sun.com/jstl/fmt" %>
<%@ taglib prefix="sql" uri="http://java.sun.com/jstl/sql" %>

<c:choose>
```

```
<c:when test="${empty param.surveyId or empty param.choice}">
  <font color="red">
    Error: survey.jsp called incorrectly!
  </font>
</c:when>
<c:otherwise>

  <sql:update>
    insert into survey_results(survey_id, choice)
      values(?, ?)
    <sql:param value="${param.surveyId}" />
    <sql:param value="${param.choice}" />
  </sql:update>

  <sql:query var="result">
    select choice, count(choice) from survey_results
      where survey_id = ?
      group by choice
    <sql:param value="${param.surveyId}" />
  </sql:query>

  <c:set var="total" value="0"/>
  <c:forEach items="${result.rowsByIndex}" var="row">
    <c:set var="total" value="${total + row[1]}"/>
  </c:forEach>

  Total votes: <c:out value="${total}"/> <br />

  <c:forEach items="${result.rowsByIndex}" var="row">
    <b><c:out value="${row[0]}"/></b> has
    <c:out value="${row[1]}"/> votes
    (<fmt:formatNumber type="percent"
      value="${row[1] / total}"/>)
    <br />
  </c:forEach>

  <hr />

  <c:forEach items="${result.rowsByIndex}"
      var="row" varStatus="s">
    <c:if test="${s.first}">
      <table>
    </c:if>

    <tr>
     <td><c:out value="${row[0]}"/></td>
     <td>
      <table>
       <tr>
        <td bgcolor="blue">
         <c:forEach
           begin="1"
           end="${row[1] * 100 / total}"> </c:forEach>
        </td>
```

1 Checks for bad input

2 Saves the user's vote

3 Retrieves survey data

4 Computes the total number of votes

5 Prints technical vote data

6 Prints graphs for vote data

```
      </tr>
      </table>
      </td>
      </tr>

   <c:if test="${s.last}">
      </table>
   </c:if>
  </c:forEach>

 </c:otherwise>
</c:choose>
```

❶ The survey.jsp page starts with an error check. If we don't receive the two parameters we need (surveyId and choice), then we don't bother going on. We put the error message in a <c:when> block and the rest of the page in <c:otherwise>. Thus, the page won't try to update or access the database unless it's given the necessary parameters.

❷ The first <sql:update> tag saves the user's vote in the database. Note that this tag—and all the database tags in survey.jsp—doesn't use a dataSource attribute. As I mentioned at the beginning of this chapter, I assume the page runs in an environment where the default database has been set up correctly. If this is not the case, you'll need to add a dataSource attribute to every <sql:query> and <sql:update> tag in the page. For information on how to do this properly, see chapter 9.

The SQL command that we use to save the user's choice is simple. Remember that the survey_results table is supposed to have a row for every individual survey response. Thus, all we need to do is add a row for the current user's vote. To do this, we use the base query

```
insert into survey_results(survey_id, choice)
  values(?, ?)
```

and send it our two parameters using <sql:param> tags.

❸ Now, after saving the new result, we want to retrieve all results for the requested survey. We do this with an <sql:query> tag that contains an <sql:param> tag to pass the survey_id number we're interested in. We use a bit of advanced SQL here, so let's go over it carefully.

Our SQL query retrieves two things from the survey_results table. It begins as follows:

```
select choice, count(choice) from survey_results
  where survey_id = ?
```

The first thing we're selecting—choice—is simple; it's the value of a column. It's clear that we're only interested in rows that have a particular survey_id.

But count(choice) is a little trickier. We want to get a count for each choice that exists for the current survey. To do so, we need to add the phrase group by choice to the SQL statement; it tells the database that we're interested in organizing the results by choice. Consider the following potential rows for survey_id=7:

survey_id	choice
7	Yes
7	No
7	Not sure
7	Not sure
7	Yes
7	Not sure
7	Yes
7	Not sure
7	Not sure

For these values, our SQL statement, which contains the group by choice clause, will produce the following results:

choice	count(choice)
Yes	3
No	1
Not sure	5

This is the virtual table we store using the <sql:query> tag's var attribute. In this case, we save a copy of this virtual table into a scoped variable called result.

❹ When we iterate over this table, we can retrieve the value of a choice with ${row[0]} and the counter for that choice with ${row[1]}. As an example of using these kinds of expressions, and because the computation will help us compute percentages later, we use a <c:forEach> loop to tally the total number of votes cast for the survey (among all the various choices). For instance, in the virtual table we just looked at, the total number of votes cast is 9.

To perform this calculation, we start by setting the scoped variable total to 0. Then, for each line of the table, we run the following tag:

```
<c:set var="total" value="${total + row[1]}"/>
```

It adds each count to the running total and, finally, leaves us with a complete count. For our sample table, we start with 0 and add 3 (the count for Yes). We then save this result in the `total` variable and loop again. The next time, we add 1 to 3, yielding 4. Finally we add 5 to 4, yielding the grand total, 9. At the end of the `<c:forEach>` loop, the `total` variable holds the final tally.

❺ To print the numeric voting data that we first presented in figure 12.2, we use another `<c:forEach>` loop. As I mentioned, we can access the choice's value with `${row[0]}` and its count with `${row[1]}`. Instead of tallying numbers internally, the second `<c:forEach>` loop prints out data for the user based on this information. First, we print the raw information; without the formatting tags, this is just

```
<c:out value="${row[0]}"/> has <c:out value="${row[1]}"/> votes
```

For instance, it could print text like this:

```
Yes has 3 votes
```

After printing this raw information, we print some calculated information. Percentages are a useful way to represent parts of a whole. For instance, 3 out of 9 total votes is about 33%. We supply a simple calculation, and the `<fmt:formatNumber>` tag takes care of printing the number appropriately:

```
<fmt:formatNumber type="percent" value="${row[1] / total}"/>
```

The expression `${row[1] / total}` represents the piece of the pie (so to speak) that's occupied by the current row. That is, `row[1]` represents the current row's count, and `total`—which results the first `<c:forEach>` loop—stores the total number of votes. The `<fmt:formatNumber>` tag takes care of rounding, localizing, and formatting the number so that it looks suitable for the user.

❻ Finally, to display a graph for the voting data, we get creative. Consider the following `<c:forEach>` loop:

```
<c:forEach begin="1"
    end="${row[1] * 100 / total}"> </c:forEach>
```

This loop doesn't print out new and interesting values each time it runs. Its only goal is to print out the text ` `, which represents a *nonbreaking space* character in HTML. (For our purposes, a non-breaking space is a space character the browser can't easily ignore.) This loop is only dynamic in that it decides how many times to print out ` ` depending on the value of its `end` attribute. In this case, we print a number of spaces proportional to the percentage of votes that the current row received.

Because we've included this loop in a table cell with a specific background color—`<td bgcolor="blue">`—the number of spaces that we print leads to a wider or narrower column inside the table cell.[1]

Thus, we get a virtual bar graph—with almost no work, and certainly with no special graphics. We produce the bar graph from figure 12.2 just by printing the appropriate number of spaces for each survey result.

Although this technique is something of a dirty trick, it's remarkably flexible. Suppose we wanted to overlay percentages and numbers on the bar graph. We could do so simply by inserting some new tags into the inner `<table>`, as follows:

```
<table>
  <tr>
    <td bgcolor="blue">
      <c:forEach
        begin="1"
        end="${row[1] * 100 / total}"> </c:forEach>
      <font color="white">
      <fmt:formatNumber type="percent"
        value="${row[1] / total}"/>
      </font>
    </td>
  </tr>
</table>
```

Adding this `<fmt:formatNumber>` tag produces the output shown in figure 12.3.

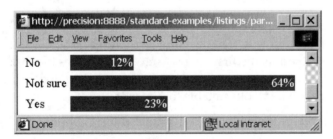

Figure 12.3 It's easy to modify the display of the bar graph by adding tags. For instance, we can overlay percentages on the bar graph we produce. The bar graph is printed with a `<c:forEach>` tag that outputs a dynamic number of spacing ( ) characters. This is something of a dirty HTML trick, but it's cute enough to merit the example.

---

[1] If you're an HTML guru, you might have noticed that we need to use a `<table>` within a `<table>` to achieve our custom spacing; this is one way to indicate to the browser not to line up all of the outer table's columns. I mention this fact but don't dwell on it, because this isn't a book about HTML tricks. Nonetheless, this is one HTML trick that I don't mind including; it's both useful and cute.

Of course, nothing requires you to use HTML kludges to display graphs of data. You can use a calculation similar to that in the `<c:forEach>` tag's end attribute—`${row[1] * 100 / total}`—inside a `height` or `width` attribute for an HTML image tag. For instance:

```
<img src="blue.jpg" height="5"
  width="<c:out value="${row[1] * 100 / total}"/>"/>
```

This `<img>` tag will dynamically size an image based on a calculation whose result we output to the page.

NOTE   Remember that for non-JSTL tags, you can't simply include an expression in an attribute; you need to use a `<c:out>` tag to print dynamic data. JSP 1.3 may alter this requirement, but it is still necessary in all earlier versions of JSP. For instance, under JSP 1.2, you can't write

```
<img src="blue.jpg" height="5"
    width="${row[1] * 100 / total}"/>
```

Of course, the look and feel of your own survey.jsp page is up to you. You could add your site's regular header and footer to the page, along with navigational links, advertisements, or other information.

12.2 A message board

Another web-site feature that helps build communities is a message board, guest book, or other similar facility to let users read and post messages. A messaging system is typically divided into forums, or message boards, that group related messages. For instance, if you're creating a site for a news organization, you might have a different message board for every article. If you sell software, you might have a message board for each of your company's products.

In this section, we'll create a simple messaging system. There's no end to how such a system could grow; you could support threaded messages, searches, administrative tools, and so on. Here, we'll just show the basic framework for such a system; thus this section's pages might be more appropriate as a guest book than a message forum.

12.2.1 What our message board looks like

Our message board will be designed so that it's easy to link to from any of your pages. In figure 12.4, you see a link that tells users they can discuss a news article. When users click this link, a new window for the appropriate message board pops

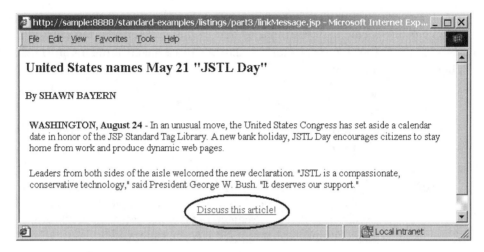

Figure 12.4 It's easy to add support for our message board to any web page. Simply add a link where it's appropriate. You'll see what form this URL takes in section 12.2.3.

up. If this board doesn't have any messages yet, then users are invited to be the first to post a message (figure 12.5). Otherwise, users see prior messages and can add to the discussion (figure 12.6).

Figure 12.5
Users who ask for an empty forum are told that they can be the first user to post a message in the forum.

Figure 12.6
When a forum contains messages, users see those messages and can add to the discussion using a simple HTML form.

12.2.2 *Setting up the message database*

Just as with the survey system we built in section 12.1, our message-board application uses a single database table. We call this table messages. You can create it using the following SQL command:

```
create table messages (
  message_board integer,
  sent_date timestamp,
  author varchar(30),
  subject varchar(30),
  body varchar(255)
)
```

Table 12.2 shows more information about the database table that this command creates.

The 30-character limits on the length of the author's name and the message's subject are probably reasonable, but the 255-character limit on the length of the body is somewhat limiting. I haven't used a different type to store message bodies because the database types that allow longer limits are woefully variable among different databases. In Oracle, you might use the LONG type; in PostgreSQL, it's TEXT; and in hsqldb, it's LONGVARCHAR. Although details like this are important for real-

Table 12.2 Our message-board application's database table (messages) stores one row for every message. Each row contains the author, subject, and body of the message, as well as the date posted and a number that identifies the message board to which the message has been posted.

Column name	Type	Purpose
message_board	INTEGER	Indicates what message board the message is part of
sent_date	TIMESTAMP	Records when the message was posted
author	VARCHAR(30)	Records the name of the user who posted the message
subject	VARCHAR(30)	Contains the subject of the message
body	VARCHAR(255)	Contains the body of the message

world applications, they're beyond the scope of this book. Fortunately, limiting message bodies to 255 characters will still let us write and test our message board.

To help you see what the message table stores, here's a sample set of rows that the table could store. These rows represent a hypothetical discussion between two users over the course of a day or two:

message_board	sent_date	author	subject	body
4	2002-08-21 20:43:30.0	Bob Jones	What a dumb product!	Why would I need a telephone cleaner?
4	2002-08-21 20:49:32.0	Customer Support	The product fills a niche.	Some people have dirty telephones.
4	2002-08-22 09:10:02.0	Bob Jones	Oh, I see.	Thanks.

This table only shows rows for a particular message board (board number 4), but the messages table can simultaneously manage multiple message boards. In this way, it's similar to the survey_results table from section 12.1, which could store results for many surveys at once.

12.2.3 *Linking to appropriate message boards*

As with our survey application from section 12.1, you don't need to do anything to create a message board; you just need to decide on a number and begin using it. This number might come from another source; for instance, you might use product numbers for a message board about products, or article numbers for a message board about articles—assuming you have separate databases that store products or articles. Alternatively, you could simply manage the numbers yourself, manually.

Once you've settled on a number for a board, it's easy to provide a link to it, like the one in figure 12.4. We can use the `<c:url>` tag from chapter 5, but suppose we need to create a link from a static HTML page. In that case, we can create a normal, static HTML hyperlink:

```
<a target="_blank" href="viewMessages.jsp?messageBoard=2">
  Discuss this article!
</a>
```

The only interesting thing about this hyperlink is the highlighted part—the section that begins with `?`. As you first saw in chapter 5, you can add a `?` to a URL to send it request parameters manually. If you add

```
?length=30&width=5&height=2
```

to a URL that points to a JSP page, then when the page loads, it will have a `length` parameter equal to `30`, a `width` parameter of `5`, and a `height` parameter of `2`. For example, the expression `${param.length * param.width * param.height}` would equal 300.

In this case, we want to set the `messageBoard` parameter to the number for the message board to which we want to create a link.

Note how we use the `target="_blank"` attribute for the `<a>` tag that we used for `<form>` in section 12.1. This attribute causes the message board to open in a new window instead of using the current window. Of course, you don't have to use this attribute; but in many cases, it's convenient if a message board opens in a new browser window instead of interrupting the rest of your application. If you don't plan to open separate windows, you need to add navigational information to the viewMessage.jsp page that we'll look at in the following section; popping up a new window lets you avoid spending too much time on customizing the navigation in the message-board window.

12.2.4 *How the message board works*

Figure 12.7 shows the flow of our message-board application. Individual pages link to the viewMessages.jsp page. These pages use the `messageBoard` parameter to tell viewMessages.jsp what board to use. The viewMessages.jsp page displays the appropriate board's messages, and it includes an HTML form that points to post-Message.jsp, which adds a message to the database and then forwards back to view-Messages.jsp.

Let's begin by looking at viewMessages.jsp in listing 12.2.

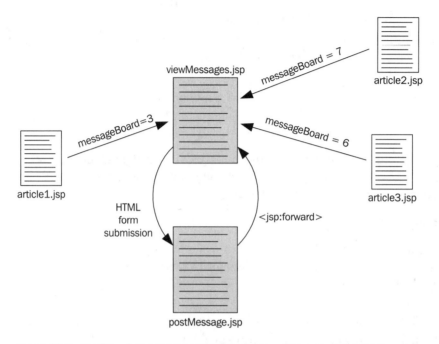

Figure 12.7 The flow of our message-board application. Users start at outside pages, which link to viewMessages.jsp, passing in a messageBoard parameter. This page shows users the requested board's messages and lets the user post a message by submitting a form to postMessage.jsp. After it posts a message, postMessage.jsp forwards the user to viewMessages.jsp.

Listing 12.2 viewMessages.jsp: a page that displays messages from a message board

```
<%@ taglib prefix="c" uri="http://java.sun.com/jstl/core" %>
<%@ taglib prefix="sql" uri="http://java.sun.com/jstl/sql" %>

<c:choose>
  <c:when test="${empty param.messageBoard}">
    <font color="red">
      Error: viewMessages.jsp called incorrectly!
    </font>
  </c:when>
  <c:otherwise>

    <sql:query var="result">
      select * from messages
        where message_board = ?
        order by sent_date
      <sql:param value="${param.messageBoard}" />
    </sql:query>
```

❶ Retrieves the board's messages

```
<c:choose>
  <c:when test="${result.rowCount == 0}">        ❷ Checks whether the board
    <p>                                              has any messages
      Currently, there are no messages in this message board.
      Be the first to post a message by filling in the form
      below!
    </p>
  </c:when>
  <c:otherwise>
    <c:forEach items="${result.rows}" var="row">
      <p>
      From: <c:out value="${row.AUTHOR}" /> <br />
      Date: <c:out value="${row.SENT_DATE}" /> <br />     ❸ Prints each
      Subject: <c:out value="${row.SUBJECT}" /> <br />       message
      <blockquote>
          <tt><c:out value="${row.BODY}" /></tt>
      </blockquote>
      <hr />
    </c:forEach>
  </c:otherwise>
</c:choose>

<form method="post" action="postMessage.jsp">     ❹ Lets a user enter
  <p>                                                 a new message
  <b>New message</b> <br />
  Name: <input type="text" name="name" /> <br />
  Subject: <input type="text" name="subject" /> <br />
  <textarea cols="30" rows="5" name="body"></textarea> <br />
  <input type="hidden" name="messageBoard"
    value="<c:out value="${param.messageBoard}" />" />   ❺ Passes the
  <input type="submit" value="Post!" />                     current board
  </p>                                                       number
</form>

    </c:otherwise>
</c:choose>
```

❶ After confirming our parameters using a technique that should look familiar by now, we perform a simple SQL query against our database, finding all messages associated with our `messageBoard` parameter. We use the SQL clause `SELECT *`, which retrieves all columns from the database. Unlike in the survey application from section 12.1, we'll refer to each row's columns by name (for instance `${row.name}`) instead of by number (as in `${row[1]}`).

Note that the SQL query controls the order in which messages display. In listing 12.2, the messages will be displayed in chronological order, starting with the oldest. If you wanted to reverse the order, you could change the final line in the SQL query to

```
order by sent_date desc
```

The SQL keyword desc stands for *descending* and reverses the natural ordering of a column.

❷ We want to print a special message for the user if the forum doesn't yet contain any messages for the supplied messageBoard parameter. We determine this condition by checking to see if the rowCount property of <sql:query>'s result is 0. The rowCount property contains the number of messages in the forum.

❸ Within a <c:forEach> loop, we print each message's name, date, subject, and body. (The example uses column names, not numbers, as promised.) The date is printed as a string whose precise format depends on the database we're using. We could format the date cleanly using <fmt:parseDate> and <fmt:formatDate>, but I've left that step out for simplicity—and because I don't know what database you'll be using.

❹ At the bottom of the page, we print a straightforward HTML form that points to our other page, postMessage.jsp. (See figure 12.7.)

❺ This form is fairly run-of-the-mill, except for one technique it demonstrates. When the postMessage.jsp page posts a message, it needs to know what message board to use. More specifically, it expects a messageBoard parameter just like viewMessages.jsp does. Because the goal of our form is always to let the user post a message into the current forum, we simply pass our forum's number to the next page using an <input type="hidden"> form field. We do so by printing out the value of ${param.messageBoard} into the value attribute for this form field.

Posting messages

The page that posts messages, postMessage.jsp, is about as simple as viewMessages.jsp. For its place in our message-board system, see figure 12.7. This page's job is simple: it accepts a message to be posted (as described by its request parameters), saves the message in the database, and then forwards the user to viewMessages.jsp. Listing 12.3 shows this page.

Listing 12.3   postMessage.jsp: a page that posts messages to a message board

```
<%@ taglib prefix="c" uri="http://java.sun.com/jstl/core" %>
<%@ taglib prefix="fmt" uri="http://java.sun.com/jstl/fmt" %>
<%@ taglib prefix="sql" uri="http://java.sun.com/jstl/sql" %>

<c:choose>
  <c:when test="${empty param.messageBoard or
                  empty param.name or
```

```
                empty param.subject or
                empty param.body}">
    <font color="red">|#1
       Error: you need to enter a name and subject. Please
       go back and try again.
    </font>
  </c:when>
  <c:otherwise>

     <jsp:useBean id="currentDate"
       class="java.util.Date"/>

     <sql:update>
       insert into
         messages(message_board, sent_date, author, subject, body)
         values(?, ?, ?, ?, ?)
       <sql:param value="${param.messageBoard}"/>
       <sql:dateParam value="${currentDate}"/>
       <sql:param value="${param.name}"/>
       <sql:param value="${param.subject}"/>
       <sql:param value="${param.body}"/>
     </sql:update>

     <jsp:forward page="viewMessages.jsp" />
  </c:otherwise>
</c:choose>
```

❶ Simple, brusque validation

❷ Records the current date

❸ Sends the current date to the database

❹ Forwards to the first page

❶ The postMessage.jsp page begins with a simple and convenient validation from our perspective but a somewhat brusque and inconvenient one from the user's. To the application flow from figure 12.7, we could add the extra cycle shown in figure 12.8; we already demonstrated this technique in chapter 11, so we don't need to do so again here.

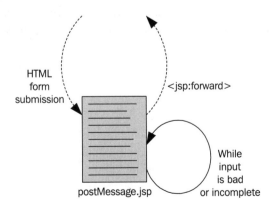

Figure 12.8
The postMessage.jsp page from listing 12.3 validates its input, but it displays only a crude validation message; essentially, it says, "Something's wrong; go fix it," instead of helping the user to do so. As an exercise, you could apply chapter 11's form-validation technique to this page, which would cause it to cycle until its input is successful.

❷ Recall from chapter 10 that we can use the `<jsp:useBean>` tag to record the current date in a scoped variable. Because we want to store the date that the user posted a message, we use this feature of `<jsp:useBean>` and save a scoped variable called `currentDate`.

❸ We send this saved date to the database using a subsequent `<sql:dateParam>` tag.

❹ Once our `<sql:update>` has completed, we return the user to the viewMessages.jsp page. Thus, users get to see their new messages immediately, among the other messages in the forum. As always, the viewMessages.jsp page will need a `messageBoard` parameter to know what board to display. However, because request parameters (just like request-scoped attributes) travel through `<jsp:include>` and `<jsp:forward>` tags, we don't have to do any extra work to pass postMessage.jsp's own `messageBoard` parameter back to viewMessages.jsp. It happens automatically.

We could pass information back to viewMessages.jsp from postMessage.jsp using an appropriately scoped variable (for instance, a request-scoped or session-scoped variable), but because viewMessages.jsp already takes a parameter that's easy for us to set, we don't need to bother.

12.3 *Summary*

In this chapter's examples, we touched on the following points:

- It's surprisingly easy to produce something like an online survey—with calculations, tallies, and even clever HTML bar graphs—using JSTL.

- Relational databases are flexible. Don't just treat them like simple spreadsheets or databases. Sometimes, simple but generic tables lead to flexible, reusable pages.

- A JSP page that has query parameters will automatically pass these parameters to the target page of a `<jsp:forward>` tag. Of course, two pages can also communicate using request, session, or application scope—but if a page is already designed to accept parameters, sometimes it's easier to use them than to invent a new mechanism.

13

Case study in
building a web site

This chapter covers...

- Designing a reusable layout
- Plugging modular channels into a web site
- Registering and authenticating users
- Personalizing a web site

301

So far, you've seen how to use JSTL to solve specific problems and to write individual applications. Now, let's look at how to tie it all together.

In this chapter, we'll build a simple web portal, like the one shown in figure 13.1. You've probably run into portals before, such as my.yahoo.com or my.netscape.com. To be honest, I'm not an enthusiastic user of portals. I often keep 12 different browser windows open at once, and I know almost all the URLs I use by heart—so I don't need a single site to tie things together for me. But apparently, lots of users do. They feel more comfortable with a central, customizable site that becomes their home on the web.

Whether you use portals or not, writing one in JSTL will be a good way to tie our separate applications into a single web site. We'll essentially use JSTL to create a primitive content-management system that lets us plug in new channels to our master web site. We'll also see how to register users, let them log in, and personalize the site for them.

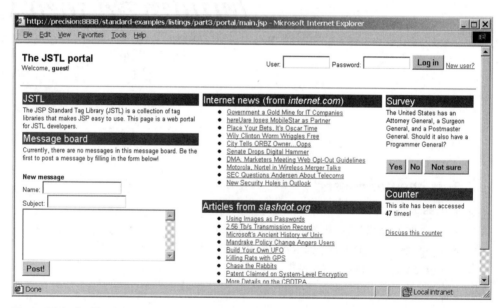

Figure 13.1   In this chapter, we design a simple web portal that combines some features we've written into a single web page. This portal uses JSTL to manage the layout and lets you insert pluggable *channels* as you see fit.

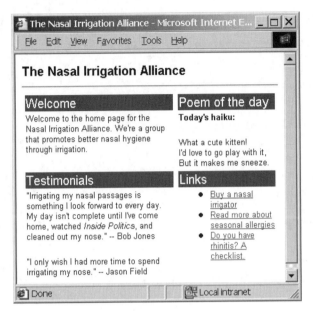

Figure 13.2
In section 13.1, we use JSTL to help organize some simple, static content. Every individual table cell—or channel—in this window is just a simple, static HTML page. These pages are imported into a central layout using <c:import>. Organizing a site like this, even when the content isn't particularly dynamic, makes it easier to maintain.

13.1 *Managing the layout*

We'll begin by using JSTL to print out a simple, static site that has the look and feel of a web portal, but without any personalization or particularly dynamic content. That is, we'll use JSTL just to help with our site's organization and layout.

Look at figure 13.2. This is a simple (albeit somewhat odd) web page. You don't need JSTL to produce it; it's just HTML, with a few `<table>` tags and other straightforward formatting. However, a page like this might be unwieldy to edit frequently. If you wanted to change the Poem of the Day, for instance, you'd have to open the file, find the right spot, and make a change. And if you accidentally erased a `</tr>` tag, you'd ruin the formatting for the entire page. Furthermore, whoever makes changes to the file would need to learn about its overall structure; it's not easy to delegate the management of different table cells, or *channels*, to different people. The department that's responsible for the Testimonials channel has to work in the same file as the guy who updates the links.

13.1.1 *A framework for channels*

To address these problems, we can use JSTL tags to help us manage our information. We'll first create a framework that makes it easy to organize, add, and remove channels. Listing 13.1 shows an example of such a framework.

Listing 13.1 simplePortal.jsp: a file that makes it easy to add and remove channels

```jsp
<%@ taglib prefix="c" uri="http://java.sun.com/jstl/core" %>
<html>
<head>
 <title>The Nasal Irrigation Alliance</title>
 <style>
   body,td {
     font-family: arial,verdana,helvetica,sans-serif;
     font-size: 8pt;
     vertical-align: top;
   }
   .heading {
     background-color: #444444;
     color: #ffffff;
     font-family: arial,verdana,helvetica,sans-serif;
     font-size: 12pt;
     font-stylet: bold;
   }
   h1 {
     font-size: 12pt;
     margin-bottom: 0px;
   }
   h2 {
     font-size: 10pt;
     margin-bottom: 0px;
   }
 </style>
</head>
<body>
<h1>The Nasal Irrigation Alliance</h1>
<hr />

<table width="100%">

 <tr>
  <td width="60%">
   <c:import url="channel.jsp">
    <c:param name="headline" value="Welcome" />
    <c:param name="page" value="welcome.html" />
   </c:import>
   <c:import url="channel.jsp">
    <c:param name="headline" value="Testimonials" />
    <c:param name="page" value="quotes.html" />
   </c:import>
  </td>
  <td width="40%">
   <c:import url="channel.jsp">
    <c:param name="headline" value="Poem of the day" />
    <c:param name="page" value="poetry.html" />
   </c:import>
```

Imports a single
channel

```
    <c:import url="channel.jsp">
     <c:param name="headline" value="Links" />
     <c:param name="page" value="links.html" />
    </c:import>
   </td>
  </tr>

 </table>

 </body>
 </html>
```

Overall, this page is straightforward. It uses inline formatting instructions (the `<style>` tag) written in the Cascading Style Sheets (CSS) language to establish some basic formatting rules, and it structures the bulk of its body into a simple HTML `<table>`. This table has only one row; it's there just to establish a chosen horizontal spacing. This row has two columns: one that's intended to take up 60% of the browser window (`width="60%"`) and one that takes up the remaining 40%.

In fact, the only part of this page that's interesting to us is the small amount of dynamic content. Within each table cell, we import two channels. Every channel has two characteristics:

- A *headline*, which is the text that displays in the horizontal bar we use to introduce a channel. For instance, "Welcome" and "Poem of the Day" are headlines.

- A source *page*, from which the content comes. For instance, one page might contain the text in the Welcome channel ("Welcome to the home page..."), and another could contain the haiku.

One thing about the `<c:import>` tags might look strange: they all import the same page, channel.jsp. That's because every channel uses the same basic layout—gray headline bar with white text, followed by regular body text. How does channel.jsp differentiate between the channels? By accessing the parameters we pass it using the `<c:param>` tags. This way, each time we import channel.jsp, it can display a different headline and print content from a different source page.

13.1.2 Modular channels

Now, let's look at how channel.jsp works. It's a simple page, shown in listing 13.2.

Listing 13.2   channel.jsp: a page to print each channel

```
<%@ taglib prefix="c" uri="http://java.sun.com/jstl/core" %>     Retrieves
<c:import var="body" url="${param.page}"/>                   ⟵  the content
```

```
<table width="100%">
 <tr>
  <td class="heading">
    <c:out escapeXml="false" value="${param.headline}"/>        ◁─┐ Prints the
  </td>                                                            │  headline
 </tr>
 <tr>
  <td>
    <c:out escapeXml="false" value="${body}"/>        ◁─┐ Prints the
  </td>                                                  │  content
 </tr>
</table>
```

The channel.jsp page just prints a headline and a body. The important thing about channel.jsp is that it contains all the HTML formatting markup needed to produce a channel. Each channel is an HTML `<table>` that's designed to fill its entire table cell (from the earlier simplePortal.jsp page), so the `<table>` tag has a `width="100%"` attribute. This table has two rows: one to produce the headline, and one for the body. The headline is set to use the formatting defined for `"heading"` (`class= "heading"`), which we defined in simplePortal.jsp:

```
.heading {
  background-color: #444444;
  color: #ffffff;
  font-family: arial,verdana,helvetica,sans-serif;
  font-size: 12pt;
  font-stylet: bold;
}
```

This formatting accounts for the white-on-gray appearance of each headline. Because channel.jsp is included directly into the outer simplePortal.jsp page, we can take advantage of CSS classes (like heading) that we defined in the `<style>` tag in simplePortal.jsp.

Abstracting the procedure for displaying a channel into channel.jsp keeps the main simplePortal.jsp page simple. Using channel.jsp lets us avoid repetitive formatting logic in the main page, allowing simplePortal.jsp to act as a straightforward catalog of channels. The body of simplePortal.jsp contains minimal HTML formatting; it looks almost like a configuration file describing the channels to import. Using channel.jsp, we avoid a hard-to-manage page containing tables within other tables.

There's one more interesting thing about channel.jsp: we've set `escapeXml= "false"` in both of the `<c:out>` tags, because we want to allow HTML formatting in the headline and body of each channel. (Bodies will almost always contain HTML

Figure 13.3
If we remove the
`escapeXml="false"`
attribute from the `<c:out>`
tag that produces each
channel's body, we see the
raw HTML formatting that
was used to produce each
channel.

markup; headings will do so less frequently, but we don't want to prevent ourselves from formatting a headline with, for instance, `<i>` or `<u>` tags.)

As I mentioned before, the channel.jsp page knows what information to print by checking its request parameters. It imports the page specified by the request parameter `page` and prints the headline from the parameter `headline`. Note that we could have used the `<c:import>` tag directly in the body of the table (without saving the page we imported in the `body` variable), but the way it's currently arranged is more instructive. If you experiment with channel.jsp, try removing the `escapeXml="false"` attribute from the second `<c:out>` tag; you'll get output that looks like figure 13.3.

Individual channels

Our top-down view of simplePortal.jsp doesn't end with channel.jsp. As I mentioned, channel.jsp doesn't display any content of its own, other than a headline and the HTML formatting for a channel. The final content for our simple portal, as figure 13.4 demonstrates, comes from individual, target pages.

The simplePortal.jsp page decides what pages should ultimately be used as channels. For instance, in listing 13.1, our page created four channels. The first channel's content comes from welcome.html, the second from quotes.html, and so on. In this example, these are just local files in the same directory as the portal, but they could be anywhere else; these files could be loaded from a different directory on the same web server, or even from a completely different web server. Instead of

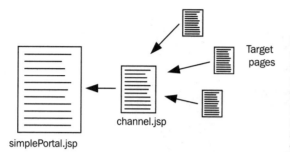

Figure 13.4
Our simple portal pulls information from many individual pages, but these pages are all funneled through channel.jsp to provide the right formatting. The result is the consistent appearance shown in figures 13.1 through 13.3.

specifying a simple filename like quotes.html, we could use a full, absolute URL like the following in the original `<c:param>` tag in simplePortal.jsp:

```
http://my.other.server/quotes/quotes.html
```

Using absolute URLs lets your portal pull content from other servers on your network.

Currently, the target pages contain nothing more than static HTML formatting and simple content; they're just regular HTML pages. However, these pages will be inserted in the middle of a table cell in the final simplePortal.jsp page, so it's inappropriate to import entire pages—those with `<html>` and `<body>` tags, for instance.

As an example of a page designed to be a portal channel, here are the simple, static contents of the poetry.html page:

```
<b>Today's haiku:</b>

<p>
  What a cute kitten! <br />
  I'd love to go play with it, <br />
  But it makes me sneeze. <br />
</p>
```

As you can see, the final pages don't know anything about the portal's overall table formatting; they contain only minimal HTML formatting. Therefore, we can change the way pages are displayed in simplePortal.jsp without having to modify any HTML formatting in the target pages.

Adding error checking

As it stands now, an error that occurs during channel.jsp's `<c:import>` tag will cause the whole portal to fail to load. To address this issue, we should wrap it in `<c:catch>` and print out an appropriate error message, like this:

```
<c:catch var="error">
  <c:import var="body" url="${param.page}"/>
</c:catch>
<c:if test="${not empty error}">
```

```
  <c:set var="body">
    This channel failed to load.  Sorry.
    <!-- Here's why: <c:out value="${error}"/> -->
  </c:set>
</c:if>
```

Instead of simply importing the page, we now catch errors and check for them. If an error occurs, we set the body to contain a brief error message. (We put a more verbose error message into an HTML comment so the user doesn't have to see it by default.) Suppose we now try to include a channel whose page doesn't exist:

```
<c:import url="channel.jsp">
 <c:param name="headline" value="Today's news" />
 <c:param name="page" value="nope.jsp" />
</c:import>
```

If the file nope.jsp doesn't exist in the current directory, then with the channel.jsp page in listing 13.2, the entire portal will fail to load. With our new changes, the user will see a channel like the one in figure 13.5. The error's still there, but it doesn't prevent the entire portal page from loading.

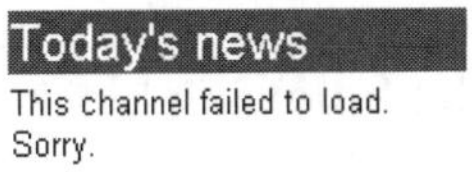

Figure 13.5
Using <c:catch>, we can limit the scope of errors that a channel encounters to that channel alone. Instead of preventing the entire portal page from loading, channel.jsp can catch and print a friendlier error message.

Today's news
This channel failed to load.
Sorry.

13.2 *Adding dynamic content*

So far, our target pages have been simple, static HTML files; they haven't contained dynamic content of their own. But the `<c:import>` tag lets us include JSP files just as easily as HTML files, so the target pages can easily be JSP pages, and they can contain all the dynamic content you'd like.

13.2.1 *Including RSS channels*

What would a portal be without including a few Rich Site Summary (RSS) channels? (An original, interesting one, perhaps—but that's beside the point.) Many portals rely on news feeds and other RSS channels. We discussed how to process RSS in chapter 8; now, let's look at how to include it in our portal. (You might want to review the example at the end of chapter 8 before reading this one.)

Because the theme of this chapter involves organizing content, let's take a step back and figure out the best way to include RSS channels in the portal. One way to include RSS files would be for each target page to import and format a particular

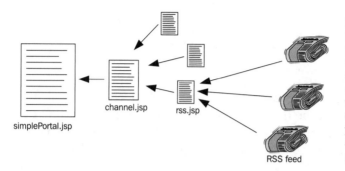

Figure 13.6
Instead of having each target page fetch its own RSS feed, we can centralize the logic in a single page (rss.jsp). The rss.jsp page is to RSS feeds what channel.jsp is to channels: it serves as a single focal point for the formatting and other logic needed to print RSS channels.

RSS feed. For instance, we could have rss1.jsp, which prints a global news feed, and rss2.jsp, which displays technology news.

The problem with this approach is that we end up duplicating effort. The files rss1.jsp and rss2.jsp would probably be the same, except for the URL from which they retrieve their RSS feeds. This duplication would make the pages harder to manage. If we wanted to change how our RSS feeds looked, we'd have to edit multiple pages—one for each feed. Instead, why not use a single page—say, rss.jsp—to print content from multiple RSS feeds? (See figure 13.6.)

This single rss.jsp page will need a way for us to tell it what RSS feed it should retrieve, each time we load it. As you might have guessed, a request parameter is a great way to pass this kind of information. Consider the following block of tags, which we could add to simplePortal.jsp:

```
<c:import url="channel.jsp">
 <c:param name="headline"
   value="Articles from <i>slashdot.org</i>" />
 <c:param name="page"
   value="rss.jsp" />
 <c:param name="rssUrl"
   value="http://www.slashdot.org/slashdot.rdf"/>
</c:import>
```

The first two `<c:param>` tags are straightforward: we'd like to insert a channel headlined "Articles from *slashdot.org*" coming from rss.jsp. The third parameter indicates the URL for the RSS file we'd like rss.jsp to retrieve. However, we're passing this parameter to channel.jsp, not directly to rss.jsp. The channel.jsp page doesn't care about this parameter, so it simply ignores it. When channel.jsp uses a `<c:import>` tag, however, the parameter is passed straight through to rss.jsp. Thus, we have no problem communicating with rss.jsp from simplePortal.jsp, even though there's a page (`channel.jsp`) between the two.

Now, we're ready to look at the page that does the RSS importing. It's similar to the one from chapter 8; I include it here only to make the concepts concrete. Listing 13.3 shows the rss.jsp page, which fetches the URL from its `rssUrl` parameter and formats the RSS file as a bulleted list.[1]

Listing 13.3   rss.jsp: a channel that fetches and displays RSS feeds

```
<%@ taglib prefix="c" uri="http://java.sun.com/jstl/core" %>
<%@ taglib prefix="x" uri="http://java.sun.com/jstl/xml" %>

<c:import var="xml" url="${param.rssUrl}" />
<x:parse var="rss" xml="${xml}" />

<ul>
<x:forEach select="$rss//*[name()='item']">
  <li>
    <a href="<x:out select="./*[name()='link']"/>">
      <x:out select="./*[name()='title']" />
    </a>
  </li>
</x:forEach>
</ul>
```

This rss.jsp page was used to read the RSS feeds shown in figure 13.1's portal. The middle column contains two RSS feeds: one from internet.com and another from slashdot.org.

13.2.2 *Including other dynamic content*

To produce figure 13.1, we included an entire message board as a portal channel. Specifically, we imported a message board from chapter 12's messaging system, using tags like this:

```
<c:import url="channel.jsp">
 <c:param name="headline" value="Message board" />
 <c:param name="page" value="viewMessages.jsp?messageBoard=1" />
</c:import>
```

TIP   Note how we pass a `messageBoard` parameter within `<c:param>`'s value attribute. Doing so might seem tricky, but all we're doing is causing channel.jsp to fetch viewMessages.jsp and send it a parameter (as part of the URL) when it does so.

---

[1] For information on how the XPath expressions work, see chapters 7 and 8.

Because message boards in chapter 12's message system can grow without bound, you normally wouldn't include an entire board in a single portal channel; but you could if you wanted to. (Instead, you'd probably link to a forum, the way the whimsical "Discuss this counter" link in figure 13.1 does.)

Our survey application from chapter 12 integrates cleanly, as well. Simply ask the survey question in a channel that includes an appropriate HTML <form>, and have the form open in new window—a technique you saw how to handle in chapter 12.

In figure 13.1, we also included chapter 9's counter in a channel. Let's look more closely at how to do this; it's a good end-to-end example of including dynamic content in the portal.

To begin with, we modify the counter example from chapter 9 to print the count, not simply to store the value as a scoped variable. The result is the counter.jsp page from listing 13.4.

Listing 13.4   counter.jsp: a channel that adds a counter to the portal

```
<%@ taglib prefix="c" uri="http://java.sun.com/jstl/core" %>
<%@ taglib prefix="sql" uri="http://java.sun.com/jstl/sql" %>

<sql:transaction>

  <sql:update>
    update counter set counter = counter + 1
  </sql:update>
  <sql:query var="result">
    select * from counter
  </sql:query>
  <c:set var="count" value="${result.rows[0].counter}" />

</sql:transaction>

<p>
  This site has been accessed
  <b><c:out value="${count}" /></b>
  times!
</p>

<p>
 <a target="_blank"
   href="<c:url value="viewMessages.jsp">
           <c:param name="messageBoard" value="2"/>
         </c:url>">
  Discuss this counter
 </a>
</p>
```

> **NOTE** This example assumes that your application has an appropriate database set up as its default data source. If it doesn't, you'll need to use the `<sql:setDataSource>` tag that we discussed in chapter 9.

This page displays a counter and then a link that people can follow if they're inclined to engage in discussions in a forum about the counter. (From browsing the Web, I think it's clear that many people are bored enough to discuss a hit counter.)

You can include nearly any dynamic content inside a portal channel. Just as with HTML content, you can even pull it out of a JSP page from a different server.

13.3 Registering users

You've seen how to include static and dynamic content into a portal-like page, but it's not much of a portal unless it provides personalized output to users. To do this, we'll need to let the portal sign up new users.

13.3.1 Modifying the header

First, let's look at how to modify the front page to let users register and log in.

To produce the header at the top of figure 13.2, the simplePortal.jsp page uses straightforward HTML:

```
<h1>The Nasal Irrigation Alliance</h1>
<hr />
```

Compare this header to figure 13.1, which shows three separate features related to user registration:

- A greeting ("Welcome, guest!") that can be personalized ("Welcome back, Murray!")

- Boxes that let the user enter a name and password, if he or she isn't already logged in

- A link labeled "New user?" that lets new users register

To print the header at the top of figure 13.1, we can use the following text and JSTL tags:

```
<table width="100%">
<tr>
 <td>
  <h1>The JSTL portal</h1>
  <c:choose>
   <c:when test="${empty sessionScope.user}">
```

```
    Welcome, <b>guest</b>!
  </c:when>
  <c:otherwise>
    Welcome back, <b><c:out value="${sessionScope.user}"/></b>!
  </c:otherwise>
  </c:choose>
</td>
<td align="right">
<c:if test="${empty sessionScope.user}">
  <form method="post" action="login.jsp">
   User: <input type="text" name="user" size="10" />
   Password: <input type="password" name="pw" size="10" />
   <input type="submit" value="Log in" />
   <a href="register.jsp">New user?</a>
  </form>
</c:if>
 </td>
</tr>
</table>
<hr />
```

This block of code is designed to produce an HTML table that takes up the full width of the page (width="100%"). The table has one row; we use it only to split the left side of the screen from the right side. On the left side of the table, we display a greeting, and on the right, if necessary, we display a login form.

The JSTL tags are designed to behave differently depending on whether a user is logged in. To determine whether a user is logged in, we check the session-scoped variable user. We'll demonstrate later how the portal manages this variable; for now, it's enough to know that if the user hasn't yet logged in, the variable will be empty. Thus, the expression ${empty sessionScope.user} will be true only when the user hasn't logged in.

We use this fact to display a special greeting for guests on the left side of the screen, and to display a login form on the right side. (No login form is necessary when the user's already logged in, so we don't bother displaying it in that case.)

13.3.2 *The registration form*

Notice the HTML hyperlink that lets new users register:

```
<a href="register.jsp">New user?</a>
```

This link takes users to a page that looks like figure 13.7. This page is produced by a JSP page called register.jsp that works just like the "junk email registration" form

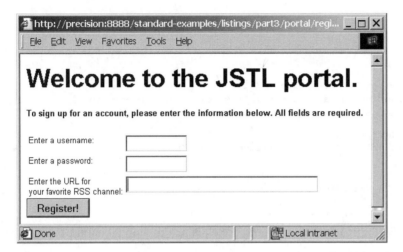

Figure 13.7   To let our portal personalize itself to our users, we need to ask them to register. Registration involves letting the user choose a username, a password, and the URL for an RSS channel they'd like to display.

from chapter 11. However, it's more intricate than that example. The register.jsp page is shown in listing 13.5.

Listing 13.5   register.jsp: a page that registers users and validates their entries

```
<%@ taglib prefix="c" uri="http://java.sun.com/jstl/core" %>

<c:if test="${param.submitted}">
  <c:if test="${empty param.name}" var="noName" />
  <c:if test="${empty param.pw}" var="noPw" />
  <c:if test="${empty param.url}" var="noUrl" />

  <c:if
    test="${not (noName or noPw or noUrl or
                 requestScope.takenName)}">
    <c:set value="${param.name}" var="name" scope="request"/>
    <c:set value="${param.pw}" var="pw" scope="request"/>
    <c:set value="${param.url}" var="url" scope="request"/>
    <jsp:forward page="doRegister.jsp" />
  </c:if>
</c:if>

<html>

<head>
 <style>
   body, td {
     font-family: arial,verdana,helvetica,sans-serif;
     font-size: 8pt;
```

Validates
input

```
      vertical-align: top;
    }
  </style>
</head>
<body>
<h1>Welcome to the JSTL portal.</h1>
<p><b>To sign up for an account, please enter the information
below.  All fields are required.</b></p>

<form method="post">
<input type="hidden" name="submitted" value="true" />
<table>
 <tr>
  <td>Enter a username:</td>
  <td>
    <input type="text" name="name" size="10"
      value="<c:out value="${param.name}"/>"
    />
    <c:if test="${noName}">
      <br /><font color="red">You must enter a username</font>
    </c:if>
    <c:if test="${requestScope.takenName}">
      <br /><font color="red">Sorry, that username
        is already taken. Please choose another.</font>
    </c:if>
  </td>
 </tr>
 <tr>
  <td>Enter a password:</td>
  <td>
    <input type="password" name="pw" size="10"
      value="<c:out value="${param.pw}"/>"
    />
    <c:if test="${noPw}">
      <br /><font color="red">You must enter a password</font>
    </c:if>
  </td>
 </tr>
 <tr>
  <td>Enter the URL for <br />your favorite RSS channel:</td>
  <td>
    <input type="text" name="url" size="40"
      value="<c:out value="${param.url}"/>"
    />
    <c:if test="${noUrl}">
      <br /><font color="red">You must enter a url</font>
    </c:if>
  </td>
 </tr>
</table>
<input type="submit" value="Register!" />
```

**Validates
forwarded
information**

```
</form>

</body>
</html>
```

Most of this page should be familiar from our prior experience in chapter 11. The only thing that's different about register.jsp is that it refers to a request-scoped attribute called takenName. It does this twice. First, in its initial validation, it refuses to pass the user on to doRegister.jsp if takenName is true. Then, it prints out a special error message if takenName is true.

From the special error message that prints, you can probably figure out what the takenName variable represents: it's true if the user has entered a username that has already been taken by another user. But what sets this scoped variable, and how does it do so?

The doRegister.jsp page sets the scoped variable. When the user enters values for all three form fields, we forward the user to doRegister.jsp. Normally, doRegister.jsp just adds the new user to a database and bounces the user back to the main

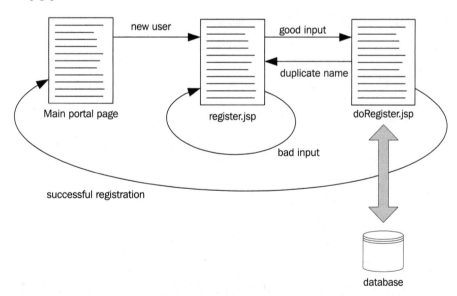

Figure 13.8 New users who try to register with the portal need to fill out the information in the form presented by register.jsp. If the user enters valid information, then register.jsp forwards to doRegister.jsp. Normally, doRegister.jsp adds the user to the database and returns the user to the main portal page. However, if the user enters a duplicate username, doRegister.jsp forwards the user back to register.jsp and gives him a chance to choose a new name.

portal page. However, if the user's chosen name has already been taken by some-one else, doRegister.jsp forwards back to register.jsp after setting the takenName variable. Thus, doRegister.jsp lets register.jsp reprint the form, but it feeds the page special information so that it knows how to instruct the user. Figure 13.8 summa-rizes the flow of pages that new users encounter.

13.3.3 Saving the registration

The doRegister.jsp page is shown in listing 13.6. As with the other database exam-ples in this part of this book, it assumes that your application has a sensible default database set up. If not, then you'll need to use the <sql:setDataSource> tag to set up a database connection.

Listing 13.6   doRegister.jsp: adds a new user to the portal's database

```
<%@ taglib prefix="c" uri="http://java.sun.com/jstl/core" %>
<%@ taglib prefix="sql" uri="http://java.sun.com/jstl/sql" %>

<sql:transaction isolation="serializable">
  <sql:query var="result">
    select user from users where user=?
    <sql:param value="${requestScope.name}"/>
  </sql:query>
  <c:if test="${result.rowCount > 0}"
        var="takenName"
        scope="request">
    <jsp:forward page="register.jsp" />
  </c:if>
  <sql:update>
    insert into users(user, password, rss)
      values(?, ?, ?);
    <sql:param value="${requestScope.name}"/>
    <sql:param value="${requestScope.pw}"/>
    <sql:param value="${requestScope.url}"/>
  </sql:update>
</sql:transaction>
<c:set var="user" scope="session" value="${requestScope.name}"/>
<jsp:forward page="main.jsp"/>
```

The doRegister.jsp page reads all of its data from request-scoped variables that were previously set by register.jsp. The page receives the following three variables:

- requestScope.name—The user's chosen username
- requestScope.pw—The user's chosen password
- requestScope.url—The URL for the RSS channel the user chose

First, the page checks to see whether `requestScope.name` already exists in the user database. If it does, then it returns the user to register.jsp after setting the request-scoped variable `takenName`. The way doRegister.jsp does this is interesting:

```
<c:if test="${result.rowCount > 0}"
      var="takenName"
      scope="request">
  <jsp:forward page="register.jsp" />
</c:if>
```

The same `<c:if>` tag that decides whether to forward back to register.jsp sets the request-scoped `takenName` to `true`. If the `<c:if>` tag's condition is satisfied—if the result includes one or more rows, indicating that the chosen username clashes with an existing one—then `takenName` will also be set to `true` by the `<c:if>` tag. Thus, if the `<jsp:forward>` tag is ever reached, `takenName` will be `true`.

Finally, if the user's chosen name isn't a duplicate, doRegister.jsp adds the new user to the database and returns the user to the main portal page. Before doing so, it sets the session-scoped variable `user` equal to the user's new name. This action has the effect of logging the user in, which is convenient: why make users log in right after they've registered?

You might have noticed that we use an `<sql:transaction>` tag to surround all these operations. This tag, with the attribute `isolation="serializable"`, helps prevent against the unlikely event that two users register the same name at once. The read and the subsequent write are treated as a single transaction, so that if one user has just caused the page to read the username "Bob", no other page can create the same username. The username is effectively reserved for the user as soon as we check to see whether it's a duplicate.

13.3.4 *The user database*

The user database is straightforward. It has three columns:

Column name	Type	Purpose
`user`	`VARCHAR(20)`	Username
`password`	`VARCHAR(20)`	Password
`rss`	`VARCHAR(255)`	URL for the user's chosen RSS feed

We create the table with the following SQL command:

```
create table users (
  user varchar(20) primary key,
  password varchar(20) not null,
```

```
rss varchar(255) not null
)
```

Note that we've made the `user` column a primary key. Because primary keys are unique within a table, the database serves as a last line of defense to ensure unique usernames. We could have depended on the database's ability to enforce the uniqueness of usernames instead of performing a query to determine whether the user's chosen name exists. That is, we could have eliminated the `<sql:transaction>` and `<sql:query>` tags and used `<c:catch>` to determine whether an error occurred. But doRegister.jsp is more instructive as I've listed it, and (in my opinion) it's also better designed; it checks for a particular kind of error case (duplicate usernames) before sending data to the database. Because of this check, it's easier to report a specific error condition to the user ("Sorry, that username is already taken"); moreover, we also decrease the likelihood of ignoring a real, unexpected database error.

The old admonition to "be careful what you wish for" applies, as well as the story of the "boy who cried 'wolf.'" The problem with expecting an error from an underlying component is twofold. First, the error might not occur. Second, you might inadvertently ignore a real problem. Thus, I advise against using `<c:catch>` as a mechanism for deliberate control flow (like `<c:if>`); instead, it should be used only to respond to unexpected error conditions.

13.4 *Authenticating users*

Now that the portal can register users and their passwords in a database, let's look at how we can use this information to let users log in.

13.4.1 *Logging in users*

The login form we created in section 13.3 sends information to a page called login.jsp. This page, as shown in listing 13.7, is reasonably simple.

Listing 13.7   login.jsp: lets users log in to the portal

```
<%@ taglib prefix="c" uri="http://java.sun.com/jstl/core" %>
<%@ taglib prefix="sql" uri="http://java.sun.com/jstl/sql" %>

<sql:query var="result">
  select * from users where user=? and password=?
  <sql:param value="${param.user}" />
  <sql:param value="${param.pw}" />
</sql:query>
<c:choose>
  <c:when test="${result.rowCount > 0}">
    <c:set var="user" scope="session" value="${param.user}" />
```

```
    <c:set var="rss" scope="session"
      value="${result.rows[0].RSS}" />
  </c:when>
  <c:otherwise>
    <c:set var="failedLogin" scope="request" value="true"/>
  </c:otherwise>
</c:choose>
<jsp:forward page="main.jsp" />
```

The login.jsp page first performs a query against the user database. This query includes an SQL where clause that looks like this:

```
where user=? and password=?
```

The <sql:param> tags fill in the question marks with the supplied username and password. (The user supplies these values in the form fields at the top of figure 13.1.) The query matches a row only if both the username and the password match. This is how we handle *authentication*—the process of forcing the users to prove that they are who they say they are.

If the login succeeds—if a row is matched—then the login.jsp page sets the session-scoped user variable, which proves to the portal (and its channels, if they're interested) that a user has logged in. We also set a variable called rss with the RSS channel URL that the database associates with the user.

If the login fails, then we simply set a variable named failedLogin. This variable has *request* scope; we set it so that the main portal page—to which login.jsp forwards whether the login succeeds or fails—can print an appropriate message. For instance, we could add a tag like this to the main login page:

```
<c:if test="${requestScope.failedLogin}">
  Sorry, bad username or password.
</c:if>
```

13.4.2 *Some notes about authentication*

In sections 13.3 and 13.4, we created a simple authentication mechanism for the portal. Authentication is an important subject in its own right, and the details of it are beyond this book's scope. However, I want to say a few things about authentication that might be useful to you as you design web applications.

In many environments, you don't have to handle authentication. This will be particularly true in large environments where you're integrating your JSP pages with existing data models and services and not building an application from scratch. The JSP container can manage authentication for you, and you may be able to retrieve the name of the current user simply by using an expression like the following:

```
${pageContext.request.remoteUser}
```

Alternatively, back-end Java logic may manage authentication and set some information in the session scope for you to use.

One principle for authentication is important to keep in mind: don't reinforce your front door but leave your back door wide open. If you handle authentication at a single page in your application, consider what might happen if a user tried to access one of your other page's URLs directly. Using session-scoped variables is a good idea because users can't set scoped variables directly. Similarly, using a parameter to pass a secure username from one page to another is a very bad idea, because users *can* set parameters.

A final note: in some environments, network security is important. Sending a cleartext password to a web site might not be acceptable in some environments. You may have noticed that some web pages have URLs that start with *https* instead of *http*. These URLs use the Secure Sockets Layer (SSL), which is a mechanism that can provide both encryption and authentication for the Web.

Overall, be careful when handling the authentication of users. In other words, don't use the system that we built here to protect your valuable assets until you've thought long and hard about computer security!

13.5 *Personalizing the site*

The portal and any channel can use the session-scoped `user` variable to determine who (if anyone) is logged in and react accordingly. Channels and the portal can also use other session-scoped variables to configure themselves.

You've already seen one simple example of this kind of personalization. The header for the main portal page that we added in section 13.3 will print a customized greeting for the user. For example, instead of saying, "Welcome, guest!" it will say, "Welcome back, Shawn!" if I log in.

Let's look at a few other examples of personalization.

13.5.1 *Filling in a form automatically*

Look again at figure 13.1. The first column contains a message board from chapter 12's messaging system. Normally, users need to enter a username when posting a message. But because the portal might know who's logged in, let's let the messaging system take advantage of that fact.

To add this capability, we can take the line in the message system's viewMessage.jsp page that reads

```
Name: <input type="text" name="name" />
```

and replace it with this:

```
Name: <input type="text" name="name"
  value="<c:out value="${sessionScope.user}"/>" />
```

If this new line runs and nobody's logged in, it will result in

```
value=""
```

This result is fine, because it's the default behavior of `<input type="text">`. If a user is indeed logged in, however, we instead get

```
value="username"
```

where `username` is the current user's name. This result leads to the personalized output shown in figure 13.9.

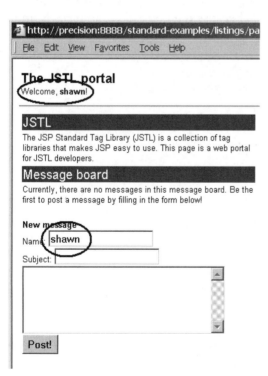

Figure 13.9
Because the portal knows who's logged in, individual channels don't need to ask separately; they can take advantage of the centralized authentication by referring to a portal-managed, session-scoped variable.

13.5.2 *Displaying a chosen RSS feed*

When users sign up using our register.jsp page, they also supply the URL for an RSS channel they'd like to view. You saw earlier how to include the RSS feed from Slashdot that appears in figure 13.1:

```
<c:import url="channel.jsp">
 <c:param name="headline"
   value="Articles from <i>slashdot.org</i>" />
 <c:param name="page"
   value="rss.jsp" />
 <c:param name="rssUrl"
   value="http://www.slashdot.org/slashdot.rdf"/>
</c:import>
```

But instead of Slashdot (which can sometimes get tedious), let's show the RSS channel the user chose. Note that we can't simply write

```
<c:param name="rssUrl" value="${sessionScope.rss}"/>
```

because we need to take into account the possibility that the user isn't logged in and thus that no session-scoped variable named rss is present. We can't include tags like <c:choose> inside <c:import> because the body of <c:import> is, in its familiar syntax, intended only for <c:param> tags. So, instead, we can do this:

```
<c:choose>
 <c:when test="${not empty sessionScope.rss}">
  <c:set var="userRss" value="${sessionScope.rss}"/>
 </c:when>
 <c:otherwise>
  <c:set var="userRss"
    value="http://www.slashdot.org/slashdot.rdf"/>
 </c:otherwise>
<c:choose>
<c:import url="channel.jsp">
 <c:param name="headline"
   value="Current RSS feed" />
 <c:param name="page"
   value="rss.jsp" />
 <c:param name="rssUrl" value="${userRss}"/>
</c:import>
```

We use a <c:choose> tag to decide which RSS feed to use. If a user is logged in, we note that user's preference; otherwise, we default to using Slashdot's URL (http://www.slashdot.org/slashdot.rdf).

With this change to the main portal page, users can receive custom news based on the URL they entered. For instance, if I signed up to the portal using the URL http://politicalwire.com/headlines.xml, which offers current political headlines, I'd

Current RSS feed

- In Massachusetts, Romney Readies Attacks On Democrats
- Democrats Receive Record Soft Money Contribution
- Ken Starr To Lead Court Fight Against Campaign Finance Reform
- Another Political Web Site Folds
- In Maryland, O'Malley Hints He Might Run For Governor
- Kerry Steps Up Criticism Of Bush In New Interview
- Lott's Anger At Daschle Grows
- In Florida, Democrats Fret Over Reno's Campaign
- Fight Over Ridge's Status Escalates
- In Pennsylvania, Democratic Primary Tightening
- In Illinois, Republicans Try To Unify After Bitter Primary
- In Massachusetts, Romney Will Not Pick Running Mate
- Bush Will Sign Campaign Finance Reform Bill
- Bullish Year For Business Candidates
- In New York, McCall Has Narrow Lead Over Cuomo

Figure 13.10
Because the portal records user preferences, it can display a user-chosen RSS feed—like this list of political headlines.

get the output shown in figure 13.10. New users who come to the portal will still see the links from www.slashdot.org.

13.6 *Summary*

In building and expanding an online portal, we encountered the following ideas:

- Using JSTL's `<c:import>` tag can help you organize your pages. You can separate commonly reused fragments and include them multiple times into your pages, modifying their behavior by sending them different request parameters each time.

- The `<c:catch>` tag is useful to ensure that an error in one such fragment (like channel.jsp) doesn't lead to an error for your whole page.

- It's easy to roll your own simple authentication system to register and log in users using JSTL's SQL tags.

Part 4

JSTL for programmers

Parts 1 through 3 of this book have covered everything that web-page authors need to know about JSTL. But if you're a Java programmer, JSTL offers you a few special features.

In part 4, we present more advanced material. None of this material is necessary to use JSTL, but you might find it useful if you're a programmer who wants to get the most out of JSTL. First, we discuss some more advanced uses of JSTL than you saw in parts 1 through 3. Then, we examine ways to configure JSTL tags and otherwise assist the page authors you work with. For instance, you can use Java code to manage locales, time zones, and databases so that your page authors don't have to. Part 4 shows you how.

Finally, we explore how JSTL makes it easier to write custom JSP tags. If you've been intimidated by the JSP Tag Extension API, then you will probably appreciate JSTL's more convenient APIs for iteration and conditional tags.

If you're not a programmer, don't despair. You won't need to know any of the material in these chapters. However, I certainly encourage you to be ambitious: Java isn't that hard to learn, and JSTL is designed to make things easier—for programmers, too. If you don't know Java, I suggest you start with a good introductory book on Java, like Peter van der Linden's *Just Java*.[1] Then, feel free to wade into part 4's material. My hope is that you'll find it more interesting and helpful than you expected.

---

[1] Prentice Hall, 2001.

Control and performance

This chapter covers...

- Mixing Java code and JSTL
- Exposing data for JSTL tags
- Advanced features of JSTL tags
- Configuring JSTL

JSTL was designed to be easy to use even if you don't know anything about Java. But if you do know Java, then you can take advantage of features that help you fine-tune JSTL's behavior and performance. If you know the difference between a `java.lang.String` and a `java.io.Reader`, this chapter is for you.

We'll begin by looking at how to integrate JSTL tags with *scripting elements*—Java code embedded directly into your pages. In most cases, JSTL and custom tag libraries make scripting elements obsolete. However, if you're a lone Java developer who also writes web pages, then scripting elements might lie on a path of least resistance for you. Or you might need to use scripting elements to communicate with an older tag library. Either way, this chapter shows you how to mix JSTL tags and embedded Java in your web pages.

Then, we'll look at some advanced features of JSTL. These features can help you squeeze extra performance and flexibility out of JSTL tags.

Finally, we'll discuss how you can help control and configure page authors' environments. If you're a back-end Java developer, JSTL lets you set up default database connections, locales, and other items for your pages. It also lets you place restrictions on JSP pages, which can be helpful in enforcing your organization's web-design policies.

14.1 Scripting elements and the JSTL rtexprvalue libraries

Scripting elements let you add Java code directly to your JSP pages. Although JSTL tags cause Java code to run behind the scenes, scripting elements are different: they let you insert literal Java code alongside your static HTML text. For instance, the scripting elements in the following code are set in boldface type:

```
<% Date d = new Date(); %>
It's now <%= d %>; do you know where your children are?
```

There are three kinds of scripting elements:

- *Scriptlets*—Scriptlets, the most general scripting elements, let you embed arbitrary Java statements into your page. For instance, the following scriptlet is taken from a JSP page I wrote long ago; its goal was to help my page format a date using a particular time zone:

```
<%
  Date now = new Date();
  TimeZone tzUser = TimeZone.getTimeZone(request.getQueryString());
  DateFormat df = DateFormat.getDateTimeInstance(DateFormat.MEDIUM,
    DateFormat.MEDIUM);
%>
```

- *Scripting expression*—Scripting expressions work like the `<c:out>` tag: they output the result of an expression in the middle of your page. But whereas `<c:out>` uses JSTL's expression language, JSP scripting expressions use Java as their language.[1] Scripting expressions start with `<%=` and end with `%>`. For instance, the following text includes a scripting expression:

```
Good morning, Mr. <%= user %>.
```

- *Declaration*—A declaration is designed to let you declare Java methods and fields that can be used later in your page. Declarations start with `<%!` and end with `%>`.

This book doesn't discuss the details of how scriptlets and other scripting elements work. If you want more information about scripting expressions, books like *Web Development with JavaServer Pages*[2] cover them in detail. The purpose of this section is just to show you how to integrate scripting elements with JSTL, assuming you already know how they work.

14.1.1 *Warning against scripting expressions*

Advanced JSP users may feel comfortable adding Java to their web pages, but most authorities on JSP pages believe that scriptlets and other scripting elements make JSP pages harder to maintain. When a page mixes HTML and Java code, the page often becomes difficult to read, edit, or test. Implementation logic is mingled with presentation text, meaning that anyone who needs to maintain the page must the skills both of a page designer and a Java programmer.

JSTL was designed to make JSP pages easy to develop without using any Java code. JSTL therefore encourages Java web-development teams to separate back-end *business logic* (written in Java) from presentation logic (written with JSTL and HTML). In large organizations that employ separate teams of Java developers and HTML authors, this approach can lead to a productive division of labor.

However, although pages that contain Java code have fallen out of favor, eliminating Java from web pages entirely might be too extreme in your environment. Therefore, even though I encourage you to try writing JSP pages without scriptlets, this section shows you how to integrate them with JSTL tags.

---

[1] Technically, JSP supports languages other than Java too, although this support, in general, constitutes little more than lip service. For all practical purposes, JSP uses Java as its scripting language.

[2] Duane Fields, Mark Kolb, and Shawn Bayern, 2nd ed. (Manning Publications, 2001).

14.1.2 JSTL's dual libraries

To work better with scripting expressions, every JSTL tag library has a twin that uses scripting expressions (`<%= … %>`) instead of the JSTL expression language. Recall from chapter 2 that JSTL offers four tag libraries:

- The core library
- The XML-processing library
- The text-formatting and internationalization library
- The database library

Each of these libraries has a counterpart that's identical, except that every attribute that accepts a JSTL expression in the familiar library accepts, instead, a scripting expression in the twin library. Formally, when a tag accepts a scripting expression for an attribute, that tag is said to accept an *rtexprvalue*, or *request-time expression value*. For instance, the following tag uses an rtexprvalue:

```
<fmt_rt:formatNumber value="<%= netWorth %>"/>
```

Table 14.1 lists the four rtexprvalue-oriented JSTL libraries.

Table 14.1 For each JSTL tag library that we discussed earlier in this book, JSTL supports a twin rtexprvalue library that accepts Java expressions instead of JSTL expressions. This table lists the URIs and suggested prefixes of the four JSTL rtexprvalue libraries.

JSTL tag library	Suggested prefix	URI	Example tag
Core library (iteration, conditions, and so on)	`c_rt`	http://java.sun.com/jstl/core_rt	`<c_rt:forEach>`
XML processing library	`x_rt`	http://java.sun.com/jstl/xml_rt	`<x_rt:forEach>`
Internationalization (i18n) and formatting	`fmt_rt`	http://java.sun.com/jstl/fmt_rt	`<fmt_rt:formatDate>`
Database (SQL) access	`sql_rt`	http://java.sun.com/jstl/sql_rt	`<sql_rt:query>`

Importing the rtexprvalue libraries is as simple as importing the familiar libraries you've already seen. For instance, chapter 2 showed how to import the core library:

```
<%@ taglib prefix="c" uri="http://java.sun.com/jstl/core" %>
```

To import the rtexprvalue version of the core library, you'd instead write the following:

```
<%@ taglib prefix="c_rt" uri="http://java.sun.com/jstl/core_rt" %>
```

Then, if you wanted to use the `forEach` tag in the core library, you'd write

```
<c_rt:forEach ...>
```

instead of

```
<c:forEach ...>
```

For example, if we wanted to loop over a collection of products stored in the session-scoped variable named `products`, we'd normally write

```
<c:forEach items="${sessionScope.products}" var="product">
  <c:out value="${product}" />
</c:forEach>
```

With the rtexprvalue library, we could instead write

```
<c_rt:forEach
    items='<%= session.getAttribute("products") %>'
    var="product">
  <%= pageContext.getAttribute("product") %>
</c_rt:forEach>
```

This book doesn't describe how JSP's implicit objects, such as `pageContext` and `session`, work. The goal here is to show you how the JSTL rtexprvalue libraries accept input, assuming you already know how to write rtexprvalues.

14.1.3 *Scripting variables and* *<jsp:useBean>*

Referring to scoped variables from within Java scripting elements can be inconvenient. For instance, in the last example, we used the following rtexprvalue:

```
<%= pageContext.getAttribute("product") %>
```

This seems like a lot of trouble just to retrieve the `product` variable. To make it easier to manage variables, JSP introduces the idea of a *scripting variable*—a variable you can access by its name, as in

```
<%= product %>
```

Because of the way JSP works, we can easily create a scripting variable using a scriptlet:

```
<% String product = pageContext.getAttribute("product"); %>
```

This scriptlet creates a Java variable, and thus a scripting variable, named `product`, which we can use later in our pages. But this also seems like a lot of work for a simple task.

Fortunately, there are easier ways. Custom tags can also produce scripting variables, but in recognition of the diminishing role of scriptlets and scripting expressions, no JSTL tags take advantage of this ability. Therefore, if you want to create a scripting variable based on a scoped variable exposed by a JSTL tag, you'll need to do so yourself. To do so, you can use `<jsp:useBean>`, a standard JSP tag.

Like `<jsp:include>` and `<jsp:forward>`, the tags we discussed in chapter 2, the `<jsp:useBean>` tag is automatically available to you in any JSP page. Its options are complicated and already covered in detail by many JSP books; for our purposes, we're concerned only with its simplest usage:

```
<jsp:useBean id="variable name" type="variable type"/>
```

In this syntax, *variable name* is the name of the scripting variable you want to expose, and *variable type* is the Java type of that variable—for instance, `java.lang.String` or `java.util.Date`.

When used in this way, `<jsp:useBean>` attempts to locate a scoped variable using the value of its `id` attribute, and it creates a scripting variable associated with this scoped variable. For instance, if we wanted to create and use a scripting variable named `product` in a `<c_rt:forEach>` loop similar to the last one, we could write

```
<c_rt:forEach
    items='<%= session.getAttribute("products") %>'
    var="product">
  <jsp:useBean id="product" type="com.jstlbook.Product"/>
  Your product is <%= product %>.
</c_rt:forEach>
```

The `<jsp:useBean>` tag creates a scripting variable named `product`, which we can use in subsequent scripting elements. Note that you have to specify manually the type of the scripting variable you want to create; JSTL can't shield you from the details of data types when you insist on using scripting variables.

With the syntax we've described, the `<jsp:useBean>` tag can, despite its name, be used to expose any object, whether or not you think of that object as a JavaBean. For instance, `<jsp:useBean>` works fine with `java.lang.String`, `java.util.Date`, or whatever data types you have. Chapter 10 already showed you how to use `<jsp:useBean>` with `java.util.Date`, but we used a different syntax (the `class` attribute instead of the `type` attribute) for it there.

14.2 Modifying properties with `<c:set>`

Shifting gears a little, we'll now begin to examine some advanced features of JSTL tags. In most cases, these tags will already be familiar, but we'll introduce attributes that let you gain more control over their behavior or performance. First, we look at an advanced feature of the `<c:set>` tag.

In chapter 3 and throughout the book, you've seen how the `<c:set>` tag can set scoped variables. It also has an advanced syntax that lets you modify a property of an existing scoped variable. Instead of specifying the `var` and `scope` attributes, you can use two different attributes: `target` and `property`. Unlike `var` and `scope`, both of these attributes accept any valid JSTL expressions. The `target` attribute points to the variable you'd like to alter, and `property` resolves to the name of the property of `target` you want to change.

For example, suppose `${user}` points to a JavaBean or `Map` that stores information about the current user. Imagine this variable has an `iq` property that stores the user's IQ. Using the syntax for `<c:set>` presented in chapter 3, we don't have any fine-grained control over this property. We can replace the entire `user` variable with `<c:set>` or even remove it with `<c:remove>`, but if the user does something brilliant or spectacularly stupid, we have no way of adjusting the `iq` property alone.

The `target` and `property` attributes give us this power. To add five points to the user's IQ, we can use the following tag:

```
<c:set value="${user.iq + 5}" target="${user}" property="iq"/>
```

As with the familiar use of `<c:set>`, `value` accepts any JSTL expression, and you can also use the tag's body to supply a value.

14.3 Advanced techniques for importing text

Like all JSTL tags, the `<c:import>` tag's first priority is ease of use. However, `<c:import>` has a few advanced attributes you can use to gain greater control over the way the tag operates. These attributes aren't intended for everyone, but you might find them useful if you're an advanced JSP user.

14.3.1 Representing imported text as a java.io.Reader

Normally, when you use the `<c:import>` tag's `var` attribute to save imported data to a scoped variable, the tag simply exposes a `java.lang.String` that stores all the content that the tag retrieves. If you use `<c:import>` to retrieve large amounts of data, however, storing the data as a string might not be efficient. Strings take up memory, and they also take time to process.

To address this issue, the `<c:import>` tag has a `varReader` attribute for exposing information as a `java.io.Reader` object. A reader can be more efficient than a string because it doesn't require `<c:import>` to read and buffer the entire content retrieved from a URL. Instead, it simply opens the connection and lets another tag read the data. This process is both faster and less memory intensive than buffering the data into a string.

Typically, `<c:import>` does not accept any text or other tags in its body, except for `<c:param>`. However, when you specify `varReader`, the tags or scripting elements that use the exposed reader must appear within the `<c:import>` tag's body.

This is a requirement because the `<c:import>` tag needs to ensure that it has an opportunity to close the `Reader` object to prevent resource leaks. Therefore, it cannot simply expose a reader to an entire page on an open-ended basis; the reader might never be used or closed. Instead, `<c:import>` only lets page authors use the reader within its body, and it destroys the reader before the tag finishes.

For example, suppose we want to import some data with `<c:import>` and then feed that data to a custom tag called `<custom:process>`. Using the syntax we presented in chapter 6, we'd write the following:

```
<c:import url="target.jsp" var="data"/>
<custom:process data="${data}"/>
```

Note that the hypothetical `<custom:process>` tag needs to understand JSTL's expression language and accept `java.lang.String` objects from its `data` attribute.

Now, imagine that the target.jsp page includes megabytes of data. The last example might not run efficiently, so instead, we can use a reader:

```
<c:import url="target.jsp" varReader="data">
  <custom:process data="${data}"/>
</c:import>
```

Here, `<custom:process>` needs to accept a `java.io.Reader`; instead of simply using the value of a string, it needs to read characters from this reader. It appears in `<c:import>`'s body so that when the `</c:import>` tag is finally reached, the reader can be destroyed.

When you expose a reader to the `<c:import>` tag's body, you can't use `<c:param>` in that same body. This limitation arises because `<c:import>` needs to open the connection and expose a reader immediately, before its body begins to execute. If it had to wait for `<c:param>` tags, it couldn't do this. Thus, `<c:param>` tags are outlawed in this case. If you want to send parameters to a URL and also expose a reader for the URL, you'll need to build up the URL beforehand using `<c:url>`, as follows:

```
<c:url value="http://url" var="url" >
  <c:param name="name1" value="value1"/>
  <c:param name="name2" value="value2"/>
</c:url>
<c:import url="${url}" varReader="reader">
  <custom:process data="${reader}"/>
</c:import>
```

WARNING   Don't use this pattern with relative URLs, because `<c:url>` adds the name of the current web context to URLs. This will confuse `<c:import>`.

One final note of caution: `varReader` may not be effective when you import relative URLs. It works fine, but under most implementations of JSTL (including the reference implementation), it won't be any faster than using a simple string.

14.3.2 *Character encoding*

Let's look at another advanced feature: `<c:import>` gives you control over what character set to use if you import from a URL that offers binary data. If you've programmed in Java, you might be familiar with the difference between an `Input-Stream` and a `Reader`. Specifically, both classes let you read data, but `InputStream` returns binary data, whereas `Reader` returns text characters. If you're retrieving data from a URL and this data begins with the character "S", then a `Reader` object simply provides the "S" to you. (Think of this "S" almost like a high-level object; you can treat it as if it represents some real-world entity without worrying about how it's stored internally by the computer.) `InputStream`, however, returns a simple byte, like 01010011—or, because it's usually convenient to interpret bytes as numbers—83. But 83 isn't a character; it's still just a number. To convert it to a character, you need to use a *character encoding*, otherwise known as a *character set*. (In the character set that's most widely used, 83 represents the character "S".)

Some resources can return characters to you directly. In particular, if you import a JSP page with `<c:import>`, and the page resides in the same JSP container as the one you're writing, then the two pages communicate using characters, and no character encoding is necessary. The target page simply sends characters like "S" and "T", and you don't need to interpret them; you can immediately use them as characters.

But when you import files over the network—for example, every time you use an absolute URL—the data is transferred over a binary medium, and you must use a character encoding to figure out how to interpret the data. Picture a URL as returning a series of numbers to you: 87, 72, 89, and so on. You need a character encoding to figure out what these numbers mean.

By default, `<c:import>` usually does a pretty good job of interpreting these numbers. When you load an absolute URL from a web server, this absolute URL has a chance to declare its character encoding. Picture it responding by saying something like this: "Here are some bytes, encoded using the ISO-8859-4 character set: 87, 72, 89, ..." The `<c:import>` tag receives this message and normally can decipher the bytes.

However, in some situations you want to specify a character encoding yourself. In particular, sometimes a URL doesn't declare its character encoding appropriately. In this case, `<c:import>` falls back to a decoding that works *most* of the time. This encoding is called ISO-8859-1, and it represents a character encoding used widely in the United States and Western Europe. Because this default encoding isn't appropriate in all circumstances—say, if you're downloading the original Russian text of *Crime and Punishment* from a server in St. Petersburg—the <c:import> tag lets you override the default. (Incidentally, the text of *Crime and Punishment* is long enough that it's a great example of something you'd want to use a reader for, instead of a string!)

To do so, simply specify a value for the charEncoding attribute. To specify a character set, use its name, as in charEncoding="ISO-8859-4". (You can also use an expression, as long as it resolves to the name of a valid character encoding.)

For cases where an encoding is not necessary—for instance, if you're importing a local JSP page—the charEncoding attribute is ignored.

14.4 Advanced XML parsing and manipulation

The XML-manipulation tags that we discussed in chapter 8 work fine in most situations. However, if you need to handle very large XML documents, these tags offer a few attributes to let you squeeze out extra performance. In addition, <x:parse> and <x:transform> have attributes that help you deal with complex XML documents that include or otherwise refer to documents (much as JSP pages that use <c:import> do).

14.4.1 XML data formats

Few computer technologies have generated as much enthusiasm as XML. A side effect of the massive hype is that dozens of different styles of parsing XML have emerged. XML files are simple text files, but when programs work with them, they do so using an amazingly large array of strategies. Even in Java, a platform that has encouraged standardization, there are half a dozen standard ways to parse and manipulate XML documents.

Therefore, when you read about JSTL's XML tags in chapter 7, you might have wondered what format JSTL uses to store and retrieve XML documents as scoped variables. For instance, consider the following tag:

```
<x:parse var="tasks">
  <todoList>
    <task>Shave the dog</task>
    <task>Clean the ceiling</task>
    <task>Rotate the couch's pillows</task>
  </todoList>
</x:parse>
```

It's clear that this `<x:parse>` tag stores a scoped variable named `tasks`. It's even clear that this variable will be stored in the page scope. But what is the Java data type of the `tasks` variable?

It's up to the individual implementation of JSTL that you're using. By default, JSTL isn't designed to produce a specific kind of XML type that's usable by other tags. It just needs to make sure that it can communicate with itself consistently. Therefore, if we write

```
<%= pageContext.getAttribute("tasks").getClass().getName() %>
```

which is a Java expression that prints out the name of the `tasks` variable's Java class, our results could vary from one implementation or version of JSTL to another. JSTL gives this considerable flexibility to implementations to encourage runtime efficiency. Mandating a particular Java type would restrict an implementation's ability to adapt to new XML-parsing technologies or to choose a type that it knows how to handle efficiently.

Normally, you don't have to worry about the data types that JSTL uses to store XML documents. (This is why the topic never came up in chapter 8.) But if you need JSTL's tags to interoperate with other XML tags, then you can't use the default behavior of `<x:parse>`, because you don't know what type of objects `<x:parse>` will produce.

For cases where you need to interoperate, the `<x:parse>` tag provides a `varDom` attribute (along with a `scopeDom` attribute). This attribute works just like `var`, but instead of exposing an implementation-specific type, it exposes an instance of `org.w3c.dom.Document`, which is part of Java's standard support for a technology known as the *Document Object Model* (DOM). A DOM representation of an XML document isn't particularly efficient in terms of either space or time—to put it bluntly, DOMs are big and slow—but it serves as a useful *lingua franca* for XML. To let the `<x:parse>` tag expose XML data for a custom tag library or other custom code to use, you can specify the `varDom` attribute instead of `var`. For instance:

```
<x:parse varDom="tasks">
  <todoList>
    <task>Shave the dog</task>
    <task>Clean the ceiling</task>
    <task>Rotate the couch's pillows</task>
  </todoList>
</x:parse>
```

Now, the `tasks` variable is guaranteed to implement the `org.w3c.dom.Document` interface.

JSTL's support for DOM works in both directions: not only does `<x:parse>` expose a DOM when its `varDom` attribute is used, but JSTL's other XML-support

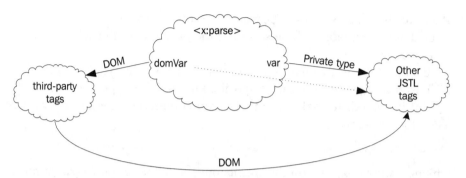

Figure 14.1 The `<x:parse>` tag can use any data type to represent XML for variables exposed through its `var` attribute. JSTL tags like `<x:out>` and `<x:if>` can use these data types, but other tags cannot. For this reason, `<x:parse>` lets you expose a standard DOM through its `varDom` attribute. To ensure interoperability, JSTL tags accept DOM objects as well as whatever private type `<x:parse>` exposes for them.

tags—for instance, `<x:set>` and `<x:out>`—all accept DOM objects as well. Figure 14.1 summarizes the ways that XML data can flow among tags.

Therefore, for your own Java code to interact with JSTL, you need to use DOM. See appendix D for pointers to more information on DOM objects.

14.4.2 *Telling `<x:parse>` where a document came from*

The `<x:parse>` tag has a `systemId` attribute that lets you tell the tag where your raw XML text came from. In many cases, `<x:parse>` couldn't care less about where you got your document; it's like a broker at a pawn shop who accepts the television and hub caps you offer without asking how they came into your possession.

However, if your document refers to other documents and resources using relative paths, you'll need to use the `systemId` attribute to tell `<x:parse>` where you found the document. This path can be either relative or absolute. Here's an example:

```
<c:import var="cnn" url="http://www.cnn.com/cnn.rss"/>
<x:parse var="cnnXml"
  xml="${cnn}"
  systemId="http://www.cnn.com/cnn.rss"/>
```

If the file at http://www.cnn.com/cnn.rss points to another document with a relative URI like style.xsl or /data/header.xml, passing the document's full URI to `<x:parse>` helps the tag find your document's dependencies.

Similarly, the `<x:transform>` tag accepts one attribute to specify a full URI for its XML document (`xmlSystemId`) and another for its XSLT stylesheet (`xsltSystemId`).

When you use relative paths for the `systemId`, `xmlSystemId`, and `xsltSystemId` attributes and operate on documents that contain relative URIs, JSTL interprets such URIs as if they refer to resources in your web application. This is a convenient and powerful illusion; it means you can use entity references like the following:

```
<!ENTITY included SYSTEM "/target.xml">
```

If your document contains this declaration and you parse it with a `systemId` of `/myContext/page.xml`, then the entity will refer to the target.xml file at the root of your web application. This process lets you avoid using absolute URIs in your XML documents, which is useful because you need to change cross-references that use such URIs any time your application moves.

When you use the `xsltSystemId` attribute, XSLT tags like `<xsl:include>` and `<xsl:import>`, as well as the XSLT `document()` function, can work with relative URIs too.

14.4.3 *Efficient parsing with org.xml.sax.XMLFilter*

The `<x:parse>` tag has another advanced attribute: `filter`. You can use this attribute to supply an object that implements the `org.xml.sax.XMLFilter` interface. This interface lets you provide Java logic that implements a SAX-based filter for XML documents. The details of programming an XML filter are beyond the scope of this book, but if you're familiar with them (or if someone hands you an `XMLFilter` object) then the filter attribute can be useful in getting your pages to run faster.

From a performance perspective, a filter is useful primarily because it lets you cut down the size of a document. Say you've downloaded an XML document representing the entire text of *Hamlet*, but you're only interested in lines of the play that are spoken by Hamlet himself. You could use an XML filter to throw away the rest of the document, which could vastly reduce the size of the DOM (or other object) that JSTL has to keep in memory to represent the document. If you perform multiple operations on this document after parsing it, then cutting down its size can lead to noticeable performance improvements.

You might wonder why `<x:parse>` bothers to accept a `filter` attribute when you can already filter documents using XPath and the `<x:set>` tag. The reason is twofold. First, XPath can only operate after the entire document is parsed, but important performance improvements can be gained during parsing itself, before the document is ever exposed to an `<x:set>` tag. Second, you might want to filter a document using something other than XPath—for instance, using arbitrary Java code. In such cases, the `org.xml.sax.XMLFilter` interface can be useful.

JSTL 1.0 doesn't provide any standard XML filters you can use in your pages. However, the JSTL reference implementation provides an example of a filter that might be useful. As an example filter for the JSTL reference implementation, I designed and implemented a small language called SPath. SPath lets you filter a document based on a subset of XPath's syntax—corresponding roughly to the portion of XPath we discussed chapter 7. (This isn't a coincidence; it's the subset of XPath that I think is most useful in most situations.)

You can experiment with the SPath filter by copying the spath.tld file from the src/org/apache/taglibs/standard/extra/spath directory of the reference implementation's source code distribution, available from http://jakarta.apache.org/taglibs, to your web application's WEB-INF directory. Then, you can import SPath's small tag library into your page using the spath prefix with the following directive:

```
<%@ taglib prefix="spath" uri="/WEB-INF/spath.tld" %>
```

After this, you're free to use a tag called `<spath:filter>` in your page. The `<spath:filter>` tag takes two attributes: `select`, which lets you specify an expression in the small SPath language, and `var`, which lets you expose a filter. You can use the tag as follows:

```
<spath:filter select='//customer[@id="525"]' var="spath"/>
<x:parse xml="${bigDocument}" var="filtered" filter="${spath}"/>
```

These two lines have a very similar effect to the following:

```
<x:parse xml="${bigDocument}" var="unfiltered"/>
<x:set select='$unfiltered//customer[@id="525"]' var="unfiltered"/>
```

However, for large documents, the former example should run much faster than the latter; it applies an XMLFilter before the document is ever exposed, instead of simply applying an XPath expression to pare down an already large document.

NOTE   I said the two examples have a "very similar effect"—not an identical effect. The reason for the difference is somewhat technical. The first example exposes an entire document (in a variable called `filtered`), whereas the second exposes the root XML element of a document (in a variable called `unfiltered`). This might not seem like a big difference, but XPath draws a distinction between the *root node* of a document and the same document's root element. If the variable `filtered` points to the root node of a document, you can expose the document's root element as a variable called `doc` by using the following tag:

```
<x:set select="$filtered/node()" var="doc" />
```

The XPath expression in this tag works because in XPath, the root element is a child of the root node. If this concept still seems inscrutable, don't worry; you can get along fine without understanding the details.

14.4.4 *Efficient transformations with javax.xml.transform.Result*

If you're familiar with the Transformation API for XML (TrAX), which is part of the Java API for XML Processing (JAXP), you know that a special attribute of the `<x:transform>` tag is designed to make it easier for you to pipeline XSLT transforms and otherwise gain more control over your XSLT transformations. In particular, `<x:transform>` has a `result` attribute that accepts any implementation of `javax.xml.transform.Result`. In TrAX, the `Result` interface lets you plug in your own logic to accept the result of a transformation.

The `result` attribute is mutually exclusive with `var`. Thus, `<x:transform>` can, in general, output its results in three different ways; but each individual `<x:transform>` tag must choose one of them, as shown here:

Attributes specified	`<x:transform>`'s behavior
Neither `var` nor `result`	Prints the document to the JSP page immediately
`var`	Saves the document to the variable named by `var`
`result`	Sends the result directly to the TrAX object passed in using `result`

When you use `var`, `<x:transform>` exposes the result of the transformation as a DOM object (implementing `org.w3c.dom.Document`). Therefore, the `result` attribute is useful both to gain efficiency and to interoperate with any custom TrAX logic you have.

14.5 *Deciphering requests with <fmt:requestEncoding>*

Most of JSTL's formatting tags are straightforward and don't require any advanced understanding. But I've left an entire tag, `<fmt:requestEncoding>`, for this chapter, because understanding it fully—like the `charEncoding` attribute of `<c:import>`—requires a reasonably subtle understanding of character sets.

Earlier in this chapter, I mentioned that when you import a file over the network, the `<c:import>` tag must use a character encoding to decipher it. But requests for your JSP pages come in over the same network, so requests need a character encoding to be deciphered correctly. Just like some URLs, some web browsers fail to declare an appropriate encoding for the bytes they send to you. This failure typically shows up as an inability to read foreign characters in request parameters. For instance, you might use an expression like `${param.firstName}` and get garbage instead of the Cyrillic character you (and your Russian user) were expecting.

To instruct JSTL to interpret parameters with a particular character encoding, you can use the `<fmt:requestEncoding>` tag. Table 14.2 lists its single attribute.

Table 14.2   `<fmt:requestEncoding>` tag attribute

Attribute	Description	Required	Default
value	The name of a character encoding to decode the request	No	*Automatic*

The most specific use of `<fmt:requestEncoding>` is to invoke it with a `value` attribute:

```
<fmt:requestEncoding value="UTF-8"/>
```

This tag instructs JSTL to use the UTF-8 character encoding to interpret all request parameters. Of course, the `value` attribute can come from a JSTL expression, so you don't have to specify it literally.

If your JSP environment has been set up appropriately, `<fmt:requestEncoding>` can also attempt to manage appropriate character encodings automatically. In such cases, you can specify the tag with no attribute:

```
<fmt:requestEncoding/>
```

This simple tag tries to figure out the right character set to use automatically, the way most other JSTL formatting tags do. You'll finally see, in section 14.6.1, some of the mechanisms the formatting tags use to figure out so much information automatically.

14.6 *Exposing data to JSP pages*

Throughout this book, we've used the JSTL expression language to access Java-Beans and other kinds of Java data. JSTL makes JavaBeans, `java.util.Lists`, `java.util.Maps`, and other data types extremely simple to access from a web-page author's perspective. Now, it's time to look at how to fulfill the programmer's end of the contract. This section explains how to expose data to JSTL tags in a manner they can easily understand.

This section assumes that you know Java, at least at a beginner's level. To get the most out of this section, you should also have some familiarity with writing Java servlets and servlet listeners.

14.6.1 *Saving data to a scope*

The JSTL expression `${user}` refers to the scoped variable `user`. Your Java code can set such scoped variables in order to expose information to a JSP page. Once you've exposed variables, you can provide a list of them to page authors, who will then be able to display your data using appropriate HTML or other markup.

In this section, I'll show you how to write to scoped variables from a servlet. I don't talk about listeners, and we won't discuss the details of servlets; my goal is to show you how to add data to scopes. For more information on servlets and listeners, see *Web Development with JavaServer Pages.*

When you write a servlet, you typically extend the `HttpServlet` class and override the `doGet()` method, the `doPost()` method, or both. These two methods accept the same arguments: an `HttpServletRequest` object that represents the request for the servlet, and an `HttpServletResponse` object that represents the servlet's response to the browser. The definition of a `doPost()` method in a servlet might look like this:

```
protected void doPost(HttpServletRequest request,
                      HttpServletResponse response)
      throws ServletException, IOException {
   // method body
}
```

Within the method's body, we have access to the parameters we've declared: `request` points to the object representing a browser's request for our servlet, and `response` helps us manage our response.

Assuming we've already written a servlet that knows how to instantiate or retrieve data, let's look at how we can expose this data to a JSP page before forwarding to it. Suppose we've declared a `doPost()` method using the arguments just described and that this method retrieves an object called `user`. The easiest scope to write to is the request scope. To store this object as a request-scoped variable named `currentUser`, we'd write the following:

```
request.setAttribute("currentUser", user);
```

To store the same object in session scope, we'd write:

```
request.getSession().setAttribute("currentUser", user);
```

To store `user` in application scope, we could write

```
request.getSession().getServletContext().
  setAttribute("currentUser", user);
```

This isn't the most elegant way to write to the application scope, but the other techniques require more planning and are beyond this book's scope. (This cries out for a play on words, but I'll spare you from having to read one.)

Note, again, that there is no page scope for a servlet; the servlet isn't a JSP page. Page scope only works from within a page; it's not useful for communicating from a servlet.

Once you expose data like this, a JSP page to which you forward can access the data using expressions like `${currentUser}`, `${requestScope.currentUser}`, and so on.

Incidentally, servlets can also read data from the various scopes. Instead of using the `setAttribute()` call, you can use `getAttribute()`, which takes only a single argument: the name of the scoped variable you're trying to retrieve.

Again, this wasn't meant to be a general introduction to using servlets with JSP pages, just a quick pointer on how to set scoped variables.

14.6.2 *Exposing dynamic data structures*

Now that you can expose data to JSP scopes, you might wonder what kind of data you should expose. To operate well with JSTL's expression language, the easiest thing to do is to expose objects from the Java 2 Collections API. This API contains a number of classes that hold data for you, and JSTL is designed to work with most of them.

In particular, there are two kinds of `Collections` classes you can easily use to expose data for use with the JSTL expression language. The first is called a `List`, and as its name implies, it stores a list of objects. For instance, if we have three strings that we want to expose to the user, we can create a `List`, add items to it, and then expose the entire list at once. To do so, we can write code like this:

```
List l = new ArrayList();
l.add(string1);
l.add(string2);
l.add(string3);
request.setAttribute("strings", l);
```

NOTE   This example assumes that `java.util.List` and `java.util.Array-List` are imported into your Java source file. You can ensure this by adding the following to the top of your file:

```
import java.util.List;
import java.util.ArrayList;
```

Some people like to import entire packages at once. You can do so with a single statement:

```
import java.util.*;
```

Some programmers and style guides discourage this sort of bulk import, but for core classes like those in Java's standard `java.util` package, there isn't much harm in importing everything.

Once you expose your list using the previous code, a page author could access it using expressions like `${strings[0]}`, `${strings[1]}`, and so on.

In some ways, `java.util.Map` objects are more flexible than `java.util.List` objects. They let you store pairs of items, where each item has a name and a value. Maps are therefore useful when you have a collection of objects to expose and you want to give each a name. For instance, we might use a map to associate ZIP codes with city names. We can create a map as follows:

```
Map m = new HashMap();
m.put("11791", "Syosset, NY");
m.put("06510", "New Haven, CT");
m.put("33767", "Clearwater, FL");
```

NOTE   As before, you'll need to make sure that `java.util.Map` and `java.util.HashMap` are imported into your Java source.

Exposing this map in the session scope lets page authors access the pairs of ZIP codes and place names. For instance, if we store the map as a session-scoped variable named `zips`, then the following tag will print out `"New Haven, CT"`:

```
<c:out value='${sessionScope.zips["06510"]}'/>
```

14.6.3 *Writing JavaBeans*

Sometimes, you want to expose one of your own Java classes to a page author. Doing so can be more efficient and convenient than creating maps and lists for all of your application's data. You can expose any Java object as a scoped variable, but simply exposing an object doesn't mean that JSTL will be able to do anything useful with it. If you want your object's data to be easily readable by page authors, you'll need to follow a few conventions when designing your classes.

Fortunately, these conventions are straightforward. The rules are laid out by the JavaBeans specification (this might sound intimidating, but it's not). You don't have to jump through any complicated hoops to write a JavaBean; in fact, whether a class is a JavaBean or not is something of a blurry distinction these days. For JSTL's purposes, you'll just need to follow a few simple rules.

Think of your class as a collection of *properties* you want to expose. For instance, if you're writing a class to represent a customer, your `Customer` class might have properties like `firstName`, `lastName`, `birthdate`, and so on. Then, to make sure the JSTL expression language can access your class's data, you need to make sure your methods follow a specific pattern: they should have names that begin with the word `get`, followed by the name of a single property. The first letter of the property should be capitalized. For instance, to expose the `lastName` property, your method should be called `getLastName()`.

Furthermore, your "get" methods—formally called *getters* or *accessors*—should not accept any arguments. They can return any type of object, but they must return something; they should not be declared `void`. Thus, a valid definition for a Java-Bean-style accessor would be:

```
public String getLastName() {
  return lastName;
}
```

The method can run whatever logic we want it to run before it returns a value, but as a matter of style, running a getter method shouldn't have any lasting effect. For instance, you shouldn't perform a database update from a getter method.

If our object has such a `getLastName()` method, then it exposes a `lastName` property to the JSTL expression language. For instance, if our object is exposed as the session-scoped variable `user`, then a page author could write `${session-Scope.user.lastName}`. When this expression runs, it will call our `getLastName()` method and return whatever data we return. If your getter method returns another object of yours, and this object has its own getter methods, then page authors can construct long expressions to navigate your objects.

The JavaBeans specification also let you expose boolean data using a method that returns `boolean` and starts with the word `is`, as in `isRegistered()` or `isSmart()`.

NOTE   The JavaBeans specification allows you to use methods with any name as getters, but using names that don't start with `get` or `is` requires more work. Only methods that begin with `get` or `is` will work, by default, as getters.

Although writing simple JavaBean-style accessor methods is simple, the full set of rules for programming JavaBeans can be complicated. Normally, you don't have to worry about these rules, but they may sometimes get in your way. For example, the JavaBeans specification also specifies *setter* methods—methods that begin with `set` and that let you change a bean property. These methods aren't supposed to matter when you're trying to expose data, but they can sometimes hinder a property you're trying to expose. For instance, one of the JavaBeans specification's rules says that the data types for a setter and a getter method must match. Suppose a class has the following methods:

```
public String getLastName();
public void setLastName(Object o);
```

In this case, because the type of the setter method's argument (`Object`) doesn't match the type returned from the `getLastName()` method, the JavaBeans machinery that operates behind the scenes in the JSTL expression language won't recognize `lastName` as a property. Expressions like `${sessionScope.user.lastName}` won't work for such an object. Accidental clashes like this happen rarely, but they can be very confusing when they do come up.

14.7 Configuring JSTL

As I've emphasized throughout this book, JSTL's major goal is simplicity for the page authors that use it. So, JSTL tries to hide as many background details as possible. In chapter 9, for example, I mentioned that JSTL's database tags can use a default database if one is configured by a back-end Java developer. In this section, we'll look at how you—as a back-end Java developer—can provide a useful default environment for JSTL page authors you work with. Like the previous section, this section assumes you know how to write servlets and listeners in Java.

14.7.1 Providing default information to JSTL tags

Some JSTL tags—particularly those in the database and formatting libraries—look for *configuration variables* that can be set by behind-the-scenes Java code. These variables let you store data that alters JSTL's behavior. Each configuration variable has a specific name and affects a specific feature of JSTL, although a single configuration variable may have an effect on multiple tags.

How JSTL organizes configuration variables

Every JSTL configuration variable has a name that begins with `javax.servlet.jsp.jstl`. JSTL looks for configuration variables in the following places, in order:

- Page scope
- Request scope
- Session scope
- Application scope
- Context-initialization parameters

The four scopes should be familiar from their usage in this book. As you'll see in a moment, context-initialization parameters can be set in your web application's WEB-INF/web.xml file, otherwise known as its *deployment descriptor.*

Once a JSTL tag finds a configuration variable in one of the locations just listed, it stops looking. Therefore, setting a configuration variable in session scope overrides any value for the same parameter in page scope. Similarly, if you set any scoped variable for a configuration variable, that variable overrides the context-initialization parameter with the same name.

Scoped variables

In section 14.6, we discussed how to manage scoped variables. However, you can't set configuration variables manually using the techniques from that section. Instead, you must use the utility methods that JSTL provides for setting configuration variables. These methods are found in the `javax.servlet.jsp.jstl.core.Config` class. This class has four static methods you can use to set configuration data for JSTL; table 14.3 describes these methods.[3]

Table 14.3 JSTL provides the following four methods in the class `javax.servlet.jsp.jstl.core.Config` to let you provide configuration data to JSTL tags behind the scenes. You can use these methods to set up default databases, modify your pages' default locales, and establish other useful defaults for your pages.

Method	Description	Where it's useful
`set(PageContext pc, String name, Object value, int scope)`	Sets a configuration variable in any scope. For the `scope` attribute, you can pass the value `PageContext.PAGE_SCOPE`, `PageContext.REQUEST_SCOPE`, `PageContext.SESSION_SCOPE`, or `PageContext.APPLICATION_SCOPE`.	Scriptlets, tag handlers
`set(ServletRequest request, String name, Object value)`	Sets a configuration variable in request scope. You pass in a `ServletRequest` object.	Servlets, listeners
`set(HttpSession session, String name, Object value)`	Sets a configuration variable in session scope. You pass in an `HttpSession` object.	Servlets, listeners

---

[3] Appendix B describes the other methods in the `javax.servlet.jstl.core.Config` class.

Table 14.3 JSTL provides the following four methods in the class `javax.servlet.jsp.jstl. core.Config` to let you provide configuration data to JSTL tags behind the scenes. You can use these methods to set up default databases, modify your pages' default locales, and establish other useful defaults for your pages. *(continued)*

Method	Description	Where it's useful
`set(ServletContext application, String name, Object value)`	Sets a configuration variable in application scope. You pass in a `ServletContext` object.	Servlets, listeners

When you use the methods of this `Config` class, you don't need to know the name of the variable you want to set. Instead, you can refer to the variable using a constant—a `final` variable—in the `Config` class. For example, suppose we're writing a servlet and need to set a variable called `javax.servlet.jsp.jstl.sql.maxRows`. (You'll see in section 14.6.2 what this variable is for.) To set this variable in session scope, we could write

```
Config.set(session,
           "javax.servlet.jsp.jstl.sql.maxRows",
           new Integer(500));
```

However, as long as we've imported the `javax.servlet.jsp.jstl.core.Config` class into our Java source code with a line like this

```
import javax.servlet.jsp.jstl.core.Config;
```

then we can use a constant in the `Config` class instead of this variable's name:

```
Config.set(session,
           Config.SQL_MAX_ROWS,
           new Integer(500));
```

For each configuration variable we discuss in the following sections, we'll show both its name and the constant in `Config` that represents it.

Initialization parameters

Context-initialization parameters are specified in your application's web.xml file. The web.xml file is located in your application's WEB-INF directory, and it contains information that the container can use to tailor your application's environment. (For full information on web.xml files, see *Web Development with JavaServer Pages*.) Here, we'll just show enough of the file's syntax that you can configure initialization parameters.

A reasonably minimal web.xml file looks like this:

```
<?xml version="1.0" encoding="ISO-8859-1"?>
<!DOCTYPE web-app
```

```
    PUBLIC "-//Sun Microsystems, Inc.//DTD Web Application 2.3//EN"
    "http://java.sun.com/j2ee/dtds/web-app_2_3.dtd">
<web-app>
  <description>
    My web application.
  </description>
  <context-param>
    <param-name>my.initialization.parameter</param-name>
    <param-value>my.parameter.value</param-value>
  </context-param>
</web-app>
```

The tags that create an initialization parameter are highlighted. They appear within the `<web-app>` element. The outer tag, `<context-param>`, declares a single context-initialization parameter. This tag has two children: `<param-name>`, which specifies the name of the parameter, and `<param-value>`, which specifies the value of the parameter. Our sample web.xml file sets the parameter named `my.initialization.parameter` to a value of `my.parameter.value`.

The constants declared in the `Config` class aren't relevant when setting configuration variables using context-initialization parameters.

JSTL expressions can access context-initialization parameters directly using the `initParam` implicit object, as in `${initParam["my.initialization.parameter"]}`. However, page authors don't need to access configuration variables manually; their defaults take effect automatically.

14.7.2 *Managing database access*

Now that we've looked at how to set configuration variables, let's see what specific variables JSTL looks for. JSTL's database tags support the variables listed in table 14.4.

Table 14.4 JSTL's database tags support configuration variables to help you set up default databases for your pages and to help prevent against runaway queries.

Variable constant	Variable name	Purpose
`Config.SQL_DATA_SOURCE`	`javax.servlet.jsp.jstl.sql.dataSource`	Default `DataSource` object or path
`Config.SQL_MAX_ROWS`	`javax.servlet.jsp.jstl.sql.maxRows`	Default value for `<sql:query>`'s `maxRows` attribute

Default DataSource

The `javax.servlet.jsp.jstl.sql.dataSource` variable (`Config.SQL_DATA_SOURCE`) lets you install an object that represents your pages' default database. This variable is called `dataSource` because it is designed primarily to accept a `javax.sql.Data-Source` object. A `DataSource` object can support connection pooling, or it can be a naïve implementation useful for prototyping or small applications.

However, if you don't have a `DataSource` object in hand, JSTL lets you specify two other types of information in the `SQL_DATA_SOURCE` variable:

- If you're using a JSP container that also supports the Java 2 Enterprise Edition (J2EE), you can specify a string that's a Java Naming and Directory Interface (JNDI) path to a `DataSource` (such as `jdbc/MyDataSource`).

- You can specify a string that describes how to connect to a database manually, using the old JDBC `java.sql.DriverManager` facility. `DataSources` are more flexible and powerful than `DriverManager`, but JSTL lets you use it in case you don't care about the performance advantages of connection pooling—or if you simply don't have time to learn how to use `DataSource` objects with your environment's databases.

To use this last option, you can set the variable—using either `Config.set()` or your application's deployment descriptor—to a string of the following form:

```
url,driver,user,password
```

Each of these options matches an attribute of the `<sql:setDataSource>` tag we discussed in chapter 9. In this string, `url` is required, and all the other elements are optional. You can use two sequential commas $(,,)$ if you want to leave out a field. For instance, the string

```
jdbc:foo,,shawn,jstl
```

uses a `url` of `jdbc:foo`, a username of `shawn`, and a password of `jstl`—but it specifies no driver. (Recall from chapter 9 that you don't need to specify a driver if you can be sure it's already been loaded elsewhere.)

The advantage of using strings like this over the `<sql:setDataSource>` tag is that you can hide the information from your JSP pages. Using the configuration variable, for example, lets you change the parameters behind the scenes without having to tell the user. You could even start with a simple string containing manual JDBC instructions and switch later to a `DataSource` as your application grows.

In many applications, listeners are the ideal place to initialize and expose `Data-Source` objects. For instance, you might want to expose a `DataSource` hard-wired to a particular username for each new user session. Or, you can expose a single `Data-Source` for your entire application.

Default result-size limitation

In chapter 9, we examined the `maxRows` attribute for the `<sql:query>` tag. This attribute helps prevent runaway queries by truncating a result that's bigger than expected. If you want to set an application-wide default policy for `maxRows`, you can do so using the `javax.servlet.jsp.jstl.sql.maxRows` (`Config.SQL_MAX_ROWS`) variable. To be blunt, it can be useful when you don't trust page authors you work with to properly set `maxRows`; you might find the configuration variable useful if your pages have a tendency to engage in runaway queries, filling up your server's memory needlessly.

For example, to limit the default size of results to 500 rows for the entire application, we could write

```
Config.set(context,
        Config.SQL_MAX_ROWS,
        new Integer(500));
```

where `context` is an instance of `HttpServletContext`.

14.7.3 *Managing internationalization*

JSTL also supports several configuration variables for the formatting and internationalization library. They are listed in table 14.5.

Table 14.5 JSTL's formatting tags use configuration variables to let you describe default locales, time zones, and other features of an internationalized application.

Variable constant	Variable name	Purpose
`Config.FMT_TIME_ZONE`	`javax.servlet.jsp.jstl.fmt.timeZone`	Default time zone
`Config.FMT_LOCALE`	`javax.servlet.jsp.jstl.fmt.locale`	Default locale, overriding browser
`Config.FMT_FALLBACK_LOCALE`	`javax.servlet.jsp.jstl.fmt.fall-backLocale`	*See section 14.7.3*
`Config.FMT_LOCAL-IZATION_CONTEXT`	`javax.servlet.jsp.jstl.fmt.local-izationContext`	*See section 14.7.3*

The first two of table 14.5's configuration variables are easy to understand. `Config.FMT_TIME_ZONE` specifies a time zone to use for a specific scope (such as a single session or the entire application). It accepts either a `java.util.TimeZone` object or a `String`; if it's passed a `String`, then anything that works in `<fmt:setTimeZone>`'s `value` attribute works here. (See chapter 10 for more information about how to specify time zones.)

Similarly, `Config.FMT_LOCALE` lets you override the default browser-sensing capabilities of JSTL's `fmt` tags. It accepts a `java.util.Locale` object or a `String`. If it's passed a `String`, then anything that works in `<fmt:setLocale>`'s `value` attribute works for the configuration variable, too.

The other two configuration variables are more complicated because they involve details we haven't discussed yet. The `Config.FMT_FALLBACK_LOCALE` variable doesn't override the default locale the way `Config.FMT_LOCALE` does. Instead, it provides a safety net for your application. Sometimes, an internationalization-capable formatting tag can't figure out which locale to use. For instance, the browser might have requested a locale for which Java doesn't know how to format numbers or dates, or a locale that doesn't match one of the available locales in a resource-bundle family. When this happens, JSTL uses `Config.FMT_FALLBACK_LOCALE` to recover. Thus, you can use `Config.FMT_FALLBACK_LOCALE` to establish a sensible lowest-common-denominator locale for your application.

The `Config.FMT_LOCALIZATION_CONTEXT` variable lets you specify two things. First, it accepts a `String` representing a default bundle *basename* for your application. (See chapter 10 for more information about basenames.) Second, it lets you establish a default JSTL `LocalizationContext` object. Appendix B describes `LocalizationContext` objects in more detail.

14.8 *Enforcing good page-authoring habits*

Earlier in this chapter, I advised against using scriptlets and other scripting elements. If you agree with this advice and happen to manage a web application, you might encourage your application's page designers to avoid scriptlets—in meetings, by posting signs in restrooms, or through any number of other informal strategies.

Informal encouragement doesn't always work, however. Criticizing scriptlets at meetings might not diminish their use in practice. To let you formalize your application's policies, JSTL gives you a way to help prohibit scriptlets in your application's pages.

It's important to realize that JSTL's anti-scriptlet support isn't a security measure. JSTL doesn't give you any tools that fully prevent a determined page author from using scriptlets. Instead, JSTL lets you expose a policy that page authors can implicitly accept by using your tag libraries or by including a special `<%@ taglib %>` directive in their pages.

JSP 1.2 introduced the idea of a *tag-library validator* (TLV). A validator is a class, written in Java, that reads a JSP page and decides whether it's legitimate. It can use whatever criteria it wants to determine whether the page is legitimate. For instance, TLVs are powerful enough to implement the kinds of constraints you saw for the `<c:choose>` tag in chapter 4.

JSTL provides two standard TLV classes that help you validate your pages against practices that make the pages hard to maintain. The first, called `Script-FreeTLV`, is designed to prevent pages from using scripting elements. The second, `PermittedTaglibsTLV`, limits the tag libraries that can be imported into a page; it lets you enumerate a list of appropriate tag libraries.

14.8.1 *Requiring script-free pages*

To use JSTL's validators, you must write a *tag-library descriptor* (TLD) document. We'll discuss the syntax of this document more thoroughly in chapter 15. For now, here's a cookie-cutter approach that lets you use `ScriptFreeTLV`. Simply save the document from listing 14.1 into your application's WEB-INF directory as a file called scriptfree.tld.

Listing 14.1   scriptfree.tld: TLD to discourage scripting elements

```
<?xml version="1.0" encoding="ISO-8859-1" ?>
<!DOCTYPE taglib
    PUBLIC "-//Sun Microsystems, Inc.//DTD JSP Tag Library 1.2//EN"
    "http://java.sun.com/j2ee/dtds/web-jsptaglibrary_1_2.dtd">
<taglib>
  <tlib-version>1.0</tlib-version>
  <jsp-version>1.2</jsp-version>
  <short-name>scriptfree</short-name>
  <validator>
    <validator-class>
        javax.servlet.jsp.jstl.tlv.ScriptFreeTLV
    </validator-class>
    <init-param>
      <param-name>allowDeclarations</param-name>       ❶ Allow
      <param-value>false</param-value>                    declarations?
    </init-param>
    <init-param>
      <param-name>allowScriptlets</param-name>         ❷ Allow
      <param-value>false</param-value>                    scriptlets?
    </init-param>
    <init-param>
      <param-name>allowExpressions</param-name>        ❸ Allow scripting
      <param-value>false</param-value>                    expressions?
    </init-param>
    <init-param>
      <param-name>allowRTExpressions</param-name>      ❹ Allow
      <param-value>false</param-value>                    rtexprvalues?
    </init-param>
```

```
  </validator>
  <tag>
    <name>noop</name>
    <tag-class>javax.servlet.jsp.tagext.TagSupport</tag-class>
    <body-content>empty</body-content>
  </tag>
</taglib>
```

Most of this document is boilerplate. However, it has four interesting sections, marked by the tags `<init-param>` and `</init-param>`. These sections let you configure how strict you'd like to be in monitoring against scripting elements. You can decide to limit

❶ declarations (`<%! … %>`)

❷ scriptlets (`<% … %>`)

❸ scripting expressions (`<%= … %>`)

❹ rtexprvalues (a scripting expression within a JSP tag attribute)

In the file I've shown, all of these scripting elements are prohibited; you can selectively allow them by replacing the word `false` with `true` inside the corresponding `<param-value>` tags.

If you save this file as /WEB-INF/scriptfree.tld in your web application, then scripting expressions will be prohibited from any page that uses the following directive:

```
<%@ taglib uri="/WEB-INF/scriptfree.tld" prefix="scriptfree" %>
```

As I mentioned, this limitation requires buy-in from any JSP page author whose behavior you're trying to control; a page author can always choose not to include this directive.

If you know how to write and package tag libraries (a topic we'll introduce in chapter 15) then you can include the `<validator>` element from scriptfree.tld in your own TLD files, thus requiring that anyone who uses your taglibs also *not* use scripting elements.

14.8.2 *Enumerating legal tag libraries*

JSTL's second validator lets you list the tag libraries that are valid for a particular page. Listing 14.2 shows an example that ensures no tag libraries other than JSTL's non-rtepxrvalue libraries are used in a page.

Listing 14.2 permitted.tld: TLD to constrain tag library declarations

```
<?xml version="1.0" encoding="ISO-8859-1" ?>
<!DOCTYPE taglib
    PUBLIC "-//Sun Microsystems, Inc.//DTD JSP Tag Library 1.2//EN"
    "http://java.sun.com/j2ee/dtds/web-jsptaglibrary_1_2.dtd">
<taglib>
  <tlib-version>1.0</tlib-version>
  <jsp-version>1.2</jsp-version>
  <short-name>permitted</short-name>
  <validator>
    <validator-class>
        javax.servlet.jsp.jstl.tlv.PermittedTaglibsTLV
    </validator-class>
    <init-param>
      <param-name>permittedTaglibs</param-name>
      <param-value>
        http://java.sun.com/jstl/core
        http://java.sun.com/jstl/fmt        Lists valid tag
        http://java.sun.com/jstl/sql        libraries
        http://java.sun.com/jstl/xml
      </param-value>
    </init-param>
  </validator>
  <tag>
    <name>noop</name>
    <tag-class>javax.servlet.jsp.tagext.TagSupport</tag-class>
    <body-content>empty</body-content>
  </tag>
</taglib>
```

If you save this document as /WEB-INF/permitted.tld inside your application, then any page that includes the directive

```
<%@ taglib uri="/WEB-INF/permitted.tld" prefix="permitted" %>
```

will be prevented from using anything but the tag libraries whose URIs you've listed inside the `<param-value>` element. For instance, you might list only the tag libraries that are supported at your organization. Or, if you feel particularly strongly about the caution against JSTL's database tags that I mentioned in chapter 9, you could formally discourage their use in your pages by removing the URI for JSTL's database tags (http://java.sun.com/jstl/sql) from your /WEB-INF/permitted.tld file.

14.9 *Summary*

If you're a JSTL user who knows Java, keep the following points in mind when using JSTL's advanced features:

- Scripting expressions let you incorporate Java code directly into your JSP pages, using pseudotags that look like `<% … %>` and `<%= … %>`. Using them can be convenient, but it can also make your pages difficult to maintain.

- The `<jsp:useBean>` tag acts as a bridge between JSTL and scripting expressions.

- The `<c:set>` tag lets you modify properties of JavaBeans, or values in `Map` objects, which you can reference using JSTL's expression language.

- The tag libraries for text importing and XML parsing contain a handful of extra attributes that give you more control over the libraries' behavior. Most of these advanced options are intended to help you squeeze more performance out of JSTL when it's critical that your pages run quickly.

- You can create scoped variables using servlets and listeners. To let the JSTL expression language read your data, just write classes that use JavaBean-style accessor methods, like `getUserName()`.

- You can use JSTL configuration variables to modify the behavior of the database and formatting tags behind the scenes.

- JSTL gives you tools to help discourage scriptlets and unwanted tag libraries from being used in your applications' pages.

15

Using JSTL to
develop custom tags

This chapter covers...

- The basics of tag-library development
- Tag-library descriptor (TLD) files
- Writing iteration tags
- Writing condition tags

As you've seen, JSTL gives page authors the tools they need to access databases, format text and XML, internationalize applications, and perform many other common tasks. In many cases, authors of JSP pages don't need to look beyond the flexible set of tags that JSTL offers.

However, JSTL's tags aren't meant to solve every potential problem a page author might run into. When page authors have a need that JSTL doesn't address, they depend on back-end Java programmers to fill in the gaps. For example, JSTL 1.0 doesn't offer a way to send email, read from online directories using the Java Naming and Directory Interface (JNDI), send messages using the Java Message Service (JMS), and so on. If page authors need to accomplish these tasks, they need to be helped along by back-end Java programmers in their organization (or third-party tag libraries they download or purchase).

In this chapter, we look at how JSTL makes it easier to develop custom tag libraries. At this point, I assume you have some knowledge of the Java programming language. As you'll see, JSTL lets you develop some kinds of tags without making you learn the details of JSP's complex tag-related APIs. However, under JSP 1.2, you still need to know Java to develop custom tags.

NOTE   At the time I wrote this chapter, the JSP 1.3 expert group was considering how to provide a way for non-programmers to produce custom tags using JSP instead of Java. So, under JSP 1.3, developing tags might become even easier. For the moment, though, JSTL's support for tag developers is a useful step in the right direction.

15.1 *Developing and installing tag libraries*

Tag libraries are written in Java using JSP's *tag extension API*. This API lets you develop *tag handlers*, which are Java classes that implement custom JSP tags. For instance, we might write a Java class named

```
com.jstlbook.examples.MyIfTag
```

whose code runs every time the tag

```
<book:if>
```

appears in our site's JSP pages. For such a class to be a tag handler, it must implement the `javax.servlet.jsp.tagext.Tag` interface, which is defined by the JSP specification.

15.1.1 *JSTL's support for tag-handler developers*

Writing tag handlers from scratch is not enormously difficult, but it's tricky to get right. Most Java developers can master the art of tag-handler development, but creating effective tag libraries requires specialized skills and knowledge. When you develop a traditional tag handler, you need to keep in mind somewhat complex protocols concerning the tag-handler lifecycle, the order in which methods are expected to be invoked, and so on.

To make your job easier, JSTL comes with several Java classes known as *support classes* or *base classes*. Instead of building a tag handler from scratch, you can extend, or *subclass*, one of these base classes. Therefore, for a few kinds of common tags, JSTL shields you from the details of the tag-extension API. Rather than learning how traditional tag-handler methods like `doStartTag()` and `doAfterBody()` work, you can focus on your custom code.

JSTL primarily helps you build two important kinds of tags: conditional tags and loop tags. Conditional tags, as we explained in chapter 4, let page authors make decisions within a JSP page. Loop tags, or iteration tags, help page authors cycle over data, often to build tables or lists. Before JSTL, creating these tags was possible, but the process was roundabout and indirect. With JSTL, writing a conditional tag is as simple as writing a method that returns a boolean value, and developing a tag that loops over data is as easy as providing the data you want the tag to loop over.

We'll look at how JSTL's support for tag developers works in sections 15.2 and 15.3. Before that, it will help to take a step back and learn a little more about how tag libraries work in JSP.

15.1.2 *The tag-library descriptor (TLD)*

Imagine that we've written a Java class called `com.jstlbook.example.MyIfTag`. If this class implements the `javax.servlet.jsp.tagext.Tag` interface, it has the potential to become a tag handler. However, before we can use this class as a tag handler, we need to associate it with a JSP tag library.

To make this association, we need to create a file called a *tag-library descriptor (TLD)*. A TLD is an XML document that describes the tags contained by an individual tag library. Books like *Web Development with JavaServer Pages*[1] describe the TLD in more detail, but let's look briefly at the basics.

The TLD is a straightforward XML document. (Because TLDs are XML documents, you may wish to browse chapter 2 if you're not yet comfortable with XML's

---

[1] Duane Fields, Mark Kolb, and Shawn Bayern, 2nd ed. (Manning Publications, 2001).

syntax.) Every TLD should have a header, or prologue. For JSP 1.2 TLDs, you can use the following:

```
<?xml version="1.0" encoding="ISO-8859-1" ?>
<!DOCTYPE taglib
   PUBLIC "-//Sun Microsystems, Inc.//DTD JSP Tag Library 1.2//EN"
   "http://java.sun.com/dtd/web-jsptaglibrary_1_2.dtd">
```

This header simply identifies the file as a TLD. After this header, the rest of the document is contained within a `<taglib>` element, which has two important sections. First, `<taglib>` has a few child elements that describe the tag library as a whole. Then, `<taglib>` has one or more child `<tag>` elements that define individual tags within the tag library.

Taglib-wide elements

Useful taglib-wide descriptive elements that can occur within `<taglib>` include the following:

```
<taglib>
  <tlib-version>1.0</tlib-version>
  <jsp-version>1.2</jsp-version>
  <short-name>book</short-name>
  <uri>http://jstlbook.com/tld/example.tld</uri>
  <display-name>JSTL book examples</display-name>
  <description>Taglib examples from Manning</description>

    . . .

</taglib>
```

The `<tlib-version>` element contains the version identifier for your tag library. For example, you might use 1 or 1.0 for the first version of your tag library. It doesn't matter what number you choose, but you should pick a new value for each version of your tag library that you make public. Versions facilitate documentation, testing, and final use. In contrast with `<tlib-version>`, `<jsp-version>` describes the version of JSP with which you want to use the tag library. For JSP 1.2, this element should have the value 1.2. (Note that JSTL requires JSP 1.2.)

The `<short-name>` tag contains, not surprisingly, a short identifier for the tag library. Usually, this value should be the prefix you recommend using with the tag library. Recall from chapter 2 that page authors can choose the prefixes they use. Still, you can suggest a recommended prefix, just as JSTL recommends c for the core library, sql for the database library, and so on. For this chapter's sample tag library, we choose the prefix book.

As we discussed in chapter 2, every tag library is uniquely identified by a Universal Resource Identifier (URI), which we insert into the `<uri>` element. For this chapter's sample tag library, we use the following URI:

```
http://jstlbook.com/tld/example.tld
```

After `<uri>`, the two elements `<display-name>` and `<description>` provide optional information that might be printed out by tools, such as integrated development environments (IDEs), that support JSP.

Note that the TLD `<taglib>` element can contain taglib-wide descriptor elements other than the ones we've shown here, but they're not important for our purposes. (Remember that in chapter 14, we used a `<validator>` element to introduce validation logic into a TLD.)

Elements for individual tags

In addition to these taglib-wide elements, the `<taglib>` element contains descriptions of each individual tag in the taglib. The `<taglib>` element has a child `<tag>` element for each tag. As figure 15.1 suggests, the `<tag>` element maps a tag name to a tag-handler class. Here's a sample `<tag>` element:

```
<tag>
  <name>if</name>
  <tag-class>com.jstlbook.example.MyIfTag</tag-class>
  <attribute>
    <name>test</name>
    <required>true</required>
  </attribute>
</tag>
```

Figure 15.1 represents this mapping graphically.

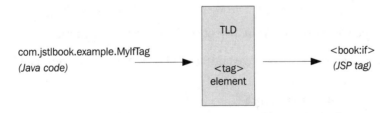

Figure 15.1 When you write a tag handler class in Java, you need to map it to a JSP tag using the `<tag>` element inside a TLD document. Only with such a mapping does the JSP container know how your tag library's tags are implemented.

The `<tag>` element's two most important children are `<name>` and `<tag-class>`, which describe the tag's name and its implementation class, respectively. These two child elements provide the mapping between tag name and tag-handler class.

For each attribute that the tag accepts, the `<tag>` element must have a child `<attribute>` element. This `<attribute>` element can contain a number of its own child elements, including `<name>` (containing the attribute's name), and `<required>` (`true` if the attribute is required, `false` otherwise).

The `<tag>` and `<attribute>` elements can contain many other elements, but they're not important for our purposes. As I mentioned, books like *Web Development with JavaServer Pages* describe the TLD in detail; we only need to cover TLD basics here.

15.1.3 *Installing and using a tag library*

Before you can use a TLD that you've written, you need to make it available to a web application. You can do this a number of ways, but we'll cover the simplest one. To use a tag library in an application, follow this procedure:

1   Copy the TLD file to your application's WEB-INF directory.

2   Install the tag handlers in WEB-INF/classes (for raw Java classes) or WEB-INF/lib (for packaged JAR files). Note that if you add the classes to WEB-INF/classes, you must create the appropriate subdirectory for your package. For instance, you would add .class files for classes in the `com.jstlbook.examples` package to the WEB-INF/classes/com/jstlbook/examples directory.

3   Instruct the page author to import the tag library using the `<%@ taglib %>` directive. However, instead of using the tag library's real URI, the page author can use the local path to the TLD file for the `<%@ taglib %>` directive's `uri` attribute. For example, if your TLD file is named example.tld and you have added it to the WEB-INF directory, then the following directive would import the tag library into a page:

```
<%@ taglib prefix="example" uri="/WEB-INF/example.tld" %>
```

The directive must appear in any page that uses the tag library.

Once you've followed these steps, page authors will be ready to use your tag library.

15.2 *Developing conditional tags*

As you saw in chapter 4, JSTL's `<c:if>` tag lets page authors introduce conditional logic into their pages. The `<c:if>` tag takes a `test` attribute that accepts conditional expressions using JSTL's expression language.

Although this expression language is useful in many situations, some pages require more specific, focused conditional logic. The expression language lets you compare two values, for example, but it doesn't let you ask all the conditional questions that Java lets you ask. That's what custom tag handlers are for.

15.2.1 A simple conditional tag

For our first example of custom conditional tags, suppose a page author for our application needs to display different data depending on whether it's the weekend or weekday. Imagine the following requirement: when a page is loaded any time between Monday and Friday, the page must print, "Our operators are standing by at this very moment." Otherwise, it should not print this message: no use inviting telephone calls when nobody's around to answer them.

We might be able to implement this functionality using the `<fmt:formatDate>` tag from chapter 10 and some clever applications of the `pattern` attribute. But although this strategy would probably be fun to implement, it would lead to an awkward, hard-to-maintain page. Instead, we'd like to create simple logic that differentiates weekdays from weekends and expose this logic to page authors who don't necessarily know how to program. That is, we want page authors to be able to write something like this:

```
<book:ifWeekday>
  Our operators are standing by at this very moment.
</book:ifWeekday>
```

The new tag, `<book:ifWeekday>`, should let its body be processed only if the current day is a weekday. Thus, on Monday through Friday, this tag will cause its body to be printed; on the weekends, it will prevent its body from printing. With this simple syntax, pages using the tag will be easy to maintain.

Before we create the `<book:ifWeekday>` tag, we need to figure out how to write code to differentiate weekends from weekdays. Ideally, we'd like to write a simple `isWeekday()` method that returns `true` on weekdays and `false` on weekends. Listing 15.1 shows one way to write such a method, spelled out in detail to make sure it's clear.

> **Listing 15.1 weekday.java: a class with a method that detects weekends**

```
package com.jstlbook.examples;

import java.util.*;

public class Weekday {

    public boolean isWeekday() {        ❶ Returns a boolean
```

```
        Calendar now = Calendar.getInstance();
        if (now.get(Calendar.DAY_OF_WEEK) == Calendar.SATURDAY)        ❷ Separates
            return false;                                                 weekends
        if (now.get(Calendar.DAY_OF_WEEK) == Calendar.SUNDAY)            from
            return false;                                                 weekdays
        return true;
    }

}
```

This class contains a single method, isWeekday(), that implements the logic we need.

❶ The isWeekday() method returns a boolean, a Java type that has exactly two values: true and false. The method uses this type because it asks a yes-or-no question: "Is today a weekday?" The question has only two possible answers.

❷ The first line of the method retrieves a Calendar object representing the current date. When Calendar.getInstance() is called, it returns a Calendar object corresponding to the current moment. We save this Calendar in a variable called now.

The rest of the method differentiates weekends from weekdays. To determine what day of week a Calendar object represents, you can call its get() method with the argument Calendar.DAY_OF_WEEK. To test this method's return value against different days of the week, you can compare it to the constants Calendar.SUNDAY, Calendar.MONDAY, and so on. In the isWeekday() method, we check to see whether the day is Calendar.SATURDAY or Calendar.SUNDAY. If it is, we return false, because these are weekend days, not weekdays. Otherwise, for all remaining days, we return true.

Turning simple classes into tag handlers

Our Weekday class provides all the necessary logic to differentiate weekends from weekdays, but it isn't useful in its current form. It's just a stand-alone class; it can't be used as a tag handler.

However, with JSTL's support for developing conditional tags, we're not far from giving page authors a tag they can use to differentiate weekends from weekdays. We've written a boolean method that answers the question—and this is all that JSTL's conditional-tag support requires.

JSTL provides an abstract class called ConditionalTagSupport in the javax.servlet.jsp.jstl.core package. In Java, *abstract classes* are classes that cannot be instantiated themselves; they must be extended, or subclassed, to be useful. ConditionalTagSupport contains a few method declarations, but we're most interested in the following:

```
protected abstract boolean condition() throws JspException;
```

The `ConditionalTagSupport` class uses this abstract method to decide whether to include its body in its JSP page. If `condition()` returns `true`, then the tag lets its body be evaluated, just like `<c:if>` when its `test` attribute evaluates to `true`. Otherwise, if `condition()` returns `false`, then the tag skips over its body.

Therefore, to implement the `<book:ifWeekday>` tag we demonstrated earlier, we just need to extend `ConditionalTagSupport` and write a `condition()` method that returns `true` for weekdays and `false` for weekends, as our `isWeekday()` method does.

Listing 15.2 shows the changes we need to make to our `Weekday` class to turn it into a `ConditionalTagSupport` tag handler.

> **Listing 15.2 WeekdayTag.java: the Weekday class converted to a tag handler**

```
package com.jstlbook.examples;

import java.util.*;
import javax.servlet.jsp.JspTagException;

public class WeekdayTag
    extends javax.servlet.jsp.jstl.core.ConditionalTagSupport {

    public boolean condition() throws JspTagException {
        Calendar now = Calendar.getInstance();
        if (now.get(Calendar.DAY_OF_WEEK) == Calendar.SATURDAY)
            return false;
        if (now.get(Calendar.DAY_OF_WEEK) == Calendar.SUNDAY)
            return false;
        return true;
    }
}
```
If we return true from here, the tag's body will run

Changes from listing 15.1 are highlighted. We now call the class `WeekdayTag` because it's conventional for tag handlers' names to end with `Tag`.

With these minor changes, we've written our first tag handler!

Writing the TLD

To expose this single tag to a web page, we need to create a tag library (a TLD) to contain it. The TLD must associate the tag and the tag-handler class that implements it. The following relatively minimal TLD will do fine:

```
<?xml version="1.0" encoding="ISO-8859-1" ?>
<!DOCTYPE taglib
  PUBLIC "-//Sun Microsystems, Inc.//DTD JSP Tag Library 1.2//EN"
  "http://java.sun.com/dtd/web-jsptaglibrary_1_2.dtd">

<taglib>
  <tlib-version>1.0</tlib-version>
  <jsp-version>1.2</jsp-version>
```
Boilerplate TLD prologue

Describes the taglib

```
<short-name>book</short-name>                              ↑ Describes
<uri>http://jstlbook.com/tld/weekday.tld</uri>              │ the taglib

<tag>
  <name>ifWeekday</name>
  <tag-class>com.jstlbook.examples.WeekdayTag</tag-class>
</tag>                                                       Creates the
</taglib>                                                    <ifWeekday>
                                                             tag
```

Note that this tag library's single `<tag>` element has no `<attribute>` children because our sample `<ifWeekday>` tag doesn't accept any attributes.

Using the tag

If we name this TLD file weekday.tld and add it to our application's WEB-INF directory, we can begin using the tag that it defines. We need to use a `<%@ taglib %>` directive to import the tag library and give it a prefix. For instance:

```
<%@ taglib prefix="book" uri="/WEB-INF/weekday.tld" %>
```

Now, our tag is accessible as `<book:ifWeekday>`. Here's a sample JSP page, from the ground up, that uses the tag:

```
<%@ taglib prefix="book" uri="/WEB-INF/weekday.tld" %>
<book:ifWeekday>
  Our operators are standing by at this very moment.
</book:ifWeekday>
```

This JSP page will print a message only on weekdays; on weekends, it will print nothing but white space.

15.2.2 A conditional tag with attributes

The `<book:ifWeekday>` tag from the last section is relatively simple—so simple, in fact, that it's hard to think of a compelling use for it in real life. Let's expand this conditional tag by allowing it to make more specific decisions about days of the week, as well as times of the day. To do this, we'll write a tag handler that accepts attributes.

Let's create a new tag called `<book:ifTime>`. This tag will take the following attributes:

Attribute	Explanation	Examples
day	Requires that the current weekday match a specific weekday. Accepts lowercase names of days.	sunday monday
before	Requires that the current hour be earlier than a specific time of day. Accepts numeric hours in military time.	6 18
after	Requires that the current hour be later than a specific time of day. Accepts numeric hours in military time.	8 20

If multiple attributes are specified, we want them all to be satisfied before the tag prints its body. For example, consider the following tags (with descriptions of when their bodies should run):

Example	Includes body only...
`<book:ifTime day="wednesday">`	on Wednesdays
`<book:ifTime day="friday"` `   before="12">`	on Fridays before noon
`<book:ifTime after="12">`	on any day, but only after noon
`<book:ifTime day="sunday"` `   after="21" before="22"/>`	on Sundays, between 9:00 p.m. and 10:00 p.m.

Thus, we can use this tag whenever we want a web page to display something for a particular interval of time. The tag could be useful for time-sensitive recurring announcements, like "Don't forget to fill out your payforms!"

The code for <book:ifTime>

To write a handler for this new tag, we'll again implement a `condition()` method. But in addition, we must process the three attributes that this tag accepts. To do so, we'll write methods named `setXxx()`, where *xxx* is the name of the attribute. For instance, for the `before` attribute, we'll write a method named `setBefore()`. (Note that in the method name, we've capitalized the leading b in `before`.)

TIP   You might recognize the form of the `setXxx()` methods from chapter 14. These methods are typical JavaBeans setter methods. Tag attributes are simply treated as JavaBeans properties: the tag handler is a bean. Therefore, any legitimate bean-style properties that the tag-handler class has can correspond to tag attributes; you just need to declare them in your TLD.

Listing 15.3 shows the Java code for our `<book:ifTime>` tag.

Listing 15.3   TimeTag.java: the handler for <book:ifTime>

```
package com.jstlbook.examples;

import java.util.*;

public class TimeTag
  extends javax.servlet.jsp.jstl.core.ConditionalTagSupport {
```

```
private int day = -1;              Variables for
private int after = -1;            attributes
private int before = -1;

public void setDay(String s) {
  if (s.equals("sunday"))
    day = Calendar.SUNDAY;
  else if (s.equals("monday"))
    day = Calendar.MONDAY;
  else if (s.equals("tuesday"))
    day = Calendar.TUESDAY;
  else if (s.equals("wednesday"))              Accepts the
    day = Calendar.WEDNESDAY;                  day attribute
  else if (s.equals("thursday"))
    day = Calendar.THURSDAY;
  else if (s.equals("friday"))
    day = Calendar.FRIDAY;
  else if (s.equals("saturday"))
    day = Calendar.SATURDAY;
  else throw new IllegalArgumentException("bad weekday: " + s);
}

public void setBefore(int i) {
  if (i < 0 || i > 23)
    throw new IllegalArgumentException("bad hour: " + i);
  before = i;
}

public void setAfter(int i) {
  if (i < 0 || i > 23)
    throw new IllegalArgumentException("bad hour: " + i);
  after = i;
}

protected boolean condition() {
  Calendar now = Calendar.getInstance();          Retrieves the
  int currentDay = now.get(Calendar.DAY_OF_WEEK); current date
  int currentHour = now.get(Calendar.HOUR_OF_DAY); and time

  if (day != -1 && currentDay != day)
    return false;

  if (before != -1 && currentHour >= before)
    return false;                               Ensures the date
                                                and time meet
  if (after != -1 && currentHour < after)       requirements
    return false;

  return true;
}
}
```

Understanding the code

The TimeTag handler is based on the same principle as the WeekdayTag handler: it extends ConditionalTagSupport and provides a condition() method that decides whether the tag should include its body. However, unlike WeekdayTag, the TimeTag handler has *setter* methods for attributes.

❶ The tag handler needs a way to remember what attributes have been sent to it. Handlers can store attributes any way they'd like. Here, we keep a single int variable for each attribute: day, before, and after. We initialize them to -1, which happens to be an invalid value for all the attributes. This way, we can compare each attribute later to -1 to determine whether it was set by the page author (or left out of the tag). If an attribute has no clearly invalid values—for instance, if you need to accept both negative and positive numbers—then you can use a separate boolean variable to record whether an attribute is set.

❷ The setDay() method accepts the day attribute. That is, if the tag is called with the attribute day="tuesday", then the tag handler can expect the setDay() method to be called with an argument of tuesday. In this method, we compare the input String to all the names of days we accept. If a match is found, we store the int that the Calendar class uses to represent the day numerically. For instance, the Calendar.SUNDAY constant int represents Sunday, Calendar.MONDAY represents Monday, and so on. If no match is found, we throw an IllegalArgumentException to indicate that our argument—the attribute the page author used—isn't valid. Thus, because of our "bad weekday" message, a page author who uses the attribute day="sundae" (a misspelling possibly arising from hunger) would receive the following error message: "bad weekday: sundae".

The setDay() method accepts a String argument because we want the page author to specify a string corresponding to a weekday.

Unlike setDay(), the setBefore() method accepts an int, not a String. We write the method this way because the only valid attributes for the before attribute are integers. We want hours to be identified by simple integers; we don't want to accept 8.5 or 8:00. This is how we decided to specify the tag's behavior earlier. There's nothing wrong with a tag that accepts other values—indeed, these other values would be convenient for page authors—but I've limited the <book:ifTime> tag's behavior for simplicity and to demonstrate int attributes.

When an attribute accepts only integer values and has a setter method whose parameter is an int, the JSP container is responsible for converting user's input into an integer. Therefore, we don't have to run Integer.parseInt() on the input ourselves; we can assume that setBefore() will only be called with an integer. Page authors who set the before attribute to something other than an integer will get a fatal error and will need to correct the problem.

❸ To implement the tests we need to conduct, we first capture the current date using the same method call in `Calendar` that we used in the `WeekdayTag` class. Here, we also record the current day and hour from the `Calendar` object we retrieve. Because the integers that `Calendar` uses for the current hour match the hours we accept— 24-hour, military time, starting with `0`—we don't need to interpret or translate the number we get back from our `Calendar` object. We can simply store it as `currentHour`. This value will therefore store the number corresponding to the current hour. For example, if it's 8:52 p.m., `currentHour` will equal `20`; it will remain `20` exactly until 9:00 p.m., at which point it will change to `21`.

❹ The heart of the `condition()` method ensures that the current time meets all of the attributes' requirements. For each potential attribute, we check whether the page author has specified it by comparing it against `-1`. (See ❶.) If the attribute has been set, then we check to make sure the attribute's requirement is satisfied. If any check fails, we return `false`; otherwise, if all the checks succeed and we reach the end of the method, we return `true`.

The TLD for <book:ifTime>

To describe the `<book:ifTime>` tag, we simply need to add the following `<tag>` element to any TLD (for example, the one we created for `<book:ifWeekday>` earlier in this chapter):

```
<tag>
  <name>ifTime</name>
  <tag-class>com.jstlbook.examples.TimeTag</tag-class>
  <attribute>
   <name>day</name>
  </attribute>
  <attribute>
    <name>before</name>
  </attribute>
  <attribute>
    <name>after</name>
  </attribute>
</tag>
```

This `<tag>` element specifies the tag's three attributes: `day`, `before`, and `after`. Note that because we don't use the `<required>` element, all of these three attributes are optional.

Using the tag

Assuming we've added the tag to our weekday.tld file and located this file in our application's WEB-INF directory, we can use the new tag as follows:

```
<%@ taglib prefix="book" uri="/WEB-INF/weekday.tld" %>
<book:ifTime day="sunday" after="21" before="22">
```

```
    "Alias" is on right now on ABC.  What are you doing
    browsing the web?
</book:ifTime>
```

Or, perhaps more usefully:

```
<%@ taglib prefix="book" uri="/WEB-INF/weekday.tld" %>
<book:ifTime day="sunday" after="3" before="4">
    Our site conducts routine maintenance between
    3:00 a.m. and 4:00 a.m. on Sundays.  During this
    time, some services may be unavailable.  We apologize
    for the inconvenience.
</book:ifTime>
```

This latter tag would display a warning notice to users, but only between 3:00 a.m. and 4:00 a.m. on Sundays.

Reporting errors in tag usage

Suppose the page author enters an invalid hour in one of the <book:ifTime> tag's attributes, as follows:

```
<book:ifTime before="25">
```

In such cases, the precise behavior is up to the JSP container on which you're running. In Jakarta Tomcat, the page author would receive an error message that looks like figure 15.2.

In figure 15.2, the text

```
Bad hour: 25
```

comes from our custom tag handler—specifically, from the following lines in listing 15.3:

```
if (i < 0 || i > 23)
    throw new IllegalArgumentException("bad hour: " + i);
```

Because this error message might be the only indication to page authors that they've done anything wrong, it's often helpful to include descriptive error messages when you throw exceptions in your tag handlers. When you add error messages to your tag handlers, consider including the following information:

- The name of the tag throwing the exception
- The name of the attribute that contains the error, if applicable
- The nature of the error (for example, a copy of the offending attribute value)
- Information about how to fix the problem.

Figure 15.2
Page authors can see the error messages that tag developers write. In this case, the text "bad hour: 25" comes from the TimeTag handler, a custom tag handler we wrote earlier in this chapter. Tag authors should take this opportunity to provide helpful, informative error messages when appropriate.

For example, the message that we use in TimeTag—bad hour followed by the offending input—is useful but not as descriptive as it could be. Instead, we could have written something like this:

```
  "<ifTime>: bad hour '" + i + "' in attribute 'before';"
+ "need an hour between 0 and 23"
```

Errors like this give page authors more information. Also, in general, such messages may be more familiar to users because they resemble the JSTL reference implementation's error messages more than a simple bad hour message does.

15.2.3 *Integrating custom conditional tags with standard tags*

As you saw during our discussions of JSTL's tags in part 2, the <c:if> and <x:if> tags let page authors expose a boolean variable using the tags' var attribute. This feature is useful primarily to store conditions that might change, and to use conditions in mutually exclusive <c:when> tags.

The ConditionalTagSupport base class will automatically expose a boolean variable whose name is the value of your tag's var attribute. (The boolean value will represent the result of your condition() method.) This free service helps you integrate your tags into `<c:when>` blocks, and it makes it easy for you to write tags that behave like JSTL's tags.

To demonstrate this functionality, let's add a few lines to the `<tag>` element for `<book:ifTime>` in our TLD. The new lines are highlighted:

```
<tag>
  <name>ifTime</name>
  <tag-class>com.jstlbook.examples.TimeTag</tag-class>
  <attribute>
   <name>day</name>
  </attribute>
  <attribute>
    <name>before</name>
  </attribute>
  <attribute>
    <name>after</name>
  </attribute>
  <attribute>
    <name>var</name>
  </attribute>
</tag>
```

This is all we need to add. The base `ConditionalTagSupport` class provides the setter method for var (`setVar()`) and exposes the variable automatically when the page author specifies a var attribute. `ConditionalTagSupport` similarly supports a `scope` attribute if you'd like to add it to your tag.

15.2.4 *Using the expression language*

JSTL 1.0 doesn't provide a standard way to use the expression language in your own tags; there is no standard JSTL API for invoking the expression language to interpret expressions within your own tags. Although JSP 1.3 wasn't yet released at the time this chapter was written, the plan is for JSP 1.3 to take care of resolving expressions for you. Thus, if JSTL 1.0 provided a standard expression API, it would be useful only under JSP 1.2, and the Java Community Process typically avoids intentionally providing legacy interfaces.

However, the lack of a standard API doesn't mean you can't accept JSTL expressions in your own tags. It just makes it hard to describe an exact procedure in this book! To use the expression language in your own tags under JSP 1.2, you'll need to use an API specific to an individual implementation of JSTL—one that decides to expose an expression-language API for you to use. The JSTL reference implementation, which is available from the Jakarta Taglibs web site at http://jakarta.apache.org/taglibs, provides such an interface.

At the time this was written, accessing the expression language using the JSTL reference implementation was simple: make sure the file standard.jar from the JSTL reference implementation is in your classpath, and call the following method in the class `org.apache.taglibs.standard.lang.support.ExpressionEvaluatorManager`:

```
public static Object evaluate(String attributeName,
                             String expression,
                             Class expectedType,
                             Tag tag,
                             PageContext pageContext)
```

The first argument, `attributeName`, is the name of the attribute you'd like to evaluate—`test`, `value`, or whatever you've called the attribute. The second argument, `expression`, is the expression to evaluate. For instance, it might be the string `"${sessionScope.customer}"`. The next argument, `expectedType`, is a `java.lang.Class` object representing the type you want the expression language to return. If you're looking for a `java.lang.String` object, you could pass the literal `java.lang.String.class` for this argument. The `tag` argument is the current instance of your tag handler; you typically use the keyword `this` for this argument. Finally, `pageContext` is your tag's `PageContext` object; normally, your tag handler will have an instance variable called `pageContext` that you can pass.

Here's an example of a call that evaluates an expression and returns a string:

```
evaluate("username",
         "${sessionScope.username.fullname}",
         String.class,
         this,
         pageContext);
```

15.3 Developing iteration tags

In addition to its support for conditional tags, JSTL makes it easier to write loop tags. JSTL provides a `LoopTagSupport` class that's almost as easy to use as `ConditionalTagSupport`.

Just as `ConditionalTagSupport` has a `condition()` method that lets you plug in your own conditional logic, `LoopTagSupport` contains several methods that let you provide items to loop over. You provide these items by implementing a few methods, and the base class automatically takes care of iterating over them. Therefore, instead of needing to control the details of JSP tag iteration, you simply provide data and let `LoopTagSupport` do the rest. In fact, `LoopTagSupport` doesn't just handle looping; it also exposes your item to its body in the same manner `<c:forEach>` does, so that page authors will be able to access your data using conventions they're already familiar with.

`LoopTagSupport` has three methods you need to supply when you write your own iteration-tag subclasses (see table 15.1).

Table 15.1 `LoopTagSupport` methods

Method	Purpose
`void prepare()`	Lets you prepare for the iteration, typically using the tag's attributes.
`boolean hasNext()`	Returns `true` when your tag has more items to iterate over, or `false` otherwise.
`Object next()`	Returns a new item each time it's called. If no new items are left (that is, if `hasNext()` would return `false`), `next()` throws a `NoSuchElementException`.

Suppose that you've designed a tag called `<example:loop>` that loops over some of your application's data. The JSP container can use the same instance of your tag handler to service multiple appearances of `<example:loop>` in your application. Therefore, your tag handler must be prepared to be called multiple times. This is the purpose of the `prepare()` method. You should use it instead of your class's constructor to set up your class for a particular invocation of `<example:loop>`. Often, you'll want to read attributes and take some action—for example, open a database connection or file—in `prepare()`. Usually, `prepare()` will modify some instance variables of your tag-handler class.

The `hasNext()` and `next()` methods function similarly to their namesakes in `java.util.Iterator`. The `hasNext()` method returns `true` or `false` depending on whether your tag has more items to iterate over, and `next()` returns the actual items to iterate over, one at a time.

Once the items are exhausted, the tag handler might be discarded. If this happens, its `release()` method will be called. The `release()` method is part of JSP's tag extension API; it's not unique to `LoopTagSupport`. You should implement `release()` if your tag needs to clean up after itself.

If the tag handler isn't discarded, it might be used again, in which case `prepare()` will be called again.

Figure 15.3 shows the order of method invocation in `LoopTagSupport`.

15.3.1 *A simple loop tag*

Let's look at an example of a simple loop tag. JSTL, appropriately, doesn't provide a tag for you to read files directly from disk. Portable web applications should never write to the disk directly; they can't be sure they'll have access to do so (or even that a writable disk is present on the server they run on).

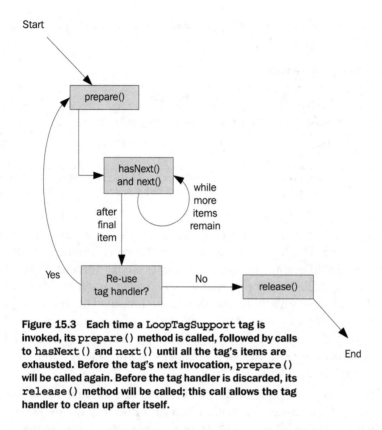

Figure 15.3 Each time a `LoopTagSupport` tag is invoked, its `prepare()` method is called, followed by calls to `hasNext()` and `next()` until all the tag's items are exhausted. Before the tag's next invocation, `prepare()` will be called again. Before the tag handler is discarded, its `release()` method will be called; this call allows the tag handler to clean up after itself.

However, writing a simple tag to loop over the lines of a disk file will show you all you need to know about the `LoopTagStatus` interface, so it's a good example. Such a tag might be useful for very small applications or prototypes, where you want to test an idea before using a real database. In an early stage of an application, you can write your data to disk files and read them in with a tag.

Our sample tag, `<book:forEachLine>`, will take a single attribute, `filename`, which accepts absolute path names pointing to disk files. For instance, on a Unix system, a page author might use the attribute `filename="/etc/passwd"` to load the Unix machine's account and password database. On Windows, you might say `filename="c:\\winnt\\system32\\drivers\\etc\\services"` to retrieve the system's list of network services.

WARNING When a backslash character (\) appears in an attribute name, as it often does when you refer to filenames on Windows machines, you need to escape the backslash character by typing it twice. If you write a tag that requires backslashes in attributes, you'll probably need to advise page authors of this rule, because they may not be aware of it if their backgrounds lie with HTML alone.

We'd like to be able to use this tag as follows:

```
<book:forEachLine var="line" filename="/etc/group">
  <c:out value="${line}"/> <br />
</book:forEachLine>
```

If `<book:forEachLine>` functions correctly, this JSP fragment will print out the entire contents of the /etc/group file in the middle of a web page. (Note that printing this information publicly is a bad idea in practice, because it gives the world a list of all user groups on the machine.) As with `<c:forEach>`, the variable named by `var` (in this case, `line`) contains the loop's current item at any given point. It can be accessed anywhere in the loop's body. Therefore, the `<c:out>` tag in this example prints the current line during each loop; finally, all lines in the file will be printed.[2]

Listing 15.4 shows the code for `ForEachLineTag`, a handler for this `<book:forEachLine>` tag.

Listing 15.4 ForEachLineTag.java: a tag handler for <book:forEachLine>

```
package com.jstlbook.examples;

import java.io.*;
import java.util.*;
import javax.servlet.jsp.JspTagException;

public class ForEachLineTag
  extends javax.servlet.jsp.jstl.core.LoopTagSupport {

  private String filename;          ❶ Stores the filename
  private BufferedReader input;        attribute

  public void setFilename(String s) {  ❷ Accepts the
    filename = s;                          filename
  }                                        attribute
```

---

[2] The /etc/group file is found on most Unix machines. If you use Windows, imagine that the value of the `filename` attribute is instead something like `"c:\\temp\\notes.txt"`.

```
protected void prepare() throws JspTagException {
  try {
    if (input != null)
      input.close();
    input = new BufferedReader(new FileReader(filename));
  } catch (IOException ex) {
    throw new JspTagException(ex.toString());
  }
}

public void release() {
  try {
    if (input != null)
      input.close();
  } catch (IOException ex) {
    // ignore
  }
}

protected boolean hasNext() throws JspTagException {
  try {
    return input.ready();
  } catch (IOException ex) {
    throw new JspTagException(ex.toString());
  }
}

protected Object next() throws JspTagException {
  try {
    return input.readLine();
  } catch (IOException ex) {
    throw new JspTagException(ex.toString());
  }
}

}
```

❸ Prepares for an iteration

❹ Cleans up when we're done

❺ Determines if there's more data

❻ Returns the next line from the file

Understanding the code

Listing 15.4 shows the code for a custom iteration tag that extends JSTL's LoopTag-Support base class. We store the value of the filename attribute in our own variable named filename (❶), which is set from the setFilename() accessor (❷). Before looping over the data, we prepare for the iteration by opening a file (❸).

We use the release() method to call the close() method (❹) for the stream we've opened. Using the simple interface that LoopTagSupport provides, we can't easily close the stream as soon as we're done with it;[3] but we want to make sure that

---

[3] If we only closed it immediately before returning false from hasNext(), we would leave it open in cases where it wasn't fully consumed.

no matter what happens, we close it before the container says it's done with us. The `release()` method handles this task. Note that we also close any old streams that we opened when `prepare()` is called again, because `prepare()` is designed to tell us that we're about to start a new loop. Thus, `prepare()` gives us a chance to clean up as well.

❺ The `hasNext()` method returns `true` if the `BufferedReader` is ready for more reading, as reported by its `ready()` method. If this method returns `true`, we infer that we have at least one more line to read.[4]

❻ Each time the `next()` method is called, it returns the line that it reads from the file, using `BufferedReader.readLine()`.

Writing the TLD

You might have noticed that whereas our earlier example of the tag's usage contained a `var` attribute, no setter method for `var` appears in listing 15.4. We can omit this method because, just as with `ConditionalTagSupport`, the `setVar()` method is supplied by `LoopTagSupport`. Therefore, to support `var`—which is typically important in an iteration tag, because it's the easiest way to access the current item—we simply need to add it to the TLD. Here's a sample TLD entry for `<book:forEachLine>`:

```
<tag>
  <name>forEachLine</name>
  <tag-class>com.jstlbook.examples.ForEachLineTag</tag-class>
  <attribute>
    <name>filename</name>
    <required>true</required>
  </attribute>
  <attribute>
    <name>var</name>
  </attribute>
</tag>
```

This TLD entry mandates the `filename` attribute but lets `var` be optional.

Using the tag

The `<book:forEachLine>` tag is useful not just to display entire files, but also to format each line of a file in general. For instance, using `<book:forEachLine>`, it's easy to turn a file delimited by commas or other separators into an HTML table.

As an example, the user database for a Unix machine is stored in /etc/passwd; each line contains colon-separated fields corresponding to information like user-

---

[4] It's conceivable, in unusual circumstances, for this type of check to result in our tag's completing before a file is truly done. However, we ignore this fringe case for simplicity.

name, user number, and so on. The following JSP fragment prints a formatted HTML table for a Unix machine's user database:

```
<table border="1">
<book:forEachLine filename="/etc/passwd" var="line">
  <tr>
    <c:forTokens items="${line}" delims=":" var="field">
      <td><c:out value="${field}"/></td>
    </c:forTokens>
  </tr>
</book:forEachLine>
</table>
```

On one of my servers, this code prints out the table shown in figure 15.4. For each line, we execute the body of <book:forEachLine>. This body contains a <c:forTo-kens> tag, so for each line of the file, we tokenize it into strings separated by colons (:). (See chapter 5 for more information about <c:forTokens>.) Finally, we print each token in a table cell.

It's easy to reuse tags for different purposes. For example, simply changing the delims=":" attribute to delims="," would allow us to print an HTML table to display a comma-delimited file. Suppose I'm a bookie who wants to avoid using a formal database; instead, I keep a list of names, money owed, and limbs broken in a comma-separated file:

```
Bob Bobson,$100,arm
David Davies,$200,leg
Peter Peters,$50,wrist
Richard Richards,$6,finger
```

I can produce the table in figure 15.5 without writing any new Java code. I simply alter the JSP fragment to look like this:

```
<table border="1">
<book:forEachLine filename="c:\\temp\\debts.csv" var="line">
  <tr>
    <c:forTokens items="${line}" delims="," var="field">
      <td><c:out value="${field}"/></td>
    </c:forTokens>
  </tr>
</book:forEachLine>
</table>
```

This fragment can print an HTML table for any comma-separated file.

Again, I should remind you that I'm not encouraging you to write tags that read from the filesystem within a web application. Reading a file is just a convenient example to demonstrate the LoopTagSupport protocol. Instead of reading files, you'll probably read relative paths within your web application using the Servlet-

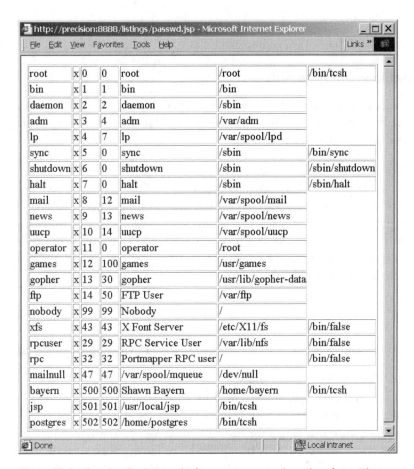

Figure 15.4 The `<book:forEachLine>` tag appears in action, formatting a Unix system's user database (/etc/passwd) into an easily readable HTML table.

Figure 15.5
It's easy to reuse `<book:forEachLine>` to print tables for different kinds of files. Here, instead of a colon-separated list of user data, we print a table for a comma-separated data file (maintained by a hypothetical bookie).

`Context.getResource()` or `ServletContext.getResourceAsStream()` method—or just use `<c:import>`!

15.3.2 *More advanced iteration tags*

The `<book:forEachLine>` tag that we developed in section 15.3.1 exercises the `LoopTagSupport` class nicely. But `LoopTagSupport` has a few more capabilities that listing 15.4 didn't demonstrate.

Tag status

As you saw in chapter 5, the `<c:forEach>` and `<c:forTokens>` tags have a `varStatus` attribute that exposes a JavaBean for the page author. This bean lets the page author determine information about the current iteration—for example, whether it's currently the first loop, the last loop, or somewhere in between. If we want `<book:forEachLine>` to expose a similar status bean, we can simply add a `varStatus` attribute to the TLD:

```
<attribute>
  <name>varStatus</name>
</attribute>
```

Just as with `var`, the `LoopTagSupport` class takes care of exposing a status bean for us.

Subsetting with begin, end, and step

We also discussed the `begin`, `end`, and `step` attributes for `<c:forEach>` and `<c:forTokens>` in chapter 5. These attributes let a page author iterate over only part of the data at hand, skipping the rest of it. We can add support for these attributes to `<book:forEachLine>`, but doing so requires more work than supporting `var` and `varStatus`. Because `LoopTagSupport` doesn't know how we want to supply the beginning, ending, and increment values for an iteration, it doesn't provide accessors like `setBegin()`, `setEnd()`, and so forth. Instead, it provides protected variables called `begin`, `end`, and `step`, and it expects us to set them if we want to use them.

However, setting these variables isn't enough. We need to do two other things:

- Inform the superclass that we've specified particular values like `begin` and `end`
- Ask the superclass to validate them for consistency (for example, `begin` can't be greater than `end`, `begin` can't be negative, and so on)

For example, if we want to accept a `begin` attribute, we can write the following setter method:

```
public void setBegin(int i) throws JspTagException {
  this.begin = i;
```

```
    this.beginSpecified = true;
    validateBegin();
}
```

Our `setBegin()` method declares `JspTagException` because `validateBegin()` may throw this exception if it decides the new value for `begin` is invalid.

You could write `setEnd()` and `setStep()` methods in the same style. Then, simply add your attributes to the TLD, and you can support iteration with subsetting, just like the core JSTL tags.

15.4 *Summary*

In this chapter, we looked at how JSTL makes it easier to develop condition and iteration tags for JSP pages. When developing tags using JSTL, keep in mind the following points:

- JSP comes with a tag-extension API for writing custom tags.
- The tag library descriptor (TLD) document maps tag handler classes to tag names. In a JSP page, the `<%@ taglib %>` directive imports a tag library by referring to its TLD.
- JSTL simplifies the process of writing tags by providing base classes that do some of the heavy lifting for you.
- JSTL's `ConditionalTagSupport` class lets you write conditional tags by supplying a `condition()` method that causes the tag to either include or skip its body.
- JSTL's `LoopTagSupport` class lets you write iteration tags by supplying items to iterate over.
- Tag handlers that extend `ConditionalTagSupport` and `LoopTagSupport` must provide accessor (`setXxx()`) methods for their own attributes, but the JSTL base classes provide `setVar()` automatically. Thus, they expose variables without your needing to do any of the work.

JSTL reference A

A.1 *Expression language syntax*

Chapter 2 covers the JSTL expression language. Section A.1 serves as a concise summary.

A.1.1 *Implicit objects*

The JSTL expression `${data}` indicates the scoped variable named `data`. Additionally, the expression language supports the following implicit objects:

Implicit object	Contains
pageScope	Scoped variables from page scope
requestScope	Scoped variables from request scope
sessionScope	Scoped variables from session scope
applicationScope	Scoped variables from application scope
param	Request parameters as strings
paramValues	Request parameters as collections of strings
header	HTTP request headers as strings
headerValues	HTTP request headers as collections of strings
initParam	Context-initialization parameters
cookie	Cookie values
pageContext	The JSP PageContext object for the current page

For example, the expression `${param.username}` indicates the request parameter named `username`.

A.1.2 *Operators*

JSTL's operators help you work with data.

Property access

To retrieve properties from collections, the JSTL expression supports the following operators:

- The dot (`.`) operator retrieves a named property. The expression `${user.iq}` indicates the `iq` property of the scoped variable named `user`.
- The bracket (`[]`) operator lets you retrieve named or numbered properties:
  - The expression `${user["iq"]}` has the same meaning as `${user.iq}`.
  - The expression `${row[0]}` indicates the first item in the `row` collection.

Checking for emptiness

The empty operator determines whether a collection or string is empty or null. For instance, ${empty param.firstname} will be true only if a request parameter named firstname is not present. JSTL expressions can also compare items directly against the keyword null, as in ${param.firstname == null}, but this is an advanced use.

Comparing variables

The JSTL expression language supports comparisons using the following operators:

Operator	Description
== eq	Equality check
!= ne	Inequality check
< lt	Less than
> gt	Greater than
<= le	Less than or equal to
>= ge	Greater than or equal to

Arithmetic

JSTL expressions can conduct arithmetic using the following operators:

Operator	Description
+	Addition
-	Subtraction
*	Multiplication
/ div	Division
% mod	Remainder (modulus)

In addition, the – operator can precede a single number to reverse its sign: ${-30}, ${-discount}.

Boolean logic

The comparison operators produce boolean expressions, and JSTL expressions can also access boolean primitives. To combine boolean subexpressions, JSTL provides the following operators:

Operator	Description
`&&` `and`	`True` only if both sides are true
`||` `or`	`True` if either or both sides are true
`!` `not`	`True` only if the expression following it is false

JSTL supports two boolean literals: `true` and `false`.

Parentheses

JSTL expressions can use parentheses to group subexpressions. For example, `${(1 + 2) * 3}` equals 9, but `${1 + (2 * 3)}` equals 7.

A.2 Core tag library

JSTL's core tag library supports output, management of variables, conditional logic, loops, text imports, and URL manipulation. JSP pages can import the core tag library with the following directive:

```
<%@ taglib prefix="c" uri="http://java.sun.com/jstl/core" %>
```

A.2.1 General-purpose tags

JSTL provides `<c:out>` for writing data, `<c:set>` for saving data to memory, `<c:remove>` for deleting data, and `<c:catch>` for handling errors.

Examples

```
Thanks for logging in, <c:out value="${name}"/>.
<c:set var="loggedIn" scope="session" value="${true}"/>
<c:remove var="loggedOut" scope="session"/>
```

Tag attributes

The `<c:catch>` tag's attribute is as follows:

Attribute	Description	Required	Default
`var`	Variable to expose information about error	No	*None*

The `<c:out>` tag's attributes are as follows:

Attribute	Description	Required	Default
value	Information to output	Yes	*None*
default	Fallback information to output	No	*Body*
escapeXml	True if the tag should escape special XML characters	No	true

The `<c:set>` tag's attributes are as follows:

Attribute	Description	Required	Default
value	Information to save	No	*Body*
target	Name of the variable whose property should be modified	No	*None*
property	Property to modify	No	None
var	Name of the variable to store information	No	*None*
scope	Scope of variable to store information	No	page

If `target` is specified, `property` must also be specified.
The `<c:remove>` tag's attributes are as follows:

Attribute	Description	Required	Default
var	Name of the variable to remove	Yes	*None*
scope	Scope of the variable to remove	No	*All scopes*

A.2.2 Conditional logic

JSTL has four tags for conditions: `<c:if>`, `<c:choose>`, `<c:when>`, and `<c:otherwise>`.

Examples

```
<c:if test="${user.wealthy}">
  You have quite a lot of money in your account.
</c:if>

<c:choose>
  <c:when test="${user.generous}">
    Why don't you give some of it to me?
  </c:when>
  <c:when test="${user.stingy}">
    You should transfer some of it to a CD.
  </c:when>
```

```
<c:otherwise>
    A money-market account looks right for you.
  </c:otherwise>
</c:choose>
```

Tag attributes

The `<c:if>` tag's attributes are as follows:

Attribute	Description	Required	Default
test	Condition to evaluate	Yes	*None*
var	Name of the variable to store the condition's result	No	*None*
scope	Scope of the variable to store the condition's result	No	page

The `<c:choose>` tag accepts no attributes.

The `<c:when>` tag's attribute is as follows:

Attribute	Description	Required	Default
test	Condition to evaluate	Yes	*None*

The `<c:otherwise>` tag accepts no attributes.

A.2.3 Looping

The core JSTL library offers two tags for looping: `<c:forEach>` for general data and `<c:forTokens>` for parts of strings.

Examples

```
<c:forEach items="${orders}" var="order">
  <c:out value="${order.id}"/>
</c:forEach>

<c:forEach begin="0" end="100">
  I will not continue to disrupt class discussions!
</c:forEach>

<c:forTokens items="a:b:c:d" delims=":" var="token">
  <c:out value="${token}"/>
</c:forTokens>
```

Tag attributes

The `<c:forEach>` tag's attributes are as follows:

Attribute	Description	Required	Default
items	Information to loop over	No	*None*
begin	Element to start with (0 = first item, 1 = second item, …)	No	0
end	Element to end with (0 = first item, 1 = second item, …)	No	*Last item in the collection*
step	Process every step items	No	1 *(all items)*
var	Name of the variable to expose the current item	No	*None*
varStatus	Name of the variable to expose the loop status	No	*None*

Either `items`, or both `begin` and `end`, must be specified.

The `<c:forTokens>` tag's attributes are as follows:

Attribute	Description	Required	Default
items	String to tokenize	Yes	*None*
delims	Characters to use as delimiters	Yes	*None*
begin	Element to start with (0 = first item, 1 = second item, …)	No	0
end	Element to end with (0 = first item, 1 = second item, …)	No	*Last item in the collection*
step	Process every step items	No	1 *(all items)*
var	Name of the variable to expose the current item	No	*None*
varStatus	Name of the variable to expose the loop status	No	*None*

A.2.4 Import and URL

The core library supports inclusion of text using `<c:import>`, URL printing and formatting with `<c:url>`, and redirections with `<c:redirect>`. All URL tags accept `<c:param>` child tags.

Examples

```
<c:import url="http://www.cnn.com/cnn.rss" var="newsfeed"/>

<a href="<c:url url="/index.jsp"/>"/>
```

```
<c:redirect url="go-away.jsp">
  <c:param name="unwantedUser" value="true"/>
</c:redirect>
```

Tag attributes

The `<c:import>` tag's attributes are as follows:

Attribute	Description	Required	Default
url	URL to retrieve and import into the page	Yes	*None*
context	/ followed by the name of a local web application	No	*Current application*
charEncoding	Character set to use for imported data (if necessary)	No	*ISO-8859-1*
var	Name of the variable to expose imported text	No	*Print to page*
scope	Scope of the variable to expose imported text	No	page
varReader	Name of an alternate variable to expose `java.io.Reader`	No	*None*

The `<c:url>` tag's attributes are as follows:

Attribute	Description	Required	Default
value	Base URL	Yes	*None*
context	/ followed by the name of a local web application	No	*Current application*
var	Name of the variable to expose the processed URL	No	*Print to page*
scope	Scope of the variable to expose the processed URL	No	page

The `<c:redirect>` tag's attributes are as follows:

Attribute	Description	Required	Default
url	URL to redirect the user's browser to	Yes	*None*
context	/ followed by the name of a local web application	No	*Current application*

The `<c:param>` tag's attributes are as follows:

Attribute	Description	Required	Default
name	Name of the request parameter to set in the URL	Yes	*None*
value	Value of the request parameter to set in the URL	No	*Body*

A.3 XML tag library

JSTL's XML-processing tag library supports parsing of XML documents, selection of XML fragments, flow control based on XML, and XSLT transformations. JSP pages can import the XML-processing tag library with the following directive:

```
<%@ taglib prefix="x" uri="http://java.sun.com/jstl/xml" %>
```

A.3.1 Parsing and general manipulation

Before you work with an XML document, it must be parsed with `<x:parse>` or back-end Java code. The `<x:out>` and `<x:set>` tags can retrieve fragments of parsed documents, whether these documents are DOM objects or a JSTL implementation's own choice of data type.

Examples

```
<c:set var="textDocument">
  <orders>
    <order>
      762 cans of low-fat yogurt
    </order>
    <order>
      6 spoons
    </order>
  </orders>
</c:set>
<x:parse xml="${textDocument}" var="xml"/>
<x:out select="$xml/orders/order[1]"/>

<x:set var="fragment" select="$xml//order"/>
```

Tag attributes

The `<x:parse>` tag's attributes are as follows:

Attribute	Description	Required	Default
xml	Text of the document to parse (`String` or `Reader`)	No	*Body*
systemId	URI of the original document (for entity resolution)	No	*None*
filter	`XMLFilter` object to filter the document	No	*None*
var	Name of the variable to expose the parsed document	No	*None*
scope	Scoped of the variable to expose the parsed document	No	*None*
varDom	Name of the variable to expose the parsed DOM	No	*None*
scopeDom	Scoped of the variable to expose the parsed DOM	No	*None*

The `<x:out>` tag's attributes are as follows:

Attribute	Description	Required	Default
select	XPath expression to evaluate as a string, often using XPath variables	Yes	*None*
escapeXml	True if the tag should escape special XML characters	No	true

The `<x:set>` tag's attributes are as follows:

Attribute	Description	Required	Default
select	Any XPath expression, often using XPath variables	Yes	*None*
var	Name of the variable to store the XPath expression's result	Yes	*None*
scope	Scope of the variable to store the XPath expression's result	No	page

If the XPath expression results in a boolean, `<x:set>` exposes a `java.lang.Boolean` object; for a string, `java.lang.String`; and for a number, `java.lang.Number`. XPath node-sets are exposed using an implementation-dependent type.

A.3.2 *Conditional logic*

Like the core library, the XML library supports four tags for conditional logic: `<x:if>`, `<x:choose>`, `<x:when>`, and `<x:otherwise>`.

Examples

```
<c:set var="textDocument">
  <orders>
    <order>
      17 carts
    </order>
    <order>
      34 horses
    </order>
  </orders>
</c:set>
<x:parse xml="${textDocument}" var="xml"/>
<x:if select="$xml//order">
  Document has at least one &lt;order&gt; element.
</x:if>

<x:choose>
  <x:when test="$xml//order[1] = '17 carts'">
    Looks like you put the carts before the horses.
  </x:when>
  <x:when test="$xml//order[1] = '49 pigs'">
```

```
    Why do you need 49 pigs?
  </x:when>
  <x:otherwise>
    I don't know <i>what</i> you ordered.
    Buy some more stuff and give us another chance
    to figure it out.
  </x:otherwise>
</x:choose>
```

Tag attributes

The `<x:if>` tag's attributes are as follows:

Attribute	Description	Required	Default
select	XPath expression to evaluate as boolean, often using XPath variables	Yes	*None*
var	Name of the variable to store the condition's result	No	*None*
scope	Scope of the variable to store the condition's result	No	page

The `<x:choose>` tag accepts no attributes.

The `<x:when>` tag's attribute is as follows:

Attribute	Description	Required	Default
select	Condition to evaluate	Yes	*None*

The `<x:otherwise>` tag accepts no attributes.

A.3.3 Loops

Like the core library, the XML-processing library supports looping over data. It provides a single tag, `<x:forEach>`, to loop over nodes in an XML document.

Examples

```
<c:set var="textOrders">
  <orders>
    <order>
      12 gallons of strawberry margarita mix
    </order>
    <order>
      6 tons of pickled sausage
    </order>
    <order>
      17 mice
    </order>
  </orders>
```

```
</c:set>
<x:parse xml="${textOrders}" var="orders"/>

You ordered:
<ul>
<x:forEach select="$orders/orders/order" var="item">
  <li><x:out select="." /></li>
</x:forEach>
</ul>
```

Tag attributes

The `<x:forEach>` tag's attributes are as follows:

Attribute	Description	Required	Default
select	XPath expression pointing to a set of nodes (often using XPath variables)	Yes	*None*
var	Name of the variable to store the current item for each loop	No	*None*

A.3.4 Transformations

JSTL provides an `<x:transform>` tag for conducting XSLT transformations from within a JSP page.

The `<x:param>` tag can set a parameter in an XSLT stylesheet.

Examples

```
<x:transform xml='${xml}' xslt='${xslt}'/>

<x:transform xslt='${xslt}'>
  <orders>
    <order>
      16 boxes of dried cheese
    </order>
    <order>
      34 live cattle
    </order>
  </orders>
</x:transform>
```

Tag attributes

The `<x:transform>` tag's attributes are as follows:

Attribute	Description	Required	Default
xml	Source XML document for the XSLT transformation	No	*Body*
xmlSystemId	URI of the original XML document (for entity resolution)	No	*None*
xslt	XSLT stylesheet providing transformation instructions	Yes	*None*

Attribute	Description	Required	Default
xsltSystemId	URI of the original XSLT document (for entity resolution and XSLT tags like `<xsl:include>`)	No	*None*
result	`javax.xml.transform.Result` object to accept the transformation's result	No	*Print to page*
var	Name of the variable to expose the transformation's result	No	*Print to page*
scope	Scope of the variable to expose the transformation's result	No	page

The `<x:param>` tag's attributes are as follows:

Attribute	Description	Required	Default
name	Name of the XSLT parameter to set	Yes	*None*
value	Value of the XSLT parameter to set	No	*Body*

A.4 *Database tag library*

JSTL's database library supports database queries, updates, and transactions. JSP pages can import this library with the following directive:

```
<%@ taglib prefix="sql" uri="http://java.sun.com/jstl/sql" %>
```

A.4.1 *Preparing databases*

For JSP pages that do not have a default database, `<sql:setDataSource>` can prepare a database for use.

Examples

```
<sql:setDataSource
  driver="org.hsqldb.jdbcDriver"
  url="jdbc:hsqldb:/home/databases/orders"
  user="sa"
  password="shhhh!"/>
```

Tag attributes

The `<sql:setDataSource>` tag's attributes are as follows:

Attribute	Description	Required	Default
driver	Name of the JDBC driver class to be registered	No	*None*
url	JDBC URL for the database connection	No	*None*

Attribute	Description	Required	Default
user	Database username	No	*None*
password	Database password	No	*None*
dataSource	Database prepared in advance (String or javax.sql.DataSource)	No	*None*
var	Name of the variable to represent the database	No	*Set default*
scope	Scope of the variable to represent the database	No	page

A.4.2 Queries and updates

JSTL can read from databases with <sql:query> and write to them with <sql:update>. These tags support SQL commands with ? placeholders, which <sql:param> and <sql:dateParam> can fill in.

Examples

```
<sql:query var="result">
  SELECT ORDER
  FROM ORDERS
  WHERE CUSTOMER_ID='52'
    AND PRODUCT_NAME='Oat Bran'
</sql:query>
<c:forEach items="${result.rows}" var="row">
  <c:out value="${row.product_name}"/>
</c:forEach>

<sql:update var="count">
  UPDATE CONVICTS
    SET ARRESTS=ARRESTS+1
    WHERE CONVICT_ID=?
  <sql:param value="${currentConvict}"/>
</sql:update>
```

Tag attributes

The <sql:query> tag's attributes are as follows:

Attribute	Description	Required	Default
sql	SQL command to execute (should return a ResultSet)	No	*Body*
dataSource	Database connection to use (overrides the default)	No	*Default database*
maxRows	Maximum number of results to store in the variable	No	*Unlimited*
startRow	Number of the row in the result at which to start recording	No	0

Attribute	Description	Required	Default
var	Name of variable to expose the result from the database	Yes	*None*
scope	Scope of variable to expose the result from the database	No	page

The `<sql:update>` tag's attributes are as follows:

Attribute	Description	Required	Default
sql	SQL command to execute (should not return a `ResultSet`)	No	*Body*
dataSource	Database connection to use (overrides the default)	No	*Default database*
var	Name of the variable to store the count of affected rows	No	*None*
scope	Scope of the variable to store the count of affected rows	No	page

The `<sql:param>` tag's attribute is as follows:

Attribute	Description	Required	Default
value	Value of the parameter to set	No	*Body*

The `<sql:dateParam>` tag's attributes are as follows:

Attribute	Description	Required	Default
value	Value of the date parameter to set (`java.util.Date`)	Yes	*None*
type	DATE[a] (date only), TIME (time only), or TIMESTAMP (date and time)	No	TIMESTAMP

a. In this appendix's tables, I list discrete sets of permissible values in ALL CAPS to help them stand out. JSTL is case-insensitive in this regard, and I encourage lowercase in practice because it makes the tags easier and more pleasant to read.

A.4.3 *Transactions*

JSTL provides an `<sql:transaction>` tag to group `<sql:query>` and `<sql:update>` into transactions.

Examples

```
<sql:transaction>
  <sql:update>
```

```
    UPDATE BALANCES
       SET BALANCE = BALANCE + 2
       WHERE USER=25
  </sql:update>
  <sql:update>
    UPDATE BALANCES
       SET BALANCE = BALANCE - 2
       WHERE USER=30
  </sql:update>
</sql:transaction>
```

Tag attributes

The `<sql:transaction>` tag's attributes are as follows:

Attribute	Description	Required	Default
dataSource	Database connection to use (overrides the default)	No	Default database
isolation	Transaction isolation (READ_COMMITTED, READ_UNCOMMITTED, REPEATABLE_READ, or SERIALIZABLE)	No	Database's default

A.5 Formatting tag library

JSTL's internationalization-capable formatting library supports localized formatting, fine-grained control over the display of numbers and dates, and internationalization of text messages. JSP pages can import this library with the following directive:

```
<%@ taglib prefix="fmt" uri="http://java.sun.com/jstl/fmt" %>
```

A.5.1 Numbers

JSTL provides the `<fmt:formatNumber>` tag to display numbers and the `<fmt:parseNumber>` tag to read numbers.

Examples

```
<fmt:formatNumber value="${balance}" type="currency"/>
<fmt:parseNumber value="${param.number}" var="numb"/>
```

Tag attributes

The <fmt:formatNumber> tag's attributes are as follows:

Attribute	Description	Required	Default
value	Numeric value to display	No	*Body*
type	NUMBER, CURRENCY, or PERCENT	No	number
pattern	Custom formatting pattern	No	*None*
currencyCode	Currency code (for type="currency")	No	*From the default locale*
currencySymbol	Currency symbol (for type="currency")	No	*From the default locale*
groupingUsed	Whether to group numbers (TRUE or FALSE)	No	true
maxIntegerDigits	Maximum number of integer digits to print	No	*None*
minIntegerDigits	Minimum number of integer digits to print	No	*None*
maxFractionDigits	Maximum number of fractional digits to print	No	*None*
minFractionDigits	Minimum number of fractional digits to print	No	*None*
var	Name of the variable to store the formatted number (as a text string)	No	*Print to page*
scope	Scope of the variable to store the formatted number	No	page

The <fmt:parseNumber> tag's attributes are as follows:

Attribute	Description	Required	Default
value	Numeric value to read (parse)	No	*Body*
type	NUMBER, CURRENCY, or PERCENT	No	number
parseLocale	Locale to use when parsing the number	No	*Default locale*
integerOnly	Whether to parse to an integer (true) or floating-point number (false)	No	false
pattern	Custom parsing pattern	No	*None*
var	Name of the variable to store the parsed number (as a text string)	No	*Print to page*
scope	Scope of the variable to store the parsed number	No	page

A.5.2 *Dates*

To read and write dates, JSTL provides `<fmt:parseDate>` and `<fmt:formatDate>`, respectively. To adjust the time zones used for reading and writing dates, JSTL offers the `<fmt:timeZone>` and `<fmt:setTimeZone>` tags.

Examples

```
<fmt:formatDate value="${birthday}"/>
   <fmt:parseDate value="${birthday}" var="date"/>

<sql:query>
   ...
      <sql:dateParam value="${date}"/>
</sql:query>
```

Tag attributes

The `<fmt:formatDate>` tag's attributes are as follows:

Attribute	Description	Required	Default
value	Date value to display	Yes	*None*
type	DATE, TIME, or BOTH	No	date
dateStyle	FULL, LONG, MEDIUM, SHORT, or DEFAULT	No	default
timeStyle	FULL, LONG, MEDIUM, SHORT, or DEFAULT	No	default
pattern	Custom formatting pattern	No	*None*
timeZone	Time zone of the displayed date	No	*Default time zone*
var	Name of the variable to store the formatted date (as a text string)	No	*Print to page*
scope	Scope of the variable to store the formatted date	No	page

The `<fmt:parseDate>` tag's attributes are as follows:

Attribute	Description	Required	Default
value	Date value to read (parse)	No	*Body*
type	DATE, TIME, or BOTH	No	date
dateStyle	FULL, LONG, MEDIUM, SHORT, or DEFAULT	No	default
timeStyle	FULL, LONG, MEDIUM, SHORT, or DEFAULT	No	default
parseLocale	Locale to use when parsing the date	No	*Default locale*
pattern	Custom parsing pattern	No	*None*

Attribute	Description	Required	Default
timeZone	Time zone of the parsed date	No	*Default time zone*
var	Name of the variable to store the parsed date (as a `java.util.Date`)	No	*Print to page*
scope	Scope of the variable to store the parsed date	No	`page`

The `<fmt:timeZone>` tag's attribute is as follows:

Attribute	Description	Required	Default
value	Time zone to apply to the body (`string` or `java.util.TimeZone`)	Yes	*None*

The `<fmt:setTimeZone>` tag's attributes are as follows:

Attribute	Description	Required	Default
value	Time zone to expose as a scoped or configuration variable	Yes	*None*
var	Name of the variable to store the new time zone	No	*Replace default*
scope	Scope of the variable to store the new time zone	No	`page`

A.5.3 *Other internationalization*

To assist with customized internationalization of applications, JSTL offers the following tags: `<fmt:setLocale>` to specify a new default locale, `<fmt:bundle>` and `<fmt:setBundle>` to prepare resource bundles for use, and `<fmt:message>` and `<fmt:param>` to output localized messages.

Examples

```
<fmt:setLocale value="en_US"/>
<fmt:setBundle basename="vulgarInsults"/>

<fmt:bundle basename="org.apache.bookies">
  <fmt:message key="threat" >
    <fmt:param value="${address}"/>
    <fmt:param value="${numberOfChildren}"/>
    <fmt:param value="${nameOfSpouse}"/>
  </fmt:message>
</fmt:bundle>
```

Tag attributes

The `<fmt:bundle>` tag's attributes are as follows:

Attribute	Description	Required	Default
basename	Base name of the resource bundle family to use in the body	Yes	*None*
prefix	Value to prepend to each key name in `<fmt:message>` subtags	No	*None*

The `<fmt:setBundle>` tag's attributes are as follows:

Attribute	Description	Required	Default
basename	Base name of the resource bundle family to expose as a scoped or configuration variable	Yes	*None*
var	Name of the variable to store the new bundle	No	*Replace default*
scope	Scope of the variable to store the new bundle	No	page

The `<fmt:message>` tag's attributes are as follows:

Attribute	Description	Required	Default
key	Message key to retrieve	No	*Body*
bundle	Resource bundle to use (JSTL `LocalizationContext`; see appendix B)	No	*Default bundle*
var	Name of the variable to store the localized message	No	*Print to page*
scope	Scope of the variable to store the localized message	No	page

The `<fmt:param>` tag's attribute is as follows:

Attribute	Description	Required	Default
value	Value of the parameter to set	No	*Body*

JSTL API (for developers)

Web-page authors are JSTL's main audience, but JSTL provides tools for back-end Java programmers as well. This appendix is a guide to JSTL's APIs, which promote convenience and interoperability with the standard tag library.

Sections B.1 and B.2 are formal, concise reviews of material already covered. Sections B.3 and B.4 show APIs not discussed in the book's main narrative and provide insight on the inner workings of JSTL.

B.1 *Configuration variables*

Chapter 14 discussed JSTL's configuration variables and showed you how to set defaults for applications. The core of JSTL's configuration support is a single class: `javax.servlet.jsp.jstl.core.Config`.

B.1.1 *The javax.servlet.jsp.jstl.core.Config class*

The `Config` class has two important components: static constants and static methods. Because the class's role is solely static, you never need to instantiate the `Config` class. Instead, you can directly call its methods and refer to its fields.

Constants

Each constant in the `Config` class represents a single configuration setting. Table B.1 lists all the constants in `Config`.

Table 15.1   Configuration variables exposed as constants in the `javax.servlet.jsp.jstl.core.Config` class. Chapter 14 discusses the meaning of each configuration variable.

Constant	Associated library	Description
SQL_DATA_SOURCE	Database	Default database (`DataSource` or `String`)
SQL_MAX_ROWS	Database	Default value for `<sql:query>`'s maxRows attribute
FMT_LOCALE	Formatting	Default locale
FMT_FALLBACK_LOCALE	Formatting	Fallback locale
FMT_LOCALIZATION_CONTEXT	Formatting	Default localization context
FMT_TIME_ZONE	Formatting	Default time zone

Using the methods in Config

The `Config` class contains methods for setting, retrieving, and removing configuration variables. Each of these methods takes an argument that we label `name`, indicating the name of the variable to retrieve or modify. The `name` argument can be any of the constants in table B.1, or you can use your own names to configure tag libraries you write.

Methods for setting configuration variables

```
static void set(javax.servlet.jsp.PageContext pageContext,
                String name,
                Object new,
                int scope)
```

This method sets the configuration variable *name* to the object *new* in the given *scope* (one of PageContext.PAGE_SCOPE, PageContext.REQUEST_SCOPE, PageContext. SESSION_SCOPE, or `PageContext.APPLICATION_SCOPE` from javax.servlet.jsp.PageContext) of *pageContext*.

```
static void set(javax.servlet.ServletRequest request,
                String name,
                Object new)
```

This method sets the configuration variable *name* to the object *new* in the request scope represented by *request*.

```
static void set(javax.servlet.http.HttpSession session,
                String name,
                Object new)
```

This method sets the configuration variable *name* to the object *new* in the session scope represented by *session*.

```
static void set(javax.servlet.ServletContext application,
                String name,
                Object new)
```

This method sets the configuration variable *name* to the object *new* in the application scope represented by *application*.

Methods for retrieving configuration variables

```
static Object find(javax.servlet.jsp.PageContext pageContext,
                   String name)
```

This method retrieves the configuration variable *name* from *pageContext*, searching the following in order: page scope, request scope, session scope, application scope, and initialization parameters. It returns `null` if no configuration variable named *name* is found.

```
static Object get(javax.servlet.jsp.PageContext pageContext,
                  String name,
                  int scope)
```

This method retrieves the configuration variable *name* from *pageContext*, looking only in the specified scope (one of `PageContext.PAGE_SCOPE`, `PageContext.`

REQUEST_SCOPE, PageContext.SESSION_SCOPE, or PageContext. APPLICATION_SCOPE from javax.servlet.jsp.PageContext). It returns null if no such configuration variable is found.

```
static Object get(javax.servlet.ServletRequest request,
                  String name)
```

This method retrieves the configuration variable name from the request scope represented by request. It returns null if no such configuration variable is found.

```
static Object get(javax.servlet.http.HttpSession session,
                  String name)
```

This method retrieves the configuration variable name from the session scope represented by session. It returns null if no such configuration variable is found.

```
static Object get(javax.servlet.ServletContext application,
                  String name)
```

This method retrieves the configuration variable *name* from the application scope represented by *application*. It returns null if no such configuration variable is found.

Methods for removing configuration variables

```
static void remove(javax.servlet.jsp.PageContext pageContext,
                   String name,
                   int scope)
```

This method removes the scoped variable name from pageContext—specifically, from the given scope (one of PageContext.PAGE_SCOPE, PageContext. REQUEST_SCOPE, PageContext.SESSION_SCOPE, or PageContext. APPLICATION_SCOPE from javax.servlet.jsp.PageContext).

```
static void remove(javax.servlet.ServletRequest request,
                   String name)
```

This method removes the scoped variable name from the request scope represented by request.

```
static void remove(javax.servlet.http.HttpSession session,
                   String name)
```

This method removes the scoped variable name from the session scope represented by session.

```
static void remove(javax.servlet.ServletContext application,
                   String name)
```

This method removes the scoped variable name from the application scope represented by application.

B.2 *Conditions and loops*

Chapter 15 explained how JSTL can help you write conditional and loop tags. Chapter 5 showed the bean exposed by the `varStatus` attribute of `<c:forEach>` and `<c:forTo-kens>`. In this section, we look more formally at the APIs associated with these features.

B.2.1 *The javax.servlet.jsp.jstl.core.LoopTag interface*

JSTL's three iteration tags (`<c:forEach>`, `<c:forTokens>`, and `<x:forEach>`) implement the `LoopTag` interface. This interface, which your own tags also implement when they extend `LoopTagSupport` (see section B.2.3), shares information about the current loop with subtags. JSTL has no tags that are intended specifically for tag bodies, although of course tags like `<c:out>` can appear as children of `<c:forEach>`. However, if you want to simplify the tags your page-author colleagues use, you can write a tag that collaborates with a parent iteration tag to determine status automatically; doing so lets page authors avoid needing to specify a `var` attribute to the parent `<c:forEach>` tag.

LoopTag has just two methods:

```
public Object getCurrent()
```

This method retrieves the current item being looped over—the one that would be exposed by `var`.

```
public LoopTagStatus getLoopStatus()
```

This method retrieves status information about the current loop and overall iteration. The `varStatus` attribute exposes a variable of this type. See section B.2.2.

These methods can be called by subtags that determine their parent or ancestor classes using the `findAncestorWithClass()` method in `javax.servlet.jsp.tagext. TagSupport`. For instance:

```
LoopTag t = (LoopTag) findAncestorWithClass(this, LoopTag.class);
Object current = t.getCurrent();
LoopTagStatus status = t.getLoopStatus();
```

B.2.2 *The javax.servlet.jsp.jstl.core.LoopTagStatus interface*

When a child tag in a loop calls `getLoopStatus()` from its parent tag, it retrieves an object implementing the `LoopTagStatus` interface. This interface has a number of methods, each of which determines some property about the current loop or the overall iteration:

```
public Object getCurrent()
```

This method is the same as `LoopTag.getCurrent()`. See section B.2.1.

```
public int getIndex()
```

This method returns the index of the current item within its containing collection, starting with `0`.

```
public int getCount()
```

This method returns the count of the current loop, starting with `1`.

```
public boolean isFirst()
```

This method returns `true` if `getCount()` would return 1, or `false` otherwise.

```
public boolean isLast()
```

This method returns `true` if the current loop will be the last one for the parent tag (in its current invocation), or `false` otherwise.

```
public Integer getBegin()
```

This method returns the value specified for the parent tag's `begin` attribute (wrapped as an `Integer`), or `null` if no value was specified.

```
public Integer getEnd()
```

This method returns the value specified for the parent tag's `end` attribute (wrapped as an `Integer`), or `null` if no value was specified.

```
public Integer getStep()
```

This method returns the value specified for the parent tag's `step` attribute (wrapped as an `Integer`), or `null` if no value was specified.

B.2.3 *The javax.servlet.jsp.jstl.core.LoopTagSupport class*

The `LoopTagSupport` class contains the following interesting methods (chapter 14 discusses them in more detail):

```
protected abstract Object next() throws JspTagException
```

This method lets you supply the next item to loop over.

```
protected abstract boolean hasNext() throws JspTagException
```

This method lets you inform the parent tag whether your iteration is ready to finish.

```
protected abstract void prepare() throws JspTagException
```

This method lets you prepare for an iteration; it's called once for each invocation of your tag.

You can set the following `protected` fields of `LoopTagSupport`:

```
protected int begin
protected int end
protected int step
```

When you have set any of these three `int` fields, you should update the corresponding `boolean` fields by setting them to `true`:

```
protected boolean beginSpecified
protected boolean endSpecified
protected boolean stepSpecified
```

Once you are finished setting `begin`, `end`, and `step`, you should also call the following methods:[1]

```
protected void validateBegin() throws JspTagException
protected void validateEnd() throws JspTagException
protected void validateStep() throws JspTagException
```

These methods will throw a `JspTagException` if the values you specified are inconsistent or meaningless.

B.2.4 *The javax.servlet.jsp.jstl.core.ConditionalTagSupport class*

The `ConditionalTagSupport` class has the following method, which chapter 14 discusses in more detail:

```
protected abstract boolean condition() throws JspTagException
```

Your conditional tags should override this method and return `true` if they want their bodies to execute, or `false` otherwise.

B.3 *Interoperating with JSTL's database tags*

Chapter 9 showed you how to access results from `<sql:query>` using JSTL's expression language. We'll now look at the structure of the bean exposed by `<sql:query>` and demonstrate how to expose your own JDBC `ResultSet` data using the same structure. This section also covers how your tags can send `?`-style parameters to `<sql:query>` and `<sql:update>`.

B.3.1 *The javax.servlet.jsp.jstl.sql.Result interface*

The `<sql:query>` tag exposes an object whose class implements the `Result` interface, which is designed to act as a bean-style interface to a `java.sql.ResultSet`. In JSTL's case, the data is cached because JSTL cannot keep the `ResultSet` open once the `<sql:query>` tag has completed its operation.

Chapter 9 discussed how to access members of this interface as JavaBean properties. Here's what the methods look like:

```
public SortedMap[] getRows()
```

---

[1] This is all admittedly a somewhat odd programming model, and I think it's my fault. Consider this an open letter of apology.

This method returns an array of rows, each of which is a `SortedMap` that has keys representing column names and values representing column data. The `Maps` are sorted by key name, case insensitively; the `Comparator` used by the `SortedMap` is the same one you can access as `String.CASE_INSENSITIVE_ORDER`.

```
public Object[][] getRowsByIndex()
```

This method returns a two-dimensional array. Each "row" in the array (such as `getRowsByIndex()[0]` or `getRowsByIndex()[1]`) represents a database row; each element in this subarray represents column data. Both indexes start with 0. Thus, `getRowsByIndex()[0][3]` is the fourth column of the first row.

```
public String[] getColumnNames()
```

This method returns an array for each column name resulting from the query. The order of these names is the same as the order of data in each sub-array returned by `getRows-ByIndex()`. For example, `getColumnNames()[0]` is the name of the first column, and `getRowsByIndex()[0][0]` is the column data for that same column (in the first row).

```
public int getRowCount()
```

This method returns the number of rows in the result from the database.

```
public boolean isLimitedByMaxRows()
```

This method returns `true` if the `Result` object was truncated by `<sql:query>`'s `maxRows` attribute, or `false` otherwise.

B.3.2 *The javax.servlet.jsp.jstl.sql.ResultSupport class*

The `Result` interface provides a convenient layer of abstraction for page authors who need to access information from databases. One of JSTL's virtues is that it's a standard, so once page authors learn how to access data from a `Result` bean using the information from chapter 9, they can access data from any JDBC-compliant database using only the `<sql:query>` tag.

To take advantage of this mind-share, you can expose your own data from back-end Java code using JSTL's `ResultSupport` class. This class has static methods that take a `ResultSet` parameter and return an object implementing JSTL's `Result` interface. After calling these methods, you can immediately close your `ResultSet` and return your JDBC connection to a database pool, thus simplifying resource management within your application. Furthermore, you need tell page authors only, "My data looks just like the variable that comes back from `<sql:query>`"; you don't have to teach them any local, idiosyncratic skills.

The `ResultSupport` class has the following two static methods:

```
static Result toResult(ResultSet rs)
```

This method returns a `Result` object based on the given `ResultSet`. Note that the `ResultSet` is consumed; it must be reset before further use (and if it is a one-way `ResultSet`, it will no longer be usable).

```
static Result toResult(ResultSet rs, int maxRows)
```

This method returns a `Result` object based on the given `ResultSet`, limiting it to `maxRows` rows if necessary. Recall that the `Result` objects returned by `ResultSupport` methods cache data. The `maxRows` parameter lets you avoid consuming too much memory as the result of a runaway query (for instance, a negligence to join two tables in a query, producing an unanticipated, unfiltered cross-product of two relations).

B.3.3 *The javax.servlet.jsp.jstl.sql.SQLExecutionTag interface*

JSTL provides two tags for setting `PreparedStatement` parameters: `<sql:param>` and `<sql:dateParam>`. However, SQL supports many data types; applications and databases may need more support. To let you plug in your own parameter tags, JSTL provides the `SQLExecutionTag` interface.

To write a custom parameter tag designed to set a ?-style parameter in a `PreparedStatement`, simply have your tag find its nearest `SQLExecutionTag` ancestor and call the following method for this ancestor:

```
public void addSQLParameter(Object value)
```

This method adds a `PreparedStatement` parameter to the SQL execution tag (typically `<sql:query>` or `<sql:update>`). The SQL tag will accept this parameter among those sent by other child tags, such as `<sql:param>`.

For instance, a custom child tag might contain the following code:

```
SQLExecutionTag t =
  (SQLExecutionTag)
    findAncestorWithClass(this, SQLExecutionTag.class);
t.addSQLParameter(myParameter);
```

B.4 *Using JSTL's localization algorithms*

To help you internationalize your applications, JSTL provides two classes related to formatting and globalization.

B.4.1 *The javax.servlet.jsp.jstl.fmt.LocaleSupport class*

JSTL uses a detailed algorithm to select which locale to use when internationalizing applications. This algorithm is designed to choose the best locale when the set of available locales to satisfy any requested operation, such as a keyed lookup of an internationalized message, does not contain the precise locale the user would prefer.

Chapter 10 glosses over these details, because they're not important to page authors; this appendix doesn't cover the behind-the-scenes algorithm, because it's not important for most programmers either. For more information, see the JSTL specification. (See appendix D for information on downloading the JSTL spec online.)

For now, it's just important to see how to interface with this algorithm. Doing so is important if you are writing code whose localization behavior should match JSTL's; this helps ensure consistency within an application.

The `LocaleSupport` class gives you access to JSTL's localization algorithm. It provides four static methods:

```
static String getLocalizedMessage(PageContext pageContext,
                                  String key)
```

This method returns a localized message for the given `key`, using the default bundle and locale retrieved through `pageContext`. Effectively, calling this method is a programmer's way to retrieve what a default `<fmt:message>` tag would print into a JSP page. If the method can't determine a default bundle, or if the relevant `Resource-Bundle` doesn't contain the given `key`, the method returns the string `"???key???"`, where *key* is the `key` you passed as a parameter.

```
static String getLocalizedMessage(PageContext pageContext,
                                  String key,
                                  Object[] args)
```

This method is just like the previous one, but it performs parametric substitution, as by the `<fmt:param>` tag. The `args` array is a list of parameters.

```
static String getLocalizedMessage(PageContext pageContext,
                                  String key,
                                  String basename)
```

This method returns a localized message for the given `key` and resource-bundle `basename`, using the given `pageContext` to determine what locale to use (according to JSTL's localization algorithm). If the relevant `ResourceBundle` doesn't contain the given `key`, the method returns the string `"???key???"`, where *key* is the `key` you passed as a parameter.

```
static String getLocalizedMessage(PageContext pageContext,
                                  String key,
                                  String basename
                                  Object[] args)
```

This method is just like the previous one, but it performs parametric substitution, as by the `<fmt:param>` tag. The `args` array is a list of parameters.

B.4.2 *The javax.servlet.jsp.jstl.fmt.LocalizationContext class*

The `LocalizationContext` class is simply a way to wrap a `java.util.Resource-Bundle`, a `java.util.Locale`, or both. Creating a `LocalizationContext` is useful for two reasons: you can either set it as the application's default `LocalizationContext` using the `Config.FMT_LOCALIZATION_CONTEXT` configuration variable, or you can give it to a page author to pass to a `<fmt:message>` tag's `bundle` attribute.

When you set the default localization context using `Config.FMT_LOCALIZATION_CONTEXT`, you affect the behavior of a number of tags. This (along with the FMT_LOCALE configuration variable) is how chapter 10 can magically invoke concepts like "the default locale," and details can be successfully hidden from page authors who may not know anything about internationalization. Setting the default `LocalizationContext` changes the default locale for the `<fmt:formatNumber>`, `<fmt:parseNumber>`, `<fmt:formatDate>`, and `<fmt:parseDate>` tags. Because a configuration variable can be applied to any scope, using `LocalizationContext` can be particularly useful if you want to adjust the default locale for a user's session; this approach may be appropriate if the user supplied a preference for a particular locale and you want to override the default preference of the user's browser. The default `LocalizationContext` also affects the default resource bundle and locale for `<fmt:message>` tags.

Instances of the `LocalizationContext` class are immutable, which means you can't change them. To obtain an appropriate `LocalizationContext` object, you must supply all relevant information via a constructor:

```
public LocalizationContext()
```

This constructor creates an empty `LocalizationContext` object.

```
public LocalizationContext(ResourceBundle bundle)
```

This constructor creates a new `LocalizationContext` with the given `bundle` (and with this bundle's locale).

```
public LocalizationContext(ResourceBundle bundle, Locale locale)
```

This constructor creates a new `LocalizationContext` with the given `bundle` and `locale`.

Once you construct a `LocalizationContext`, you can pass the new object to one of the "set" methods in `Config` (see section B.1) to establish this new `LocalizationContext` as the default. To establish a locale without a bundle, use the `FMT_LOCALE` configuration with a `Locale` object, not `FMT_LOCALIZATION_CONTEXT` with a `LocalizationContext`.

Database tags and SQL

The database tags from chapter 9 and the examples in part 3 use the Structured Query Language (SQL) to access data. This appendix shows how you can use SQL in your `<sql:query>` and `<sql:update>` tags. For more information about `<sql:query>` and `<sql:update>`, see chapter 9. If you're not familiar with SQL, this appendix will help you follow the book's examples.

NOTE   This is not meant to be a complete guide to SQL—just a crash course to help you understand this book's examples if you haven't used SQL before. For a more complete introduction to SQL, see the resources in appendix D.

C.1 SQL and `<sql:update>`

SQL has two categories of commands. Commands in its *Data Definition Language* (DDL) let you alter the structure of a database—for instance, add or remove a table. By contrast, commands in SQL's *Data Manipulation Language* (DML) let you work with data—add, modify, or remove rows, for example.

The `<sql:update>` tag supports both kinds of commands. You can therefore use `<sql:update>` not only to add data but also to change the structure of your database.

C.1.1 Managing tables

In a relational database, a table is a collection of data that's organized into *rows* and *columns.* Think of a row of data as a single record or entry, and a column as a field, or a placeholder filled in by each row.

For example, a table of users might have three columns: ID, IQ, and BLOOD_TYPE. Table C.1 shows an example, with some sample data.

Table 15.1 A simple table that lists users' ID numbers, IQs, and blood types. Relational databases store information in tables that work similarly to printed tables in books: they are divided into rows and columns.

NAME	IQ	BLOOD_TYPE
1	106	O
2	82	A-
3	164	B+
4	143	
5	128	AB+

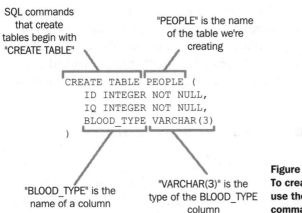

SQL commands that create tables begin with "CREATE TABLE"

"PEOPLE" is the name of the table we're creating

```
CREATE TABLE PEOPLE (
    ID INTEGER NOT NULL,
    IQ INTEGER NOT NULL,
    BLOOD_TYPE VARCHAR(3)
)
```

"BLOOD_TYPE" is the name of a column

"VARCHAR(3)" is the type of the BLOOD_TYPE column

Figure C.1
To create tables in SQL, use the CREATE TABLE command.

Creating a table

To create a table with these three columns, we can use an SQL command like that shown in figure C.1.

A CREATE TABLE command lists the columns your new table will contain. The column definitions, separated by commas, list each column's name, its data type, and any constraints that limit the data the column can store.

Like every JSP scoped variable (see chapters 2 and 4), every column has a data type. For instance, one column might require numbers, and another might require dates. Data types help a database ensure that your data makes sense. For example, if one of your tags tries to store "January 20" as a user's height, it's probably an error; the database should flag it as such and refuse to accept the data.

Table C.2 lists some common data types, although many other, convenient types exist and vary widely from database to database.

Table 15.2   Common SQL data types

SQL data type	Description	Sample value
INTEGER	Integer	6510
REAL	Floating-point number	6.02
DATE	Date only (no time)	January 20, 1986
TIME	Time only (no date)	2:05 a.m.
TIMESTAMP	Date and time	January 20, 1985 2:05 a.m.
VARCHAR(x)	String of up to x characters	"Where did I leave my hat?"

In addition to types, columns have another important property: they can be marked either as NULL or NOT NULL. A column marked NULL means that a row need not provide data for that column. For example, in table C.1, the fourth row doesn't contain any BLOOD_TYPE information. This is only possible if BLOOD_TYPE is marked NULL. Columns can enforce other kinds of restrictions, too. See appendix D for more information.

Deleting a table

If you want to delete a table and start over, the syntax is simply

```
DROP TABLE table
```

where `table` is the name of the table you want to delete. SQL also has commands for changing the structure of existing tables, but these are more advanced, and we don't discuss them here.

C.1.2   Inserting data

To add data to a table, use the INSERT command to add a row. For instance, to add the first row of data from table C.1 into the PEOPLE table we created in section C.1.1, we can use the command from figure C.2.

The general syntax for simple INSERT commands is

```
INSERT INTO table (column1, column2, …)
VALUES (value1, value2, …)
```

where `value1` corresponds to the new row's value for `column1`, `value2` corresponds to `column2`, and so on. Alternatively, you can leave out the explicit list of columns, in which case all columns in the table (in the order in which they were created using CRE-

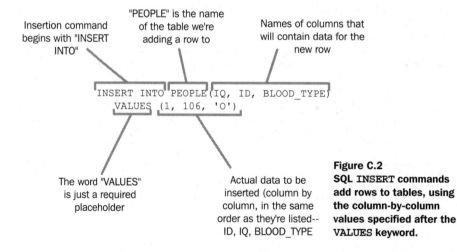

Figure C.2
SQL INSERT commands add rows to tables, using the column-by-column values specified after the VALUES keyword.

ATE TABLE) will be assumed. Thus, if we were adding to the same PEOPLE table we created earlier, the following command would be equivalent to figure C.2's:

```
INSERT INTO PEOPLE
VALUES(1, 106, 'O')
```

Note that if a column doesn't appear in the INSERT command's list of columns, it will, by default, be given the value NULL in the new row. Standard SQL and some database systems support *default values* for each column, which can be used instead of NULL when a column's value isn't explicitly specified. However, without such default values, all columns marked NOT NULL need to be given an explicit value when you insert a row into a table.

C.1.3 *Modifying data*

The SQL command for modifying data—or, to use SQL's terminology, *updating* data—is UPDATE. Its syntax is as simple as that of INSERT. In the last section, we inserted a row for a user with an IQ of 106 and a blood type of O. Now, suppose this user gets a blood transfusion that somehow changes her blood type and turns her into a genius. We need to update the database so that the user's IQ is now 182 and her blood type is AB+.

To do so, we can use the command shown in figure C.3.

The syntax for simple UPDATE commands is as follows:

```
UPDATE table
SET column1=value1, column2=value2, ...
[ WHERE conditions ]
```

The UPDATE command modifies existing rows in *table*. It sets *column1* equal to *value1*, *column2* to *value2*, and so on. By default, when no WHERE clause appears, the

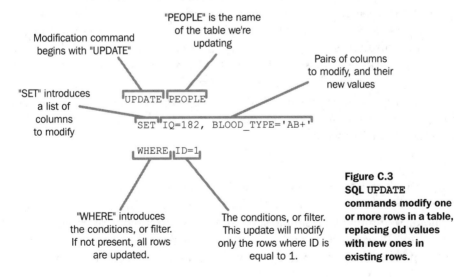

Figure C.3
SQL UPDATE commands modify one or more rows in a table, replacing old values with new ones in existing rows.

command will modify every row in the table. (Be careful! Pressing the Enter key too soon when typing SQL commands directly into a database can have disastrous effects.)

When the word WHERE does appear, it is followed by a series of conditions that filter, or limit, the rows that will be updated.

Conditions

SQL is powerful in part because it lets you handle a large number of rows at once with a simple command. In other words, if you want to change all rows where some column has a value greater than 2, you can do so in one fell swoop. You don't have to consider each row individually or loop over them all, as you might with a traditional programming language or even `<c:forEach>`.

Instead, you can write a single SQL statement that decides which rows to handle and which ones to ignore. Such statements contain a conditional expression (written in SQL) that is evaluated for every row. If the expression evaluates to true, the row is matched and processed; if it evaluates to false, the row is ignored.

When an expression is evaluated for a row, a few things happen. First, when a column name appears in the expression, the row's value for that column is substituted. For example, in the following expression the value NAME is replaced with the value of the NAME column for each row in turn:

```
NAME='David Davies'
```

Thus, the condition is true when a row's NAME column is equal to the value David Davies; it is false otherwise.

The syntax for SQL expressions is too general and complicated to cover in the space we have here, but a few other characteristics of expressions are worth mentioning. First, in SQL, literal values—such as David Davies—are surrounded by single quotation marks. This formatting contrasts with Java, which uses double quotation marks (`""`) for string literals. (XML, as you may recall from chapter 2, allows both single and double quotes for attribute values.)

Also, simple SQL expressions can be combined to form more complicated ones. For instance, if we want to find all rows where NAME equals David Davies and AGE is less than 30, we can write

```
NAME='David Davies' AND AGE < 30
```

Separating the two simple conditions with the keyword AND requires that both sides of the expression be true for the overall result to be true. (SQL supports other operators, including OR.) Individual, simple subexpressions can use operators like = (equals), < (less than), > (greater than), and <> (not equal to). You can even perform simple arithmetic on values from different columns. For example, some of an employee's retirement benefits might apply only if the employee's age and years of service total 70 or greater. We could express this condition with the following expression:

```
AGE + SERVICE > 70
```

C.1.4 Removing data

Of course, data stored in a relational database isn't permanent. You can delete it with the DELETE command, whose syntax is straightforward:

```
DELETE FROM table
[ WHERE condition ]
```

If a DELETE command appears without a WHERE clause, it deletes every row from the table. Be very careful when using DELETE, because you can easily remove all data from a table with a command like this:

```
DELETE FROM CUSTOMERS
```

This command deletes all data from the CUSTOMERS table, which probably isn't a good idea unless you're going out of business.

As with UPDATE, you can use the keyword WHERE, followed by a conditional SQL expression, to narrow the set of rows to delete. For instance, if we needed to delete all users under the age of 18, we could use the command

```
DELETE FROM PEOPLE
WHERE AGE < 18
```

C.2 SQL and <sql:query>

To retrieve data from a database, use the SQL SELECT command. Remember that, as chapter 9 showed, <sql:query>'s only job is to acquire data, not to print it out. SELECT is the SQL statement you use to tell a database what information you want to receive.

C.2.1 Basic SELECT syntax

The simplest form of the SELECT statement is

```
SELECT * FROM table
```

This simple statement retrieves all data from the table named *table*. That is, every column of every row is retrieved. To print the entire contents of a table, you can use this SELECT statement with the printQuery.jsp page from listing 9.1 in chapter 9.

Suppose, however, that you're not interested in every row. For instance, we might be a publisher releasing a new philosophical tract that we think will only interest people with an IQ over 130. (As with the other examples in this chapter,

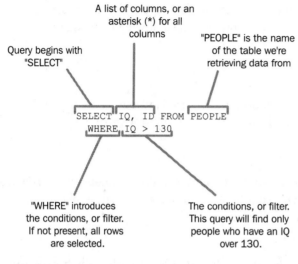

A list of columns, or an asterisk (*) for all columns

"PEOPLE" is the name of the table we're retrieving data from

Query begins with "SELECT"

```
SELECT IQ, ID FROM PEOPLE
WHERE IQ > 130
```

"WHERE" introduces the conditions, or filter. If not present, all rows are selected.

The conditions, or filter. This query will find only people who have an IQ over 130.

Figure C.4
SQL SELECT queries retrieve one or more rows from a table, often based on a conditional expression following the WHERE keyword.

don't take the subject matter too seriously.) To help us market this book effectively, we might run the SELECT query in figure C.4.

Like UPDATE commands, SELECT commands can contain a WHERE clause specifying a conditional expression. See the previous section for more information about SQL conditions.

Basic SELECT commands take the following form:

```
SELECT columns FROM table
WHERE condition
```

The list of columns can be replaced with an asterisk (*), which refers to all columns.

TIP   You might wonder why you'd ever want to avoid selecting all columns at once. After all, they might be useful even if you don't currently need them—and why bother modifying a query? If you're dealing with very large data, picking only the columns you truly care about may cause your pages to run faster. Doing so also makes your queries clearer if you have to maintain your pages. It's easier to figure out the role of SELECT LAST_NAME FROM USERS than to decide what SELECT * FROM USERS is doing in your page.

SQL SELECT statements can be considerably more complex than this simple form suggests.

Relationships between tables

One feature that makes relational databases powerful is the ability to connect, or *join*, multiple tables during a single query. For instance, suppose we have another table called ADDRESSES that, instead of storing users' IQs and blood types, stores their mailing addresses. This table might share user IDs with the PEOPLE table, so the same user would have the ID 2 in both tables. To retrieve the users' IQs and mailing addresses at the same time, we could write the following query:

```
SELECT IQ, ADDRESS
  FROM PEOPLE, ADDRESSES
  WHERE PEOPLE.ID=ADDRESSES.ID
```

C.3 SQL miscellany

When you read and write SQL statements, you should keep in mind a few useful facts about SQL's syntax.

C.3.1 White space

White space isn't significant in SQL. That is,

```
DELETE FROM CUSTOMERS
  WHERE AGE < 18
```

is equivalent to

```
DELETE
  FROM CUSTOMERS
  WHERE AGE < 18
```

and

```
DELETE FROM CUSTOMERS WHERE AGE < 18
```

White space, however, is significant inside a quoted string literal. For instance,

```
NAME='David Davies'
```

differs from

```
NAME='DavidDavies'
```

C.3.2 Case sensitivity

Whether actual SQL commands are uppercase or lowercase doesn't matter; SELECT commands can equally well begin with select. Relational database software varies widely in whether items like table names are case sensitive or insensitive, so check your database's documentation before confusing CUSTOMERS with customers. Many databases even let you configure whether matches in conditional expressions that use single-quoted substrings (like NAME='David Davies') are case-sensitive.

As I mentioned in chapter 9, when you retrieve data from an `<sql:query>` tag's scoped variable, it doesn't matter whether you use uppercase or lowercase for column names. Consider this example:

```
<sql:query var="smartUsers">
  SELECT IQ FROM PEOPLE WHERE IQ > 140
</sql:query>
<table>
<c:forEach items="${smartUsers.rows}" var="row">
  <tr>
    <td><c:out value="${row.IQ}"/></td>            ◁─┐ Uppercase
  </tr>                                                │ column name
</c:forEach>
</table>
```

This fragment is equivalent to

```
<sql:query var="smartUsers">
  SELECT IQ FROM USERS WHERE IQ > 140
</sql:query>
<table>
<c:forEach items="${smartUsers.rows}" var="row">
  <tr>
    <td><c:out value="${row.iq}"/></td>            ◁─┐ Lowercase
  </tr>                                                │ column name
</c:forEach>
</table>
```

C.3.3 *More advanced SQL*

Again, the discussion here was designed only to introduce SQL informally. I've left out complex syntax diagrams and many advanced features of the language. Also, many databases have proprietary extensions to SQL that a general introduction can't cover. JSTL is compatible with all this simple, advanced, standard, and proprietary SQL. If you're familiar with more advanced SQL—or if someone hands you an SQL query on a silver platter and says, "This is how you retrieve the blood types of all overweight executives in our company, for use in your web application"—JSTL should let you use it without a problem. The SQL is actually processed by your database, not JSTL.

C.4 *Summary*

Keep the following points in mind when thinking about JSTL, SQL, and databases:

- The Structured Query Language (SQL) is the typical way to access relational databases. SQL is divided into commands for altering a database's structure (DDL) and working with data (DML).
- To create a table, use the command CREATE TABLE.

- To delete a table, use `DROP_TABLE`.
- The SQL commands `INSERT`, `UPDATE`, `DELETE` modify data within tables.
- The `SELECT` command lets you retrieve data.
- JSTL works with whatever SQL commands your database supports. Unfortunately, although SQL is a standard language, many database vendors extend it in custom ways or fail to implement the entire standard.

References and resources

433

D.1 JSP Standard Tag Library

- JSTL in Action: *Official book web site*

  http://www.manning.com/bayern. From this site, you can download the source code, errata, and companion articles for this book.

- *JSTL 1.0*

  http://jcp.org/aboutJava/communityprocess/final/jsr052/. The readable specification for JSTL 1.0 can serve as a useful reference, particularly for some advanced details that are beyond the scope of this book.

- *Installing Tomcat and JSTL*

  http://www.manning.com/bayern/tomcat. If you need to set up a JSP container, you can access a tutorial I've posted on Manning's web site.

- *Installing the hsqldb database*

  http://www.manning.com/bayern/hsqldb. To experiment with databases, you may want to set up your own private database. The hsqldb product is a free, open-source database that's easy to set up. I describe how in an article on Manning's site.

- *JSTL reference implementation*

  http://jakarta.apache.org/taglibs/doc/standard-doc/intro.html. JSTL's reference implementation is available as open-source software through the Jakarta Taglibs project, which is part of the Apache Software Foundation. If you run your own JSP container, you can download and install updated versions of the reference implementation from this site.

- *Sun's JSP site*

  http://java.sun.com/products/jsp/. Sun Microsystems, where Java originally came from, maintains a web site to promote and inform people about JavaServer Pages (JSP). This information also may contain current information on tag libraries and JSTL.

- *Jakarta Tomcat*

  http://jakarta.apache.org/tomcat/. This is the web site for Jakarta Tomcat.

- *Jakarta Taglibs*

  http://jakarta.apache.org/taglibs/. This web site provides free, open-source tag libraries for JSP. Many libraries in Jakarta Taglibs inspired features in JSTL.

- *Web Development with JavaServer Pages 2d. ed*

  By Duane Fields, Mark Kolb, and Shawn Bayern (Manning, 2001); ISBN 193011012X. My first book with Manning, this guide covers JSP 1.2. Although JSTL hides many details of JSP, these details are useful for advanced page authors.

D.2 XML-related references

- *Online chapter on XSL Transformations*

  http://www.ibiblio.org/xml/books/bible2/chapters/ch17.html. An easy-to-read guide to XSLT, available online for free.

- *XSLT and XPath tutorial*

  http://www.vbxml.com/xsl/tutorials/intro/. Another tutorial on XSLT and XPath.

- *ZVON.org: "The Guide to the XML Galaxy"*

  http://www.zvon.org. Some people I know swear by this collection of tutorials and information about XML, particularly its information on XSLT and XPath.

- *Slashdot's RSS feed*

  http://slashdot.org/slashdot.rdf. Technology news from Slashdot, formatted in RSS.

- *RSS news*

  http://www.blogspace.com/rss/rss10. An RSS news feed about RSS feeds. On the hit show *Seinfeld*, Kramer once wanted to produce a coffee-table book about coffee tables. This is the RSS analogy.

D.3 Databases

- *Introduction to SQL: Mastering the Relational Database Language*

  By Rick F. Van der Lans (Addison-Wesley, 1999); ISBN 0201596180. This book is a readable guide to the Structured Query Language (SQL).

- *JDBC Data Access API*

  http://java.sun.com/products/jdbc/. Read more information about JDBC, Java's database-access API, on the Sun site.

- *hsqldb*

  http://hsqldb.sourceforge.net/. This is a small, free database written in Java, formerly called Hypersonic SQL. See section D.1 for a pointer to instructions on installing and configuring hsqldb.

- *Microsoft SQL Server*

  http://www.microsoft.com/sql/default.asp. This is the home page for Microsoft's database, presumptuously named SQL Server.

- *MySQL*

  http://www.mysql.com. This is the web site for a free and very popular, but overrated, database system.

- *Oracle*

  http://www.oracle.com. Oracle is the world's largest database company.

- *PostgreSQL*

  http://www.postgresql.org. This is the web site of a free, open-source, extremely high-quality database system.

D.4   Related standards

- *Hypertext Transfer Protocol (HTTP 1.1)*

  http://www.ietf.org/rfc/rfc2616.txt. The Hypertext Transfer Protocol (HTTP) is the foundation for the World Wide Web.

- *Java Community Process*

  http://www.jcp.org/. The evolution of JavaServer Pages (JSP) and the JSTL in Action (JSTL) is governed by the Java Community Process (JCP), a standards organization. Read about the future of the Java platform at the JCP web site.

- *Java APIs for XML*

  http://java.sun.com/xml/. You can read more about Java APIs for working with XML at the Java web site. Some of these Java APIs serve as foundations for JSTL's XML support.

- *JavaServer Pages 1.2*

  http://jcp.org/aboutJava/communityprocess/final/jsr053/. This site provides the JavaServer Pages (JSP) specification, version 1.2.

- *Extensible Markup Language (XML) 1.0 (Second Edition)*

  http://www.w3.org/TR/2000/REC-xml-20001006. This site lists the XML standard, in all its tedious glory.

- *XML Path Language (XPath), Version 1.0*

  http://www.w3.org/TR/xpath. JSTL adopts XPath (see chapters 7 and 8), a language for selecting XML fragments that was originally part of the XSLT standard.

- *XSL Transformations (XSLT), Version 1.0*

  http://www.w3.org/TR/xslt. JSTL includes support for XSLT (see chapter 8), a language that's primarily useful for converting XML documents from one form to another.

- *World Wide Web Consortium (W3C)*

  http://www.w3.org/. The web site for the W3C offers technical standards for XML-related technologies. In addition to the specific URLs listed earlier, you can read more about the Document Object Model (DOM) at this site.

D.5 Miscellaneous references

- *HTML and CSS reference*

  http://www.blooberry.com. The HTML and CSS guides at Blooberry are well organized and thorough.

- *Just Java*

  By Peter van der Linden (Prentice Hall, 2001); ISBN 0130320722. This book is an excellent, readable introduction to the Java programming language.

index

More Java titles from Manning

JDK 1.4 Tutorial

GREGORY M. TRAVIS
ISBN 1930110456
408 pages, $34.95
Spring 2002

Java 3D Programming

DANIEL SELMAN
ISBN 1930110359
400 pages, $49.95
Spring 2002

For ordering information visit www.manning.com

More Java titles from Manning

Instant Messaging in Java:
The Jabber Protocols

Iain Shigeoka
ISBN 1930110464
400 pages, $39.95
Spring 2002

Web Development with Java Server Pages
Second edition

Duane Fields, Mark A. Kolb, and Shawn Bayern
ISBN 193011012X
800 pages, $44.95
November 2001

For ordering information visit www.manning.com